www.wadsworth.com

www.wadsworth.com is the World Wide Web site for Wadsworth and is your direct source to dozens of online resources.

At www.wadsworth.com you can find out about supplements, demonstration software, and student resources. You can also send email to many of our authors and preview new publications and exciting new technologies.

www.wadsworth.com
Changing the way the world learns®

FROM THE WADSWORTH SERIES IN COMMUNICATION STUDIES

Gendered Lives

COMMUNICATION, GENDER, & CULTURE

SIXTH EDITION

Julia T. Wood

LINEBERGER DISTINGUISHED PROFESSOR OF HUMANITIES
THE UNIVERSITY OF NORTH CAROLINA AT CHAPEL HILL

THOMSON
WADSWORTH

Australia · Canada · Mexico · Singapore · Spain
United Kingdom · United States

Publisher: Holly J. Allen
Acquisitions Editor: Annie Mitchell
Senior Development Editor: Greer Lleuad
Assistant Editor: Breanna Gilbert-Gambacorta
Editorial Assistant: Trina Enriquez
Senior Technology Project Manager: Jeanette Wiseman
Senior Marketing Manager: Kimberly Russell
Marketing Assistant: Andrew Keay
Advertising Project Manager: Shemika Britt
Project Manager, Editorial Production: Jane Brundage

Print/Media Buyer: Rebecca Cross
Permissions Editor: Sarah Harkrader
Production Service: Vicki Moran, Publishing Support
  Services
Photo Researcher: Stephen Forsling
Copy Editor: April Wells-Hayes
Cover Designer: Gopa and Ted2, Inc.
Cover Image: "Structured Upset" by Gopa and Ted2, Inc.
Compositor: TBH Typecast, Inc.
Printer: Webcom, Ltd.

For more information about our products,
contact us at:
Thomson Learning Academic Resource Center
1-800-423-0563

For permission to use material from this text,
contact us by:
Phone: 1-800-730-2214   **Fax:** 1-800-730-2215
Web: http://www.thomsonrights.com

Library of Congress Control Number: 2003115087

ISBN 0-534-63615-2

Wadsworth/Thomson Learning
10 Davis Drive
Belmont, CA 94002-3098
USA

Asia
Thomson Learning
5 Shenton Way #01-01
UIC Building
Singapore 068808

Australia/New Zealand
Thomson Learning
102 Dodds Street
Southbank, Victoria 3006
Australia

Canada
Nelson
1120 Birchmount Road
Toronto, Ontario M1K 5G4
Canada

Europe/Middle East/Africa
Thomson Learning
High Holborn House
50/51 Bedford Row
London WC1R 4LR
United Kingdom

Latin America
Thomson Learning
Seneca, 53
Colonia Polanco
11560 Mexico D.F.
Mexico

Spain/Portugal
Paraninfo
Calle/Magallanes, 25
28015 Madrid, Spain

DEDICATION

This book is dedicated to:

Emma Goldman, Elizabeth Cady Stanton, Susan B. Anthony, Margaret Sanger, Sojourner Truth, Mary Wollstonecraft, Charlotte Perkins Gilman, Frederick Douglass, and other women and men who began the conversation about gender in this country;

and to:

Betty Friedan, Ella Baker, Marilyn French, Bill McCartney, Gloria Steinem, Jackson Katz, Ellen Goodman, Michael Kimmel, Evelyn Fox Keller, bell hooks, James Doyle, Sandra Harding, Nancy Chodorow, Robert Bly, Susan Faludi, Karlyn Campbell, Mary Daly, Madonna, and other women and men who have added to the cultural dialogue about gender;

and to:

Cam McDonald, Michelle Wood Wilco, Samuel Keenan Bingman Cox, Daniel Wood Wilco, Harrison Wood Wilco, Dylan Tyler Reich, and other boys and girls whose voices will shape the next generation's understanding of women and men, masculinity and femininity, and the meaning of gender in our society.

CONTENTS

ACKNOWLEDGMENTS

One of the most gratifying aspects of writing a book is the opportunity to thank those who have offered support, insight, and advice. First and foremost, I thank my students. The undergraduate women and men in my classes are unfailing sources of education for me. Their questions and ideas, their willingness to challenge some of my notions, and their generosity in sharing their perceptions and experiences have shaped the pages that follow—sometimes in obvious ways, sometimes subtly.

Among the undergraduate students who have pushed me to think in new ways about gender, communication, and culture are Cutler Andrews, Christina Davis, Justin Davis, Alice Newton, and Leigh Raynor. Among the graduate students who have influenced my thinking are LindaBecker Bourne, Walter Carl, Richard Danek, Nathan Epley, Natalie Fixmer, Christina Foust, Chuck Grant, Allison Howry, Chris Inman, Tim Muehlhoff, Phaedra Pezzullo, Nina Reich, Sharon Varallo, and Kate Willink.

I am fortunate to have enjoyed the professional and personal support of Holly Allen and Annie Mitchell at Wadsworth. Holly's and Annie's creativity, insights, and support have enhanced this edition immeasurably. Along with Holly and Annie, others at Wadsworth have contributed in important ways to this edition of *Gendered Lives*. They are Greer Lleuad, development editor; Breanna Gilbert-Gambacorta, assistant editor; Elizabeth Hurley, editorial assistant; Jeanette Wiseman, technology project manager; Kimberly Russell, marketing manager; Jane Brundage, production project manager; Sarah Harkrader, permissions editor; April Wells-Hayes, copy editor; and Vicki Moran, project manager.

I also thank the individuals who reviewed the first, second, third, fourth, fifth, and sixth editions of this book and who offered generous responses and insightful suggestions, which are reflected in the pages that follow. Reviewers for the first edition were Sandra Albrecht, University of Kansas; Victoria DeFrancisco, University of Northern Iowa; Bonnie Dow, University of Georgia; Valerie Downs, California State University, Long Beach; Cheris Kramarae, University of Illinois at Urbana-Champaign; Larry Lance, University of North Carolina at Charlotte; Suzanne McCorkle, Boise State University; Edward Schiappa, University of Minnesota; and Patricia Sullivan, State University of New York, the College at New Paltz. Reviewers for the second edition were Dan Cavanaugh, Southwest Texas State University;

Judith Dallinger, Western Illinois University; Bonnie Dow, University of Georgia; Kathleen Galvin, Northwestern University; Jim Hasenauer, California State University at Northridge; and Diane Umble, Millersville University. Reviewers for the third edition were Cynthia Berryman-Fink, University of Cincinnati; Pamela Cooper, Northwestern University; Jill Rhea, University of North Texas; Ralph Webb, Purdue University; and Gust A. Yep, San Francisco State University. Reviewers for the fourth edition were Bernardo Attias, California State University at Northridge; Pamela Dawes-Kaylor, Ohio State University; Michael R. Elkins, Texas A&M University at Kingsville; Maureen Keeley, Southwest Texas State University; Kelly Morrison, Michigan State University; Trevor Parry-Giles, University of Maryland at College Park; and Carol Thompson, University of Arkansas at Little Rock. Reviewers for the fifth edition were Rick Buerkel, Central Michigan University; Steve Duck, University of Iowa; Victoria Leonard, College of the Canyons; Jennifer Linde, Arizona State University; Kaye J. Nubel, Saddleback College; Bruce Riddle, Kent State University; and Eva Rose, Chaffey College. Reviewers for the sixth edition were Lisa M. Burns, University of Maryland; Nancy J. Eckstein, Wheaton College; Lindsay Hayes, University of Maryland at College Park; Pam McAllister Johnson, Kansas State University; and Valerie McKay, California State University, Long Beach.

And, always, I thank Robbie—the love of my life—for his support, criticism, and continuing interest in gender as a focus of my research and a facet of our lives.

Julia T. Wood
The University of North Carolina at Chapel Hill
December 2003

ABOUT THE AUTHOR

Dan Sears

Julia T. Wood
The University of North
Carolina at Chapel Hill

Julia T. Wood joined the Department of Communication Studies at the University of North Carolina at Chapel Hill at the age of 24. She is now the Lineberger Professor of Humanities and a professor in the Department of Communication Studies, where she teaches courses and conducts research on gender, communication, and culture, and on communication in personal relationships. During her career, she has authored 15 books and edited 8 others. In addition, she has published more than 70 articles and book chapters and has presented numerous papers at professional conferences. She has won 9 awards for undergraduate teaching and 12 awards for her scholarship.

Professor Wood lives with her husband, Robert Cox, who is also a professor of Communication Studies at the University of North Carolina at Chapel Hill. Filling out their family are Madhi "the wonder dog" and two cats, Sadie and Wicca. When not teaching or writing, Professor Wood enjoys traveling to other countries; working with prisoners in a stop violence program; conversations with students, friends, and family members; and consulting with attorneys on cases involving sex and gender issues.

GENDERED LIVES

Introduction

Opening the Conversation

Destiny is not a matter of chance, it is a matter of choice.

—WILLIAM JENNINGS BRYAN

Most textbooks open by discussing the area of study they cover, but I'd like to launch our conversation a bit differently. I think you're entitled to know something about the person behind the words you'll be reading, so I want to introduce myself and explain why I wrote this book.

We tend to think of books as impersonal sources of information. Like anything people create, however, books reflect the experiences and identities of those who create them. Authors influence books when they decide to include certain topics and omit others, to rely on particular theories, and to include some issues and exclude others. Choices about topics, writing style, and theoretical stance shape the content and overall meaning of a book. This doesn't mean books are not informative or reliable, but it does mean they reflect authors' experiences and perspectives. By telling you a little about who I am, what I believe, and why I wrote this book, I am inviting you to think about how my background, experiences, beliefs, and values have shaped the book you're reading.

Let's start with some simple demographic information. I am a European American, middle-aged, heterosexual, spiritually engaged, middle-class woman who has been in a committed relationship with Robert (Robbie) Cox for 30 years. Yet, if you think about it, this information isn't simple at all, because it implies a great deal about my identity and my experiences. For instance, I am privileged in many ways —my race, class, and sexual orientation are approved by mainstream Western culture. I am also socially disadvantaged by my sex, because women are less valued than men in Western culture. I did not earn the privileges conferred by my skin color, sexual orientation, and class, nor did I earn the inequities that come with being female. That is the nature of privilege and inequity—they are unearned. They do not reflect the achievements, efforts, or failings of individuals who enjoy or suffer them.

THE SOCIAL CONSTRUCTION OF INEQUALITY

To speak of being privileged in some ways and devalued in others does not mean I take either for granted. The fact that my sex makes me vulnerable to job discrimination, violence, and other injustices is not something I accept as unchangeable. In fact, one reason I wrote this book is that I believe we *can* bring about changes in our society. I also do not accept my privileges unreflectively. The realization that both my personal and my professional life are contoured by whether I fit what our culture arbitrarily designates as normal or superior makes me keenly aware that sex, gender, race, sexual orientation, and class profoundly influence individuals' knowledge, experience, and opportunities.

If we don't want to be limited by the horizon of our social position, we can try to learn about the experiences, perspectives, and circumstances of people in other social positions: the anger and hurt that gay men, lesbians, transsexuals, and intersexed people experience in a society that defines only heterosexuality as normal; the resentment that some heterosexual White men sometimes feel toward the enactment of laws and policies that could reduce the privileges they enjoy; the sense of restriction many women feel knowing they cannot venture out at night without risking assault; the frustration of poor and working-class citizens whose needs and circumstances often are not represented in legislation that claims to help "everyone"; what it means to be a person of color in a sea of Whiteness.

In some important ways, we cannot fully understand the lives of people who differ from us. Sensitivity and earnest efforts to understand are important, yet they cannot yield complete knowledge of the daily reality of others' lives. What we can do is realize that our feelings, identities, values, and perspectives are not everyone's. Realizing the limits of our own standpoint encourages us to learn from people who have different standpoints. We do this by respecting the different conditions that shape their lives and by recognizing that only *they* can define the meanings of their experiences, feelings, thoughts, hopes, beliefs, problems, and needs. We cannot speak for them, cannot appropriate their voices as our own. But to listen is to learn, and to learn is to broaden our appreciation of the range of human experiences and possibilities.

Realizing that inequality is socially constructed empowers us to be agents of change. We have choice about whether to accept our culture's designations of who is valuable and who is not, who is normal and who is abnormal. We don't have to treat light skin, heterosexuality, maleness, and middle-class economic status as superior or "right." Instead, we can challenge social views that accord arbitrary and unequal value to people and that limit humans' opportunities and lives. This book will help you identify ways that you can refuse to be complicit in practices that uphold inequality.

FEMINISM—FEMINISMS

Finally, in introducing myself to you, I inform you that I am a feminist. The word *feminist* is often misunderstood. Many people, like my student Andrea (see commentary), say they aren't feminists because they associate feminism with anti-male attitudes or radical acts of protest. Ironically, although many people in their twenties do not call themselves feminists, they do think that the women's movement has improved the conditions and opportunities available to women. When feminism is defined as "a movement for social, political, and economic equality of women and men," 71% of women and 61% of men say they agree with the movement (Baumgardner & Richards, 2000). This suggests that there is greater reservation about the label *feminist* than about the actual goals, values, and achievements of feminists.

When I talk with students who say they aren't feminists, we often discover that we agree on most issues relevant to gender but disagree on what feminism means. There's good reason for this. First, feminism is not one single belief or stance. Chapter 3 discusses a variety of feminist positions, and Chapter 4 explores the different stances within men's movements. Second, most people's impressions of feminism have been shaped by media portrayals of feminism and feminist movements. Beginning with the inaccurate report in the 1960s that feminists burned bras as a protest (which they did not do then), media have consistently misrepresented feminists as man-hating, tough, shrill extremists.

Media stereotypes of feminists and feminism fail to fit many women and men who define themselves as feminists. Like me, many feminists have good relationships with both women and men. Also like me, many women who label themselves feminists are feminine in many ways: They enjoy wearing feminine clothes, experimenting with hairstyles and makeup, and engaging in traditionally feminine activities such as baking bread, gardening, and interacting with children. Being feminist does not conflict with being feminine, but it does mean being reflective about how we define and embody femininity.

Because feminism means different things to different people, I should tell you how I define feminism. I see it as an active commitment to equality and respect for life. For me, this includes respecting all people, as well as nonhuman forms of life and

Andrea

I would never call myself a feminist, because that word has so many negative connotations. I don't hate men or anything, and I'm not interested in protesting. I don't want to go around with hacked-off hair and no makeup and sit around bashing men. I do think women and men are equal and should have the same kinds of rights, including equal pay for equal work. But I wouldn't call myself a feminist.

the earth itself. Simply put, my feminism means I am against oppression, be it the oppression of women, men, specific sexualities or sexual orientations, particular race-ethnicities, elderly people, children, animals, or our planet. I don't think oppression and domination foster healthy lives for individuals or societies as a whole. I believe there are better, more humane and enriching ways to live, and I am convinced we can be part of bringing these alternatives into existence. That is the core of feminism as I define it for myself. During the course of reading this book, you will encounter varied versions of feminism, which should shatter the myth that feminism means the same thing to all people and should invite you to consider where to position yourself among diverse viewpoints.

Feminism does not just happen. It is an achievement and a process. My own identification with feminism began in the 1970s, when a friend first introduced me to some readings that made me aware of discrimination against women. My initial response to this knowledge was denial; I tried to rationalize inequities or repress my knowledge of them, perhaps because recognizing them would be too painful. When denial failed to work, I entered an angry phase. I was bitter about my grow-

FYI

On Feminism

Katha Pollitt (1994), nationally syndicated columnist:

To me, to be a feminist is to answer the question "Are women human?" with a yes. It is not about whether women are better than, worse than, or identical with men. . . . It's about justice, fairness, and access to the broad range of human experience. . . . It's about women having intrinsic value as persons . . . human beings, in other words. No more, no less. (pp. xii–xiv)

Jennifer Baumgardner and Amy Richards (2000), third wave feminists:

Feminism [is] a word that describes a social-justice movement for gender equity and human liberation. . . . By feminists we mean each and every politically and socially conscious woman or man who works for equality within or outside the movement. (pp. 50, 54)

Rebecca West (1913):

I myself have never been able to find out precisely what feminism is. I only know that people call me a feminist whenever I express sentiments that differentiate me from a doormat.

The American Heritage Dictionary of the English Language (1992):

Belief in the social, political, and economic equality of the sexes. (p. 671)

ing understanding of ways in which women, including myself, were devalued. I was also angry at myself for having been unaware of society's devaluation of women and for conforming to the roles assigned to women. This anger led me to strike out, sometimes in inappropriate ways and at inappropriate targets. It was a deep anger, directed both toward discrimination against women and toward myself for having been ignorant of it for so long. I began to question conventional views of women, men, and relationships; I began to change myself and my relationships to fit my growing belief in equality between people. This angry and embittered phase was necessary for me to absorb what I was learning, but it could not lead me forward in any constructive sense.

Finally, I was able to transform the anger into an abiding commitment to being part of change, not so much for myself as for future generations. I want our society to be fairer, to respect differences, and to affirm all people more than it has historically. Years later, when I began to study gender issues, I learned that the path I had traveled to achieve my feminist identity is not uncommon (Ossana, Helms, & Leonard, 1992). Ignorance, denial, anger, internalization of new values and identities, and transformation to constructive commitment are stages many individuals go through as they dislodge one identity and worldview and embrace alternate ones.

FEATURES OF *GENDERED LIVES*

Three features distinguish this book and support the views I've just discussed. First, I include discussion of diverse classes, ethnicities, races, and sexual orientations whenever research is available. Unfortunately, there is more research on discrimination faced by women than by men, on heterosexuals than on people of other sexualities and sexual orientations, and on middle-class than on less economically comfortable citizens. By including what research there is on the range of people that make up our world, I've tried to make *Gendered Lives* reflect the diversity of human beings better than most textbooks do.

A second feature of this book is language that includes all readers. I use terms like *he and she* and *women and men* in preference to *he, mankind,* and *men.* But inclusive language means more than including women; it also means using language that refuses to go along with cultural marginalization of some groups. For instance, I refer to individuals in intimate relationships as *partners* rather than *spouses,* and I generally refer to *committed relationships* rather than *marriages.* The terms *spouse* and *marriage* exclude lesbians, transsexuals, gay men, and transgendered and intersexed people because our society denies them the legal, material, and social legitimacy accorded to heterosexuals. The terms *spouse* and *marriage* also fail to acknowledge intimate connections between people who cohabit but choose not to marry. Use of inclusive language reflects awareness of how language can exclude people.

FYI

Multicultural Perspectives on Sex and Sexual Orientation

What's feminine? What's masculine? What's gay? It depends on which culture's perspective you take.

- The Agta people in the Philippines and the Tini Aborigines in Australia see keen hunting ability as a feminine ideal (Estioko-Griffin & Griffin, 1997).

- In Melanesia young Sambian boys perform fellatio on adult men. The Sambia believe that swallowing the semen of adult men helps boys grow into healthy adult males (Herdt, 1997).

- The Society Islands of French Polynesia have three sex-based classifications: males, females, and māhū. A māhū is understood to be half woman, half man. Female-bodied māhū behave in masculine ways and have sexual relations with non-māhū females; male-bodied māhū behave in feminine ways and have sex with non-māhū males (Glenn, 2002).

- To become a man in some societies, a boy must accomplish at least one of three things: have a vision, kill an antelope, or earn enough money to support himself (Clatterbaugh, 1997).

- In Mexico and parts of Brazil, male homosexuality is defined not by male-to-male sex but by whether a man penetrates (not homosexual) or is penetrated by (homosexual) another man (Almaguer, 1993; Cantú, 2004).

- In addition to male and female, India recognizes a category of person who is a female man, called a hijra. Hijras sometimes remove their external genitalia to appear more woman-like (Herdt, 1997; Nanda, 2004).

A third way in which *Gendered Lives* reflects awareness of my own limited standpoint and my respect for those whose standpoints differ are the student voices that punctuate this book. In the pages that follow, you'll meet a lot of students—some like you, some quite different. In my course on gender and communication, students keep journals in which they write about issues that arise in our class conversations. Many of my students were kind enough to give me permission to include their words in this book. In addition, students at other campuses around the country have written to me to respond to previous editions of *Gendered Lives,* and some of their comments appear in this edition. I've tried to return their generosity by including a range of individuals and viewpoints, including ones with which I personally disagree. In fact, including ideas with which I disagree, from both students and scholars, is necessary if this book is to reflect the range of ideas about gender and communication that circulate in our culture. Hannah, a student from a Northeastern college, makes the point in her commentary.

Hannah's comment reflects a critical open-mindedness that fosters learning. As you read this book, think about research findings and students' voices, and reflect on how they are similar to or different from your own beliefs and values. To encourage you to think independently about other students' ideas, I have refrained from evaluating or interpreting the reflections that appear in this book. The students write clearly and eloquently, and I don't want to muffle their voices with my analysis. The student commentaries, my ideas, and your responses to what you read create a circle of learning in which we collaboratively explore gender, communication, and culture.

> ### Hannah
>
> When I was reading *Gendered Lives,* I had to keep reminding myself that you were presenting information and that not all points were your personal values and beliefs. I didn't agree with all of your statements or the ideas of others, like the students in their commentaries, but I learned a lot about the ways others see gender. I also learned a lot about how I think about gender by seeing what ideas I agreed with and disagreed with.

Each chapter also includes FYI features that highlight important information about gender. In each chapter, you'll also find Web sites that you may visit to learn more about particular topics. This book's emphasis on information reminds us that knowledge is a critical basis for sound opinions, attitudes, and behavior regarding gender.

Becoming Aware

Reading this book will enlarge your awareness of gender—how it is shaped and expressed in contexts ranging from the political arena to intimate relationships. The awareness you gain will enhance your understanding of yourself and your society. At the same time, you may feel unsettled as you read this book.

If you are a woman, you may find it disturbing to learn the extent to which Western culture discounts your experiences and limits your opportunities. I also realize that a number of those reading this book—both women and men—have been raped, sexually abused, sexually harassed, or battered. Some of you have eating disorders; some have suffered job discrimination; some of you have been taunted for not embodying current social expectations for males or females. Reading *Gendered Lives* is likely to stir up these issues. If you don't wish to deal with such difficult issues, then you may choose to forgo or delay study in this area. However, if you are ready to wrestle with serious personal and social matters, then this book should help you understand issues in your life as not only personal but also political. Such issues reflect widespread cultural biases that define unrealistic

FYI

Julia—the Author—Comments

Occasionally, a student tells me that *Gendered Lives* "bashes men." This comment puzzles me, because I don't think of myself as a male basher. For 30 years I've been married to a wonderful man; I have many male friends and colleagues whom I like and admire, and I've done as much to mentor male as female students. When I ask students to explain why they think the book bashes men, they tell me it gives more attention to discrimination against women than against men. They are correct in this observation, but the difference in coverage is due to findings from research.

Like any scholar, what I write depends largely on available information. Existing research shows that, although both men and women experience violence from an intimate partner, 95% of people who are known to be physically abused by a romantic partner are women (Hasenauer, 1997; Wood, 2001b). It would be inaccurate to give equal space to discussion of men and women who are physically abused by intimate partners. The same is true of sexual harassment: Although members of both sexes are sexually harassed, most victims are women. The only way I could present a gender-balanced discussion of sexual harassment would be to misrepresent facts.

This book includes information about men and men's issues—more, in fact, than any other book for a course in gender and communication. In the chapters that follow, you'll learn about men's movements, pressures men face to succeed and make money, and stereotypes that limit men in the workplace and in personal relationships.

Research I've included throughout this book shows how social expectations of women and men can restrict all of us. I hope that, as you read this book, you'll perceive that the coverage is as balanced as existing research permits.

expectations for both men and women, marginalize women, condone violence and aggression, and promote inequities.

If you are a man, reading this book may increase your awareness of ways in which cultural views of masculinity constrain your options. You may be uncomfortable learning about social expectations for men to succeed, to be self-sufficient, to repress feelings, and to put work ahead of family. You may also be surprised to learn how your sex benefits you in ways that you may not have noticed. As a result of what you read, you may become more aware of how society values some people more than others and how this different valuing affects the social, political, and economic quality of people's lives.

Becoming aware of inequities in social life may prompt you to criticize practices and attitudes that sustain discrimination and disadvantage. Realize that some people will respond negatively to thoughtful criticisms of current social attitudes and practices. Women who speak out against inequities and discrimination are sometimes accused of male bashing. Men who speak out against discrimination against women are sometimes regarded as wimps or as disloyal to men. Such responses reflect an unwillingness to engage the substance of the criticism. If you want to take an active role in shaping our shared world, you must anticipate struggles with those who are less willing to consider ideas that question familiar perspectives and ways of acting.

In his commentary, Patrick makes an important point when he says that he personally doesn't discriminate against women. We need to distinguish between the actions and attitudes of individuals and the social practices and values of our culture. This book doesn't suggest that individual men are bad, oppressive, or sexist. The point is that Western culture as a whole has constructed inequalities between women and men, and these inequalities continue in our era. The problem, then, is not rooted primarily in individual men or women. Rather, it is rooted in the social system that accords unequal value and opportunity on the basis of sex, skin color, sexual orientation, and other factors. This kind of prejudice diminishes us all. It limits our appreciation of human diversity by falsely defining a very narrow zone of what is good, normal, and worthy of respect. Regardless of whether you are privileged or oppressed by social evaluations of what is normal and good, your study of gender, communication, and culture may be unsettling. If you are seriously disturbed by what you read, you might find it helpful to talk with your instructor or to visit the counseling center at your school.

> ### Patrick
> I don't want to be lumped with all men. I am not sexist; I don't discriminate against women; I believe in gender equality and try to practice it in my relationships with women. It really makes me angry when people bash males as if we are all oppressors or something. I don't oppress women or anyone else, and I don't want to be blamed for unfair things that others do.

WHY I WROTE THIS BOOK

I've written *Gendered Lives* because I believe that change is needed in how we view and enact gender. I also believe that the knowledge in this book can empower you to think more carefully about your personal identity and our shared world. Since the first edition appeared, I've received many positive responses from students in my classes as well as from students around the nation. I've also received feedback that has helped me rethink and improve this book. I am most gratified when readers like Meghann, who attends a college in the Midwest, tell me that this book has made a difference in their lives.

> ### Meghann
> This book was an eye-opener for me. I'd never thought about how society has shaped my sense of myself as a woman or what that means. Now that I do see how society shapes me—or tries to shape me—I think more about how I want to be. I still agree with some social views of women and men, but there are others that I am starting to question. Because now I think critically about these views and their impact on me, I feel more in charge of who I am and who I will be.

Yet the book you are holding is not the one that Meghann read. Because gender, culture, and communication are always in flux, this book has changed in many ways since the first edition. It has evolved in response to changes in societies and in response to feedback from students and faculty.

CHANGES IN THIS EDITION

In addition to continuing to emphasize our potential as agents of change, this edition includes more than 300 new references to research that has been published since the fifth edition went to press or that I had not read at that time. For example, this edition gives greater attention to people who are intersexed, transsexed, and transgendered. Chapter 3 now includes expanded coverage of the third wave of U.S. feminism, which is charting an ambitious agenda for the future. I've also expanded discussion of men's movements, devoting all of Chapter 4 to them. It provides in-depth coverage of men's movements with new material on men's antiviolence organizations. Chapters 5 and 7 include enlarged discussions of fathers' influence on children, and Chapter 8 features new material on what it means to be a man in 21st-century America. I've also updated Chapter 9 to provide a more current picture of gendered dynamics in education. In making these changes, I've striven to avoid the tendency of a book to grow longer with each new edition. I've eliminated dated material and sources to make room for more current research and coverage of issues that are important in our lives today.

Another change in this edition of *Gendered Lives* is greater attention to gender beyond the boundaries of the United States. I chose not to add a chapter on intercultural gender beliefs and practices because I didn't want to separate it from discussion of issues such as families, education, relationships, and so forth. Instead, I've woven information about gender in a range of cultures into the book as a whole.

The revisions in this edition underline the urgency of change. In the chapters that follow, you'll learn about the extent to which our society creates inequities that diminish individual and collective life. Is it right, for instance, that at least 50% of women working outside of the home experience sexual harassment in their jobs? Is there any way to justify the fact that every 12 seconds, every day in the United States, a woman is battered by her intimate partner, or that each day four women die from battering? Is it fair that men who want to spend time with their families are often evaluated negatively in professional contexts? Is it fair that most of the advances won by women's movements have benefited White, middle-class women more than minority and poor women? Is there any reason why a typical woman working full time outside the home earns less than a typical man working full time? Is it right that mothers have an advantage over fathers in gaining custody of children?

If you don't want inequities such as these to continue, read on. Becoming aware of how our culture establishes and communicates inequities is necessary, but that alone will not lead to changes. In fact, concentrating exclusively on what is wrong tends to depress us and paralyze impulses toward reform. Awareness of inequities must be coupled with belief that change is possible. A bit of historical perspective should convince us of this. In the 1800s, women weren't allowed to vote—they had no voice in the government or in making laws that affected them. They also had no access to a university education, could not own property if they married, and were barred from participating in many professions. Through individual action and social movements, many of these blatant sex inequities have been changed. Since 1972, schools receiving federal funds have been required not to discriminate against women. When my mother had a child in 1958, her employer dismissed her because he believed that a mother belonged at home with her child. She had no voice and no legal recourse. We now have laws to protect women against unfair employment practices. In recent decades, sexual harassment, acquaintance rape, and marital rape have been named and recognized as illegal.

Paralleling these legal changes are substantial transformations in how we view ourselves and each other as women and men. Our culture once defined women as too frail and delicate for hard manual or intellectual work. Today, women pursue careers in business, construction, science, education, politics, and the military. Despite lingering barriers, women are doing things and defining themselves in ways not previously possible for women in the United States.

Views of men, too, have changed. At the turn of the century, our society defined manliness in terms of physical strength and bravery. Following the Industrial Revolution, the ability to earn a good salary became the social standard of manliness. Today, many men are challenging social definitions of men as income producers and are seeking greater opportunities to participate in family life and personal relationships. You have options for what you will do and who you will be that were not available to your parents.

COMMUNICATION AS THE FULCRUM OF CHANGE

Communication is the heart of social life and social change. Through communication we identify and challenge current cultural views that constrain individuals and create inequities. We also rely on communication to define alternatives to the status quo and persuade others to share our visions. For example, in the mid-1800s Elizabeth Cady Stanton and other early feminists galvanized support for the women's rights movement through their eloquent speeches. Public discourse sparks and guides collective efforts at political reform.

Other kinds of communication also instigate change. Perhaps you talk with a friend about gender inequities, and as a result your friend alters her perceptions.

Maybe a teacher discusses sexual harassment with his class, and a student is empowered to bring charges against a man who has been harassing her. You talk with your father about ways in which current leave policies disadvantage working mothers, and he persuades his company to revise its policies. Wherever there is change, we find communication. Through your public, social, and interpersonal communication, you are a powerful agent of change—someone who can transform yourself and the society in which we jointly participate.

Information is a key foundation for being an effective change agent. Before you can define what needs to be different, you must first know what exists now and what it implies. Reading *Gendered Lives* will provide a range of viewpoints on issues such as those mentioned in this introductory chapter. Then you can make informed choices about what you believe and about the identity you wish to fashion for yourself. You may decide to change how you define yourself, or you may be satisfied with your identity and the existing gender arrangements in our culture. Either stance is grounded if it is an *informed* choice—but no choice is wise if it is not based on information and serious reflection.

THE CHALLENGE OF STUDYING COMMUNICATION, GENDER, AND CULTURE

Studying communication, gender, and culture requires courage because it involves us in perplexing questions about our society and our personal identities. We must be willing to consider new ideas openly and to risk values and identities that are familiar to us. Further, with awareness comes responsibility. Once we are informed about gender and communication, we can no longer sit back passively as if this were not our concern. It *is* our concern both because it affects each of us directly and because we are part of a collective world. Thus, how we act—or fail to act—influences our shared culture.

Although studying communication, gender, and culture is disturbing, it can be very worthwhile. By questioning constructed inequality, we empower ourselves to do more than unthinkingly reproduce the cultural patterns we have inherited. By involving ourselves in communication that enlarges others' awareness and revises cultural practices, we assume active roles in creating personal and collective lives that are fairer, more humane, and infinitely more enriching than what might otherwise be possible. That is the goal of *Gendered Lives*.

DISCUSSION QUESTIONS

1. Write a paragraph explaining what it means to you to be a man or woman today. At the end of the course, you may want to review what you've written.

2. What does feminism mean to you? Write down your definition and see if it changes during the course of reading this book and taking this class.

3. Using my self-description as a guideline, consider how your identity influenced your choice to take this course as well as how it may affect your perceptions of topics in the book and the course. Have you been privileged and disadvantaged by your race, class, sex, and sexual orientation? How have your privileges and disadvantages affected your opportunities, knowledge of issues, interests, abilities, goals, and so on?

4. This is a good time to familiarize yourself with InfoTrac® College Edition. Access the InfoTrac College Edition Web page at *http://www.infotrac-college.com/wadsworth*. Type in the password from the card you received with your free subscription. You will be at the opening screen. Select Keywords and type "women and language." Read several of the articles that appear, to see the kind of current research in the area of gender, communication, and culture.

5. I explain why I use inclusive language. What do you think of modifying language to reduce exclusion? Is *partner* preferable to *spouse*? Is *he* or *she* better than *he*? Does language make a difference in how we think?

6. What changes do you think are most needed in our society? How are these related to issues of communication, gender, and culture?

1

The Study of Communication, Gender, and Culture

We are looking for permission to be more than our society tells us we are.

—STARHAWK

f you tune in to popular TV talk shows, the chances are good that you'll see guests discussing gender and communication. If you go to a bookstore, you'll find dozens of popular advice books that promise to help men and women communicate with each other. The general public's fascination with gender and communication is mirrored by college students' interest. Gender and communication is a rapidly expanding area of study in colleges and universities around the nation. Many campuses, like mine, cannot meet the high student demand for enrollment in these courses.

In this chapter we will consider how learning about relationships among gender, communication, and culture can empower you personally and professionally. Then we will look at the key concepts and vocabulary that form the framework of this book.

COMMUNICATION, GENDER, AND CULTURE AS AN AREA OF STUDY

Courses in gender, communication, and culture have grown remarkably in the past two decades due to expanded knowledge and awareness of the value of learning about this area of personal and cultural life.

■ Expanded Knowledge of Gender, Communication, and Culture

Had you attended college in the 1970s, you would not have found a textbook like this one. Classes that explore various aspects of gender have become widespread only in the last twenty years. An explosion of interdisciplinary scholarship has generated rich insight into how gender is created, sustained, and changed by communication within cultures. Research has also shown us how gender shapes individuals' communication and how, in turn, communication influences cultural views of women and men. In *Gendered Lives,* you'll encounter research that enables you to appreciate the profound connections between gender, communication, and culture.

The Value of Studying Communication, Gender, and Culture

Learning about relationships among communication, gender, and culture serves three important goals. First, it enhances your appreciation of complex ways in which cultural values and habits influence your views of masculinity and femininity and men and women. Differences between feminine and masculine communication often show up when heterosexual partners try to work through problems using distinct styles of conflict management, when male and female co-workers have different preferences for how to lead a meeting, when teachers interact differently with female and male students, when media represent men and women in sex-stereotyped ways, and when female and male political candidates say similar things but the public evaluates them differently. You can increase your understanding of personal, social, and professional life by learning about masculine and feminine communication styles and cultural views of gender.

Second, studying gender, communication, and culture will enhance your insight into yourself and your gender, both as it is now and as you may revise it. You will become more aware of ways in which cultural expectations of gender are communicated to you in your daily life. In turn, this will expand your insight into how your own communication does or doesn't conform to prevailing cultural prescriptions for gender. The knowledge you gain will enable you to make more informed choices about who you want to be and how you participate in cultural life.

Third, studying communication, gender, and culture should strengthen your effectiveness as a communicator. Learning about general differences in how women and men communicate will enlarge your ability to appreciate the distinct validity of diverse communication styles. This allows you to interact more constructively and insightfully with others whose ways of communicating may differ from your own. In an era marked by diversity, effective participation requires us to develop skill in understanding varied individuals and to cultivate a range of communication skills.

THE MEANING OF GENDER IN A TRANSITIONAL ERA

These days we hear a lot about miscommunication between the sexes. Men are often confused when women want to continue talking after men think an issue is settled; women may be frustrated when men seem not to listen or don't respond to what they say. What men and women expect of each other and themselves is no longer clear.

■ Confusing Attitudes

You probably don't subscribe to your grandparents' ideals of manhood and womanhood. You may believe that both women and men should be able to pursue careers and that both should be involved in homemaking and child care. You are not surprised when a woman knows something about car maintenance or a man prepares a good meal. These experiences and views depart from those of former generations. Americans as a whole have enlarged their perspectives on women's and men's roles and abilities.

Yet, if you're like most of your peers, there are also a number of gender issues about which you are confused. Many people believe women should have equal opportunities in public and work life but think women should not be involved in actual wartime combat. Although a majority of young adults believe both parents should participate in child rearing, most people also assume that the mother, not the father, should be the primary caregiver during the early years of children's lives (Tyre & McGinn, 2003). You may support equal opportunity but still think that colleges and universities

Michael

The other day in class we were talking about whether women should have combat duty. I'm really uncomfortable with where I stand on this, since I *think* one way, but I *feel* another. I do think women should have to serve just as much as men do. I've never thought it was right that they didn't have to fight. And I think women are just as competent as men at most things and could probably be good soldiers. But then when I think about my mom or my sister or my girlfriend being in the

(continued)

should be allowed to offer more and bigger scholarships to male athletes. You may believe that women are as effective as men in management, yet perhaps you're still more comfortable with a man as your supervisor.

When we grapple with issues like these, we realize that our attitudes aren't always clear even to ourselves. On one level many of us think women and men are equal in most respects. Yet on another level, where deeply ingrained values and beliefs reside, we may hold some very traditional views (Conway & Vartanian, 2000; Powlishta, 2000). We live in a transitional era in which we no longer accept many traditional views of women and men, yet we haven't become comfortable with alternative images. This makes our lives and our relationships interesting, unsettled—and sometimes very frustrating.

(Michael, continued)

trenches, having to kill other people, maybe being a prisoner who is tortured and assaulted, I just feel that's wrong. It doesn't seem right for women to be involved in killing when they're the ones who give life. Then, too, I want to protect my girlfriend and sister and mom from the ugliness and danger of war. But then this other part of me says, "Hey, guy, you know that kind of protectiveness is a form of chauvinism." I just don't know where I stand on this except that I'm glad I don't have to decide whether to send women into combat!

Changing Traditions

In 1995 the first woman enrolled at The Citadel, a military school that had been all male for 151 years. Times have changed. In May of 1999, the first female cadet graduated from The Citadel. She completed the training in only three years. In December of 1999, an African American woman was the first woman to graduate from The Citadel and enter full-time military service as a second lieutenant in the Marines. In the summer of 1999, a woman led the military training for new cadets. In 2000, the admissions office at The Citadel reported an increase of 33% in the number of women applicants over the previous year. According to Major General John Grinalds (2000), a faculty member at the school, allowing women to enter the school made The Citadel "stronger than ever."

And it's not just The Citadel that's changed. In 1994 restrictions on women's participation in the U.S. military were changed to open 250,000 positions to women in the armed forces (Gerber, 2003). Women now serve in a range of positions, including fighter pilot. But some American women fought for their country even when women were not allowed to do so. Even during the Civil War, a number of women disguised themselves as men in order to fight (Blanton & Cook, 2002).

 Visit The Citadel's home page at **http://www.citadel.edu.** Do the features of the site suggest that women have been well integrated into life at The Citadel?

■ Differences Between Women and Men

Are women and men really as different as pop psychologists would have us believe? Certainly there are some differences between the sexes that we need to understand. There is also substantial variation within each sex as a result of diverse experiences, heredity, sexual orientations, races, cultures, and classes. And there are many similarities between women and men—ways in which the two sexes are more alike than different.

Because there are similarities between the sexes and variations within each sex, it is difficult to come up with language for discussing general patterns of communication. Terms like *women* and *men* are troublesome because they imply that all women can be grouped together and all men can be grouped together. When we say, "Women's communication is more personal than men's," the statement is true of most, but not all, women and men. Certainly some women don't engage in personal talk, and some men do.

Thinking and speaking as if there were some stable, distinct essence that is women and some stable, distinct essence that is men is referred to as **essentializing,*** the tendency to reduce something or someone to certain characteristics we assume are essential to its nature. When we essentialize, we presume that all members of a sex are alike in basic respects (Spelman, 1988; Wood, 1993c; Young, 1992). Essentializing obscures the range of characteristics possessed by individual women and men and conceals differences among members of each sex. In this book we will discuss generalizations about women and men, but this does not imply any essential qualities possessed by all members of a sex. We'll also take time to notice exceptions to generalizations about gender—a point Elaine makes in her commentary.

To think constructively about differences and similarities, we need to understand what gender and sex are, how they are influenced by the culture in which we live, and how communication reflects, expresses, and re-creates gender in our everyday lives. In *Gendered Lives*, we'll consider different images of masculinity and femininity and examine why such diverse views exist and what practical implications they have. We will also examine both how communication shapes our gender identities and how we use communication to express our masculinity or femininity in interaction with others. A third focus of our attention will be culture,

> **Elaine**
>
> I read John Gray's book, and I could identify men and women who were just like he described them—you know, from Mars or Venus. But I also know some men who aren't at all like the ones in his book—they don't go into "caves," which Gray says all men do. And I know some women, myself included, who do go into caves—just retreat from others and conversation to sort stuff out. But Gray says women don't go into caves—they talk with others. What I think is that you can't say anything about all women or all men. There may be generalizations, but there are also exceptions.

---

* Boldfaced terms appear in the Glossary at the end of this book.

because gender is embedded within culture and reflects and shapes the values and assumptions of its cultural context.

RELATIONSHIPS AMONG GENDER, CULTURE, AND COMMUNICATION

When asked to discuss a particular aspect of nature, John Muir, founder of the Sierra Club, said he could not discuss any single part of the natural world in isolation. He noted that each part is "hitched to the universe," meaning it is connected to all other parts of nature. Gender, culture, and communication are interlinked, and they are hitched to the whole universe. Because this is so, we cannot study any one of them without understanding a good deal about the other two. What gender means depends heavily on cultural values and practices; the ways a culture defines masculinity and femininity shape expectations about how individual women and men should communicate; and how individuals communicate establishes meanings of gender that, in turn, influence cultural views. Sex, gender, culture, and communication are complex concepts that we need to define so we can share common meanings and vocabulary in the chapters that follow.

■ Sex

Although many people use the terms *gender* and *sex* interchangeably, they have distinct meanings (Reeder, 1996). **Sex** is a designation based on biology, whereas **gender** is socially and psychologically constructed. Often sex and gender go together so that most men are primarily masculine and most women are primarily feminine. In other cases a male is more feminine than most men, or a woman is more masculine than the majority of women. Sex and gender are inconsistent for transsexual individuals, who feel they are trapped in the body of one sex but identify strongly with the other sex (Fausto-Sterling, 2000; Herdt, 1996; Money, 1988). The term *gender* refers to the identities, roles, activities, feelings, and so forth that society associates with being male or female and that we as individuals learn and either internalize or challenge. This means that your gender is an area of personal choice because you can change it more easily than your sex. Because sex is the less complex concept, we'll explain it first, then discuss gender.

A person is designated male or female based on external genitalia (penis and testes in males, clitoris and vagina in females) and internal sex organs (ovaries and uterus in females, prostate in males). Genitalia and other sex markers are determined by chromosomes. Of the 23 pairs of chromosomes that direct human development, only one pair determines sex. The chromosome pair that determines sex usually has two chromosomes, and one of these is always an X. The presence or absence of a Y chromosome determines whether a fetus will develop into what we recognize as male or female. Thus, XX results in a female, and XY results in a male.

You might have noticed that I qualified discussion of genetic determination of sex by using the word *usually*. That's because there are occasional variations in the sex chromosomes. Some people have XO, XXX, XXY, or XYY sex chromosomes (Blackless, Charuvastra, Derryek, Fausto-Sterling, Lauzanne, & Lee, 2000; Dreger, 1998). All fetuses (and people) have at least one X chromosome because it carries genes essential to life (Jegalian & Lahn, 2001). Males, who typically have only a single X chromosome, are more vulnerable to a number of X-linked recessive conditions than are females, who have two X chromosomes and are unlikely to have an X-linked recessive condition on both. As long as there is a single Y chromosome, a fetus will develop into what we label male, although an XXY or XYY male may differ in some respects from an XY male.

Sexual development is also influenced by hormones. Even before birth, hormones affect us. Beginning only seven weeks after conception, hormones influence sexual differentiation in the fetus. When pregnancy proceeds routinely, fetuses with a Y chromosome are bathed in androgens that ensure development of male sex organs, and fetuses without a Y chromosome receive fewer androgens, so female sex organs develop. In some cases, however, a genetically female fetus (XX) is exposed to excessive progesterone (the synthetic form is called progestin) and may develop male genitalia. The opposite is also true: If a male fetus is deprived of progesterone during the critical period of sexual differentiation, his male genitalia may not develop and he will appear physically female (Money, 1986; Pinsky, Erickson, & Schimke, 1999).

Social Views of Intersexuality

For many years, infants who were born with ambiguous genitals routinely underwent "normalizing surgery" to reconstruct genitals to be more consistently male or female (Crouch, 1998; Kessler, 1998; Lorber, 2001; Preves, 1998).

But is it possible that intersexed people don't need to be "fixed"? Recently, a number of scholars, scientists, doctors, and laypersons have advocated acceptance of intersexuality (Preves, 2004; Sheridan, 2001). Adult intersexuals within the transgender movement challenge society's view that they are abnormal. They believe that being intersexed is not a disease or "problem"; it's just another form of human identity. In other words, as Suzanne Kessler (1998) says, "There is no one best way to be male or female or any other gender possibility" (p. 132).

In 1992 Cheryl Chase founded Intersex Society of North America (ISNA), which has three primary missions: (1) to affirm a positive identity for intersexed people; (2) to change social attitudes toward intersexuality; and (3) to stop "normalizing" surgery.

 Visit the Web site at: **http://www.isna.org**. Another site that provides information on intersexed and transgendered people is **http://www.itpeople.org.**

"Sex brought us together, but gender drove us apart."

Some children are born with some biological characteristics of each sex. Traditionally, people whose internal and external genitalia are inconsistent were called **hermaphrodites,** a term from Roman mythology. According to the myth, the god Hermes and the goddess Aphrodite had a son whom they named Hermaphroditos. When the young woman Salmacis saw Hermaphroditos, she immediately fell in love and begged the gods to join her with him so that they would never be apart. Granting Salmacis's wish, the gods joined them into a single body that was both male and female. Today the term **intersexed** is preferred by people who have some biological qualities of each sex.

The influence of hormones does not end at birth. They continue to affect our development by determining whether we will menstruate, how much body hair we will have and where it will grow, how much fat and muscle tissue we will develop, and so forth. Because male fetuses receive heavier amounts of hormones, they become sensitized to hormonal influence. Researchers currently think this may be why males are more sensitive than females to hormonal activity, especially during puberty (Jacklin, 1989; Tavris, 1992).

Because research on biological sexuality is still relatively new, there are many questions for which we lack conclusive answers. For instance, among scientists opinion is divided about whether sex hormones affect sexual orientation (Adler, 1990; Money, 1988) and cognitive abilities (Adler, 1989; Bleier, 1986). There is also controversy about whether intersexed people should be "normalized" through medical treatment (Dreger, 2000).

However strong the influence of biology may be, it seldom, if ever, determines behaviors. It *influences* behavior in greater or lesser amounts, but it doesn't *determine* behavior, personality, and so on. Biology also doesn't determine the meaning that members of a culture assign to particular behaviors—which ones are valued, which ones devalued. More important than whether biological differences exist is how we treat differences. This moves us into discussion of a second concept: gender.

■ Gender

Gender is a considerably more complex concept than sex. There is nothing a person does to acquire her or his sex. It is a classification based on genetic and biological factors, and it tends to endure over time. Gender, however, is neither innate nor necessarily stable. It is acquired through interaction in a social world, and it changes over time. One way to understand gender is to think of it as what we learn about sex. We are born male or female, but we learn to be masculine and feminine. Gender is a social, symbolic construction that varies across cultures, over time within a given culture, and in relation to the other gender. We'll elaborate these three aspects of gender.

What gender means depends on a society's values, beliefs, and preferred ways of organizing collective life. Consider current meanings of masculinity and femininity in America. To be masculine is to be strong, ambitious, successful, rational, and emotionally controlled. Although these requirements are perhaps less rigid than they were in earlier eras (House, Dallinger, & Kilgallen, 1998), they remain largely intact. Those we regard as "real men" still don't cry or need others; "real men" are successful and powerful in their professional and public lives (Kimmel, 2000a, 2000b).

Bishetta

I remember when I was very little, maybe 5 or so. My brother and I were playing outside in the garden and Mom saw us. Both of us were coated with dirt—our clothes, our skin, everything. Mom came up to the edge of the garden and shouted, "Bishetta, you get out of that garden right now. Just look at you. Now what do you think folks will think of a dirty little girl? You don't want people to think you're not a lady, do you?" She didn't say a word to my brother, who was just as dirty.

Femininity in our era is also relatively consistent with earlier views, although there is increasing latitude in what is considered appropriate for women. To be feminine is to be physically attractive, deferential, emotionally expressive, nurturing, and concerned with people and relationships (Spence & Buckner, 2000). Those who embody the cultural definition of femininity still don't allow themselves to outdo men (especially their partners), to disregard others' feelings, or to put their needs ahead of others'. "Real women" still look good, adore children, and care about homemaking. For all of the changes in our views of women and men, the basic blueprint remains relatively constant (Greenfield, 1997; Kerr, 1997, 1999).

By definition, gender is learned. Socially endorsed views of masculinity and femininity are taught to individuals through a variety of cultural means. From infancy on, we are encouraged to conform to the gender that society prescribes for us. Young girls are often cautioned, "Don't be self-ish—share with others," "Be careful—don't hurt yourself," and "Don't get dirty." They are praised for looking pretty, expressing emotions, and being nice to others. Young boys, in contrast, are more likely to be admonished, "Don't be a sissy," "Go after what you want," and "Don't cry." Usually they are reinforced for strength, independence, and success, particularly in competitive arenas.

So far we've focused on how individuals learn gender, yet gender is not a strictly personal quality. Rather, it is a complex set of interrelated cultural ideas that stipulate the social *meaning* of sex. Because social definitions of gender permeate public and private life, we see them as normal, natural, and right. When the practices and structures that make up social life constantly represent women and men in particular ways, it is difficult to imagine that masculinity and femininity could be defined differently. But, as we will see later in this chapter, masculinity and femininity come in many forms across cultures.

> ## Bob
>
> What I always thought was unfair in my family was the way my folks responded to failures my sisters and I had. Like once my sister Maryellen tried out for cheerleader, and she wasn't picked. So she was crying and upset, and Mom was telling her that it was okay and that she was a good person and everyone knew that and that winning wasn't everything. And when Dad came home he said the same things—telling her she was okay even if she wasn't picked. But when I didn't make the junior varsity football team, Dad went bonkers! He asked me what had gone wrong. I told him nothing, that other guys were just better than I had been. But he'd have none of that. He told me I couldn't give up and had to work harder, and he expected me to make the team next season. He even offered to hire a coach for me. It just wasn't okay for me not to succeed.

The fact that the social meanings of gender are taught to us does not mean we are passive recipients of cultural meanings. We make choices to accept cultural prescriptions or to modify or reject them. Individuals who internalize and embody cultural prescriptions for gender reinforce existing social views. People who reject conventional prescriptions and step outside of social meanings for gender often provoke changes in cultural views. In the early part of the 19th century, for instance, many women challenged social views that asserted that women were not entitled to vote or pursue higher education (Simon & Danziger, 1991). In defying their era's definition of women, these individuals transformed social views of women and the rights to which they are entitled.

Meanings of gender are also changed by communication that is less public and less collective than social movements. Role models, for instance, provide individuals with visible alternatives to traditional views. We also influence ideas about gender as we interact casually with friends. When one woman encourages another to be more assertive and to confront her supervisor about problems, she may instigate change in what her friend sees as appropriate behavior for women. Similarly, when one man tells another that time with his family is a top priority, his friend has to rethink and perhaps change his own views of men's roles. As these examples indicate, there is a reciprocal relationship between individual communication and cultural views of gender: Each influences the other to continuously uphold or remake the meanings of masculinity and femininity.

A good example of the way we remake the meaning of gender is the concept of **androgyny.** In the 1970s researchers coined the word *androgyny* by combining the Greek word *aner* or *andros,* which means "man," and the Greek word *gyne,* which means "woman." As you may know, androgynous individuals embody qualities that Western culture considers both feminine and masculine. For example, androgynous women and men are both nurturing and assertive, both strong and sensitive. Many of us don't want to be restricted to the social prescriptions of a single gender, and we cultivate both masculine and feminine qualities in ourselves. As Miguel points out in his commentary, there is value in the full range of human qualities—those the culture labels feminine and those it labels masculine.

To realize the arbitrariness of the meanings of gender, we need only consider varying ways different cultures define masculinity and femininity. Many years ago, anthropologist Margaret Mead (1935/1968) reported three distinct gender patterns in the New Guinea societies she studied. Among Arapesh people, both women and men conformed closely to what we consider feminine behavior. Both were passive, peaceful, and deferential, and both nurtured others, especially young children. The Mundugumor tribe socialized both women and men to be aggressive, independent, and competitive. Mothers were not nurturant and spent very little time with newborn babies, weaning them early instead. Within the Tchambuli society, genders were the reverse of current ones in America: Women were domineering and sexually aggressive, whereas men were considered delicate and taught to wear decorative clothes and curl their hair so they would be attractive to women.

In some cultures, a person's gender is considered changeable (Kessler & McKenna, 1978), so someone born male may choose to live and be regarded as female and vice versa. In other societies, notably some Native American groups, more than two genders are recognized and celebrated (Brown, 1997; Nanda, 2004; Olien, 1978). Individuals who have qualities of multiple genders are highly esteemed. I personally realized the arbitrariness of gender definitions in America when I spent some time living with Tamang villagers in the hill country of Nepal. There both women and men do what we consider sex-specific tasks. For instance, men cook and participate in raising children. Women also do these things as well as engage in heavy manual labor. In the United States, gender varies across racial–ethnic groups. In general, African American women are more assertive than European American women, and African American men tend to be more communal than White men (Gaines, 1995; Rothenberg, Schafhausen, & Schneider, 2000; V. Smith, 1998).

Even within a single culture, the meaning of gender varies over time. Views of gender in the United States were not always as distinct as they are today. Prior to the Industrial Revolution, family and work were intertwined for most people (Ryan, 1979). Thus, men and women worked together to raise crops or run businesses, and both were involved in homemaking and child rearing. Affection and expressiveness were considered normal in men as well as in women (Degler, 1980); industry and strength were attractive in women just as they were in men (Cancian, 1989; Douglas, 1977).

Emma

In my day, women were a lot different than they are today. We were quieter, and we put other people ahead of ourselves. We knew our place, and we didn't try to be equal with men. Today's women are very different. Some of the younger women in my classes put their careers ahead of marriage, some don't want children, and many think they should be as much the head of a family as the man. Sometimes I feel they are all wrong in what they want and how they are, but I have to admit that a part of me envies them the options and opportunities I never had.

The Industrial Revolution gave rise to factories and to paid labor outside the home as a primary way of making a living. With this came a division of life into separate spheres of work and home. As men took jobs outside the home, women increasingly assumed responsibility for family life. Consequently, femininity was redefined as being nurturing, dependent on men for income, focused on relationships, and able to make a good home. Masculinity was also redefined as being emotionally reserved, ambitious, and successful at work, and—especially—earning a good income (Cancian, 1989; Risman & Godwin, 2001). In her commentary, Emma, a 58-year-old, part-time student, reflects on changes in how women see themselves.

As another example of how meanings of gender change, consider how ideals of beauty for women have varied over time in the United States. In the 1950s Marilyn Monroe was widely considered the sexiest woman alive. Yet by today's standards of excessive slimness in women, she would be considered fat! These examples remind us that what we take for granted as masculine and feminine is really quite arbitrary. Meanings of gender vary across cultures and over time in any given society.

Changing views of gender as well as sex are also evident in increasing recognition of individuals who don't fit conventional definitions of male or female, masculine or feminine. We've already noted that intersexed individuals have biological characteristics of both males and females. Transgendered individuals feel their biological sex is wrong—that they are really women trapped in men's bodies or men trapped in women's bodies (Howey, 2002; Sheridan, 2001; Stryker, 1997, 1998). Transgendered people often dress and adopt the behaviors of the gender with which they identify. In the movie *Boys Don't Cry,* Hillary Swank gave a compelling portrayal of a transgendered person. Transsexuals have had surgery and hormonal

He Was a She

AP/Wide World Photos

Jazz musician Billy Tipton was born on December 29, 1914. Early in life, Billy discovered jazz, and it became a lifelong passion. In the 1950s, Billy played saxophone and piano with popular bands that performed in night-clubs throughout the West and Midwest. Eventually Billy headed up his own band, the Billy Tipton Trio.

Tipton married Kitty Oakes in 1960, and the couple raised three adopted sons. They had a traditional family life, complete with Boy Scouts, PTA, and church (Holt, 1998). In the late 1970s, Oakes and Tipton separated but remained friends. When Tipton died in 1989, the mortician discovered that he was actually a she. Jon Clark, one of Tipton's adopted sons, was stunned to learn his father was female. Clark said it had never occurred to him that his father was a woman (Middle-brook, 1998).

Clark wasn't the only one who was fooled. Dick O'Neill, who played drums with the Billy Tipton Trio for a decade, said, "I never suspected a thing." Neither did Duke Ellington or others with whom Billy played. Although some people who had attended live performances remarked that Billy had a high singing voice, none of them ever questioned that Tipton was male.

Why did Tipton live as a man—both publicly and privately? According to Kitty Oakes, social norms in the mid-20th century stipulated that only men could be jazz musicians and travel around the country with bands. To follow his love of jazz, Billy had to appear to be male. As an adolescent, Billy Tipton (who was born Dorothy Lucille Tipton) bound his breasts so that he could appear to be male and get jobs with the big bands. Later, Billy wore his hair in a crew cut and dressed in men's suits. In his private life, Billy told Kitty Oakes when they married that he'd been injured in an automobile accident and that he couldn't engage in conventional sexual activities.

treatments to make their bodies more closely match the sex with which they iden-tify (Devor, 1997). After surgery, transsexuals may describe themselves as *post-transitional males to females* (MTF) or *post-transitional females to males* (FTM). One MTF transsexual is Deirdre (formerly Donald) McCloskey, a professor of eco-nomics. According to her, surgery and hormones changed her sex, but she had to learn gender, had to learn to be feminine. She studied all of the small actions—ges-tures, facial expressions, postures—that women use and practiced them until they were second nature to her. Reflecting on this, McCloskey (1999) wrote that gender is "an accretion of learned habits, learned so well that they feel like external conditions, merely the way things are. It is a shell made by the snail and then confining it" (pp. 83–84).

Transgendered, transexed, and intersexed people challenge the idea that sex and gender are dualities—that is, that male and female, masculine and feminine are opposite, stable, and the only two possibilities (Namaste, 2000). Lane Bruner (1996) encourages us to question gender stereotypes and dichotomies because they limit our understanding of the range of possible sexualities and genders. Similarly, other cultures' views of sexuality and sexual orientation challenge views prevalent in the United States. For example, the Sambia in Melanesia consider same-sex sexual activity between males a normal part of developing an adult masculine identity (Herdt, 1997). In ancient Greece, older men with status often took young men as lovers; this was considered the ideal, the purest love relationship.

We should also realize that gender is a relational concept, because femininity and masculinity make sense in relation to each other. Our society defines femininity in contrast to masculinity and masculinity as a counterpoint to femininity. As meanings of one gender change, so do meanings of the other. For instance, when social views of masculinity stressed physical strength and endurance, femininity was defined by physical weakness and dependence on men's strengths. Perhaps you've read in older novels about women's fainting spells—the "vapors"—and the smelling salts they kept nearby to bring them out of faints. With the Industrial Revolution, sheer physical strength was no longer as important to survival, so masculinity was redefined as intellectual ability and success in earning income.

FYI

The Gender Blur

Cross-dressing is not new to our era. Throughout history, a number of people have dressed and behaved other than was typical for their biological sex (Griggs, 1998). For example, the novelist known as George Sand was actually Amandine Aurore Lucile Dudevant, a very stylish cross-dresser and an aficionado of fine cigars.

Mary Edwards Walker was the first woman commissioned as a surgeon in the Union Army in the American Civil War. To practice medicine on the field, she abandoned her petticoats for a modified version of the uniform male officers wore. Walker discovered she preferred the comfort of men's clothes, so after the war she appeared in full drag with bow tie and top hat to advocate dress reform for women. Unfortunately for Walker, public attitudes were not in her favor, and she was arrested numerous times for appearing in public dressed inappropriately for a woman.

And then there's Parinyua Kiatbusaba, a Thai gay transvestite who is called *kratoey*, which means "lady boy." Kiatbusaba also happens to be a champion kickboxer who wears lipstick, eye shadow, and pink nail polish when he goes in the ring to pummel his opponents. "Inside, I'm a woman," he says (Spayde, 1998, p. 55).

Simultaneously, women's fainting spells seemed virtually to disappear, as did their former acumen at business and family finances. In part, this happened because society relied less on physical strength to distinguish between women and men.

Let's summarize this extended discussion of gender. We have noted that gender is the social, symbolic meanings that a society confers on biological sex. These meanings are communicated through structures and practices that pervade our daily existence, creating the illusion that they are the natural, normal ways for women and men to be. Yet we've also seen that what gender means varies across cultures and over time in a particular culture, and how we conceive each gender is related to our views of the other. This reminds us that, even though what our society defines as feminine and masculine may seem natural to us, there is nothing necessary about any particular meaning given to gender. By extension, this insight suggests we have more choice than we sometimes realize in how we define ourselves and each other as men and women.

■ Culture

A **culture** consists of structures and practices that reflect and uphold a particular social order by legitimizing certain values, expectations, meanings, and patterns of behavior. Because gender is central to cultural life, a given society's views of gender are reflected in and promoted by a range of social structures and practices.

One of the primary practices that structures society is communication (Weedon, 1987). We are surrounded by communication that announces social views of gender and seeks to persuade us these are natural, correct ways for men and women to be and to behave. We open a magazine and see a beautiful, sexy woman waiting on a man who looks successful and in charge; we turn on our television and watch a prime-time program in which a husband tells of a big business coup while his wife prepares dinner for them; the commercials interspersed in the show depict women cleaning toilet bowls and kitchen floors and men going for the gusto after a pickup basketball game; we go to dinner, and our server presents the check to the man; we meet with a group of people on a volunteer project, and one of the men assumes leadership; a working woman receives maternity leave, but her husband cannot get paternity leave. Each of these practices communicates our society's views of gender.

Dympna

"In 1974 I traveled to New York for my college education. . . . I'm a member of the Ibo tribe of Nigeria, and although I've lived in the United States most of my adult life, my consciousness remains fixed on the time and place of my upbringing. . . . When I left Nigeria at 18, I had no doubts about who and what I was. I was a woman. I was *only* a woman. . . . My role was to be a great asset to my husband. . . . I was, after all, raised within the context of child brides, polygamy, clitorectomies and arranged marriages. . . . I've struggled daily with how best to raise my daughter. Every decision involving Delia is a tug of war between Ibo and American traditions."

Published as: Ugwu-Oju, Dympna (2000, December 4). My turn: Should my tribal past shape Delia's future? *Newsweek,* p. 14.

Consider additional examples of cultural practices that uphold Western views of gender. Although no longer universal, the custom whereby a woman gives up her name and takes her husband's on marriage still prevails. It carries forward the message that a woman is defined by her relationship to a man rather than by her individual identity. Within families, too, numerous practices reinforce social views of gender. Parents routinely allow sons greater freedom and behavioral latitude than they grant daughters, a practice that encourages males to be independent and females not to be. Daughters, much more than sons, are taught to do housework and care for younger siblings, thus reinforcing the idea that women are supposed to be concerned with home and family. These and other practices that we take for granted support our society's views of gender and provide guidelines for how we are supposed to live as individual men and women.

Socially endorsed meanings are also communicated through structures such as institutions, which serve to announce, reflect, and perpetuate gendered cultural views. Schools, for instance, are institutions that often reinforce established cultural prescriptions for gender. Research has shown that some teachers tend to encourage dependence, silence, and deference and frown on assertiveness in female students. Contrast this with the finding that teachers generally reward independence, self-assertion, and activity in boys (Krupnick, 1985; Sadker & Sadker, 1984). Further, studies consistently report that teachers are more likely to encourage males than females to take and compete in math courses (Caplan & Caplan, 1997; Catsambis, 1999; Sandler, 2004) and that both teachers and guidance counselors tend to foster career ambitions in male students but encourage them less in female students (Sandler & Hall, 1986; Wood & Lenze, 1991a).

Another institution that upholds gender ideology is the judicial system. Until recently, a wife could not sue her husband for rape, because intercourse was regarded as a "husband's right." Men's rights are abridged by judicial views of women as the primary caretakers of children, views that are expressed in the presumption that women should have custody of children if divorce occurs. Thus, it is difficult for a father to gain child custody even when he might be the better parent or may be in a better situation to raise children.

In many respects Western culture, as well many other cultures, is **patriarchal**. The term *patriarchy* means "rule by the fathers." In a patriarchal culture, the ideology, structures, and practices were created by men. Because America was defined by men, historically it reflected the perspectives and priorities of men more than those of women. For example, it would be consistent with men's interests to consider women property, which was the case early in America's life. Similarly, from men's point of view laws against marital rape would not be desirable. Today some of the patriarchal tendencies and practices of American culture have abated.

Through its structures and practices, especially communication practices, societies create and sustain perspectives on what is normal and right for women and men. Because messages that reinforce cultural views of gender pervade our daily lives, most of us seldom pause to reflect on whether they are as natural as they have come to seem. Like the air we breathe, they so continuously surround us that we tend to take them for granted and don't question them. Learning to reflect on cultural prescriptions for gender (and other matters) empowers you as an individual. It increases your freedom to choose your own courses of action and identity by enlarging your awareness of the arbitrary and not always desirable nature of cultural expectations.

■ Communication

The last key term we will discuss is **communication.** Communication is a dynamic, systemic process in which two levels of meanings are created and reflected in human interaction with symbols. To understand this rather complicated definition, we will focus on one part of it at a time.

Communication is a dynamic process. Communication is dynamic, which means that it continuously changes, evolves, and moves on. Because communication is a process, there are no definite beginnings or endings of communicative interactions. Suppose a friend drops by while you're reading this chapter and asks what you are doing. "Reading about gender, communication, and culture," you reply. Your friend then says, "Oh, you mean about how men and women talk differently." You respond, "Not exactly—you see, gender isn't really about males and females; it's about the meaning our culture attaches to each sex." Did this interaction begin with your friend's question, or with your instructor's assignment of the reading, or with other experiences that led you to enroll in this class?

Think also about when this communication ends. Does it stop when your friend leaves? Maybe not. What the two of you talk about may influence what you think and do later, so the influence or effect of your communication continues beyond the immediate encounter. All communication is like this: It is an ongoing, dynamic process without clear beginnings and endings.

Communication is systemic. Communication occurs in particular situations or systems that influence what and how we communicate and what meanings we attach to messages. For example, suppose you observe the following interaction. In an office building where you are waiting for an appointment, you see a middle-aged man walk to the secretary's desk and put his arm around her shoulders and say, "You really do drive me crazy when you wear that outfit." She doesn't look up from her work but responds, "You're crazy, period. It has nothing to do with what I'm wearing." How would you interpret this interaction? Is it an instance of sexual harassment? Are they co-workers who are comfortable joking about sexuality with each other? Is he perhaps not an employee but her friend or romantic partner? The only reasonable conclusion to draw is that we cannot tell what is happening or what it means to the communicators, because we don't understand the systems within which this interaction takes place.

When we say communication is systemic, we mean more than that its contexts affect meaning. Recall John Muir's statement that each part of nature is "hitched to the universe." As a system, all aspects of communication are interlinked and interactive. Who is speaking affects what is said and what it means. In the foregoing example, the secretary would probably attach different meanings to the message "You drive me crazy when you wear that outfit" if it was said by a friend or by a co-worker with a reputation for hassling women. Communication is also influenced by how we feel: When you feel tired or irritable, you may take offense at a comment that ordinarily wouldn't bother you. The time of day and place of interaction may also affect what is communicated and how our words and actions are interpreted.

The largest system affecting communication is our culture, the context within which all of our interactions take place. As we saw in the preceding section, societies' view and treatment of men and women change over time. Thirty years ago it would have been rude for a man not to open a car door for his date and not to stand when a woman entered a room. Today most people would not regard either as rude. Just a few decades ago, sexual harassment did not have a name and was not considered cause for grievance or legal action. Today, however, laws and policies prohibit sexual harassment, and employees may bring charges against harassers. The same behavior now means something different, and it may have different results from those of 10 years ago. The systems—situation, time, people, culture, and so on—within which communication occurs interact; each part affects all others.

> ### Teresa
>
> The stuff we talked about in class last time about contexts of communication helped me understand something that happens a lot. I really hate it when people call me "girl." I mean, I'm an adult, and that means I am a woman, not a little girl. People don't call 22-year-old guys "boys," do they? So it grates on me when folks say that. Except it doesn't bother me when older folks like my grandfather call me a girl. I think that doesn't irritate me because I know that "girl" means something different to him and he's of a different generation. I can't really expect someone 66 years old to understand this issue and to change a whole lifetime's habit. So I know he doesn't mean it as an insult, and I don't take it as one. But if a 20- or 30-year-old calls me "girl," I'll call them on it!

Communication has two levels of meaning. Perhaps you noticed that our definition of communication referred to meaning*s*, not just a single meaning. That's because communication has two levels of meaning. Years ago, a group of clinical psychologists (Watzlawick, Beavin, & Jackson, 1967) noted that all communication has both a content level and a relationship level of meaning.

The **content level of meaning** is its literal meaning. If Ellen says to her partner, Ed, "It's your turn to fix dinner tonight," the content level of her message is a rule about sharing cooking responsibilities and a reminder of whose turn it is. The content level also indicates what response is expected to follow from a message. In this case, both Ellen and Ed may assume he will get busy working on dinner. The content level of meaning involves a literal message and implies what response is appropriate.

The **relationship level of meaning** is less obvious. It defines the relationship between communicators by indicating each person's identity and their relationship to each other. In our example, Ellen seems to be defining the relationship as an equal one in which each partner does half of the cooking. The relationship level of meaning in her comment also suggests that she regards it as her prerogative to remind her partner when it's his turn. Ed could respond by saying, "I don't feel like cooking. You do it tonight." Here the content level is again clear. He is describing how he feels and suggesting that he will not cook. On the relationship level, however, he may be arguing about the power balance between himself and Ellen. He is refusing to accept her reminder that it's his turn to cook. If she agrees and fixes dinner, then she accepts Ed's definition of the relationship as not exactly equal. She affirms his right not to fix some of their meals and his prerogative to tell her to cook.

The relationship level of meaning is the primary one that reflects and influences how people feel about each other. It provides a context for the content level of meaning because it tells us how to interpret the literal message. Perhaps when Ed says he doesn't feel like fixing dinner, he uses a teasing tone and grins, in which case the relationship level of meaning is that Ellen should not take the content level seriously, because he's joking. If, however, he makes his statement in a belligerent voice and glares at her, the relationship level of meaning is that he does mean the content level. Relationship levels of meaning tell us how to interpret content meaning and how communicators see themselves in relation to each other.

Relationship levels of meaning are particularly important when we try to understand gendered patterns of communication. A good example is interruption. Elyse is telling Jed how her day went. He interrupts and says, "Let's head out to the soccer game." The content level of this interruption is simply what Jed said. The more important meaning of an interruption is usually on the relationship level, which in this case declares that Jed has the right to interrupt Elyse, dismiss her topic, and initiate his own. If he interrupts and she does not protest, they agree to let him control the conversation. If she does object, then the two may wind up in extended negotiations over how to define their relationship. In communication, all messages have two levels of meaning.

Meanings are created through human interaction with symbols. This premise highlights two final important understandings about communication. First, it calls our attention to the fact that humans are symbol-using creatures. Symbols are abstract, arbitrary, and often ambiguous ways of representing phenomena. For example, ♀ and ♂ are symbols for *female* and *male* respectively. Words are also symbols, so *woman* and *man* are symbols of particular physical beings. We rely on symbols to communicate and create meanings in our lives.

Because human communication is symbolic, it requires mediation, or thought. Rather than reacting in automatic or instinctive ways to communication, we usually reflect on what was said and what it means before we respond. To be interpreted, symbols require thought. Symbols can also be ambiguous; that is, their meaning may not be clear. Recall our earlier example in which a man tells a secretary, "Your outfit drives me crazy." To interpret what he said, she has to think about their relationship, what she knows about him, and what has occurred in their prior interactions. After thinking about all of these things, she'll decide whether his comment was a joke in poor taste, a compliment, sexual harassment, or a flirtatious show of interest from someone with whom she is romantically involved. Sometimes people interpret what we say in a manner other than what we intended because symbols are so abstract and ambiguous that more than one meaning is plausible.

The second implication of the premise that we create meanings through interaction with symbols is that the significance of communication is not in words themselves. Instead, in the process of communicating with one another, humans *create* meanings. Our verbal and nonverbal behaviors are not simply neutral expressions of thoughts but imply values and judgments. How we express ourselves influences how we and others feel about what we communicate. The statement "You're a feminist" can create different impressions, depending on whether the vocal inflection suggests interest, shock, disdain, or admiration. Calling a woman "aggressive" conjures up an impression that is different from the impression created by calling her "assertive." A man who interacts lovingly with his child could be described as either "nurturing" or "soft," and the two descriptions suggest quite different meanings. People differ in their interpretations of identical messages. One woman is insulted when a man opens a door, whereas another considers it rude if a man doesn't hold a door for her. One person finds it entirely appropriate for a woman manager to give orders, but another employee thinks she's acting unfeminine. The meaning of communication depends on much more than verbal and nonverbal behavior; it arises from human interpretation.

The fact that symbols are abstract, ambiguous, and arbitrary makes it impossible to think of meaning as inherent in symbols themselves. Each of us constructs an interpretation of communication by drawing on our past experiences, our knowledge of the people with whom we are interacting, and other factors in a communication system that influence our interpretations. Because the meaning we attach to communication is rooted in our own perspectives, we are inclined to project our own thoughts, feelings, desires, and so forth onto others' messages. Differences in interpretation are the source of much misunderstanding between people. However, you can become a more effective communicator if you keep in mind that people differ in how they perceive and interpret communication. Reminding yourself of this should prompt you to ask for clarification of another person's meaning rather than assuming your interpretation is correct. Similarly, we should check with others more often than we sometimes do to see how they are interpreting our verbal and nonverbal communication.

SUMMARY

In this chapter we began to explore the nature of communication, gender, and culture. Because each of us is a gendered being, it's important to understand what gender means and how we can be more effective in our communicative interactions within a culture that is also gendered. The primary focus of this chapter was introducing four central concepts: sex, gender, culture, and communication.

Sex is a biological classification, whereas gender is a social, symbolic system through which a culture attaches significance to biological sex. Gender is something individuals learn; yet, because it is constructed by cultures, it is more than an individual quality. It is a whole system of social meanings that specify what is associated with men and women in a given society at a particular time. We also noted that meanings of gender vary over time and across cultures. Finally, we found that gender is relational, because femininity and masculinity gain much of their meaning from the fact that our society juxtaposes them.

The third key concept, culture, refers to structures and practices, particularly communicative ones, through which a society announces and sustains its values. Gender is a particularly significant issue in our culture, so there are abundant structures and practices that serve to reinforce our society's prescriptions for women's and men's identities and behaviors. To understand what gender means and how meanings of gender change, we must explore cultural values and the institutions and activities through which those are expressed and promoted.

Finally, we defined communication as a dynamic, systemic process in which meanings are created and reflected in human interaction with symbols. In examining the dimensions of this definition, we emphasized the fact that communication is a symbolic activity, which implies that it requires reflection and that meanings are variable and constructed rather than inherent in symbols themselves. We also saw that communication can be understood only within its contexts, including the especially important system of culture.

This chapter provides a foundation. In the following chapters we will examine ways in which individuals learn gender, the differences and similarities in feminine and masculine communication, and a range of ways in which gendered communication and identities punctuate our lives.

KEY TERMS

androgyny, 24
communication, 30
content level of meaning, 31
culture, 28
essentializing, 18
gender, 19

hermaphrodite(s), 21
intersexed, 21
patriarchal, 29
relationship level of meaning, 32
sex, 19

DISCUSSION QUESTIONS

1. If you have traveled to other cultures, what differences in views of women and men did you notice between those cultures and your own?

2. Use your InfoTrac College Edition to access Mary Hale's 1999 article, "He says, she says: Gender and the workplace." What does Hale identify as primary differences between men's and women's gender issues in the workplace? Do you foresee these changing in the next decade?

3. Talk with your parents and your grandparents or people of their generations. Ask them what it meant to be a woman or man when they were your age. How are their views different from yours? How do you think the next generation's views about communication, gender, and culture may differ from yours?

4. Type the keyword *transsexual* into the EasyTrac option on your InfoTrac College Edition. Scroll through the listings until you find an article by Sara Riemensnyder in the June 2002 issue of *Reason* entitled "Gender bender: Marriage rights." What would you have done if you had been the judge in J'Noel Gardiner's case?

5. How comfortable are you with current views of masculinity and femininity? Which ones do you find restrictive? Are you doing anything to change them in society's view or to resist them in defining your own personal identity?

2

Theoretical Approaches
to Gender Development

There is nothing so practical as good theory.

—KURT LEWIN

A student of mine named Jenna recently told me that she didn't like studying theory because it had nothing to do with "real life." But the premier social scientist Kurt Lewin disagreed when he insisted, "There is nothing so practical as good theory." What he meant, and what I tried to explain to Jenna, is that theories are very practical. They help us understand, explain, and predict what happens in our lives and the world around us. Although we sometimes think theories are removed from the real world, actually they pertain directly to our everyday lives.

THEORETICAL APPROACHES TO GENDER

A **theory** is simply a way to describe, explain, and predict relationships among phenomena. Each of us uses theories to make sense of our lives, guide our attitudes and actions, and predict others' behavior. Although our theories are not always consciously held, they still shape our conduct and expectations. And in this sense, theories are very practical.

Among the theories that each of us has are the ones we use to make sense of men's and women's behaviors. For instance, assume that you know Kevin and Carlene, who are 11-year-old twins. In many ways they are alike, yet they also differ. Carlene is more articulate than Kevin, and she tends to think in more creative and integrative ways. Kevin is better at solving analytic problems, especially mathematical ones. He also has better developed muscles, although he and Carlene spend equal time in athletics. How you explain the differences between these twins reflects your implicit theory of gender.

If you subscribe to biological theory, you might note that different cognitive strengths result from differential hemispheric specialization in male and female brains. You might also reason that Kevin's greater muscle development results from androgens, which encourage musculature, whereas estrogen programs the body to develop less muscle and more fat and soft tissue.

Then again, perhaps you think there is another reason for the differences between Kevin and Carlene. Knowing that researchers have shown that teachers and parents tend to encourage analytic problem solving in boys and creative thinking in girls, you might explain the twins' different cognitive skills as the result of learning and reinforcement. The same explanation might be advanced for disparity in their muscle development, because you could reason that Kevin is probably more encouraged and rewarded than Carlene for engaging in activities that build muscles.

A third way to explain differences is to point out the likelihood that each twin identifies with same-sex role models. If so, we would predict that Kevin imitates the qualities of men he chooses as models—physical strength and logical thinking. Identifying herself with women, Carlene is more likely to emulate feminine models. These are only three of many ways we could explain the differences between Kevin and Carlene. Each represents a particular theoretical viewpoint—a way of understanding the relationship between gender and people's behaviors and abilities. None of the three is clearly right or even more right than the others. Each viewpoint makes sense, yet each is limited, which suggests that an adequate explanation may involve several theories.

It's important to realize that theories do more than provide explanations. Our theories about sex and gender affect our thoughts and behaviors. How we explain the twins' differences is likely to influence how we treat them. If you think the differences in muscle development are determined by biology, then you probably would not push Carlene to work out more in order to cultivate muscles. On the other hand, if you think differences result from learning and role models, you well might encourage Carlene to develop her muscles and Kevin to think more creatively. If you believe women have a natural maternal instinct (biological theory), then you might not expect fathers to be equal caretakers. A different set of expectations would arise if you theorize that women are taught to nurture and that men can learn this too. If you think males are more aggressive because of their higher levels of testosterone, then you are apt to tolerate rowdiness in boys and men and to discourage it in girls and women. The theories you hold consciously or unconsciously influence how you see yourself as a woman or man, what you expect of women and men generally, and what possibilities you see as open to each sex. Because the theories we hold do affect our perceptions, behaviors, and expectations, it's important to examine them carefully. That is the goal of this chapter.

There are many theories about gender and its relationship to culture and communication. Because each theory attempts to explain only selected dimensions of gender, different theories are not necessarily in competition with one another to produce *the* definitive explanation of how gender develops and what it means. Instead, theories often complement one another by sharpening our awareness of multiple ways in which communication, sex, gender, and culture interact. Thus, as we survey alternative theoretical approaches, you shouldn't try to pick the best or right one. Instead, pay attention to the limitations and insights of each theory of gender development so that you can decide which theories are stronger and which fit together to provide a richly layered account of the gendering process and the critical role of communication in it.

Theories about gender development and behavior can be classified into three broad types: those that focus on the biological bases of gender, those that emphasize the interpersonal origins of gender, and those that concentrate on cultural influences on gender development. Within these broad categories, a number of specific theories offer insight into factors and processes that contribute to the gendering of individuals. As we discuss these, you will probably notice both how they differ in focus and how they work together to create an overall understanding of gender development.

BIOLOGICAL THEORIES OF GENDER

Perhaps the first attempt to explain general differences between women and men was **biological theory.** This approach maintains that the biological characteristics of the sexes are the basis of gender differences. Biologically based theories focus on how X and Y chromosomes and hormonal activities influence a range of individual qualities from body features to thinking and motor skills.

In recent years biological explanations have been increasingly overshadowed by theories that emphasize socialization (Stumpf & Stanley, 1998). However, it would be unwise to discount biological factors altogether. The jury is still out on some of the connections that may exist between biology and gender, but research clearly demonstrates some biological influences on human behavior.

One focus of biological theories is the influence of sex chromosomes. As we saw in Chapter 1, most males have an XY chromosome structure. Most females have an XX chromosome structure because they inherit an X chromosome from each parent. Genetic evidence (Tanouye, 1996) shows that several genes controlling intelligence are located only on X chromosomes. This implies that some aspect of males' intelligence is inherited from their mothers, whereas females may inherit their genetic intelligence from both parents. Genetic researchers have also reported that the primary gene responsible for social skills is active only on the X chromosome

FYI

The Claims of Sociobiology

One of the more controversial theories of sex and gender differences is sociobiology (also called evolutionary theory) (Barash, 2002; Barash & Lipton, 2002; Segerstråle, 2000). According to sociobiology, differences between women and men are the inevitable result of genetic factors that aim to ensure survival of the fittest. Put plainly, Harvard entomologist E. O. Wilson, who founded sociobiology, explains that it is "the systematic study of the biological basis of all social behavior" (1975, p. 4).

A key claim of sociobiology is that women and men follow distinct reproductive strategies in an effort to maximize the chance that their genetic lines will continue (Barash & Lipton, 2002; Buss, 1994, 1995, 1996, 1999; Buss & Kenrick, 1998). For men, the best strategy is to have sex with as many women as possible in order to father many children with their genes. Because men produce millions of sperm, they risk little by impregnating multiple women. Women, however, usually produce only one egg during each menstrual cycle during their fertile years, so the best evolutionary strategy for them is to be highly selective in choosing sex partners and potential fathers of their children.

Sociobiology has at least as many critics as proponents. Some scholars (Futuyama & Risch, 1984) point out that the theory fails to account for sexual behavior that occurs without the goal of reproduction—and sometimes in an active effort to avoid that outcome! Also, note critics of the theory, social evolution is not the same thing as biological evolution (Newcombe, 2002).

(Langreth, 1997). This may explain why women, who have two X chromosomes, are generally more adept and comfortable than men in social situations.

A second focus of biological theories is the role of hormonal activity in shaping sex-related behaviors. Sex hormones affect development of the brain as well as the body. For instance, estrogen, the primary female hormone, causes women's bodies to produce "good" cholesterol and to make their blood vessels more flexible than those of men (Ferraro, 2001; Shapiro, 1990). Estrogen also strengthens the immune system, making women generally less susceptible to immune disorders and more resistant to infections and viruses. Thus, it is not surprising that, from the fetal stage throughout life, men are more vulnerable to some physical problems than are women (Jacklin, 1989). Estrogen also accounts for fat tissue around women's hips, which provides cushioning to a fetus during pregnancy, and there is some preliminary support for the claim that estrogen impedes liver functioning so that women eliminate alcohol more slowly than men and thus may react more quickly to alcohol consumption (Lang, 1991).

Male sex hormones also have some documented effects as well as some controversial possible influences. After surveying an extensive amount of research on sex

Used by permission of John L. Hart FLP, and Creators Syndicate, Inc.

hormones, Carol Tavris (1992) concludes that men, like women, have a hormonal cycle. And, like women, men's hormonal cycles affect their behavior. Males who use drugs, engage in violent and abusive behavior, and have behavior problems tend to be at their cycle's peak level of testosterone, the primary male hormone. A study of 1,706 men from ages 39 to 70 found that men with higher levels of testosterone engaged in more dominant and aggressive behavior" ("Study Links High Testosterone," 1991).

Higher levels of testosterone are also linked to jockeying for power, attempts to influence or dominate others, and physical expressions of anger (Cowley, 2003; Schwartz & Cellini, 1995). Another study ("Study Links Men's Cognitive Abilities," 1991) reported that men have better spatial abilities at low points in their hormonal cycle. Additional research indicates that hormones influence cognitive abilities that range from decoding nonverbal communication to judging moving objects (Halpern, 1996; Kimura, 1999; Saucier & Kimura, 1998). Preliminary research also suggests that hormonal activity may influence transsexualism (Diamond, 1997).

A third focus of biological theories of difference is brain structure and development, which appear to be linked to sex. Research indicates that, although both women and men use both lobes of the brain, each sex tends to specialize in one. Men generally have greater development of the left lobe of the brain, which controls linear thinking, sequential information, and abstract, analytic reasoning. Specializing in the right lobe, women tend to have greater aptitude for imaginative and artistic activity, for holistic, intuitive thinking, and for some visual and spatial tasks (Joseph, 2000; Mealy, 2000; Rugg, 1995). Research indicates that women tend to use both sides of their brains to do language tasks, whereas men are more likely to use only the left sides of their brains. Further, women's brains do not have to work as hard as men's brains to figure out others' emotions (Begley, 1995; "Gender Difference," 1995).

Linking the two lobes of the brain is a bundle of nerves and connecting tissues called the corpus callosum (Figure 2.1). Women generally have greater ability to use this structure and to access the distinct capacities of both lobes (Fausto-Sterling, 2000). For instance, a recent report ("Men Use Half a Brain to Listen,"

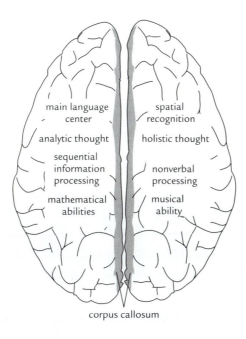

Figure 2.1 Structure of the Human Brain

2000) involving brain scans showed that men used mostly the left lobes of their brains when they were listening, whereas women used both lobes of the brain to listen. This finding does not mean that men listen less fully or less well than women. It means only that women and men, in general, use different parts of their brains when they listen.

Are differences in how we use our brains indisputable evidence of the force of biology? Not necessarily. The splenium, a thick, rounded fold of connecting tissues in the corpus callosum, is larger in most women, which may account for their greater verbal abilities (Hines, 1992; Konner, 2003). However, the splenium changes as a result of experience, which implies that we can develop it by using it, just as we use exercise to develop other muscles in our bodies.

Research on brain development also suggests there may be differences between the brains of heterosexuals and gays. The National Academy of Sciences (Elias, 1992) reports that sexual orientation may be strongly influenced by biology. Examinations of brains revealed that a band of fibers called the anterior commissure, which is part of the tissues connecting brain lobes, is significantly larger in gay men than in either heterosexual men or women. Dean Hamer headed a National Cancer Institute research project that examined the genes of 40 pairs of gay brothers. Only 7 of the 40 pairs did not have a genetic marker on the tips of their X chromosomes (Allman, 1993). The researchers hypothesize that prenatal hormones may influence development of the anterior commissure. We don't yet

FYI

Biological Differences That Make a Difference

Although men and women are alike in many respects, research (Ferraro, 2001; Fisher, 2000; Hales, 1999; Legato, 1998; Reiss, 2000; Wartik, 2002; Wheeler, 1998) suggests that there are some significant biological sex differences:

- Women are more likely than men to experience pain. Their pains are also less likely to be taken seriously by doctors.

- Women are more likely than men to suffer from migraine headaches and lupus; men are more likely than women to suffer from cluster headaches.

- On average, women's brains are smaller than men's; women's brains are also more densely packed with neurons than men's.

- Men's livers metabolize most drugs, including alcohol, more quickly than women's.

- Women and men typically have different symptoms of heart attack. Women's symptoms include shortness of breath, jaw pain, backache, and extreme fatigue. Men's primary symptom is usually chest or arm pain.

- Women are more likely to develop melanoma, but men are more likely to die from this skin cancer.

- Women are more likely to suffer from depression and anxiety, whereas men are more subject to violent behavior and abuse of drugs, including alcohol.

know if, like the splenium, the size of the anterior commissure is influenced by use. If it is, then biology alone doesn't account for differences in anterior commissures or, perhaps, in sexual orientation.

The force of biology is evident in efforts to change the sex of children. Perhaps the most famous case is that of Joan-John (Leo, 1997). When John was 8 months old, his penis was destroyed in a surgical accident. Following doctors' advice, John's parents decided to have "normalizing surgery" performed on John. His testicles were removed, a vagina was surgically created, and John was renamed Joan. Joan did not take to being a girl. Her preferred toys were trucks and guns, and she routinely ripped off the dresses her parents made her wear. Joan also insisted on urinating standing up. Even hormonal treatments and therapists could not convince Joan to accept being a girl. Finally, at age 14, Joan's father told her that she had been born a boy. For Joan-John, things now made sense. John had a mastectomy, took male hormone shots, and began living as a male. At age 25, John married a woman with children, and he continues to live as a man.

In summary, biological theories of gender attribute masculine and feminine qualities and abilities to genetics and biology. Specifically, it appears that chromosomes, hormones, and brain structure may affect physiology, thinking, and behavior. Biological theory is valuable in informing us about genetic and biological factors that may influence our abilities and options. Yet, biological theories tell us only about physiological and genetic qualities of men and women *in general*. They don't necessarily describe individual men and women. Some men may be holistic, creative thinkers, whereas some women, like Luanne, may have the mental and physical qualities necessary to play football.

Although virtually no researchers dispute the influence of biology on gender, there is substantial controversy about the strength and immutability of biological forces. Those who hold an extreme version of biological theory maintain that our chromosomes and other biological factors program, or determine, masculine and feminine behavior. A greater number of researchers argue that biology is substantially edited by environmental factors. Based on a 12-year study of adolescent males and females, psychologist David Reiss (2000) stated emphatically that biology is not destiny. By extension, a majority of current researchers think that differences between the sexes are at least partially created by environmental factors (Fausto-Sterling, 2000; Lippa, 2001; Martin & Doka, 2000; Reiss, 2000). To consider how environmental forces may mitigate biological

Luanne

When I was in high school, I wanted to play football. My folks were really cool about it, since they'd always told me being a girl didn't mean I couldn't do anything I wanted to. But the school coach vetoed the idea. I appealed his decision to the principal as sex discrimination (my mother's a lawyer), and we had a meeting. The coach said girls couldn't play football as well as guys because girls are less muscular, weigh less, and have less dense bodies to absorb the force of momentum. He said this means girls can be hurt more than guys by tackles and stuff. He also said that girls have smaller heads and necks, which is a problem in head-to-head contact on the field. My dad said the coach was talking in generalizations, and he should judge my ability by me as an individual. But the coach's arguments convinced the principal, and I didn't get to play, just because women's bodies are generally less equipped for contact sports.

endowments, we turn to theories of interpersonal and cultural influences on gender.

INTERPERSONAL THEORIES OF GENDER

A number of theorists have focused on interpersonal factors that influence the development of masculinity and femininity. From their work, two major theoretical views have emerged to explain how individuals become gendered. Psychodynamic theory emphasizes interpersonal relationships within the family that affect a child's sense of identity, particularly his or her gender. Psychological theories stress learning and role modeling between children and a variety of other people, including parents. I'll introduce both theories here and pursue them in greater detail in subsequent chapters.

■ Psychodynamic Theories of Gender Development

Originally advanced by Sigmund Freud (1957), **psychodynamic theory** focuses on family and psychic dynamics that influence individuals' development, including their gender identities. More recent work has refined psychodynamic theory to compensate for some of Freud's oversights, particularly his misunderstanding of women's development.

Psychodynamic theories state that relationships, especially the earliest ones, are central to the development of human personality, specifically gender identity. For most children, the most important early relationship is with the primary caretaker, typically the mother. That relationship fundamentally influences how an infant comes to define herself or himself and on how she or he understands interactions with others.

Psychodynamic theorists think that development of a sense of self and a gender identity occur as an infant internalizes the views of others around him or her. So, for example, infants who are lovingly nurtured by parents tend to incorporate the parents' views into their own sense of self, and they regard themselves as valuable and worthy. In addition, parents' tendencies to nurture, compete, cooperate, express affection, and so forth are internalized so that the child develops these capacities as part of herself or himself. Internalizing others is not merely acquiring roles; it creates the basic structure of the psyche—the core self.

Psychodynamic theory explains the development of masculine or feminine identity as the result of different kinds of relationships that typically exist between mothers and children of each sex. According to Nancy J. Chodorow (1989), one of the most widely respected psychodynamic theorists, the key to understanding how family psychodynamics create gender lies in realizing that "we are all mothered by women, . . . [and] women rather than men have primary parenting responsibilities" (p. 6). Because the mother herself is gendered, she tends to form distinctly different relationships with sons and daughters. Consequently, male and female infants follow different developmental paths depending on the specific relationship each has with the mother.

Between a mother and daughter there is a fundamental likeness that encourages close identification. Mothers generally interact more with daughters, keeping them physically and psychologically closer than sons. In addition, mothers tend to be more nurturing and to talk more about personal and relationship topics with daughters than with sons. This intense closeness allows an infant girl to import her mother into herself in so basic a way that her mother becomes quite literally a part of her own self. Because this internalization occurs at a very early age, a girl's first efforts to define her own identity are suffused with the relationship with her mother. The fact that girls generally define their identities within a relationship may account for women's typical attentiveness to relationships (Lorber, 2001; Surrey, 1983).

The relationship between a mother and son typically departs from that between a mother and daughter. Because they are not the same sex, full identification may not be possible. Theorists (Chodorow, 1978, 1999; Miller, 1986; Surrey, 1983) suggest that infant boys recognize in a primitive way that they differ from their mothers. More important, mothers realize the difference, and they reflect it in their interactions with their sons. In general, mothers encourage more and earlier independence in sons than in daughters, and they talk less with sons about emotional and relationship matters.

How do most young boys formulate a masculine gender identity? Because they cannot define it through the relationship with their mothers as daughters typically do, boys pursue a different path. To establish his independent identity, a boy must differentiate himself from his mother—he must declare that he is not like her. The idea that a boy must renounce his mother to establish masculine identity underlies the puberty rites of many cultures (French, 1992; Gaylin, 1992). Whether a boy rejects his mother or merely differentiates himself from her, becoming independent of others is central to the initial development of a masculine identity and the sense of autonomous power that comes with it (Kaschak, 1992).

Identity, of course, is not static or fixed in the early years of life. The initial self that we construct continues to grow and change throughout life as we interact with others and revise our sense of who we are. Yet, psychoanalytic theorists maintain that the identity formed in infancy is fundamental. They see it as the foundation on which later views of the self are erected. Thus, although identity clearly evolves, it does so on a foundation laid in infancy.

According to psychodynamic theorists, as infants mature, they carry with them the basic identity formed in the pivotal first relationship with their mothers. As girls become women, they elaborate their identities in connections with others, and relationships tend to figure prominently in their values and lives. As boys grow into men, they

> ### Abe
>
> I remember something that happened when I was a little kid. Mom had taken me to the playground, and we were playing together. Some other boys started teasing me, calling me "mama's boy." I remember thinking I had to stop playing with Mom if I wanted those other boys to accept me.

too elaborate the basic identity formed in infancy, making independence central to their values and lives. This major difference in self-definition suggests that close relationships may mean quite different things to masculine and feminine persons. For someone who is feminine, intimate relationships may be a source of security and comfort, and they may affirm her (or his) view of self as connected with others. In contrast, someone with a masculine orientation may feel that relationships stifle the independence essential to a strong identity (Gilligan, 1982; Lorber, 2001; Rubin, 1985; Wood & Lenze, 1991b).

A primary value of this theory of gender development is that it highlights the importance of relationships in cultivating gender. Whether or not we agree with the extent of the influence psychodynamic theorists accord to relationships, their insights into this area are important to an overall understanding of gender. As we will discover later in this chapter, a number of other scholars who represent distinct theoretical schools of thought also focus on relationships.

■ Psychological Theories of Gender Development

Psychological theories also focus on interpersonal bases of gender, but they do not emphasize intrapsychic processes as do psychodynamic explanations. Instead, psychological theories of gender highlight the influence of communication on gender.

Social learning theory. Developed by Walter Mischel (1966) and others (Bandura, 2002; Bandura & Walters, 1963; Burn, 1996), **social learning theory** claims that individuals learn to be masculine and feminine (among other things) through observation, experimentation, and responses from others. Children imitate the communication they see on television and in parents, peers, and others. At first, young children are likely to mimic almost anything. However, people around them will reward only some of children's behaviors, and those behaviors that are reinforced tend to be repeated. Thus, social learning suggests that others' communication teaches boys and girls which behaviors are appropriate for them. Because children prefer rewards to punishments and neutral responses, they are likely to develop gendered patterns of behavior that others approve.

According to social learning theory, then, young girls tend to be rewarded when they are polite, considerate, quiet, emotionally expressive, and obedient—all qualities associated with femininity. They tend to get fewer positive responses if they are boisterous, independent, unconcerned with others, or competitive—qualities associated with masculinity. As parents and others reinforce in girls what is considered feminine and discourage behaviors and attitudes that are masculine, they shape little girls into femininity. Similarly, as parents communicate approval to boys for behaving in masculine ways and curb them for acting feminine—for instance, for crying—they influence little boys to become masculine.

Mark Breedlove, a behavioral endocrinologist, says, "We're born with predispositions, but it's society that amplifies them, exaggerates them" (Blum, 1998, p. 46). In other words, tendencies to be aggressive or nurturing are shaped and elaborated by parents, peers, and other people. A good example of this comes from a report by Deborah Blum, a Pulitzer Prize–winning science writer. Blum calls our attention to studies of girls with a condition called congenital adrenal hypoplasia, which means they have higher levels of testosterone than is typical for girls. These girls are more interested in trucks and toy weapons than most little girls are, and they engage in rougher play. Yet, as they interact with other girls, their peers socialize them toward behaviors, games, and preferences more traditional for girls (Blum, 1997, 1998).

You may have noticed that social learning theory views children as relatively passive in the learning process. It suggests they more or less absorb a gender identity in response to external stimuli such as rewards and punishments from parents and other people in their world. Social learning theory also suggests that the reinforcement process continues throughout life with messages that reinforce femininity in women and masculinity in men.

> **Victoria**
>
> When I was little—like 4 or 5 maybe—if I got dirty or was too loud, Mama would say, "That's no way for a lady to act." When I was quiet and nice, she'd say, "Now you're being a lady." I remember wanting Mama to approve of me and trying to act like a lady. But sometimes it was hard to figure out what was and wasn't ladylike in her book. I had to just keep doing things and seeing how she responded until I learned the rules.

Cognitive development theory. This theory also focuses on how individuals learn from interaction with others to define themselves, including their gender. Unlike social learning theory, however, **cognitive development theory** assumes that children play active roles in developing their own identities. Researchers claim that children use others to define themselves because they are motivated by an *internal desire* to be competent, which in Western culture includes knowing how to act feminine or masculine.

The foundations of cognitive development theory were established by Lawrence Kohlberg (1958), Jean Piaget (1932/1965), and Carol Gilligan and her associates (1982; Gilligan & Pollack, 1988). Research shows that children go through several stages in developing gender identities (Wadsworth, 1996). From birth until about 24 to 30 months, they search others' communication for labels to apply to themselves. When they hear others call them a "girl" or "boy," they learn the labels for themselves. Then children actively look for same-sex models they can imitate (Levy, 1999).

A key developmental juncture occurs very early in life, by age 3 or earlier (Dubois, Serbin, & Derbyshire, 1998; Warm, 2000). At this point, a child develops **gender constancy,** the understanding that he or she is a male or female and that this will not change. Given this, say cognitive development theorists, children develop a high internal motivation to learn how to be competent in the sex and gender assigned to them (Levy, 1998). Boys and girls now devote themselves to identifying behaviors and attitudes others consider masculine and feminine and to learning to enact them. Same-sex models become extremely important as gauges whereby young children figure out what behaviors, attitudes, and feelings go with

Over break I was visiting my sister's family, and her little boy attached himself to me. Wherever I went, he was my shadow. Whatever I did, he copied. At one point, I was dribbling a basketball out in the driveway, and Derrick got it and started dribbling. I egged him on, saying "Attaboy! What a star!" and stuff like that, and he just grinned real big. The more I praised him for playing with the ball, the harder he played. It was really weird to see how much influence I had over him.

their gender. For young girls, mothers may be the primary source of information about femininity. Likewise, little boys study their fathers and other important males in their world to learn what counts as masculine.

As children mature, they continue to seek role models to become competent at masculinity and femininity (Burn, 1996; Martin, 1994, 1997). Perhaps you, like many adolescents, studied teen magazines and watched movies and television to figure out how to be successful as a boy or girl. We look for models for everything from how to style our hair and do the latest dances to how to feel about various things. At young ages, boys learn that aggressiveness is masculine and leads to popularity (Good, 2000). Girls learn that it's feminine to dress up, put on makeup, and do other things to be physically attractive (Franzoi & Koehler, 1998). Children quickly figure out gender rules. It's feminine to squeal or scream at the sight of bugs or mice, but boys who do so are quickly labeled sissies. It's acceptable—if not pleasant to everyone—for adolescent boys to belch, but a teenage girl who belches would most likely be criticized. There is also evidence that children who witness violence between their parents may follow the model and enact violence in their own intimate relationships (Mihalic & Elliot, 1997).

In studying how senses of morality and relationships develop, Carol Gilligan and her colleagues (1982; Gilligan & Pollack, 1988) theorized that most females are socialized to value connections with others, to communicate care and responsiveness, and to preserve relationships. Males are more likely to value autonomy and to communicate in ways that preserve their independence from others. Each sex learns what society expects of her or his gender, and most decide to act in ways that are consistent with social views of gender.

In summary, psychological theories emphasize the power of others' communication to teach lessons about gender and provide models of how to enact masculinity and femininity. Once gender constancy is established, most children strive to develop communication, attitudes, goals, and self-presentations consistent with the gender they consider theirs.

CULTURAL THEORIES OF GENDER

A third group of theorists focuses on understanding gender from a cultural or cross-cultural perspective. Cultural scholars do not necessarily dispute biological and interpersonal factors but assume that they are qualified by the influence of culture. Because it incorporates other theories, the cultural perspective is a particularly comprehensive approach to understanding what gender means in any society at a specific time (Davis & Gergen, 1997; Deaux & La France, 1998; Unger, 1998).

Of the many cultural contributions to knowledge about gender, we will focus on three. First, we'll look at findings from anthropology to discover what cross-cultural research tells us about gender. Next, we will explore symbolic interactionism, which concentrates on how individuals acquire cultural values so that most of us adopt the identities our culture designates as appropriate for our gender. Finally, we'll look at standpoint theory, a recent approach that augments the insights of symbolic interactionism and anthropology.

■ Anthropology

Anyone who has been outside the United States knows that traveling prompts you to learn not only about other countries but also about your own. When confronted with different values and ways of doing things in a foreign culture, you see the norms of your own society in a new and usually clearer light. This holds true of gender. Our views of gender in 21st-century America are clarified by considering what it means elsewhere—how other cultures view gender and how women and men in other cultures express gendered identities.

In Chapter 1, I mentioned the pioneering anthropological work of Margaret Mead (1935/1968), in which she discovered distinct meanings of gender in three different societies. Much work has followed Mead's. In foraging or hunter-gatherer societies, there is the least gender division and, therefore, the greatest equality between women and men (Lepowsky, 1998). Horticultural and pastoral societies also tend to be egalitarian, although less so than purely foraging cultures. Agrarian peoples generally have a pronounced system of gender stratification in which women are subordinate to men in status and rights. Finally, industrial–capitalist societies distinguish clearly between the genders and confer different values on women and men (O'Kelly & Carney, 1986).

Many societies have views of gender that differ from those currently prevalent in the United States. Tahitian men tend to be gentle, mild tempered, and non-aggressive, and it is entirely acceptable for them to cry, show fear, and express pain (Coltrane, 1996). The Mbuti, a tribe of pygmies in central Africa, don't discriminate strongly between the sexes. Both women and men gather roots, berries, and nuts, and both hunt (Coltrane, 1996). One African group is structured so that young boys are responsible for taking care of babies; in this society, unlike our own, young boys are actually more nurturant than young girls (Whiting & Edwards, 1973). The Mukogodo people in Kenya place higher value on females than males; as a result, daughters are given greater attention and medical care than sons (Cronk, 1993).

No Maternal Instinct

In some small Brazilian towns, mothers routinely let sickly children die, even when a simple solution of sugar and salt could save them (Cordes, 1994). During the Renaissance, parents of all classes frequently abandoned babies—900 children a year were left in just three foundling homes in Florence (Thurer, 1994).

Maternal instinct is a cherished ideal in modern Western society, but there is no convincing evidence that women have this alleged instinct. Instead, recent research increasingly suggests that society constructs views of what counts as good mothering, and these views vary across time and cultures.

Scholars who have studied the social construction of motherhood warn that the current Western expectations of mothers can be harmful to real-life mothers (Kaplan, 1992; Roth, 1994; Scheper-Hughes, 1994). Many women with children find it impossible to meet the romanticized views of mothers as unselfish, always nurturing, and exclusively devoted to their families. At the same time, prevailing social expectations fail to define a central role for fathers in caring for children. Whether we look in Brazil or in the United States, it's important to remember that mothering—and fathering—are socially shaped.

Another example of how cultural attitudes vary comes from a group of villages in the Dominican Republic where it is common for males to be born with undescended testes and an underdeveloped penis. Because this condition is not rare, the society doesn't regard it as abnormal. Instead, boys born with this condition are raised as "conditional girls," who wear dresses and are treated as girls. At puberty, a secondary tide of androgens causes the testes to descend, the penis to grow, and muscle and hair typical of males to appear. At that point, the child is considered a boy—his dresses are discarded, and he is treated as a male. Members of the society call the condition *guevedoces,* which means "testes at 12" (Blum, 1998).

Native American tribes offer yet another cultural construction of gender. According to Angela Gonzales and Judy Kertész (2001), prior to contact with Western Europeans, many (but not all) Native American groups had long-established matrilineal systems of inheritance, property ownership, and social status. These tribes were not necessarily matriarchal (in which females have greater power than males), but they were matrilineal because lines of kinship were traced through females, not males. Many of the tribes also viewed women as relatively autonomous, in direct contrast to the views of Western Europeans who colonized the United States.

Perhaps the most important lesson we can draw from anthropological studies is that cultures profoundly shape gender identity. Amazingly few sex differences have been found across a range of societies, and the ones that have been documented tend to be small (Adler, 1991). For instance, both boys and girls in most cultures show tendencies to nurture and to be aggressive. What differs is the extent to which particular cultures encourage these qualities in children of each sex.

■ Symbolic Interactionism

Symbolic interactionism is a very broad theory developed by George Herbert Mead, which holds that by communicating we learn who we are and what that means in the culture into which we have been born. Because newborns do not enter the world with a sense of self as distinct from the world, they learn from others how to see themselves. As parents and others interact with children, they literally tell them who they are. A child is described as big or dainty, delicate or tough, active or quiet, and so on. With each label, others offer the child a self-image, and children internalize others' views to arrive at their own understandings of who they are. Communication is the central process whereby we gain a sense of who we are; from the moment of birth, we engage in interaction with others, especially parents, who tell us who we are, what is appropriate for us, and what is unacceptable.

Research has shown that views of gender are communicated by parents through their responses to children (Chodorow, 1978, 1989; Shapiro, 1990), through play activities with peers (Maccoby, 1998; Powlishta, Serbin, & Moller, 1993), and through teachers' interactions with students (Sandler, 2004; Wood, 1996b; Wood & Lenze, 1991b). Learning gender occurs as others define children by sex and link sex to social expectations of gender. "You are Mommy's helper in the kitchen," mothers may say to daughters, telling young girls it is appropriate for them to be involved in domestic activities. When young boys carry in packages after shopping, parents often praise them by saying, "You're such a strong little man." This links strength with being male. At school, young girls are likely to be reprimanded for roughhousing as a teacher tells them, "That's not very ladylike." Boys engaged in similar mischief more often hear the teacher say with some amusement, "You boys really are rowdy today." Notice that responses from others, such as teachers, not only reflect broad cultural values but also provide positive and negative rewards, consistent with social learning theory. In play with peers, gender messages continue. When a young girl tries to tell a boy what to do, she may be told, "You can't boss me around. You're just a girl." Girls who fail to share their toys or show consideration to others may be

Mark

I see how gender roles work in my own family. My mother works full time, and she's still the one who fixes all the meals and does all the shopping and most of the housework. Both she and Dad seem to accept that as the way things are supposed to be. Last year her mother had a stroke, and since then Mom's been doing another job—taking care of her mother. Every day she goes by to see how Grandma is, and she shops for her and cleans her house as well as ours. Dad has told her she's doing too much, and it's clearly taking a toll on Mom. But I don't think she feels she can do less. And it doesn't seem to have occurred to Dad that he could do more to help. When I asked her why she was doing so much, she told me Grandma expected her help and needed it, and she felt that way too. I don't know how long Mom can keep taking care of everybody else without breaking down, herself.

told, "You're not being nice;" yet this is considerably less likely to be said to young boys. Thus, children learn what is expected of them and how that is related to being masculine or feminine.

An important contribution to a cultural theory of gender is the concept of **role** —specifically, roles for women and men. A role is a set of expected behaviors and the values associated with them. In an insightful analysis, Elizabeth Janeway (1971) identified two dimensions of roles. First, roles are external to individuals because a society defines roles in general ways that transcend particular individuals. Roles are assigned to individuals by the society as a whole. Thus, for each of us there are certain roles that society expects us to fulfill because of society's definition of us.

Within our culture, one primary way to classify social life is through gender roles. Women are still regarded as caretakers (Wood, 1994b), and they are expected to provide most of the care for infants, elderly relatives, and others who are sick or disabled. If a child is sick, the mother is generally expected to take time from work or other activities to care for the child (Cancian & Oliker, 2000; Hewlett, 1991). If parents or in-laws need help, it is the daughter or daughter-in-law who is expected to, and who generally does, provide the help, regardless of the costs to her personal and professional life (Aronson, 1992; Wood, 1994b). Even in work outside the home, cultural views of femininity are evident. Women remain disproportionately represented in service and clerical jobs, whereas men are moved into executive positions in for-profit sectors of the economy. Women are still asked to take care of social activities on the job, but men in equivalent positions are seldom expected to do this.

Men are still regarded as the primary breadwinners for families. Thus, it is seen as more acceptable for a woman than a man not to have an income-producing job (Tyre & McGinn, 2003). Some women today regard a career as an option, something they may or may not do or might do for a while and then focus full time on raising a family. Very few young men regard working as optional. To fulfill the masculine role successfully, a man must work and bring in an income; the feminine role does not require this.

Not only are roles assigned by society, but their value is defined as well. Within Western culture, the feminine role remains subordinate to the masculine role. Men are still regarded as the heads of families even if their wives earn more money than they do. Men, more often than women, are seen as leaders and given opportunities to lead. Further, the work that men do is more highly regarded by the society than is the work assigned to women. Society teaches women to accept the role of supporting, caring for, and responding to others. Yet that is a role clearly devalued in the United States. Competing and succeeding in work life and public affairs are primary roles assigned to men, and to those roles prestige is attached.

A second important dimension of role is that it is internalized. For social specifications of behaviors to be effective, individuals must internalize them. At very young ages, girls understand that they are supposed to be nice, put others' needs ahead of their own, and be nurturing, whereas boys understand that they are supposed to take command and assert themselves. As we take cultural scripts for gender inside of ourselves, we learn not only that there are different roles for men and women but also that unequal values are assigned to them. This can be very frustrating for those who are encouraged to conform to roles that are less esteemed.

Although gender is clearly influenced by family psychodynamics, learning, and cognitive development in interpersonal settings, those relational contexts themselves are part of a larger society whose values they echo and perpetuate. Symbolic interactionism underlines the fact that gender is socially created and sustained through communication that encourages us to define ourselves as gendered and to adopt the roles that society prescribes for us.

■ Standpoint Theory

A final contribution from the cultural perspective is **standpoint theory** (Collins, 1986; Harding, 1991, 1998; McClish & Bacon, 2002), which offers insights into how a person's location within a culture shapes his or her life. Standpoint theory focuses on how gender, race, and class influence our positions in society and the kinds of experiences those positions foster.

Standpoint theory amends symbolic interactionism by noting that the social world consists of very different positions within social hierarchies. We may all understand that our culture attaches different values to different classes and races, but each of us experiences being only in a certain race and class. An individual's standpoint in a society guides what she or he knows, feels, and does and shapes an individual's understanding of social life as a whole.

Standpoint theory dates back to the writings of 19th-century German philosopher Georg Wilhelm Friedrich Hegel (1807). Hegel noted that society as a whole recognized the existence of slavery but that its nature was perceived quite differently depending on whether one's position was that of master or slave. From this insight, Hegel reasoned that, in any society where power relationships exist, there can be no single perspective on social life. Each person sees society as it appears from the perspective of his or her social group, and every perspective is limited. All views are partial because each reflects a particular standpoint within a culture stratified by power.

A particularly important implication of standpoint theory is that, although all perspectives on social life are limited, some are more limited than others. Those in positions of power have a vested interest in preserving their place in the hierarchy, so their views of social life are more distorted than the views of persons who gain little or nothing from existing power relationships. Another reason that those in subordinate groups may have fuller understandings is that they have to understand both their own perspective and the viewpoints of those who have more power. To survive, subjugated persons have to understand people with power, but the reverse is not true.

Standpoint theory claims that marginalized groups have unique insights how a society works. Women, minorities, gays and lesbians, people of lower socioeconomic class, intersexuals, and others who are outside of the cultural center may see the society from a perspective that is less distorted, less biased, and more layered than those who occupy more central standpoints. Marginalized perspectives can inform all of us about how our society operates. María Lugones and Elizabeth Spelman (1983) point out that dominant groups have the freedom *not* to try to understand the perspective of less privileged groups. They don't need to learn about others in order to survive.

According to standpoint theory, different social groups like women and men develop particular skills, attitudes, ways of thinking, and understandings of life as a result of their standpoints. Patricia Hill Collins (1986, 1998) uses standpoint theory to show that Black women scholars have special insights into Western culture because of their dual standpoints as "outsiders within," that is, as members of a minority group (African Americans) who hold membership in majority institutions (higher education). Similarly, in his *Autobiography of an Ex-Coloured Man* (1912/1989), James Weldon Johnson reflected that "I believe it to be a fact that the coloured people of this country know and understand the white people better than the white people know and understand them" (p. 22).

An intriguing application of standpoint logic came from Sara Ruddick's (1989) study of mothers. Ruddick concluded that the demands of their role lead mothers to develop what she calls "maternal thinking," which consists of values, priorities, and understandings of relationships that are specifically promoted by the process of taking care of young children. Ruddick argues that what we often assume is a maternal instinct that comes naturally to women is actually a set of attitudes and behaviors that arise out of women's location in domestic, caregiving roles. Supporting Ruddick's finding is work by Sandra Bem (1993), who claims that what we view as maternal instinct is really the result of placing women in roles requiring caregiving. Ruddick's view of learned maternal inclinations is limited by race and class bias because she focused on the mothering of middle-class White women. In a study of African American mothering, Alison Bailey (1994) found that ethnicity also shapes perspectives on mothering.

The impact of standpoint on nurturing ability is further demonstrated by research on men in caregiving roles. In her research on single fathers, Barbara Risman (1989) found that men who are primary parents are more nurturing, attentive to others' needs, patient, and emotionally expressive than are men in general and as much so as most

Kim

My mother never finished college, but she sure understands the standpoint theory we talked about. The thing she drilled into us as kids was "Don't ever judge others until you've been in their shoes." She said that all the time, and I still hear it in my head whenever I start to judge somebody who's different from me. I think there's a lot to this idea, since the situations people are in do affect how they think and what they are like, and if you haven't been in a situation, you can't judge somebody who has. You can't even understand him or her really.

women. Other studies (Downey, Ainsworth-Darnell, & Dufur, 1998; Kaye & Applegate, 1990) found that men who care for elderly people enlarge their capacities for nurturing.

Standpoint research also calls into question the extent to which biology influences gendered behavior. Some biological theorists claim that men's testosterone levels cause them to be aggressive toward others. Yet those findings must be qualified by noting that men in higher socioeconomic classes did not display more aggression when their testosterone was high. This suggests that their standpoint in society included socialization that it is inappropriate to behave aggressively. They had learned not to be violent and aggressive even when their testosterone rose.

It would be incorrect to think that an individual is shaped by a single standpoint. All of us occupy multiple standpoints that overlap and interact. For example, an African American man's knowledge and identity are shaped by race, sexual orientation, and gender standpoints. Because standpoints interact and affect one another, this man's masculine gender identity is different from that of a European American man. As cultural studies scholar Craig Calhoun (1995) notes, no person is determined by a single category.

The cultural perspective broadens our understandings by demonstrating that gender is a set of social expectations and values that are systematically taught to individuals. Cultural views of gender reflect three related research traditions. From anthropology, we gain insight into the arbitrary and variable nature of gender by seeing how variably it is defined in diverse cultures. Symbolic interactionist theory offers an understanding of culture as a whole and the key role of communication in socializing new members into the understandings and values of a common social world. Finally, standpoint theory adds the important realization that individuals' positions within a society influence how they see social life and how they define their roles, activities, priorities, and feelings. This is a particularly important point because women and men typically occupy different standpoints in our society.

SUMMARY

In this chapter we have considered different theories that offer explanations of relationships among communication, gender, and culture. Rather than asking which is the *right* theory, we have tried to discover how each viewpoint contributes to overall understandings of how gender develops. By weaving different theories together, we gain a powerful appreciation of the complex individual, interpersonal, and cultural origins of gender identity. The cultural perspective seems broadest, because it incorporates interpersonal and biological theories yet also goes beyond them. The remainder of this book reflects the view that gender (not sex) is culturally constructed and that the meanings a culture assigns to femininity and masculinity are expressed and sustained through communication.

A key point to keep in mind is that the theories work together to explain both gender and sex differences. For instance, more girls and women, particularly those who are athletes, suffer knee injuries, especially one known as ACL (anterior cruciate ligament). In an N.C.A.A. study of ACL problems in basketball players from 1994 to 1998, women players were nearly three times more likely to suffer ACL injuries than men. For soccer players, the risk for females is even greater (Jacobson, 2001; Scelfo, 2002). The fact that women suffer more ACL injuries than men suggests that there may be a sex difference—a biologically based difference between women's and men's knees. However, socialization may also be a factor. Dr. William Garrett, a sports medicine surgeon, has studied films of women and men engaged in sports. In an interview with me (Garrett, 2001), he noted that women and men athletes hold their bodies differently. Men, he says, are looser and tend to move and stand with their knees slightly bent. Women are more likely to keep their legs and knees straight and to maintain more rigid posture. Loose posture and bent knees reduce stress on the knee and thus reduce the risk of ACL injury. Biology doesn't seem to explain the differences in posture and knee positioning. It's likely that both result from early socialization in how girls and boys are supposed to act, stand, sit, run, and so forth. Thus, what seems a purely biological effect may also reflect interpersonal and social influences.

With this theoretical background, we are now ready to consider contexts in which gender is formed and communicated as well as ways in which individuals accept or resist cultural directives for masculinity and femininity. The next chapter builds on this one by exploring how communication within rhetorical movements has challenged and changed social views of men and women.

KEY TERMS

biological theory, 38
cognitive development theory, 47
gender constancy, 47
pyschodynamic theory, 44
role, 52

social learning theory, 46
standpoint theory, 53
symbolic interactionism, 51
theory, 36

DISCUSSION QUESTIONS

1. Distinguished anthropologist Ruth Benedict said that "the purpose of anthropology is to make the world safe for difference." Having read this chapter, how would you explain this statement?

2. Think about your relationship with your parents. How were your connections to your father and mother different? How were they similar? How did sex and gender influ-

ence each relationship? If you have siblings of the other sex, how were their relationships with your parents different from yours?

3. Use your InfoTrac College Edition to read Linda Carli's 2001 article "Gender and Social Influence" in the *Journal of Social Issues*. In which contexts did she find that males and females exerted more influence? How would Carli's findings be explained by each of the following theories: biological theory, social learning theory, and symbolic interaction theory?

4. How has your standpoint been shaped by your gender, sexual orientation, and race? In turn, how has your standpoint affected how you see yourself, others, and social life? As a man or a woman, what do you think you understand particularly well? About what do you not have much insight? Relate this to standpoint theory.

5. Watch men and women athletes as they play their sports. Do you see the differences in posture and knee position that Dr. Garrett found in his research?

3

The Rhetorical Shaping of Gender:
Women's Movements in America

The truth is that none of us can be liberated if other groups are not.

—GLORIA STEINEM

In the last chapter we saw that communication in society influences individuals' gender identities. Equally important is how individuals' communication shapes society's views of masculinity and femininity. In this chapter and the next one we'll look closely at how individuals have changed cultural views of gender and men and women.

Once women could not vote in America; now they can. Once women routinely experienced discrimination on the job; now we have laws that prohibit sex discrimination in employment. Changes such as these do not just happen. Instead, they grow out of rhetorical movements that alter cultural understandings of gender and, with that, the rights, privileges, and roles available to women and men. Insight into communication, gender, and culture is enhanced by knowledge of how rhetorical movements have sculpted and continue to sculpt social views of men and women.

Rhetoric is persuasion; rhetorical movements are collective efforts that use persuasion to challenge and change existing attitudes, laws, and policies. In this chapter we will consider a number of women's movements that have altered the meaning, roles, status, and opportunities of women in America. In Chapter 4 we'll explore men's movements that seek to persuade society to particular views of masculinity. As we survey these rhetorical movements, you'll discover that they are anything but uniform. They advocate diverse views of gender and pursue a range of goals. Insight into the range of rhetorical movements about gender may allow you to define more clearly where your own values and goals place you within the range of movements about gender.

THREE WAVES OF WOMEN'S MOVEMENTS IN AMERICA

A widely held misconception is that the women's movement in America began in the 1960s. This, however, disregards over a century's history in which women's movements had significant impact. It also implies that the women's movement is a single thing, when actually there have been and are multiple women's movements.

Rhetorical movements to define women's nature and rights have occurred in three waves. During each wave, two distinct ideologies have informed movement goals and efforts at change. One ideology, called **liberal feminism,** holds that women and men are alike and equal in most respects. Therefore, goes the reasoning, they should have the same rights, roles, and opportunities. A second, quite different ideology, referred to as **cultural feminism,** holds that women and men are essentially different. If the sexes differ in important ways, then they should have different rights, roles, and opportunities. We'll see that these conflicting ideologies lead to diverse rhetorical goals and strategies.

THE FIRST WAVE OF WOMEN'S MOVEMENTS IN THE UNITED STATES

Roughly spanning the years from 1840 to 1925, the first wave of women's movements included both liberal and cultural branches. Ironically, the conflicting views of these two movements worked together to change the status and rights of women in society.

▥ The Women's Rights Movement

What we now call the **women's rights movement**—activism aimed at enlarging women's political rights—grew out of women's efforts in other reform movements. Many women in the early 1800s participated in movements to end slavery (abolition) and ban consumption of alcohol (temperance, or prohibition) (Fields, 2003; Million, 2003; Yellin, 1990). These early reformers discovered that their efforts to instigate changes in society were hampered by their lack of a legitimate public voice. They realized that a prerequisite for their political action was securing the right to speak and vote so that they had a voice in public life (Sarkela, Ross, & Lowe, 2003).

In 1840 Lucretia Coffin Mott was a representative to the World Anti-Slavery Convention in London (Campbell, 1989a), but she was not allowed to participate, because she was a woman. At the convention, Mott met Elizabeth Cady Stanton, who had accompanied her husband (who was a delegate), and the two women discussed the unfairness of Mott's exclusion. In the years that followed, Mott and Stanton worked with others to organize the first women's rights convention.

Held in New York in 1848, the Seneca Falls Convention marked the beginning of women's vocal efforts to secure basic rights in America—rights granted to White men by the Constitution. Lucretia Coffin Mott, Martha Coffin Wright, Mary Anne McClintock, and Elizabeth Cady Stanton collaboratively wrote the keynote address, entitled the "Declaration of Sentiments." Ingeniously modeled on the Declaration of Independence, the speech, delivered by Stanton, proclaimed (Campbell, 1989b, p. 34):

> We hold these truths to be self-evident: that all men and women are created equal; that they are endowed by their Creator with certain inalienable rights, that among these are life, liberty, and the pursuit of happiness.

Continuing in the language of the Declaration of Independence, Stanton catalogued specific grievances women had suffered, including denial of the right to vote, exclusion from most forms of higher education, restrictions on employment, and denial of property rights upon marriage. Following Stanton's oration, 32 men and 68 women signed a petition supporting a number of rights for women. Instrumental to passage of the petition was the support of former slave Frederick Douglass (Campbell, 1989b).

Although Douglass supported women's rights, it does not signify widespread participation of Black citizens in the women's rights movement. Initially, there were strong links between abolitionist efforts and women's rights. However, the links dissolved as many abolitionists became convinced that the movement for Black men's voting rights had to precede women's suffrage. In addition, many Black women thought the women's rights movement focused on White women's circumstances and ignored grievous differences caused by race. Forced to choose between allegiance to their race and allegiance to their sex, most Black women of the era chose race. Thus, the women's rights movement became almost exclusively White in its membership and interests.

The Seneca Falls Convention did not have immediate political impact. Women's efforts to secure the right to vote based on the argument that the Constitution defined suffrage as a right of all individuals fell on deaf ears. At that time in America's history, women were still not considered individuals but rather the property of men. In 1872, two years after Black men received the right to vote, Susan B. Anthony and other women attempted to cast votes at polls but were turned away and arrested. Not until 48 years later would women gain the right to vote, in part as a result of a second and quite distinct women's movement.

■ The Cult of Domesticity

Many women in the 1800s did not believe that women and men were equal and alike in important respects. As cultural feminists they believed that, compared to

Ain't I a Woman?

Isabella Van Wagenen was born as a slave in Ulster County, New York, in the late 1700s. After she was emancipated, Van Wagenen moved to New York City and became a Pentecostal preacher at the age of 46. She preached throughout Northern states, using the new name she gave herself: Sojourner of God's Truth. She preached in favor of temperance, women's rights, and the abolition of slavery.

On May 28, 1851, Truth attended a women's rights meeting in Akron, Ohio. Throughout the morning she listened to speeches that focused on White women's concerns. Here the historical account splits. Some historians (Painter, 1996) state that Sojourner did not speak at the meeting and someone else gave the speech that is widely credited to Truth. Other scholars state that Sojourner Truth delivered the speech, "Ain't I a Woman?" Whether given by Truth or another person, the speech pointed out the ways in which White women's situations and oppression are different from those of Black women. The speech eloquently voiced the double oppression suffered by Black women of the time (Folb, 1985; Hine & Thompson, 1998; hooks, 1981):

> That man over there says that woman needs to be helped into carriages, and lifted over ditches, and to have the best place everywhere. Nobody ever helps me into carriages or over mud-puddles, or gives me any best place. And ain't I a woman?
>
> I have ploughed, and I planted, and gathered into barns. . . . And ain't I a woman? I have borne thirteen children and seen them most all sold off into slavery, and when I cried out with a mother's grief, none but Jesus heard. And ain't I a woman?

men, women were more moral, nurturing, concerned about others, and committed to harmony. Believing the ideal of "true womanhood" (Welter, 1966) to be domesticity, these women were part of a movement feminists now refer to as the *cult of domesticity.*

Belief in women's moral virtue led cultural feminists to form various reform organizations to fight for prohibition, child labor laws, rights of women prisoners, and policies of peace. Like members of the women's rights movement, the cult of domesticity focused on the lives and concerns of White women. Their efforts at reform largely neglected the fact that Black women confronted far more basic injustices and suffered fundamental deprivations of liberty, food, shelter, and medical care.

Ironically, the conservative ideology of the cult of domesticity was critical to securing women's right to vote. Movement members argued that allowing women to vote would curb the corruption of political life. Women's moral virtue, they claimed, would reform the political world that had been debased by immoral men. This rhetorical strategy was instrumental to women's struggle to gain political

FYI

Reproductive Rights

Birth control has been a priority of women's movements. In the 19th century, Elizabeth Cady Stanton insisted that "voluntary motherhood" was a prerequisite of women's freedom (Gordon, 1976). Later, Margaret Sanger emerged as the most visible proponent of women's access to birth control. Her work as a nurse and midwife made her painfully aware that many women, particularly immigrants and poor women, died in childbirth or as a result of illegal abortions (Chesler, 1992). In speeches throughout America and Europe, Sanger advocated birth control for women. In her periodical publication, *The Woman Rebel,* Sanger declared, "A woman's body belongs to herself alone. It is her body. It does not belong to the Church. It does not belong to the United States of America or any other government on the face of the earth. . . . Enforced motherhood is the most complete denial of a woman's right to life and liberty" (1914, p. 1).

During the second wave of feminism in the United States, feminists again protested for safe, accessible birth control and abortion for all women. In 1969, a group of feminists disrupted the New York state legislature's expert hearing on abortion reform—the experts who had been invited to address the legislature consisted of 14 men and one nun (Pollitt, 2000). The protesters insisted that none of the experts had personal experience with what reproductive choices mean. Four years later the landmark case of *Roe v. Wade* established abortion as a woman's right. Yet, 30 years after that case was decided, abortion is still not available to all women who are citizens of the United States. In 1997, Congress banned access to privately funded abortions at overseas military hospitals, prohibited insurance for federal employees from covering abortion, and greatly restricted abortions for Medicaid recipients ("*Roe v. Wade* at twenty-five," 1998).

Not all feminists believe that women should have access to abortion. Groups such as Feminists for Life argue that abortion is wrong and antithetical to feminine values.

franchise. On August 26, 1920, the constitutional amendment granting women the right to vote was passed.

Although the combined force of the cultural and liberal women's movements was necessary to win suffrage, the deep ideological chasm between these two groups was not resolved. Nor did securing voting rights immediately fuel further efforts to enlarge women's rights, roles, influence, and opportunities. Few women exercised their hard-won right to vote, and in 1925 an amendment to regulate child labor failed to be ratified, signaling the close of the first wave of women's movements.

After this, women's movements in the United States were relatively dormant for nearly 35 years. This time of quiescence in women's movements resulted from several factors. First, America's attention was concentrated on two world wars. During that time, women joined the labor force in record numbers to maintain the economy while many men were at war. Between 1940 and 1944, 6 million women went to work—a 500% increase in the number of women in paid labor (Harrison, 1988; Klein, 1984).

In postwar America men's professional opportunities expanded tremendously while women's shrank. More than 2 million women who had held jobs during the wars were fired, and their positions were given to male veterans (Barnett & Rivers, 1996). The view of the man as the family breadwinner became the ideal. During these years, only 12% of married women with children under the age of 6 were employed outside of their homes (Risman & Godwin, 2001).

T HE SECOND WAVE OF WOMEN'S MOVEMENTS IN THE UNITED STATES

Roughly spanning the years between 1960 and 1995, a second wave of women's movements surged across America. As in the first wave, both liberal and cultural ideologies coexisted in the second wave. Also as in the first wave, the second wave sprang from different sources, sought diverse goals, and used distinct rhetorical strategies.

Radical Feminism

The first form of feminism to emerge in this century was **radical feminism**, which grew out of New Left politics that protested the Vietnam War and fought for the civil rights of Blacks. Women participated side by side with men in New Left struggles but didn't have equality with them. They did the same work as their male peers and risked the same hazards of arrest and physical assault, but New Left men treated women as subordinates. Men dominated New Left leadership, whereas women activists were expected to make coffee, type news releases and memos, do the menial work of organizing, and be ever available for the men's sexual recreation. Women were generally not allowed to represent the movement in public—their voices were not recognized or respected.

In 1964, women in the Student Nonviolent Coordinating Committee (SNCC) challenged the sexism in the New Left, but most male members were unresponsive. Stokely Carmichael, a major leader for civil rights, responded to women's demands for equality by telling them that "the position of women in SNCC is prone." (He actually meant *supine*—on their backs.) In 1965, women in the Students for a Democratic Society (SDS) also found no receptivity to their demands for equality (O'Kelly & Carney, 1986). Outraged by men's disregard for their rights and men's refusal to extend to women the democratic, egalitarian principles they preached, many women withdrew from the New Left and formed their own organizations. These radical feminists' most basic principle was that oppression of women is the fundamental form of oppression on which all others are modeled (Dow, 2000; Du Plessis & Snitow, 1999; Willis, 1992).

Anna

I remember when the second wave of feminism started. I was in college then. I'd never thought about women being oppressed. I'd never questioned women's place in society. Two of my close friends and I were protesting for civil rights. The men in our group always asked us to go get coffee or food or whatever. We started talking about that—why was it that we were supposed to wait on them? If all of us were working to end discrimination based on race, why were they practicing discrimination based on sex? That was when I first became aware of sexism and when I became a feminist.

The crux of radical feminism was the confronting of women's oppression with revolutionary analysis, politics, and demands for changes in women's place in society and relationships between women and men (Barry, 1998a). In 1968 these women held their first national meetings, where they began to chart the principles and practices that would define radical feminism. Central to what they created were new forms of communication that reflected their politics. A primary radical feminist communication technique was the "rap" group or consciousness-raising group, in which women gathered to talk informally about personal experiences with sexism. Radical feminists' commitment to equality and their deep suspicion of hierarchy led them to adopt communication practices that ensured equal participation by all members of rap groups. For instance, some groups used a system of chips in which each woman was given an equal number of chips at the outset of a rap session. Each time she spoke, she tossed one of her chips into the center of the group. When she had used all of her chips, she could not contribute further, and other, less outspoken women had opportunities to speak. This technique was valuable because it recognized the importance of women's voices, encouraged individual women to find and use their voices, and taught women to listen to and respect each other.

Consciousness-raising groups were leaderless, as were working committees in radical feminist organizations. Reflecting disillusion with the vying for power that

The Famous Bra Burning (That Didn't Happen!)

One of the most widespread misperceptions is that feminists burned bras in 1968 to protest the Miss America pageant. That never happened. Here's what did.

In planning a response to the pageant, protesters considered a number of strategies to dramatize their disapproval of what the pageant stood for and how it portrayed women. They decided to protest by throwing false eyelashes, bras, and girdles into what they called the Freedom Trash Can. They also put a crown on an animal labeled Miss America and led it around the pageant. In early planning for the protest, some members suggested burning bras, but this idea was abandoned (Hanisch, 1970; Oakley, 2002). However, a reporter heard of the plan and reported it as fact on national media. Millions of Americans accepted the report as accurate, and even today many people refer to feminists as "bra-burners."

characterized organizations like SDS and SNCC, leaderless discussions were structured so that participants had equal power. A third innovative communication form of radical feminists was guerrilla theater, in which they engaged in public communication to dramatize issues and arguments. Protests against the Miss America pageants in 1968 and 1969, for instance, included throwing cosmetics and constrictive underwear for women into trash containers to demonstrate rejection of the view of women as sex objects.

Perhaps the most important outcome of this movement was identifying the structural basis of women's oppression. The connection between social practices and individual women's situations was captured in radical feminists' declaration that "the personal is political." Through consciousness raising and collective efforts, radical feminists launched a women's health movement that helped women recognize and resist doctors' sexist and dictatorial attitudes and become knowledgeable about their own bodies (Boston Women's Health Club Book Collective, 1976; The Diagram Group, 1977). Although radical feminists' refusal to formally organize limited their ability to affect public policies and structures, they offered—and continue to offer—a profound and far-reaching critique of sexual inequality.

The Guerrilla Girls

Radical feminists are not confined to history. Some radical feminists continue to boldly challenge sexism, racism, and other kinds of discrimination. One radical feminist group is the Guerrilla Girls, an anonymous organization that campaigns against sexism, racism, and elitism in the art world (Guerrilla Girls, 1995).

They first captured public attention in the 1980s when they protested the Museum of Modern Art's exhibit entitled "International Survey of Contemporary Art." The Guerrilla Girls plastered posters throughout public places in New York City. The posters featured one nude woman from the Met's exhibit, but her head was covered by a guerrilla mask. Armed with equal measures of information, sarcasm, and humor, the posters asked, "Do women have to be naked to get into the Metropolitan Museum?" Following the question were statistics on the number of women artists (5) and women nudes (85) in the museum's exhibit (Kollwitz & Kahlo, 2003). The press appreciated the media-savvy tactics of the Guerrilla Girls and gave them good coverage. The Guerrilla Girls remain anonymous, insisting that their identities are irrelevant and that they want to focus on the issues, not on themselves. This mystery, of course, enhances public interest in the Guerrilla Girls, who appear on talk shows and give public lectures—all done while wearing masks to preserve anonymity.

 The Guerrilla Girls continue their work to serve, in their words, as "the conscience of the art world." Visit their Web site at: **http://www.guerrillagirls.com.**

■ Liberal Feminism

A second major form of second-wave feminism is *liberal feminism,* which advocates for women's equality in the world outside of the home, especially the workplace.

Today in the United States, 70% of women participate in the paid labor force (Ehrenreich, 1999), and they make up 60% of that work force (U.S. Bureau of Census, 1998). The high number of women in the U.S. work force stems from two distinct factors. First, the model of a one-earner household was never feasible for many working-class families (Stacey, 1990). Second, many women work because they enjoy the stimulation, status, and sense of achievement that comes with paid employment. It was this second factor that fueled the second wave of liberal feminism.

In the mid-1900s many middle-class White women were economically comfortable, but they didn't feel entirely fulfilled by their domestic roles. Surrounded by children and hardworking husbands, with matching appliances in their three-bedroom, suburban ranch houses and station wagons in the driveways, society told these women they were living the American Dream. But many of these middle-class homemakers were not happy. They loved their families and homes, but they also wanted an identity beyond the home. So they were not only unhappy, but they felt guilty that they were not satisfied with the American Dream. Because most of these women felt guilty about their dissatisfaction, they kept their feelings to themselves. Consequently, most individual women didn't realize that many other women also felt unfulfilled.

The liberal feminist movement crystallized in 1963 with publication of Betty Friedan's landmark book, *The Feminine Mystique.* The book's title was Friedan's way of naming what she called "the problem that has no name," by which she meant the vague, chronic discontent that many middle-class American women felt. Friedan named the problem and defined it as a political issue, not a personal one. She pointed out that the reasons women were not able to pursue personal development were political: American institutions, especially laws, kept many women confined to domestic roles with no opportunity for fulfillment in arenas outside of home life.

Acting according to the liberal tenet that women and men are alike in important respects and are therefore entitled to equal rights and opportunities, the movement initiated by Friedan's book is embodied in NOW, the National Organization for Women, which works to secure political, professional, and educational equity for women. Founded in 1966, NOW is a public voice for equal rights for women. It has been effective in gaining passage of laws and policies that enlarge women's opportunities and protect their rights.

Liberal feminism identifies and challenges institutional practices, policies, and laws that exclude women from positions of influence in public and professional life (Brownmiller, 2000; Rosen, 2001). The rhetorical strategies of this movement

Who Was Betty Friedan?

Betty Friedan was a key figure in second-wave feminism (Hartman, 1998; Hennesee, 1999; Horowitz, 1998). Born Bettye Naomi Goldstein in Peoria, Illinois, in 1921, she engaged in nightly conversations about politics with her father while her beautiful, fashionable mother looked with disappointment at Bettye's physical appearance.

Bettye enrolled in Smith College, where she was the star student in the psychology department. After dropping the "e" from her name, Betty became the editor-in-chief of the Smith College newspaper, which she used as a platform for espousing her views on Smith's secret societies, pacifism, and international politics.

In 1942, Goldstein graduated with highest honors and began graduate studies at the University of California at Berkeley. In her first year she was offered the most prestigious graduate fellowship in the field of psychology. She declined the scholarship, left school, and moved to New York City, where she met and married Carl Friedan, a theatrical director. The marriage was not happy, and there were incidents of violence.

Friedan worked as a journalist until 1952, by which time she was pregnant with her second child and McCarthyism had eclipsed feminism and leftist politics. Compelled to live in the suburbs, she wrote for women's magazines. But Friedan was unhappy with her life in the suburbs. She questioned other Smith graduates and discovered that they too were discontented with having given up their careers for their families. These conversations led her to write *The Feminine Mystique,* in which she addressed "the problem that has no name," thus giving it a name and giving impetus to the second wave of feminism in the United States.

include lobbying, speaking at public forums, drafting legislation, and holding conventions where goals and strategies are developed. Liberal feminism appeals to people who believe that women and men should have equal opportunities to participate in cultural life.

Initially, liberal feminism focused almost exclusively on issues in the lives of women who were White, middle class, heterosexual, able bodied and young or middle aged (Hooyman, 1999). In response to criticism of this narrow focus, liberal feminism began to pay more attention to and devote more political effort to issues faced by women who are not White, middle class, heterosexual, able bodied and young. As a result, liberal feminism has become more inclusive of diverse women and the issues in their lives.

Yet liberal feminism has little to offer people who believe that women and men have different needs and abilities and should be treated differently. For those who believe the sexes are basically different, various forms of cultural feminism are more compelling.

The National Organization for Women was established on June 30, 1966, in Washington, D.C. at the Third National Conference on the Commission on the Status of Women. Among the 28 founders of NOW were Betty Friedan, its first president, and the Reverend Pauli Murray, an African American woman who was an Episcopal minister. Murray co-authored NOW's original mission statement, which begins with this sentence: "The purpose of NOW is to take action to bring women into full participation in the mainstream of American society now, exercising all privileges and responsibilities thereof in truly equal partnership with men." Among NOW's achievements:

- Passage of the 1963 Equal Pay Act

- Amendment of the Civil Rights Act of 1964 to include sex, along with race, religion, and nationality, as an illegal basis for employment discrimination

- Modification of Executive Order 11246 to prohibit gender discrimination in employment by holders of federal contracts

- Support of federally financed child-care centers so women can work outside the home

- Identification of and publicity about sexism in children's books and programs so that parents and teachers can make informed choices about media for their children

- Influence on reforms in credit and banking practices that disadvantage women

- Enlargement of women's opportunities to participate in sports

- Support for women who seek elective and appointive public office

 Visit the NOW Web site at **http://www.now.org.**

■ Separatism

Some women believe, as first-wave cultural feminists did, that women are fundamentally different from men in the value they place on life, equality, harmony, nurturance, and peace. Finding that these values gain little hearing in a patriarchal, capitalist society, some women form all-women communities in which feminine values can flourish without intrusion from men and the aggressive, individualistic, oppressive values associated with Western masculinity. **Separatists** strive for lifestyles and communities in which women live independently in mutual respect and harmony.

Separatists believe it is impossible or a poor use of their generative energies to attempt to reform America's patriarchal culture. Instead, they choose to separate from mainstream society and form communities that value women and strive to live in harmony with people, animals, and the earth. In adopting this course of action, separatists limit their potential to alter dominant social values. Because they do not assume a public voice to critique the values they find objectionable, they exercise little political influence. Yet their very existence defines an alternative vision of how we might live—one that speaks of harmony, cooperation, and peaceful coexistence of all life forms.

Lesbian Feminism

Arguing that only women who do not orient their lives around men can be truly free, **lesbian feminists** define themselves as woman identified. Although not all lesbians ally themselves with feminism, many do so because of a shared commitment to ending discrimination against women. Many lesbian feminists are also committed to political activism designed to improve the conditions of women's lives. They join groups ranging from mainstream to radical (Taylor & Rupp, 1998). Some people argue that lesbians should keep their sexual lives private, just as heterosexuals do. In response, lesbian feminists point out, "That's exactly the point: We don't think employers and others should be able to pry into our private lives and deny us jobs and housing because of the gender of our sweethearts" ("A New Court Decision," 1992).

For lesbian feminists, the primary goals are to live as woman-identified women and to make it possible for women in committed, enduring relationships to enjoy the same property, insurance, and legal rights granted to heterosexual spouses. The rhetoric of lesbian feminists has two characteristic forms. First, lesbian feminists use their voices to respond to social criticism of their sexual orientations. Second, some lesbian feminists adopt proactive rhetorical strategies to assert their value, rights, and integrity.

Revalorism

One outcome of many first- and second-wave women's movements is enlarged respect for music, literature, and art created by women whose creative, artistic work has been silenced or ignored for centuries (Aptheker, 1998).

Revalorists aim to increase society's appreciation of women and their contributions to society. Drawing on standpoint theory, which we discussed in Chapter 2, revalorists believe that women's traditional role as caregivers has led them to develop values that are more nurturing, supportive, cooperative, and life-giving than the values men learn

> ### Regina
>
> I don't see much to be gained by having equal rights to participate in institutions that are themselves all wrong. I don't believe dog-eat-dog ethics are right. I don't want to be part of a system where I can advance only if I slit somebody else's throat or step on him or her. I don't want to prostitute myself for bits of power in a business. I would rather work for different ways of living, ones that are more cooperative like win-win strategies. Maybe that means I'm a dreamer, but I just can't motivate myself to work at gaining status in a system that I don't respect.

through participation in the public sphere. Sara Ruddick (1989), for instance, claims that the process of mothering young children cultivates "maternal thinking," which is marked by attentiveness to others and commitment to others' health, happiness, and development. Karlyn Khors Campbell's *Man Cannot Speak for Her* (1989a, 1989b) document women's rhetorical accomplishments that have been excluded from conventional histories of America. Another example, from a different field, is physicist Evelyn Fox Keller's (1983, 1985) efforts to make known Barbara McClintock's brilliant work in genetics, which most science textbooks disregard. In documenting women's contributions, revalorists aim to render a more complete history of America and the people who compose it.

Some revalorists also celebrate women's traditional activities. Carol Gilligan (1982), for instance, highlights women's commitment to caring. Mary Belenky and her colleagues (1986) identify ways of knowing that may be more characteristic of women than men. The broad goal of revalorists is to increase the value that society accords to women and the skills, activities, and philosophies derived from women's traditional roles.

Revalorist rhetoric is consistent with the goal of heightened public awareness of and respect for women and their contributions to society. First, revalorists often use unusual language to call attention to what they are doing. For instance, they talk about *re-covering*, not recovering, women's history, to indicate that they want to go beyond patriarchal perspectives on history. Second, revalorists affirm the integrity of women and their contributions by supporting exhibitions of women's traditional arts such as weaving and quilting and public festivals that highlight women's creative expression. Perhaps the best-known example of this is the Lilith Fair, an annual music festival. Third, revalorists enter into debates in an effort to secure unique legal rights for women; for instance, they argue that laws must recognize that only women bear children and thus have special needs that must be legally protected.

Some feminist scholars are concerned that celebrating women's traditional activities and roles may have repressive potential, because it seems to value what historically has resulted in oppression (Boling, 1991; Wood, 1994b). For instance, caring for others may reflect skills women developed to please those who controlled their lives—sometimes literally. Revalorists respond to this criticism by arguing that *not* to celebrate women's traditional activities is to participate in widespread cultural devaluations that have long shaped perceptions of women. This controversy is part of the ongoing cultural conversation about the meaning and value of femininity.

▪ Ecofeminism

Sharing some of the ideology of revalorists but also charting new ground are the ecofeminists. Ecofeminism's official inception is usually dated to 1974, when Françoise d'Eaubonne published *La Feminisme ou la Mort,* which translates to mean *Feminism or Death*. This book provided the philosophical foundation for **ecofeminism.**

Ecofeminism has been developed by U.S. feminist thinkers such as Rosemary Radford Reuther and influential French feminists, including Françoise d'Eaubonne, Luce Irigaray, and Hélène Cixous. Feminists on both continents highlight the connection between efforts to control and subordinate women and the quest to dominate nature (perhaps not coincidentally called "Mother Earth"). Rosemary Radford Reuther (1974, 1983, 2001), a Christian and theological scholar, argues that the lust to dominate has brought the world to the brink of a moral and ecological crisis in which there can be no winners and all will be destroyed.

Ecofeminism unites the intellectual and political strength of feminist thought with ecology's concerns about our living planet. According to Judith Plant, a fortuitously named early proponent of ecofeminism (Sales, 1987, p. 302),

Sandy

Before taking this course, I had never heard the word *ecofeminist,* but it pretty much fits me. I was raised on a farm, where I spent a lot of time feeding and playing with the farm animals. I was 7 years old when I saw a hog slaughtered. I became vegetarian on the spot. I didn't want to be part of that kind of suffering. Growing up on a farm also made me sensitive to land—if you take care of the soil, it will take care of you. I believe women and men are equal, but I didn't identify with feminism—at least not the feminism I learned about in school. It was too argumentative, too confrontational for me. But ecofeminism is different. It's about living in harmony with others and the natural world. That fits me and my values.

[This movement] gives women and men common ground. . . . The social system isn't good for either—or both—of us. Yet we are the social system. We need some common ground . . . to enable us to recognize and affect the deep structure of our relations with each other and with our environment.

Ecofeminists believe that domination and oppression are wrong and destructive of all forms of life, including the planet. Reuther (1975), for instance, claims that "the project of human life must cease to be seen as one of 'domination of nature,' or exploitation. . . . We have to find a new language of ecological responsiveness, a reciprocity between consciousness and the world system in which we live" (p. 83).

For ecofeminists, oppression itself, not particular instances of oppression, is the primary issue. They believe that, as long as oppression is culturally valued, it will be imposed on anyone and anything that cannot or does not resist. Thus, women's oppression is best understood as a specific example of an overarching cultural ideology that idolizes oppression in general. Many individuals who stood against specific types of oppression have redefined themselves as ecofeminists (Chase, 1991). For instance, many animal rights activists, vegetarians, and peace activists have joined the ecofeminist movement. In fact, prominent first-wave feminists such as Charlotte Perkins Gilman, Susan B. Anthony, and Mary Wollstonecraft thought that vegetarianism and animal rights were integral to a feminist agenda (Oakley, 2002).

The goals of this movement flow directly from its critique of cultural values. Ecofeminists seek to bring themselves and others to a new consciousness of humans' interdependence with all other life forms. To do so, they speak out against values that encourage exploitation, domination, and aggression and show how these oppress women, men, children, animals, plants, and the planet itself. Ecofeminists argue that the values most esteemed by patriarchal culture are the ones that will destroy us (Diamond & Orenstein, 1990; Gaard & Murphy, 1999; Mellor, 1998; Warren, 2000).

▇ Womanism

Another group of second-wave activists identifies themselves as **womanists** to differentiate themselves from White feminists. Criticizing mainstream feminists for focusing almost exclusively on White, middle-class women and their issues, some African American women see womanism as addressing both their racial and gender identities (Guy-Sheftall, 2003; Radford-Hill, 2000). Their goals are to make others aware of the exclusionary nature of feminism as it has been articulated by middle-class White women and to educate others about the ways in which gender and racial oppression intersect in the lives of women of color.

Womanists assert that second-wave liberal feminism represents only the experiences, concerns, and circumstances of members of the privileged race in America. bell hooks (1990) notes that African American women's oppression cannot be addressed by a feminist agenda that is ignorant of how racism and sexism come together in the lives of Black women. Because of their commitment to racial unity, some Black women are reluctant to criticize sexism in Black men (Collins, 1996).

Black women in America have a distinctive cultural history that is seldom recognized, much less addressed, by the White middle-class women who have dominated both waves of American women's movements. In neglecting the experiences of non-White, non-middle-class women, mainstream feminists may inadvertently participate in the very kind of oppression they claim to oppose (Rothenberg, Schafhausen, & Schneider, 2000). Some race-related differences in women's lives are that Black women as a group are more often single, have less formal education, bear more children, are paid less, and assume more financial responsibility for supporting families. Many Black women don't identify with feminist agendas that ignore their experiences (Findlen, 1995; Logwood, 1997; Morgan, 2003; Winbush, 2000).

Beginning in the 1970s, a number of African American women who were disenchanted with White middle-class feminism but who were committed to women's equality began organizing their own groups (B. Smith, 1998). Feminist organizations such as Black Women Organized for Action and the National Black Feminist Organization sprang up and quickly attracted members. In addition to focusing on race, these organizations cut across class lines to include working-class women and to address issues of lower-class African American women. Their goals include reforming social services to respond more humanely to poor women and increasing training and job opportunities so that women of color can improve the material conditions of their lives. Womanists' rhetorical strategies include consciousness-raising and support among women of color, lobbying decision makers for reforms in laws, and community organizing to build grassroots leadership of, by, and for women of color.

In 1997, African American women organized a march to celebrate and nourish community among African American women. Following the second Million Man

> ### Lashenna
>
> NOW's answer to African American women is just a trickle-down theory. Whatever big gains and changes NOW makes in the lives of middle-class White women are supposed to trickle down to us so we get a little something too. Well, thanks, but no thanks, I say. NOW and all those White feminist movements ignore the issues in Black women's lives. We have to deal not only with gender, but with race as well. Unlike a majority of White women, many African American women are faced with economic disadvantages, single parenthood, factory or housekeeping jobs, and little education. I have family members who face one or more of these problems. I don't want White women's trickle-down theory. I want a bottom-up theory!

FYI

To Be Womanish, to Be a Womanist

Alice Walker is credited with coining the term *womanism* as a label for Black women who believe in women's value, rights, and opportunities. According to Walker, Southern Black women often said to their daughters, "You acting womanish," which meant the daughters were being bold, courageous, and willful. To be womanish is to demand to know more than others say is good for you—to stretch beyond what is prescribed for a woman or girl (Collins, 1998). In her 1983 book *In Search of Our Mothers' Gardens*, Walker writes, "Womanist is to feminist as purple is to lavender" (p. xii).

Reprinted with special permission from Clay Bennett.

March, which we'll discuss in the next chapter, the **Million Woman March** was held in Philadelphia on October 24 and 25, 1997. Powered by grassroots volunteers who built support in their localities, the steering committee for the Million Woman March was made up not of celebrities but of average women who worked at unglamorous jobs and lived outside the spotlight. The march de-emphasized media hype in favor of woman-to-woman sharing of experiences, hopes, and support. Perhaps the spirit of the Million Woman March is best summed up by Irma Jones, a 74-year-old woman who had marched with Dr. Martin Luther King, Jr., from Selma to Montgomery. After the Million Woman March, Jones said, "I'm glad we did this before I died. People say black women can never get together. Today, we got together, sister" (Logwood, 1998, p. 19).

■ Multiracial Feminism

Building on womanism's critique of exclusions in mainstream feminism, **multiracial feminism** emphasizes multiple systems of domination that affect the lives of women and men (Anzaldúa & Keating, 2002; Collins, 1990, 1998; Hurtado, 2001; Morgana & Anzaldúa, 1983; Ryan, 2004). Leaders of this movement prefer the term *multiracial* to *multicultural* because they believe that race is a particularly potent power system that shapes people's identities and opportunities (Zinn & Dill, 1996).

At the same time, multiracial feminists insist that race cannot be viewed in isolation. Although especially important from their perspective, race intersects other systems of domination in ways that affect what race means. For instance, an Asian American will experience his or her race differently, depending on whether he or she is unemployed or a member of the professional class, the working class, or the middle class.

Also central to the multiracial feminist movement is emphasis on women's agency. Despite the constraints imposed by systems of domination, women of color have often resisted their oppressions. Even when they operated within abhorrent systems of domination such as slavery, women of color found ways to care for themselves and their families and to contribute to their communities. In highlighting how women of color have resisted oppression, multiracial feminists highlight the strengths of women.

Multiracial feminists challenge categories that structure how we think about gendered identities. Multiracial feminists insist that gender does not have universal meaning—instead, what gender means and how it affects our lives varies as a result of economic class, sexual orientation, race, and so forth. Gloria Anzaldúa (1999), a Chicana feminist, resists being categorized only according to her sex or her race-ethnicity or her sexual orientation. She insists that, on its own, each category misrepresents her identity because her race-ethnicity affects the meaning of being a woman and a lesbian; her sex affects the meaning of her race-ethnicity and sexual orientation; and her sexual orientation affects the meaning of being a woman and a Chicana. Yen Le Espiritu (1997) makes the same argument about Asian American women and men, as does Minh-ha Trinh (1989) about Vietnamese women.

For multiracial feminists, the key to understanding anyone's identity lies in the *intersection* of multiple categories such as gender, race-ethnicity, sexual orientation, and economic class. This leads multiracial feminists to write and talk, not about women or men as broad groups, but about more precise and complex categories such as Black working-class lesbians and middle-class, heterosexual Chicanas. Articulating multiracial feminism's goals, Gloria Anzaldúa (2002) states that it must "incorporate additional underrepresented voices" (p. B11).

Multiracial feminists have contributed significantly to feminist theory and practice by challenging the idea of a "universal woman" and showing

---

Katie

I like the ideas of the multiracial feminists. I agree that race cuts across everything else. I'm middle class, but my life isn't the same as a White middle-class girl's, because I'm Asian American. It's like the issues in my life aren't just about my sex; they're also about my race. I can talk to Black or Hispanic girls, and we have a lot in common—more than I have in common with most White girls. You just can't get away from the issue of race unless you're White.

---

that many groups are disadvantaged by a "matrix of domination" (Zinn & Dill, 1996; Hurtado, 2001). This important insight compels us to recognize how intersections among multiple social locations, or standpoints, shape individual lives and structure society.

Power Feminism

The 1990s gave birth to a new movement called **power feminism.** Although this movement labels itself feminist, a number of feminists consider it antagonistic to the enduring concerns of feminism. Writing in 1993, Naomi Wolf argued that it is self-defeating to focus on social causes of inequities and harm that women suffer. As an alternative, Wolf advocates power feminism, which contends that society doesn't oppress women because women have the power to control what happens to them.

Wolf urges women to "stop thinking of themselves as victims" and to capitalize on the power inherent in their majority status ("What About This Backlash?" 1994). To add credibility to her views, Wolf links herself with the Reverend Jesse Jackson, a passionate champion of those who have had little power. Wolf quotes Jackson as having said, "You're not responsible for being down, you are responsible for standing up" ("What About This Backlash?" 1994, p. 15). Although Jesse Jackson and, before him, the Reverend Martin Luther King, Jr., urged Blacks to resist oppression, neither claimed that racial oppression results from the passive acceptance of those who suffer it.

Power feminism is more closely linked to the ideas of Shelby Steele (1990), a conservative African American who claims that racial discrimination is no longer part of society but only a paranoid victim psychology in the heads of Blacks and other minorities. Following in Steele's footsteps, Wolf tells women that the only thing holding them back from equality is their own belief that they are victims.

Katie Roiphe is another visible proponent of power feminism. In her 1993 book, *The Morning After: Sex, Fear, and Feminism on Campus*, Roiphe denied that rape is widespread on campuses and in society. She argues that the term *rape* is being misused to describe normal sexual relations. Roiphe asserts that Take Back the Night marches, annual nonviolent protests that began in 1978 to speak out against rape, are self-defeating because "proclaiming victimhood" does not project strength. Roiphe ignores the fact that for many people Take Back the Night marches reflect and fuel activism, not victimhood.

Folana

The only people I know who talk the power feminist talk have never been raped and never been slapped in the face with discrimination. They think their success and safety is a result of their own efforts and that any woman or minority person who hasn't achieved what they have just didn't try. I'll bet a lot of them would drop the power feminist line if they got raped. That might make them see that women and minorities don't have as much power as people like Wolf and Roiphe. As for me, I don't think of myself as a victim, but I know I'm vulnerable just because I'm Black and a woman.

Power feminism ignores pervasive social factors that historically and currently aggrieve women as a group (Bowman, 1994; Franek, 1994; hooks, 1994; Wood, 1996a). As *New York Times* columnist Anna Quindlen (1994) points out, "No one should ever discount the reason so many women can so easily see themselves as victims. It is because, by any statistical measure, they so often are" (p. A23). It is naive to think that personal will alone can always prevent women from being targets of violence.

There is a big difference between identifying a moment in which one was a victim, on the one hand, and adopting the status of victim as an identity, on the other hand. Bryn Panee, a student of mine, clarified this distinction when she reported on her experiences as a rape crisis counselor: "Every turnaround case, where a woman is able to make the transformation from a helpless victim to an empowered survivor, could not have happened if she did not recognize she was a victim of a horrible crime" (1994, n.p.).

Power feminism may appeal to women like Naomi Wolf and Katie Roiphe, who are White, upper-class, successful, and well educated. It is less helpful to women who do not enjoy Wolf's privileges. Feminist theorist bell hooks ("What About This Backlash?" 1994) says power feminism is endorsed by "people who have access to power. Naomi presents herself as speaking for the masses, but she is speaking first and foremost for her own class interests" (p. 15). Perhaps that is why power feminism is embraced mainly by White, heterosexual, middle- and upper-class individuals who have little or no personal experience with devaluation, discrimination, and sexual violation.

■ The Third Wave of Women's Movements in the United States

The second wave of liberal feminism continues to be active today. At the same time, a third wave of feminism has emerged. Building on second-wave radical and liberal feminism and the insights of womanists and multicultural feminists, **third-wave feminism** includes women of different ethnicities, abilities and disabilities, classes, appearances, and sexual orientations. But third-wave feminism is not simply an extension of the goals, principles, and values of the second wave (Bailey, 1997; Ehrenreich, 1990; Fixmer, 2003; Fixmer & Wood, in press; Hernández & Rehman, 2002; Howry & Wood, 2001). The rising generation of feminists has a distinct agenda and a distinct way of pursuing it.

Natalie

I really appreciate what the '60s women's movement did to make my life better, but I can't identify with it. My life is different than my mother's and so are the issues that matter to me. Mom fought to get a job. I want a job that pays well and lets me advance. Mom worked really hard to find day care for her children. I want to have a marriage and a job that allows me not to have to rely on day care. Her generation fought to make it okay for women not to marry. My generation wants to figure out how to make marriages work better, more fairly. Different generations. Different issues.

Because this movement is new, its agenda and rhetorical strategies are less clear than those of other women's movements we've discussed. It's also unclear at this time whether the third wave will remain a single movement or break into different branches with their own ideologies and goals. At this early stage we can identify four features of this wave and a fifth feature that is embraced by some third-wave feminists.

Remaking Solidarity to Incorporate Differences Among Women

Rather than treating women as a homogeneous group, third-wave feminists recognize that women differ in many ways, including race, class, sexual orientation, body shape and size, and (dis)ability. Coming of age in an era sharply infused with awareness of differences, third wavers claim they have "a very different vantage point on the world than that of our foremothers. . . . We find ourselves seeking to create identities that accommodate ambiguity and our multiple positionalities" (Walker, 1995, p. xxxiii). The rising generation of feminists is figuring out how to speak about and for women as a group while simultaneously recognizing differences among women (Dicker & Piepmeier, 2003; Fixmer, 2003).

Building Coalitions

A second defining feature of third-wave feminism is a commitment to building alliances with men and other groups that work against various kinds of oppression. The second wave focused primarily on the needs and rights of White women, which fueled some tensions between women and men, and between White, heterosexual women and other women. Third wavers want to get beyond the exclusiveness that characterized earlier feminist movements.

According to third-wave writers, struggling to understand and incorporate differences can lead to a deep appreciation of intersections between various forms of privilege and oppression, what Patricia Hill Collins (1986) has referred to as the "matrix of domination." In Mocha Jean Herrup's (1995) words, third-wave feminists need to "realize that to fight AIDS we must fight homophobia, and to fight homophobia we must fight racism, and so on. . . . oppression is interrelated" (p. 247).

Third-wave feminists are also committed to building positive connections with men as their friends, romantic partners, co-workers, brothers, and fathers. But, warn these women, "We can't do the work for men, and we won't try. Social change requires efforts from *both* sides. We want to meet men in the middle, not do all the adjusting ourselves" (3rd Wave, 1999). In their zine, *Bust,* and their book, *The Bust Guide to the New Girl Order* (1999), Debbie Stoller and Marcelle Karp observe that trying to balance work and family has been almost exclusively a concern of women. They argue that it should equally be a concern of men because women and men are in it together.

The 3rd WWWave

The 3rd WWWave Web site declares, "We are the women coming of age now. We are putting a new face on feminism, taking it beyond the women's movement that our mothers participated in, bringing it back to the lives of *real women* who juggle jobs, kids, money, and personal freedom in a frenzied world."

 Visit the site at **http://www.io.com/~wwwave/.**

◼ Integrating Theory Into Everyday Practices

Although appreciative of the achievements of earlier waves of feminism, third-wave feminists believe that women still don't have a"complete package of entitlement" (Griffin, 1996, p. 116). Third wavers insist that the reforms won by the second wave have not been woven into everyday life. According to Shani Jamila (2002), laws no longer permit race and gender to be used as automatic barriers, but women and minorities still experience injustices that are subtle and outside legal censure. Third wavers emphasize the rift between legality and reality, theory and practice, structural changes and everyday life. For them, a key goal is to incorporate the structural changes wrought by the second wave into material, concrete life and all of its moments.

◼ The Political Is Personal

The politics of third wavers reflects the belief that the means of exerting power and privilege are no longer centered in institutions such as the law. Instead, argue third wavers, power is decisively dispersed—it is exercised and resisted in concrete, local situations, in particular moments. Inverting the second wave insight that "the personal is political," third wavers believe the political is personal. Jennifer Baumgardner and Amy Richards (2000) declare that, for third-wave feminists, "our politics emerge from our everyday lives" (p. 18). In other words, personal actions are a key way to instigate change in both individual and collective lives (Fixmer & Wood, in press).

Theorizing their politics from the ground up, young feminists insist that their politics must be rooted in the personal, bodily resistance to oppressive ideologies. In a stunning essay that explicitly links social constructions of female beauty to eating disorders that jeopardize millions of women's health, Abra Fortune Chernik (1995) writes, "Gazing in the mirror at my emaciated body, I observed a woman held up by her culture as the physical ideal because she was starving, self-obsessed and powerless, a woman called beautiful because she threatened no one except herself" (p. 81). After recognizing the connection between cultural codes for femininity and her own body, Chernik responded in a way that was both personal and political: "Gaining weight and getting my head out of the toilet bowl was the most political act I have ever committed" (p. 81). Many self-identified third-wave feminists are committed to personal action, which they regard not as distinct from, but as deeply connected to, political change. Borrowing bell hooks' (2000b) term "door-to-door feminism," Lisa Bowleg (1995) uses her voice to "inform and educate," and she has "challenged my family and friends" (pp. 51–52). And Mocha Jean Herrup (1995) notes that, "social change is not just about the kind of political action brought about by group action. Politics is also interpersonal—about how we talk to each other and how we relate to one another" (pp. 249–250).

Celebrating Girl Culture

Departing notably from mainstream second-wave feminism, some, although not all, third-wave feminists embrace aspects of traditional "girl culture." In a conversation I had with Jennifer Baumgardner and Amy Richards, the authors of *ManifestA* (2000), they pointed out that the second wave of the movement disparaged pop culture, but the third wave seeks to engage it and shape it to suit women. Some third-wave feminists celebrate their femininity and sexuality. For instance, some third wavers say Madonna has shown that "the trappings of femininity could be used to make a sexual statement that was powerful, rather than passive" (Karp & Stoller, 1999, p. 45). The blending of serious issues and "girl culture" is one of the earmarks of several new magazines for girls and women. Alongside articles about glitter nail polish and cool clothes is serious advice about issues such as racism, eating disorders, and self-empowerment (Kuczynski, 2001). For some young feminists, it's possible—and fun—to be both fashionable and feminist (Waggonner & Hallstein, 2001).

Energetic, humorous, thoughtful, angry, sassy, hopeful, and passionate—the new feminists are committed to activist feminist work (Heywood, 1998; Heywood & Drake, 1997). As they voice their concerns and carry out their politics, they will remake feminism to resonate with the priorities of their generation.

SUMMARY

The "women's movement" is really a collage of many movements that span more than one and a half centuries and include a range of political and social ideologies. The different goals associated with women's movements are paralleled by diverse rhetorical strategies ranging from consciousness-raising to public lobbying and stump speaking. The issue of whether a person is a feminist is considerably more complicated than it first appears. Whether or not you define yourself as a feminist, you have some views of women's identities, rights, and nature. It may be that each of us needs to ask not just whether we are feminists but *which kind* of feminist we are.

KEY TERMS

cultural feminism, 59
ecofeminism, 71
lesbian feminists, 69
liberal feminism, 59
Million Woman March, 74
multiracial feminism, 74
power feminism, 76

radical feminism, 63
revalorists, 69
separatist(s), 68
third-wave feminism, 77
womanists, 72
women's rights movement, 59

DISCUSSION QUESTIONS

1. How have your views of feminism changed as a result of reading this chapter?

2. Choose the PowerTrac search option in your InfoTrac College Edition. Select title and type in "Seneca Falls Revisited." Then view the text of Lisa Marsh Ryerson's speech, "Seneca Falls Revisited: Reflections on the Legacy of the 1948 Women's Rights Convention." Pay particular attention to the excerpts from Elizabeth Cady Stanton's speech that appear in Ryerson's speech.

3. What do you see as the most important issues for feminism in the 21st century in the United States? What kinds of discrimination and oppression still limit women economically, personally, educationally, professionally, and politically?

4. To what extent do you think we should work to ensure that women have equal rights and opportunities within existing systems (liberal feminism) or should work to change the systems to incorporate traditionally feminine values and concerns (cultural feminism)?

4

The Rhetorical Shaping of Gender: Men's Movements in America

Injustice anywhere is a threat to justice everywhere.
—MARTIN LUTHER KING, JR.

In this country men historically have been less involved than women in gender movements. In part this is because men—at least, White men—already had the rights and privileges that have been and continue to be the goal of women's movements. During the first wave of women's movements, most men opposed women's efforts to gain rights, although a few, like Frederick Douglass, actively supported women's struggle to be recognized as equal. During the second wave of U.S. women's movements, a number of men supported liberal feminism; many joined NOW (National Organization for Women) and other groups to work with women for equality.

During the second wave of women's movements in America, a number of men began to explore their own gender. They worked to identify and challenge the ways that masculinity has been constructed in America. Since the 1970s men have formed groups that articulate distinct agendas and explore issues in men's lives. Some men's groups want to reinvigorate traditional images of masculinity, while others aim to remake the meaning of masculinity in America.

Like the women's movement, the men's movement is really a collection of different movements with different views of men and diverse, sometimes deeply conflicting, political and personal goals and rhetorical strategies. Also like women's movements, men's movements are evolving, with new ones constantly arising. In the 1990s, for instance, both the Promise Keepers and the Million Man March emerged as distinct movements about and for men.

Interest in masculinity and men's issues has led to research and to the establishment of new journals. The most prominent two are *The Journal of Men's Studies* and *Men and Masculinities.* The growing body of research on men and masculinities provides a basis for education; colleges and universities across the United States now offer men's studies courses, which are increasingly popular on many campuses.

The men's movement is not independent of the women's movement. As we will see in this chapter, men's movements tend to form in reaction to particular branches of women's movements and particular issues pursued by women's movements. Some branches of the men's movement ally themselves with feminist groups; others fiercely reject feminism and feminists. We will discuss three broad types of men's movements: profeminist, masculinist, and antifeminist (Hagan, 1998).

PROFEMINIST MEN'S MOVEMENTS

Although only one sector of men's movements shares the liberal or egalitarian ideology of liberal feminism, it is the most enduring branch and one with which many men identify. Referred to as **male feminists** or profeminist or progressive men, this branch of men's movements emerged from the upheaval of the 1960s. Although many men in student activist organizations like SNCC and SDS ridiculed women who accused them of sexism, not all New Left men responded negatively. A number of them recognized the truth of the women's charges, and they were ashamed when confronted with the hypocrisy of their political efforts to end discrimination while discriminating against women.

These men worked to bring their attitudes and behavior in line with the egalitarian ideology they espoused. Later generations of male feminists, including many men in their twenties today, attribute their feminism to parents and teachers who modeled egalitarian, nonsexist attitudes and practices. One of the most recent anthologies of third-wave feminism (Hernández & Rheman, 2002) includes essays by male feminists, who believe that women and men should enjoy the same privileges, opportunities, rights, roles, and status in society. For the most part these men have linked themselves and their rhetoric to mainstream liberal feminism. Out of this perspective, two distinct concerns emerge, one focused on women and the other on men.

Bill

I can't remember when I wasn't a feminist. It's as much a part of me as being a man or a Christian. My parents both work, Mom as a lawyer and Dad as an accountant. I grew up seeing my mother as strong and achieving and loving, just as Dad was. I grew up seeing my mother express her ideas articulately and seeing my father respect what she said and did. She listened when he talked; he listened when she did. When I was a kid, sometimes Mom worked late and Dad was in charge of fixing dinner for me and my brother. Other times Dad worked late and Mom was in charge. Both of them knew how to take care of us. Both of them were successful outside of the home. I grew up seeing that women and men are equal. How could I not be a feminist?

Because they believe in the equality of the sexes, male feminists support women's battles for equitable treatment in society (Doyle, 1997), and participated in efforts to increase women's rights during the second wave of U.S. feminism. During the 1972 campaign to ratify the ERA (Equal Rights Amendment), many men gave time, effort, and financial resources to the battle for legal recognition of women's equality. They joined women on public platforms to advocate for women's equality and rights. Today most male feminists endorse efforts to gain equal pay for equal work, to end discrimination against qualified women in academic and professional contexts, and to increase parental leaves and affordable child care.

One rhetorical strategy used by some profeminist men is performing a **traitorous identity,** in which a member of a group criticizes particular attitudes and actions that are common and accepted among members of that group. For example, a Christian man of my acquaintance often speaks out at Christian conferences to criticize the ways in which many Christians discriminate against gays. Another example comes from Larry May, author of *Masculinity and Morality* (1998a). May notes that at meetings he attends male speakers sometimes make sexist jokes or comments. The humor in sexist (and racist) jokes and statements depends on the preexistence of sexist and racist attitudes in listeners (Ryan & Kanjorski, 1998). May points out that, if a woman objects to the sexist comments, many men roll their eyes or dismiss her as being overly sensitive or "unable to take a joke." However, May says that when he or other men criticize the sexism, both the speaker and other men in the audience look ashamed. According to May, men find it easy to dismiss women's criticism of sexism but difficult to dismiss the same criticism when it comes from "one of us."

Another kind of communication employed by male feminists is personal persuasion to convince friends and co-workers to alter discriminatory attitudes and practices. For instance, one of my friends who considers himself a feminist talked with several of his colleagues about his disapproval of his firm's policy of paying women less than it paid men in equivalent positions. He thought the action was wrong, and he used his voice and his credibility to persuade other people. Another man, Scott Straus (2004), used his voice on campus to criticize fraternities. Later he wrote an article in which he criticized men in the fraternity to which he had belonged for practices such as bragging about who had sex with whom and rating female students' attractiveness.

Another interest of male feminists is their personal growth beyond restrictions imposed by society's prescriptions for masculinity. Because they believe that men and women are alike in most ways, male feminists want to develop the emotional capacities that society approves in women but discourages in men. Specifically, many male feminists claim that social expectations of masculinity force men to repress their feelings, and this diminishes men's humanity and makes their lives less satisfying than they could be (Avery, 1999; Hudson & Jacot, 1992).

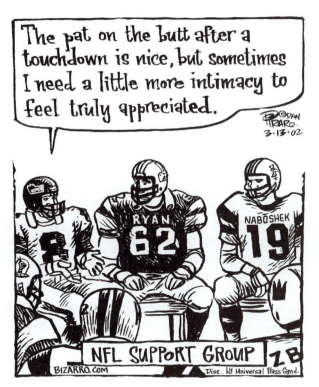

Copyright © Don Piraro. Reprinted with special permission of King Features Syndicate.

Agreeing with liberal feminist women, men in this movement regard cultural prescriptions for gender as toxic to both sexes. Whereas for women social codes have restricted professional development and civic rights, for men they often seal off feelings (Brod, 1987; Hearn, 1987). Male feminists think that, in constricting men's ability to understand and experience many emotions, society has robbed them of an important aspect of what it means to be human. A major goal of male feminists is changing this. They encourage men to get in touch with their feelings and to be more sensitive, caring, open, and able to engage in meaningful, close relationships.

The male feminist movement includes both organized political efforts and informal, interpersonal communication. Formal, public action in this movement dates to 1975, when the first Men and Masculinity Conference was held in Tennessee. The conference has met annually since then to discuss the meaning of masculinity, to establish a network of support for men, and to identify and talk about problems and frustrations inherent in our culture's definition of masculinity and the roles and activities appropriate for men (Doyle, 1997; Messner, 2001). We will look more closely at two particular profeminist organizations.

■ NOMAS

One of the most prominent male feminist organization is NOMAS, the National Organization for Men Against Sexism. This association sponsors workshops with speakers and group discussions to expand men's awareness of ways in which their emotional development has been hindered by restrictive social views of masculinity. In addition, the workshops attempt to help men change this state of affairs by offering guidance in becoming more feeling and sensitive. Often these groups serve as safe testing grounds in which men can experiment with expressing their feelings, needs, and problems.

Although members of NOMAS believe that some qualities traditionally associated with masculinity, such as courage and ambition, are valuable in women as well as in men, it condemns other conventionally masculine qualities such as aggression, violence, and emotional insensitivity. One of the major achievements of NOMAS is its Fathering Task Group. This group issues a newsletter called *Fatherlove,* which promotes nurturance of children and involvement of fathers (Doyle, 1989).

For 30 years NOMAS has held an annual conference on men and masculinity. Three issues consistently arise as priorities for discussion and action at these conferences. One is ending violence against women by analyzing the relationship between cultural codes for masculinity and men's violence against women. A second high-priority issue is working to end men's homophobic attitudes and the cruel, sometimes deadly, attacks on gays that stem from these attitudes. The third recurrent issue at NOMAS conferences is continuing to develop and enrich men's studies at colleges and universities throughout the United States. NOMAS's annual conferences allow members to work on social change through political and educational activism.

About NOMAS

The National Organization for Men Against Sexism defines itself as an activist organization that promotes positive changes in men. NOMAS is pro-men, pro-women, and pro-gay in its philosophy. Through formal and informal efforts NOMAS attempts to bring about personal, political, and social changes that foster equality of men and women and gay and straight people.

Information on the organization's goals, activities, and membership procedures may be obtained by contacting the national organization:

NOMAS 798 Pennsylvania Avenue, Box 5, Pittsburgh, PA 15221

 Visit NOMAS' Web site at **http://www.nomas.org.**

Members of NOMAS engage in a variety of rhetorical strategies. One is informal group discussions where men meet to explore the joys, frustrations, privileges, and problems of being men and of prevailing views of masculinity. Modeled on the consciousness-raising groups popular with many second-wave feminists, these groups encourage men to talk about what our society expects of men and the problems these expectations create. Through discussion, men pursue their goal of getting in touch with their emotions. They try to learn how to talk openly with other men about feelings, fears, concerns, and frustrations. Men are socialized to avoid topics like these because such subjects increase vulnerability and reflect a need for others, which violates social expectations of independence. Through these informal discussions, men explore with one another what they feel and how they might change attitudes and behaviors they find unworthy in themselves as individual men and in society overall.

Members of NOMAS also speak publicly in support of women's rights and men's personal development. In addition, NOMAS members are often involved in educational outreach programs that raise awareness of issues such as men's violence and that seek to persuade other men to become involved with changing destructive views of masculinity. Finally, members of NOMAS often enact traitorous identities to challenge everyday incidents of sexism and devaluation of women.

■ Men's Antiviolence Groups

Many profeminist men are particularly committed to ending men's violence against women. Like Kevin, whose commentary appears on this page, they believe that violence against women is not just a "woman's issue." These men reason that, since the majority of violence against women (as well as men) is enacted by men, it is an issue for men. Two specific men's antiviolence programs deserve our attention.

The White Ribbon Campaign. Perhaps you've noticed that some men wear white ribbons between November 25 and December 6. Those who do are stating that they identify with the **White Ribbon Campaign** (**WRC**), an international group of men who are working to end men's violence against women (www.whiteribbon.com, accessed May 20, 2003). Formed in 1991, the WRC is the largest men's antiviolence group in the world.

Kevin

If someone had told me five years ago I would say I'm a feminist, I wouldn't have believed it. Four years ago my little sister was raped. I was enraged and I felt totally powerless to help her, which was hard for me to deal with. I thought I was supposed to solve the problem, make things right, get the guy who did it. But I couldn't. I went with my sister to the rape crisis center and began to learn how bad the problem is. I began to see that the problem wasn't just the guy who raped her. It's the way that most men are socialized, including me—my wanting to be in control and *get* the guy who raped her. Gradually I got more involved with others who want to end violence against women. Ending it has to start with men, not women. Men have to take responsibility for looking at how masculinity is viewed in society, and we have to take responsibility for changing that.

The WRC began when a group of Canadian men felt they had to respond to an appalling incident of violence against women. On December 6, 1991, 14 women were massacred in what came to be called the Montreal Massacre. They were students in the Engineering School at the Université de Montreal. The murderer felt that engineering was a man's field in which women had no rightful place, so he removed them from the school—and from life. At first only a handful of men composed the group, which believed that men had a responsibility to speak out against men's violence against women. Designating a white ribbon as the symbol of men's opposition to men's violence against women, after only six weeks of planning this small group convinced more than 100,000 Canadian men to wear white ribbons. According to the white ribbon Web site, "wearing a white ribbon is a symbol of a personal pledge never to commit, condone, nor remain silent about violence against women" (www.whiteribbon.com, 2003). Since the WRC was founded in Canada in 1991, it has spread to many other countries. Local chapters in some countries select Father's Day and Valentine's Day for WRC events that emphasize men's caring and investment in positive, loving relationships.

But wearing a white ribbon for one or two weeks a year is not the only rhetorical strategy used by the WRC. Members also develop and present antiviolence workshops in schools, communities, and places of employment. In the workshops, WRC members demonstrate that violence is overwhelmingly committed by men, and they then encourage men in attendance to take responsibility for stopping it. Men are encouraged to become part of the solution to men's violence by speaking out against men's violence and by talking with other men about the issue. The workshops focus not only on physical violence such as battering and rape, but also on emotional violence, sexual harassment, sexist humor, and other practices that devalue and harm women.

A third rhetorical strategy of the WRC is to emphasize that they are not "male bashers." On their Web site (http://www.whiteribbon.com), they state:

> We are not male bashers, because we're men, working with men, who care about what happens in the lives of men. The majority of men are not violent. At the same time, we do think that many men have learned to express their anger or insecurity through violence. Many men have come to believe that violence against a woman, child, or another man is an acceptable way to control another person.

A final strategy of the WRC is to be vocal and active in supporting women's groups. Members of the WRC acknowledge that women, particularly feminists, have a long-standing involvement in ending violence against women and have greater expertise than members of the WRC. The WRC campaign works closely and supportively with a variety of women's groups that focus on violence against women. Yet the WRC does not invite women to join. They see the organization as a campaign of men and aimed at men. It aims to emphasize that *men* specifically oppose violence against women.

The WRC has been widely praised by both women and men. Many women's groups are pleased that some men are taking a firm and vocal stance against men's violence (Lansberg, 2000). Yet one criticism has been voiced, particularly by some men involved in efforts to end violence against women. The problem, they say, is that the WRC doesn't go far enough. It implies that most men are nonviolent and that only the few violent men need to be changed. In an analysis of the WRC, Cutler Andrews (2003) concludes that "violence is not just a way in which some men express their masculinity. Violence is an essential component of normative masculinity" (p. 52). In other words, he believes that the WRC errs in assuming that violence is a problem only for a few men. Andrews argues violence is inherent in social norms for masculinity.

Mentors in Violence Prevention. Andrews' reservations about the WRC are shared by Jackson Katz, who has developed a distinct approach to ending male violence against women. Katz is one of the principal workers in the male movement to end male violence against women. He gives workshops and speeches all over the world, and he trains men in mentoring other men to reject men's violence. **Mentors in Violence Prevention (MVP)** aims to educate men about socialization that links masculinity to violence and aggression and to motivate men to reject violence in themselves and other men (Katz, 2000).

The MVP program has two key foci. First, it aims to teach men that aggression and violence are closely linked to cultural views of masculinity and thus are part of routine masculine socialization. In other words, the MVP program focuses on normative masculinity—on the ways in which violence is seen as a normal part of manhood in our society (Katz & Jhally, 1999, 2000). From sports to the military, masculine socialization teaches boys that violence is an appropriate means of gaining and maintaining control over others and of winning—whether it's winning on the football field or the battlefield.

The second focus of the MVP program is calling attention to the role of bystanders in preventing violence. Jackson and other MVP trainers reject the idea that only those who actually commit violence are blameworthy. In many cases, for violence to be committed, there must be bystanders who approve, encourage, condone, or just remain silent, claims Katz (2000). You understand Katz's point if you have seen the film *The Accused,* which dramatizes the true story of a gang rape in New Bedford, Massachusetts. The men who committed the gang rape egged each other on and cheered each other's assaults on the victim (played by Jodie Foster in the film). Further, there were other men who did not participate in the rape but stood by, doing nothing to stop it. This is what Katz means by *bystander behavior.* He wants men to take responsibility not only for refraining from violence but also for refusing to allow or condone other men's violence.

Profeminist men's groups, including NOMAS, WRC, and MVP, share the belief that current views of masculinity in Western culture are toxic for all of us, men and women alike. They also share a commitment to challenging and changing how the culture and individuals in it define and enact masculinity. In stark contrast to profeminist groups are those in the masculinist branch of men's movements. We turn now to those.

MASCULINIST MEN'S MOVEMENTS

A number of men's groups fit within the second camp of men's movements. These groups, labeled **masculinist** (Fiebert, 1987), believe that men suffer from gender discrimination. Masculinists also believe that men should have "men-only" spaces such as the Boy Scouts and fraternities where men are free of women and femininization (Hagan, 1998). Masculinist men generally consider profeminist men soft. Masculinists accuse them of being male-bashers who fuel negative stereotypes of men. A primary rhetorical strategy of masculinists is verbally attacking men who define themselves as male feminists.

Masculinists and profeminist men also differ in their attitudes toward homophobia and gay men. The masculinist camp does not focus on homophobia, which profeminist men see as underlying all men's—gay and straight alike—inability to form close relationships with other men. The issue of gay rights is not a primary concern for most masculinist men, who tend to either ignore or denounce gay men. Profeminist men, in contrast, are committed to supporting gay concerns, challenging men's homophobic attitudes, and eliminating discrimination against gay men (Lingard & Douglas, 1999).

■ Free Men

One of the most conservative groups subscribing to masculinist ideology is the **Free Men.** It includes specific organizations such as MR, Inc. (Men's Rights, Incorporated); the National Coalition for Free Men; and NOM (National Organization of Men). Free Men aim to restore men's pride in being "real men." By "real men,"

Contacting Free Men

The National Coalition of Free Men welcomes inquiries and comments about its work. You can visit its Web site to learn more about its activities and to consider joining the group:

 www.ncfm.org.

FYI

Have American Men Been Betrayed?

In 1991 prize-winning journalist Susan Faludi published *Backlash: The Undeclared War Against American Women,* in which she documented cultural practices that demean women and thwart their progress. Eight years later, she published *Stiffed: The Betrayal of the American Man* (1999), in which she argues that a significant number of men today feel that America has betrayed them.

Based on interviews, observations, and other research, Faludi concludes that many men feel that society has broken its contract with them. No longer can they count on loyalty from a company that they commit to. No longer do many men engage in work that has immediate meaning and satisfaction for them. No longer is being a breadwinner enough to be considered a good man; now they must also be involved fathers and husbands. Faludi argues that the traditional rules for being a man no longer hold, yet a new set of rules hasn't emerged. The result, she claims, is confusion, frustration, and a profound sense of powerlessness.

this group means men who fit the traditional macho image—tough, rugged, invulnerable, and self-reliant. Free Men see male feminists as soft and unmanly and denigrate them with epithets such as "the men's auxiliary to the women's movement" (D. Gross, 1990, p. 12). In fact, Free Men say that profeminist men are not part of the men's movement at all. Interestingly, when some Free Men took the name NOM for one of their organizations, the feminist men who had originally called *their* organization NOM changed their group's name to NOMAS to emphasize that they were in favor of *changing* traditional men's roles, not reinforcing them.

Free Men think that discrimination against men is far greater and more worthy of attention and correction than is discrimination against women. These men say that "it is actually *women* who have the power and *men* who are most oppressed by the current gender arrangements" (Messner, 1997, p. 41). The oppression that Free Men claim men suffer includes the military draft, shorter life spans, more health problems, and child custody laws that favor women (Whitaker, 2001).

According to Free Men, the primary burden of masculinity is the provider role, which makes men little more than meal tickets whose worth is measured by the size of their paychecks and their professional titles. Warren Farrell (1991), for instance, claims that men are relentlessly oppressed by the "24-hour-a-day psychological responsibility for the family's financial well-being" (p. 83). Farrell claims that "almost all men see bringing home a healthy salary as an obligation, not an option." Many men believe a woman will not love them if they are not successful and good providers. The pressure to be a good provider—and the difficulty of fulfilling that role—is exacerbated in times of economic downturn (Faludi, 1999).

Specific issues such as the provider burden, however, are subordinate to Free Men's overriding concern that American men are being robbed of their masculinity. Targeting feminism as the primary source of men's loss of their masculinity, masculinists claim that "men have been wimpified. They've been emasculated" (D. Gross, 1990, p. 13). Given this perspective, it's not surprising that Free Men oppose affirmative action, forced collection of alimony and child support, and a single-sex military (Kimmel, 1996).

Longing for the return of traditional roles and men's unquestioned supremacy in society and the home, Free Men want women to accept subordinate roles and to be deferential to men. With this, they believe, men will regain their rightful places as heads of families and unquestioned authorities. At the same time, they think their superiority to women should not be tied to the breadwinner role as a particular facet of traditional manhood. To advance their agenda, Free Men engage in rhetoric ranging from lobbying for reform of laws they claim discriminate against men to condemning feminist men and women in public and private communication.

■ Mythopoetic Men

Another branch of the men's movements that has garnered much publicity is the **mythopoetic movement,** founded by poet Robert Bly. In the 1960s Bly was a peace activist. During the 1970s he was a public advocate for a feminine, peace-loving way of being, and he held Great Mother conferences (Oakley, 2002). A decade later Bly championed quite a different set of ideas that blended neoconservative politics with some of the ideology of the Free Men. The mythopoetic movement is less interested in social change than in men's personal growth, wholeness, and bonding in all-male gatherings (Silverstein, Auerbach, Grieco, & Dunkel, 1999). Mythopoetics want men to rediscover the deep, mythic roots of masculine thinking and feeling, which they believe will restore men to their primordial spiritual, emotional, and intellectual wholeness (Keen, 1991).

Mythopoetics agree with feminist women and men that the current male role is toxic, yet they don't agree with feminists about the nature of the toxicity. Mythopoetics argue that the traditional masculine ideal was not only not toxic but positive. They claim that ideal manhood existed during ancient times and the Middle Ages, when men were self-confident, strong, and emotionally alive and sensitive. As exemplars of ideal manhood, mythopoetics cite King Arthur and the

Facts About the Mythopoetic Movement

Mythopoetics have a strong following (Adler, Doignan-Cabrera, & Gordon, 1991; Bonnett, 1996; Messner, 1997b).

■ More than 50,000 men have participated in nature retreats at a cost of more than $200 per participant.

■ *MAN!* the national quarterly devoted to the movement, has more than 3,500 subscribers.

■ *Wingspan,* another national quarterly of the movement, has a (free) circulation of more than 125,000 readers.

■ In the Northeast alone, over 163 mythopoetic groups have been formed.

■ Robert Bly's book *Iron John* enjoyed over 30 weeks on the best-seller list.

■ Mythopoetics are largely White and middle class.

 To read a short biography of Robert Bly, go to **http://www.robertbly.com/biography.html.**

Knights of the Round Table, Henry David Thoreau, Walt Whitman, and Johnny Appleseed (D. Gross, 1990).

Mythopoetics think men's formerly profound connections to the earth and to comradeship with other men were ripped asunder by modernization, the Industrial Revolution, and feminism. Men were taken away from their land and, with that, from ongoing contact with life itself and their roles as stewards of the land (Kimbrell, 1991). At the same time that men were isolated from their earthy, natural masculinity (D. Gross, 1990), industrialization separated men from their families. When men began working outside of the home, young boys lost fathers who could initiate them into manhood and teach them how to relate spiritually and emotionally to other men.

Although mythopoetics believe that men have been separated from their feelings, their views depart dramatically from those of profeminist men (Keen, 1991; Mechling & Mechling, 1994). Like Free Men, Bly and his followers lay much of the blame for men's emotional deficits on feminism. Bly says that in male feminists "there's not much energy" (Wagenheim, 1990, p. 42). Stating this view more strongly, some mythopoetics charge that "the American man wants his manhood back. Period. . . . [F]eminists have been busy castrating American males. They poured this country's testosterone out the window in the 1960s" (Allis, 1990, p. 80). So one rhetorical strategy of mythopoetics is to ridicule male (as well as

Father Loss

Do social prescriptions for masculinity undermine men's ability to mourn the loss of their fathers? Neil Chethik (2001) thinks there may be a connection between socialization that teaches men to be strong and avoid close ties with other men and men's difficulty in grieving when their fathers die. Chethik surveyed more than 300 men and conducted in-depth interviews with 70 men to learn how they dealt with their fathers' deaths. He found that, no matter how many years have passed since the father died, sons continue to yearn deeply for connections with their fathers. Chethik found that many men try to follow social prescriptions for masculinity: They don't talk about their grief, don't cry, and don't show how much they hurt. Instead, they buck up and carry on, keeping their grief silent. Chethik reports that many men grieve and heal by reflecting quietly or by taking up hobbies that give them a sense of connection with their fathers.

female) feminists and to provide a counterstatement to male feminists' public arguments about masculinity.

What do mythopoetics advocate for masculinity? They insist men need to recover the *distinctly male mode of feeling,* which is fundamentally different from the female feelings endorsed by profeminist men. Men need to reclaim courage, aggression, and virility as masculine birthrights and as qualities that can be put to the service of bold and worthy goals as they were when knights and soldiers fought for grand causes.

Central to modern man's emotional emptiness, argues Bly, is **father hunger,** a grief born of yearning to be close both to actual fathers and to other men and to build deep, spiritual bonds between men. To remedy this, Bly and other leaders of the movement urge men to get in touch with their grief and, from there, to begin to rediscover their deep masculine feelings and spiritual energies. An especially influential form of persuasion by mythopoetics is Robert Bly's book *Iron John,* which is the major rhetorical text of this movement. This book, which explains mythopoetic views and recounts ancient myths of manhood, was a national bestseller for over 30 weeks, indicating that it appealed to a wide audience.

To facilitate this process, workshops and retreats allow men to "come together in nature alone, in the absence of women and civilization" (D. Gross,

Chuck

Bly's ideas sound pretty strange to me. I can't identify with chanting in the woods with a bunch of other guys to find my manhood. Heck, I didn't know I'd lost it! But if I were to be serious about this stuff, I guess I'd say there might be something to it. I mean, I do like to get together with brothers in my fraternity, and being with a group of just men does have a different kind of feeling than being with women or women and men. Like we're more uninhibited, more rough, and more loud than when girls are around. I guess I do feel more manly or something in those groups.

(continued)

1990, p. 14). In the natural world, men can recover the sense of brotherhood and distinctively male feelings repressed by industrialization and feminism. At nature retreats, men gather in the woods to beat drums, chant, and listen to poetry and mythic stories, all designed to help them get in touch with their father hunger and move beyond to positive masculine feeling. As this suggests, favored mythopoetic forms of communication are storytelling, chanting, and affirming the deep roots of distinctively masculine feelings.

The mythopoetic movement is not without critics. Michael Schwalbe's book *Unlocking the Cage* (1996) offers an inside look at the mythopoetic movement. For three years Schwalbe belonged to a men's support group, attended another men's group devoted to drumming, and participated in week-long men's retreats. Schwalbe discovered that many of these men had been harmed by distance and sometimes abuse from fathers. He concludes that these men were drawn to the mythopoetic movement because it offered primitive rites of masculinity that their fathers had not provided. Schwalbe criticizes mythopoetics for being unwilling to confront issues of gender inequality and for their participation in sustaining that inequality (Avery, 1999).

> (Chuck, continued)
>
> Another thing that interests me about what Bly says is the stuff about absent fathers. I'm not sure I'd go so far as to say I have the father hunger he talks about or that I have deep grief, but I do feel my father and I should have been closer. I never saw much of him when I was growing up. He worked all day and wanted to relax at night, not spend time with us kids. I wish I'd known him better—in fact, I still do wish it. I think a lot of guys feel that way.

■ Promise Keepers

In 1990 Bill McCartney, who was then head football coach at the University of Colorado, and his friend Dave Wardell were on a three-hour car trip to a meeting of Christian athletes in Pueblo, Colorado. On that trip, the two men conceived the idea of filling a stadium with Christian men. Later that year, McCartney and Wardell motivated 72 men to pray and fast about the idea of men coming together in Christian fellowship. The first **Promise Keepers** event in 1991 drew 4,200 men. Two years later McCartney achieved his goal of filling the 50,000-seat Folsom Field. In 1994, the Promise Keepers were ready to spread out. They had seven sites at which more than 278,000 men came together to pray and commit themselves to being Promise Keepers. Promise Keeper events such as "Stand in the Gap," "Storm the Gates," and "The Challenge" draw thousands of men each year (Shimron, 1997, 2002; Wagenheim, 1996).

According to Bill McCartney, many men have fallen away from their responsibilities as men. He says, "Men have been irresponsible. They have abandoned the home. They've chased careers. Their word wasn't good anymore. They've been unfaithful" ("Promise Keepers," 1997, p. 14A). Whereas mythopoetics see reconnecting with nature as the way for men to regain their wholeness, Promise Keepers see reconnection to God's commandments as the path. Based on evangelical Christianity, the movement urges men to be the leaders of their families because it reflects the "God-given division of labor between women and men" (Messner, 1997b, p. 30). Following the Christian path requires men to be good husbands, fathers, and members of communities. Each Promise Keeper makes seven promises (Shimron, 1997):

1. To honor Jesus Christ through worship, prayer, and obedience to God's word through the power of the Holy Spirit

2. To pursue vital relationships with other men, understanding that they need brothers to help them keep their promises

3. To practice spiritual, moral, ethical, and sexual purity

4. To build strong marriages and families through love, protection, and biblical values

5. To support the mission of his church by honoring and praying for his pastor and by actively giving his time and resources

6. To reach beyond any racial and denominational barriers to demonstrate the power of biblical unity

7. To influence his world for good, being obedient to the Great Commandment (see Mark 12:30–31) and the Great Commission (see Matthew 28:19–20)

Supporters of Promise Keepers believe that the movement is good for men and families. They say it champions values that build strong families and strong communities. In their opinion, Promise Keepers is a call for male responsibility (Whitehead, 1997). Furthermore, a number of women who are married to Promise Keepers say their marriages have improved since their husbands joined the movement (Cose, 1997; Griffith, 1997; Whitehead, 1997; Shimron, 2002).

Yet others voice reservations about the Promise Keepers. They ask why women can't attend Promise Keepers meetings. The Promise Keepers' answer is to quote Proverbs: 27:17: "Iron sharpens iron, and one man sharpens another." This reflects Promise Keepers' belief that men should lean on each other, not on women, in their quest to be good men—men can hold each other accountable in ways women can't (Shimron, 2002). Another question asked by people who have reservations about the Promise Keepers is, Why can't husbands and wives be equals (Ingraham, 1997)? McCartney responds, "When there is a final decision that needs to be made and they can't arrive at one, the man needs to take responsibility" ("Promise Keepers," 1997, p. 14A). Critics charge that "taking responsibility" is a code term for denying women's equality, voices, and rights.

Another reservation about Promise Keepers is that the group may be elitist. The great majority of Promise Keepers are White and middle or upper class economically. (Admission to a Promise Keeper event was $69 in 2002 (Shimron, 2002).) Gay men and those who support gays are uncomfortable with the Promise Keepers' view that homosexuality is a sin and that gays therefore are leading immoral lives. Finally, some critics regard Promise Keepers as more a conservative political movement than a social and spiritual movement (Cose, 1997; Whitaker, 2001). In response to criticism, Promise Keepers has made efforts to broaden

Cassie

Last summer my church had a Promise Keeper rally. I belong to the Praise Team, which is a church chorus, and we were asked to sing at the beginning of the rally. After we sang, I and two other women on the Praise Team were told we had to leave. We were led to a room where the wives and girlfriends of the men at the rally were waiting. We were told that the rally was just for men and we had to stay in that room and pray for the men until the rally was over and someone came to tell us we could come out.

I was very confused. I wanted to hear the rally too. Why weren't women allowed to hear it? Why were the organizers so extreme about excluding women? Why were we told to pray *for* the men but not allowed to pray *with* them?

its membership to include men of different races and to soften its rhetoric about husbands leading wives.

■ The Million Man March

Just as many African American women feel that feminism doesn't speak to or for them, many African American men feel that mainstream men's movements don't fit their histories and lives (Hammer, 2001). In the fall of 1995, Minister Louis Farrakhan, leader of the Nation of Islam, and the Reverend Benjamin Chavis, Jr., organized the first **Million Man March.** Their goal was for Black men of all religions and classes to fill the Mall of the nation's capital. The goals of the 1995 meeting were for Black men to atone for sins and reconcile with one another. Spike Lee's film *Get on the Bus* (1997) offers a dramatic documentation of this first march.

At the march, organizers encouraged men to pledge themselves to spiritual transformation and political action. Specifically, organizers called for the men to register to vote, fight drugs in their lives and communities, and stand against unemployment and violence. Men were asked to recommit themselves to their wives and families and to active involvement in their churches and communities.

The Million Man March was not a one-time event. Additional marches were held in years following; each time, the crowd stretched from the steps of the Capitol nearly to the Washington Monument. Those who attended found something they could identify with in this movement—something that could guide their lives and give them meaning. The Million Man March has been widely praised as a positive, uplifting movement for Black men. Yet there have been criticisms. One is that women are excluded from Million Man Marches. Some women think there is irony in asking men to leave home and be with other men in order to commit to their wives and families. Another criticism was advanced by Glenn Loury (1996), who is African American and a professor of economics. He is concerned that this movement encourages Black men to base their rage on the racial identity of those who suffer rather than to rage against suffering and inequity no matter who is the victim. Finally, some people criticize the Million Man March for being antifeminist and antigay and for holding overly conservative views of families and women (Messner, 1997b).

The inaugural Million Man March in 1995 seemed to strike a chord with other groups. Since that march, America has seen a Million Woman March in Philadelphia, a Million Youth March in Harlem, a Million Mom March in Washington, and most recently, in 2000, a Million Family March ("Million Family March," 2000).

Michael

I attended the Million Man March a couple of years ago, and it was the most important event of my life. It was wonderful to see so many Black men in one place—all there to unite with one another and to change our world. The whole mood was one of total brotherhood. It strengthened my pride in being a Black man and my feeling that I can build a life around strong spiritual values.

ANTIFEMINISM: THE BACKLASH

Feminist movements have brought about substantial changes in women's lives. Women's economic opportunities and rewards are better, although still not equal to men's; laws now prohibit discrimination in educational and work contexts; and many women's self-esteem has grown with the positive image of women and femininity promoted by women's movements. In fact, the very successes of feminism have led to an intense antifeminist movement, also called the **backlash** against feminism.

Antifeminism is a movement that opposes any measures that advance women's equality, status, rights, or opportunities. Antifeminist attitudes exist much of the time. Antifeminist movements, however, have taken formal shape in only two periods, which coincide with the first and second waves of women's movements in the United States (Blee, 1998).

Rather than in formal groups, antifeminism usually surfaces in individual and group practices that attempt to demean feminism and obstruct efforts to achieve equality between the sexes. Reflecting antifeminist values are media misrepresentations of women's successes and problems, judicial rulings that reduce women's freedoms, covert business practices that restrict women's opportunities, governmental actions that make it difficult for women to gain economic security without abandoning parental responsibilities, and popular book writers who scapegoat feminism as the source of problems ranging from loneliness to delinquent children.

In 1994, *Backlash* magazine debuted with the announced goal of returning women and men to their traditional roles. Two years later, in 1996, David Gelernter wrote an article for a mainstream magazine, entitled "Why Mothers Should Stay Home." In this article, Gelernter argues that mothers who work outside the home are selfish and irresponsible, and he claims that many problems in families are the direct result of women's employment outside the home. Gelernter and others who engage in antifeminist rhetoric believe that homemaking and raising children are exclusively the responsibilities of mothers and that feminism has enticed women to abandon these womanly responsibilities.

In addition to dispersed antifeminist practices, there have been three more formal antifeminist movements.

The Antisuffrage Movement

The first formal example of antifeminism was the **antisuffrage movement,** which aimed to prevent women from gaining the right to vote in the United States. Immediately following the Seneca Falls Convention in 1848, vocal opposition to women's suffrage surfaced. Both men and women claimed that allowing women to vote as well as to pursue higher education and own property would be in contradiction to women's natural roles as wives and mothers. By the 1870s opposition to women's suffrage was formalized in public organizations that were often led by the wives of socially prominent men (Blee, 1998). The best known antisuffrage organization was the National Association Opposed to Women's Suffrage, which claimed to have 350,000 members (Blee, 1998).

The antisuffrage movement reached its apex between 1911 and 1916. During those years, antisuffragists associated their cause with preserving the home and protecting the nation against socialism. Although the reasoning was never clear, antisuffragists argued that giving women the vote would increase the number of voters who were inclined toward socialism (Blee, 1998). The movement disbanded after women won the right to vote in 1920.

■ Fascinating, Total, Surrendered Women

A second antifeminist movement emerged in the 1970s when Marabel Morgan launched the Total Woman movement and Helen Andelin founded the Fascinating Womanhood movement, both of which advocated women's return to traditional attitudes, values, and roles. The Total Woman movement (Morgan, 1973) stressed the conventional social view of women as sexual objects and urged women to devote their energies to making themselves sexually irresistible to men. One example of advice given to women was to surprise their husbands by meeting them at the door dressed only in Saran Wrap. Fascinating Womanhood (Andelin, 1975) was grounded in conservative interpretations of biblical teachings, and it emphasized women's duty to embody moral purity and submit to their husbands.

Although many people saw Fascinating Womanhood and Total Woman movements as laughable and regressive, some women (and men) found them appealing. Over 400,000 women paid to take courses that taught them to be more sexually attractive and submissive to their husbands (O'Kelly & Carney, 1986). Primary support for these courses and the ideologies behind them came from women who were economically dependent on husbands and who embraced conservative values.

Movements that urge women to return to traditional roles were not restricted to the 1970s. The same ideas resurfaced in the 2001 book, *The Surrendered Wife: A Practical Guide for Finding Intimacy, Passion, and Peace with Your Man* (L. Doyle). This book, like the earlier two that it echoes, counsels women to abandon the myth of equality if they want happy marriages (Clinton, 2001). Women are advised to let their husbands lead the family and to accommodate their husbands.

■ The STOP ERA Campaign

Another instance of backlash was the STOP ERA movement, which also emerged in the 1970s. Taking to the public platform, the most prominent spokesperson

FYI

The Text of the Equal Rights Amendment

Equality of the rights under the law shall not be denied or abridged by the United States or by any State on account of sex.

for Stop ERA, Phyllis Schlafly, traveled around the nation to persuade people that feminism was destroying femininity by turning women into men. She told women to return to their roles as helpmates and homemakers and affirmed men's traditional roles as heads of families. Ironically, although Schlafly argued that women should be deferential and that their place was in the home, her own activities belied this advice. In speaking forcefully in public, she violated her own advice on feminine style. Further, her speaking schedule kept her on the road or writing much of the time, so she was unable to devote much time to being a homemaker or mother.

The STOP ERA movement carried out its work not only through Schlafly's public speaking but also through lobbying of legislators and courting the media. STOP ERA members warned legislators and the public that passing ERA would undercut men's willingness to support children, allow women to be drafted, threaten the family, and permit sex-integrated restrooms (Mansbridge, 1986). Like the antisuffrage movement in the 1800s and early 1900s, the STOP ERA movement was supported by men and women who believed in traditional families. Also like the previous antifeminist movement, STOP ERA was funded largely by corporate leaders and other people in the upper economic class who did not see the ERA as consistent with their economic and political interests (Blee, 1998; Klatch, 1998).

■ The Contradictory Claims of Antifeminism

In her 1991 book *Backlash: The Undeclared War Against American Women*, Pulitzer Prize–winning journalist Susan Faludi identifies two arguments that characterize the antifeminist or backlash movement. Faludi also notes that they are internally contradictory. On one hand, a good deal of antifeminist rhetoric defines feminism as the source of women's problems, including broken homes, tension between spouses, and delinquent children. According to this claim, in encouraging women to become more independent, feminism has turned women into fast-track achievers who have nothing to come home to but microwave dinners. Antifeminists argue that, rather than helping women, feminism has created more problems for them and made their lives miserable. They conclude that the solution to these problems is to renounce feminism.

A second antifeminist claim directly contradicts the first one by arguing that women have never had it so good. The media proclaim that women have won their battles for equality, they have made it, all doors are open to them, and they can have it all. Pointing to the gains in status and opportunities won by feminists, antifeminists assert that all inequities have disappeared and that there is no longer any need for feminism. This line of rhetoric has been persuasive with some people, particularly women who have benefited from feminism. Yet, if women have full equality, why is one woman in four the victim of assault by a man? If women have full equality, why does the average woman make 86 cents for doing the same job the average man is paid a dollar for doing? If women have full equality, why do women still perform most of the child-care and housekeeping tasks in two-earner families?

SUMMARY

Men's movements, like those focused on women's issues, are diverse and even contradictory. Some men consider themselves feminists, work with women for gender equality in society, and attempt to become more sensitive. Other men see feminism as a primary source of men's problems, and they feel threatened by women's progress toward equal status. Men's movements range from efforts to advance women's rights and status to active attacks on women's resistance to traditional, subservient roles. Members of men's movements engage in public and private forms of communication that contribute to the cultural conversation about gender —its meaning and its affect on the individual men and women who live under its edicts.

In this and the preceding chapter we've discussed a wide range of women's and men's movements, as well as the antifeminist movement. Through communication in private and public settings, these movements delineate multiple versions of femininity and masculinity and seek to persuade us to adopt certain points of view. As the conversation evolves, new voices will join existing rhetorical efforts to define the meaning of masculinity and femininity and the rights, roles, and opportunities available to women, minorities, men, lesbians, and gay men. It's up to you to define your role in the cultural conversation about gender. Some people will be passive listeners. Others will be critical listeners who reflect carefully on the points of view advanced by these rhetorical movements. And still others will claim a voice in the conversation and will be part of active rhetorical efforts to define gender. What role will you choose?

KEY TERMS

antifeminism, 99

antisuffrage movement, 99

backlash, 99

father hunger, 94

Free Men, 90

male feminists, 83

masculinist, 90

Mentors in Violence Prevention
(MVP), 89

Million Man March, 98

mythopoetic movement, 92

Promise Keepers, 95

traitorous identity, 84

White Ribbon Campaign (WRC), 87

DISCUSSION QUESTIONS

1. Before you read this chapter, did you know that there were so many men's movements with such diverse goals? What does limited knowledge of men's movements imply about biases in media and education?

2. Use your InfoTrac College Edition to read Michael Messner's 1998 article "The limits of 'the male sex role': An analysis of men's liberation and men's rights movements" in the June 1998 issue of *Gender and Society*. Are Messner's analyses of newsletters and magazines distributed by men's liberation (male feminist) and men's rights (masculinist) groups consistent with what you read in this chapter?

3. Which of the men's movements do you find most consistent with your own values? Do you think men should work to restore traditional male prerogatives and social power, become more sensitive themselves, or change society?

4. Follow up on the discussion of men's movements presented in this chapter by visiting the Web sites of one branch of the men's movement. Addresses for the sites appear in the FYI boxes in various sections of the chapter.

5. Speculate about the future of men's movements in the next decade. What cultural trends might influence them?

5 Gendered Verbal Communication

The tongue has the power of life and death.
—Proverbs 18.21

onsider these five sentences:

I now pronounce you man and wife.

Bob baby-sat his son while his wife attended a meeting.

Anna Kournikova is sports' hottest pinup girl.

Freshmen find it difficult to adjust to college life.

We reached a gentlemen's agreement on how to proceed.

Each of these sentences reflects a cultural assumption about women and men—who they are and what they are supposed to do and not do. In the first one, did you notice that *man* designates an individual, whereas *wife* defines a person only by her relationship to the man? In the second sentence, the use of the word *baby-sat* implies that the father was performing a special service, one we usually pay for; have you ever heard a mother's care for her children called baby-sitting? The third sentence defines a highly accomplished tennis player in terms of appearance, diverting attention from her athletic skills and sports victories. Unless the fourth sentence refers to first-year students at an all-male school, the word *freshmen* erases first-year female students. Finally, the term *gentlemen's agreement* reflects the cultural association between men and business activities.

In this and the following chapter, we examine how communication reflects and expresses cultural views of gender. This chapter focuses on verbal communication, and Chapter 6 concentrates on nonverbal communication. We will probe how verbal and nonverbal communication reflect and shape cultural understandings of masculinity and femininity. In addition, we will consider how individuals embody cultural expectations about communication—that is, how individual women's and men's communication reflects or challenges cultural prescriptions for femininity and masculinity.

VERBAL COMMUNICATION EXPRESSES CULTURAL VIEWS OF GENDER

Communication is symbolic behavior. The ability to think and communicate symbolically allows us to plan, invent, envision new possibilities, and remake ourselves and our world. Although all language is symbolic, not all symbols are linguistic. For instance, art and dance are symbolic. Both represent feelings and ideas, and both require interpretation. In this chapter, our focus is on language, one of the most complex symbol systems we have. Our nature as symbolic beings transforms us from biological creatures, who respond to the concrete world as it exists, into thinking beings who interpret, interact with, and remake our personal and social worlds.

In his analysis of humans' use of symbols, philosopher Ernst Cassirer (1978) observed that symbols allow us to define, organize, and evaluate phenomena, think hypothetically, and reflect on ourselves. Discussing these implications of symbolic behavior will illuminate ways in which verbal communication expresses cultural views and expectations of women and men.

■ Language Defines Gender

We use symbols to define, or name, objects, people, feelings, experiences, and other phenomena. We cannot describe the world in its total complexity, so we label, or name, only some phenomena. As symbolic interaction theory points out, we name those things or aspects of things that we've learned are important in society's perspective. Western society includes language that devalues and sometimes erases women. In so doing, it represents men and their experiences as the standard.

Male generic language excludes women. Male generic language purports to include both women and men, yet it refers specifically only to men. Examples of male generic language are nouns such as *businessman, chairman, mailman,* and *mankind,* and pronouns such as *he* used to refer to both women and men. Some people think there is no problem with male generic language because everyone understands that women are included in terms such as *mankind* and *chairman.* This viewpoint, however, is not supported by research on how people interpret male generic language.

Research demonstrates that, when people hear or read male generic language, they think first or only of men, not women. In a classic study of the effects of male

Andy

For a long time, it seemed really clear to me that a word like *mankind* obviously includes women or that *chairman* can refer to a girl or a guy who chairs something. I thought it was pretty stupid to hassle about this. Then last semester I had a woman teacher who taught the whole class using *she* or *her* or *women* whenever she was referring to people, as well as when she meant just women. I realized how confusing it is. I had to figure out each time whether she meant women only or women and men. And when she meant women to be general, I guess you'd say generic for all people, it still made me feel left out. A lot of the guys in the class got pretty hostile about what she was doing, but I kind of think it was a good way to make the point.

generics (Schneider & Hacker, 1973), children were asked to select photographs for a textbook with chapters entitled "Urban Man" and "Man in Politics" or "Urban Life" and "Political Behavior." The children nearly always chose pictures of men when the titles included male generic language. When the titles did not refer only to men, the children chose more photographs that portrayed both sexes. The language in the titles shaped what they thought was appropriate to include in the chapters.

Other researchers (Beal, 1994; Gastil, 1990; Hamilton, 1991; Switzer, 1990) who have conducted similar studies have found that male generic language leads many people to perceive males, not females, as included. In a particularly interesting study, students from first grade through college were asked to make up a story about an average student. When the instructions referred to the average student as *he*, only 12% of students composed a story about a female. However, when the instructions defined the average student as *he or she*, 42% of the stories were about females (Hyde, 1984).

One of the effects of male generic language is to make men seem more prominent and women less prominent than they are in real life (Henley, 1989). This affects comprehension of language, views of personal identity, and perceptions of women's presence in various spheres of life. Exclusionary language in classrooms may lead women students to wonder if they are included in discussions of freshmen, businessmen, and so forth. This year, a graduate student who studies with me earned her master's degree. She said to me, "Julia, I'm not a master. Why hasn't the degree been renamed to include women?" I didn't have a satisfactory answer.

Because there is convincing evidence that male language is not perceived as generic, most authorities on writing style don't allow male generic language. Most dictionaries now avoid male generics and other sexist language. In addition to avoiding man-linked words, new dictionaries caution against other ways of defining men as the standard and women as the exception. For instance, they discourage **spotlighting**—the practice of highlighting a person's sex. Terms such as *lady doctor* and *woman lawyer* define women as the exception in professions and thereby reinforce the idea that men are the standard.

Language defines men and women differently. A second way that language expresses cultural views of gender is by defining men and women in different ways. Women are frequently defined by appearance or by relationships with others, whereas men are more typically defined by activities, accomplishments, or positions.

FYI

Parallel Language?

Parallel language is equivalent terms. For instance, *male* and *female* are equivalent, or parallel. But what about some other allegedly parallel terms?

Masculine Term	Feminine Term
Master	Mistress
Sir	Madam
Wizard	Witch
Patron	Matron

Media offer countless examples of defining women by their physical qualities. Headlines announce "Blonde Wins Election," causing us to focus on the candidate's sex and physical appearance rather than her qualifications and plans for office. Coverage of women's sports, which is disproportionate compared with that of men's sports, frequently focuses on women players' appearance rather than their athletic skills. Stories about female athletes often emphasize wardrobes ("Chris is changing her style with a cool new outfit"), bodies ("She's gotten back in shape and is looking good on the field"), and hairstyles ("When she stepped on the court, fans noticed her lightened hair"), whereas stories about male athletes focus on their athletic abilities ("He sunk two dream shots").

In the opening of this chapter, you read the statement, "Anna Kournikova is sports' hottest pinup girl." That statement appeared in Frank Deford's article about Kournikova published in the June 2000 issue of *Sports Illustrated*. In that article, photos showed Kournikova in a long black dress with a slit and in a sultry pose. In addition to calling her "sports' hottest pinup girl" (p. 98), Deford referred to her as "the Jezebel of sweat" (p. 98) and stated that "on the court she is like a trim sloop, skimming across the surface" (p. 99). Kournikova is physically stunning, and she herself accents that. However, that isn't why she was featured in *Sports Illustrated*. In focusing more on her sex appeal than on her skill on the courts, Deford defined her as more a woman than a tennis player. Can you imagine such descriptions of any male athlete featured in *Sports Illustrated*?

Similarly, coverage of women in professional and political life regularly directs attention to appearance, which inclines readers to notice women's looks more than issues germane to news stories. Even when describing women who have been raped or abused, media reports often include extraneous and irrelevant information on the victims' appearance and dress (Carter, 1998; Meyers, 1997). As I was writing this book, my newspaper carried a story about a series of interviews with

Hillary Rodham Clinton. The opening line in the article described Clinton as appearing "in her tasteful pantsuits and soft makeup." The article went on to note that "She never looked better, with a clipped, highlighted hairstyle framing her face and deep primary colors setting off her blue eyes" (Gutzman, 2003, p. 3E). Describing an accomplished senator in this way reflects the cultural view of women as decorative objects whose worth hinges on physical appeal.

Language in media and everyday conversations also reflects social views of women as passive and men as active. Think about discussions of sexual activity that you've heard or in which you've participated. Have you noticed that people say, "He laid her," "He balled her," "He screwed her," "She got laid," and "He made love to her"? Each of these phrases suggests that in sexual activity men are active whereas women are passive.

Our language also reflects society's view of women as defined by their relationships with others rather than as independent agents. News reports are more likely to include personal information, such as marital status and information about children, when covering women newsmakers than when covering men newsmakers (Carter, 1998). In prime-time television, even professional women are often depicted primarily in interpersonal contexts, and their appearance is highlighted (Lott, 1989; Merritt, 2000). For instance, in the formerly popular sitcom Ally McBeal's legal knowledge and ability were overshadowed by emphasis on her appearance and personal life.

The cultural association of women with relationships is explicitly expressed in the words *Miss* and *Mrs.*, which designate marital status. There are no parallel words that define men in terms of whether they are married. The alternative term *Ms.* to designate a woman without identifying her by her marital status is a relatively new addition to the language and not yet fully accepted. It was not until 1987 that the *New York Times* would print *Ms.* if a woman preferred that title (Stewart, Stewart, Friedley, & Cooper, 1996). The extent to which our society defines women by marriage and family is further evidenced in the still-prevalent tradition of a wife's adoption of her husband's name upon marrying. Symbolically she exchanges her individual identity for one based on her relationship to a man: Mrs. John Smith.

There are a number of alternatives to the traditional ways of naming ourselves (Foss, Edson, & Linde, 2000; Fowler & Fuehrer, 1997). Some

Brian

I never considered whether my wife would take my name. I just assumed she would. I'm proud of my family and I feel tied to who we are, and my family name represents that. I always thought it would be a great honor for a woman to have my family name. But my fiancée doesn't feel the same way. She says she's proud of her name too, that it's who she is too. I can understand that in a way, but still it seems like she should want to take my name. She turned the tables on me by asking if I would take her name.

Sandra

It has never occurred to me that I wouldn't take my husband's name when I marry. It just seems right to me for us to have the same last name once we become our own family. I want us to be one, and the best way to express that is by taking his name.

FYI

What's in a Name?

During the 1970s several states declared that they did not require women to assume their husbands' last names on marrying. Other states, however, insisted that a woman must assume her husband's last name on marrying (Scheuble & Johnson, 1993). Only in 1975 was the issue resolved of whether a woman is legally required to assume her husband's last name. Then, a Hawaiian statute requiring women to give up their birth names on marriage was ruled unconstitutional (Schroeder, 1986).

Research by Laura Stafford and Susan Kline (1996) shows that some men are not comfortable being married to a woman who keeps her birth name. They report that men, more than women, say they would question a woman's commitment if she did not adopt her partner's name. Although men felt more strongly about this than women, a majority of both sexes surveyed favored a woman's taking her partner's last name. Additional research (Klein, Stafford, & Miklosovik, 1996) revealed that women's decisions to retain their birth names or adopt their husbands' last names are influenced by the value attached to heritage and tradition, the importance of professional identity, desire for a new personal identity, views of marriage and family, and practical issues.

women choose to retain their birth names when they marry. A number of men and women adopt hyphenated names such as Johnson-Smith to symbolize the family heritage of both partners. In some countries, such as Spain, both the mother's and father's family names are used to construct children's family names. Another alternative, one less often practiced so far, is renaming oneself to reflect **matriarchal** rather than patriarchal lineage. (The term *matriarchy* means "rule by the mothers"; it generally refers to systems of ideology, social structures, and practices that are created by women and reflect the values, priorities, and views of women as a group.) This involves changing a last name from that of the father's family to that of the mother's. Because that course of action, however, still reflects male lineage—that of the mother's father—some women use their mothers' first names to create a matrilineal last name: for example, Lynn Edwards's daughter, Barbara, might rename herself Barbara Lynnschild. In coming years no doubt we will see other alternatives to traditional naming practices. Their existence reminds us of both the importance we attach to naming and our power to use language creatively.

Language names what exists. Finally, consider the pivotal power of language to make us aware of phenomena. We notice what we name and tend not to recognize or reflect on phenomena we leave unnamed. Spender (1984b) argues that not to name something is to deny that it exists or matters—to negate it. The power of naming is clear with sexual harassment and date rape. For most of history, sexual

Susan

When we were talking about how naming makes us aware of things, it rang a bell for me. My first semester here, I had a lab instructor who made me really uncomfortable. I was having trouble with some of the material, so I went to see him during office hours. He moved away from his desk and sat beside me. Then he sort of touched my arm and knee while I was trying to show him my work. I felt really bad. Then he started cornering me after class and suggesting we get lunch together. I didn't know what to do. Finally, one day he stopped me after class and told me that he might be able to help me with my grade if I would go out with him that weekend. And you know what? I still didn't understand what was happening. I knew I didn't want to date him, and I knew he could hurt my grade, but I didn't know it was sexual harassment. If that happened again today, I'd know what to call it, and I'd also know I could do something about it. So I understood the stuff about names being important.

harassment occurred frequently, but it was unnamed (Wood 1992b, 1993f). Because it wasn't named, sexual harassment was not visible or salient, making it difficult to recognize, think about, discipline, or stop.

Why was sexual harassment unnamed for so long? People in power name what affects or matters to them (Coates, 1997; Spender, 1984a). Because historically men have held most of the power in professional life, and because sexual harassment was rarely a problem for them, it was unnamed. If sexual harassment was discussed at all, it was with language that obscured its violating nature and its ugliness. Phrases such as *making advances, getting out of line,* and *being pushy* fail to convey the abusiveness of sexual harassment. Only when the term *sexual harassment* was coined was it defined as unwanted behavior that ties sexuality to security and advancement. And only with this awareness were efforts to redress sexual harassment devised.

Similarly, the term *date rape* was coined only recently. Women who were raped by their dates had no socially recognized way to name what had happened to them. They had to deal with their experience without language to define and help them think about grievous violations that often had lifelong repercussions (Wriggins, 1998). These two examples make clear the power of naming: It allows us to see more clearly what exists and to think about it in ways possible only with symbolic designation.

■ Language Organizes Perceptions of Gender

We use language to organize experience and perceptions. Suzanne Langer (1979), a distinguished philosopher of language, points out that symbols allow us to translate concrete sense data into symbolic forms so that we can conceive of and reflect on them. The organizing function of language expresses cultural views of gender by stereotyping men and women and by encouraging polarized perceptions of sex and gender.

Stereotyping gender. Because symbols are abstract, they allow us to think in general ways and to understand broad concepts like democracy, freedom, religion, and

FYI

Language: Victims, Survivors, or . . .

How should we refer to people who are raped or physically assaulted? Should we call them *victims*? Should we call them *survivors*? For most crimes, there is no controversy about language—the target of the crime is called a victim. With sex-related crimes, however, there is a heated debate about language and its effects (Lamb, 1999). Some scholars, counselors, and activists think that the term *victim* is dangerous because it reinforces sex stereotypes of women as powerless and vulnerable. It also fuels criticism of feminism as too focused on women as victims. The term *survivor,* on the other hand, emphasizes the fact that the target of a sex-related crime survived, which suggests strength and resilience. Others who study or work with targets of violent sex-related crimes say the term *victim* is appropriate at the time of the violence. The person was a victim when the violence happened. Also, they note, *victim* is more useful for getting funds—groups such as rape crisis centers and battered women's shelters can qualify for "victim services funds," but there are no funds for "survivor services."

Perhaps we need to devise language that can represent different points in a person's experience. Someone who is raped may be a victim at one moment and a survivor later. Or maybe we need language that can indicate a person can be simultaneously a victim and a survivor (Reich, 2003).

gender. Although our ability to think in broad categories is useful in many ways, it is also the source of stereotypes, which sometimes misrepresent individuals. A **stereotype** is a generalization about an entire class of phenomena based on some knowledge of some members of the class. For example, if most women you know aren't interested in sports, you might stereotype women as uninterested in sports. This stereotype could keep you from noticing that many women engage in sports and enjoy attending athletic events. Relying on stereotypes can lead us to overlook important qualities of individuals and to perceive them only in terms of what we consider common to a general category.

Verbal communication often stereotypes women as emotional and men as rational; men are stereotyped as strong, women as weaker ("the weaker sex"). Stereotypes such as these limit perceptions of others and of ourselves. For instance, women's arguments are sometimes dismissed as being emotional when in fact they involve evidence and reasoning (Mapstone, 1998). The stereotype of women as emotional can lead people to judge women's ideas in terms of the stereotype, not the reality. A man who has an emotional outburst may be perceived as forcefully stating his ideas, because he is seen through the stereotype of men as rational.

Encouraging polarized thinking. In organizing thinking, language may also encourage **polarized thinking,** which is conceiving of things as absolute opposites.

DILBERT reprinted by permission of United Feature Syndicate, Inc.

More than many languages, English emphasizes polarities. Something is right or wrong, good or bad, appropriate or inappropriate. Our vocabulary emphasizes all-or-none terms and includes few words that indicate degrees. This makes it difficult for us to think in terms of variation and range (Bem, 1993).

Polarized language and thought are particularly evident in how we think about gender: People are divided into two sexes, male and female, which are translated into two genders, masculine and feminine. Men who don't conform to social views of masculinity and women who don't conform to social views of femininity are often judged negatively. Research indicates that women who use the assertive speech associated with masculinity are frequently perceived as arrogant and rude, whereas men who employ the emotional language associated with femininity are often perceived to be "wimps" or gay (Rasmussen & Moley, 1986).

Language labels us as either feminine or masculine. In reality, of course, most of us have a number of qualities, some of which our society designates as feminine and some as masculine. Our culture's binary labels for sexual identity encourage us not to notice how much variation there is among women and among men (Lorber, 2001). For instance, Namaste (2000) points out that transgendered people are erased because the only linguistic options for them are *men* and *women,* neither of which describes their full identities. Likewise, people who are intersexed or trans-sexed don't fit into the male-female dichotomies of our language. Awareness of our language's polarizing tendencies allows us to question dichotomous conceptions of sex and gender.

■ Language Evaluates Gender

Language is not neutral. It reflects cultural values and is a powerful influence on our perceptions. Related to gender, much of our language devalues females and femininity by trivializing, deprecating, and diminishing women and anything defined as feminine.

Women are often trivialized by language. Numerous terms label women as immature or juvenile *(baby doll, girlie, little darling)* or equate them with food *(dish, feast for the eyes, good enough to eat, sugar, sweet thing, cookie, cupcake, hot tomato, honey pie)* and animals *(catty, chick, pig, dog, cow, bitch)*. Women are often described as possessions. Susan A. Basow (1992) notes that history books' accounts of the settling of America include statements such as "Pioneers moved West, taking their wives and children with them" (p. 142). This description suggests that only men were pioneers; women and children were possessions the male pioneers took along.

Language sometimes trivializes women's accomplishments or activities. For instance, not long ago on my campus, two administrators—one woman and one man—spoke out sharply against a particular proposal. The local newspaper reported that the male administrator "expressed deep concern and outrage," whereas the woman "was piqued." To label her as *piqued* implies that her response to the proposal was frivolous, lightweight, and not to be taken seriously.

Language used to refer to women may also express negative values. One researcher (Stanley, 1977) found 220 terms for sexually permissive women but only 22 for sexually promiscuous men. Although there are derogatory terms for men *(wimp, bastard)*, there are fewer of them, especially terms that devalue promiscuity in men. Women are further deprecated when topics of particular importance to women are treated as insignificant. Frequently, women newsmakers and issues that affect

> **Anthony**
>
> Until we talked about language in class, I hadn't really thought about the double standard for sexually active girls and guys. Or if I had thought about it, I probably would have said that the double standard doesn't exist anymore. Our discussion got me thinking, and that's not really true. Guys who have sex with a lot of girls are *studs* or *players*. Girls who have sex with a lot of guys are *sluts* or *easy*. It's not as bad as it used to be, but I guess there still is kind of a double standard.

women are not covered or are sequestered in the lifestyle sections of newspapers (Danner & Walsh, 1999). Diminutive suffixes designate women as deviations from the standard (male) form of the word: *suffragette, majorette.* Calling women "girls" (a term that technically refers to a female who has not gone through puberty) defines them as children, not adults.

■ Language Enables Hypothetical Thought

Symbols allow **hypothetical thought,** which is conceiving of things that do not exist in the moment. Because symbols are abstract, they allow us to think not only about what is but also about what will or might be and what has been. In turn this enables us to think of past, present, and future and to conceive of alternatives to current states of affairs. To understand the power of hypothetical thought, consider your own commitment to earning a college degree and launching a career. Although the degree and career have no current basis in concrete reality, their *possibility* is real enough to you to motivate years of work.

Hypothetical thought has been influential in changing the meanings of gender. As we saw in Chapter 3, many first-wave feminists envisioned the day when women could vote, attend universities, and own property. Imagining these possibilities inspired the courage and effort required to change social views of femininity. Antifeminists, too, rely on hypothetical thinking in their efforts to define gender. They recall former times when women were subservient, and they try to persuade others to restore that vision of femininity. People engage in hypothetical thinking to define and work toward alternatives to prevailing views of gender.

Hypothetical thought is important in crafting our personal gender identity as well as social views of gender. Each of us has to decide what it means to be a woman or a man. We understand society's views and expectations, yet we are not compelled to accept them. Sometimes we challenge cultural definitions of gender and define our personal identities outside of culturally approved prescriptions. What are your ideals of femininity and masculinity? In entertaining this question, you are engaging in hypothetical thought, which opens possibilities for defining yourself that transcend those endorsed by society.

■ Language Allows Self-Reflection

Because we are symbol users, we name not only phenomena around us but also ourselves. If we don't like the self we are, we can change it. We do this by combining our capacities for self-reflection and hypothetical thought. For instance, one alternative to traditional sex-typing is androgyny (see Chapter 1). Androgynous people possess qualities the culture defines as masculine *and* feminine instead of only those assigned to one sex. Androgynous women and men are, for example, both assertive *and* sensitive, both ambitious *and* compassionate (Bem, 1993).

The Report Card on Androgyny

Androgynous individuals tend to be more successful personally and professionally because they are able to communicate in a range of ways and respond to diverse others with flexible skills that meet the demands of various situations.

- Androgynous women and men have higher self-esteem and are better personally adjusted than sex-typed individuals (Heilbrun, 1986; Heilbrun & Han, 1984; Hemmer & Kleiber, 1981; Jackson, 1983; Lamke, 1982; Waterman & Whitbourne, 1982).

- In the workplace, androgynous individuals are more flexible and effective interacting with a range of people (Heath, 1991; Wheeless, 1984). Androgynous communication is particularly tied to women's professional success (Hall & Taylor, 1985; Mills & Bohannon, 1983).

- Androgynous individuals and feminine-typed individuals of both sexes have happier marriages than masculine-typed individuals (Ickes, 1993).

- Androgynous people are more likely to be successful in their professional and personal lives than are sex-typed individuals (Heath, 1991).

Many women and men decide not to limit themselves only to those qualities society associates with one gender.

Not everyone thinks androgyny the best alternative to rigid sex roles. Kate Bornstein (1994) argues that androgyny is "a trap of the bipolar gender system, as it further establishes the idea of two-and-only-two genders" (p. 115). Lane Bruner (1996) agrees that androgyny is based on false dichotomies and dualities. Larry May (1998b) has different reservations about androgyny. He thinks androgynous men and women are too much alike. Instead, he suggests that men should define themselves within what he calls a "progressive male standpoint" that encourages men to adopt some traditionally masculine qualities, such as ambition and competitiveness, but to reject other traditionally masculine qualities, such as domination and violence. May's vision of ideal masculinity calls on men to "accept responsibility for the men they are and to strive toward the men they can become" (p. 151). Because May's research focuses on men, he has not defined a parallel progressive female standpoint. You might want to think about which traditionally feminine qualities would and would not fit within a progressive female standpoint.

Language Is a Process

We've seen that language expresses cultural views of gender and tends to reproduce them. Yet language is not static. Instead, we continuously change language to reflect our changing understandings of ourselves and our world. When we find existing language inadequate or undesirable, we change it. We reject terms we find objectionable (*girl,* male generics), and we create new terms to define realities we think are important *(sexual harassment, Ms., androgyny, womanism).* As we modify language, we modify how we see ourselves and our world. Further, we shape meanings in the culture at large.

Gendered Interaction: Masculine and Feminine Styles of Verbal Communication

In addition to expressing cultural views of gender, language reflects our own gendered identities. The ways we communicate place us inside or outside the social views of masculinity and femininity. In the pages that follow, we'll explore masculine and feminine styles of speech and some of the confusion that results from differences between them. We want to understand how each style evolves, what it involves, and how to interpret verbal communication in ways that honor the standpoints of those using it.

■ Gendered Speech Communities

Suzanne Langer (1953, 1979) asserted that culture, or collective life, is possible only to the extent that a group of people share a symbol system and the meanings encapsulated in it. Langer's attention to the ways in which language sustains cultural life is consistent with the symbolic interactionist and cultural theories that we discussed in Chapter 2. William Labov (1972) extended Langer's ideas by defining a speech community as a group of people that shares norms about communication. By this, he meant that a **speech community** exists when people share understandings about goals of communication, strategies for enacting those goals, and ways of interpreting communication.

It's obvious that we have entered a different speech community when we travel in countries whose languages differ from our own. Distinct speech communities are less apparent when they rely on the same language but use it in different ways and attach different meanings to language. Yet there are speech communities defined by race-ethnicity, sexual orientation, economic class, and gender. As we noted in previous chapters, the standpoint we occupy influences what we know and how we act. Standpoint theory also implies that distinct communication styles evolve out of different standpoints.

Studies of gender and communication convincingly show that most girls and women and boys and men are socialized into distinct speech communities (Campbell, 1973; Coates, 1986, 1997; Coates & Cameron, 1989; Johnson, 2000). To understand these different communities, we will first consider how we are socialized into feminine and masculine speech communities. After this, we will explore divergence in how women and men typically communicate. Please note the importance of the word *typically* and other words that indicate we are discussing general differences, not absolute ones. Not all women learn and use a feminine style of communication, and not all men learn or choose to adopt a masculine style of communication. We'll discuss gendered speech communities into which *most*—but not all— women and men are socialized.

■ The Lessons of Children's Play

Initial insight into the importance of children's play in shaping patterns of communication came from a classic study by Daniel Maltz and Ruth Borker (1982). As they watched young children engaged in recreation, the researchers were struck by two observations: Young children almost always play in sex-segregated groups, and girls and boys tend to play different kinds of games. Maltz and Borker found that boys' games (football, baseball) and girls' games (school, house, jump rope) cultivate distinct ways to communicate.

More recent research on children's play confirms Maltz and Borker's original findings. Sex-segregated groups remain the norm for children in the United States (Clark, 1998; Goodwin, 1990; Gray & Feldman, 1997; Kovacs, Parker, & Hoffman, 1996; Maccoby, 1998; McGuffey & Rich, 2004; Moller & Serbin, 1996). Even children as young as 2 or 3 years old (about the time that gender constancy develops) show a preference for same-sex playmates (Martin, 1991, 1994, 1997; Ruble & Martin, 1998).

Boys' games. Boys' games usually involve fairly large groups—nine individuals for each baseball team, for instance. Most boys' games are competitive, have clear goals, involve physically rough play, and are organized by rules and roles that specify who does what and how to play (Alexander & Hines, 1994; Pollack, 2000).

Because the games boys typically play are structured by goals, rules, and roles, there is little need to discuss how to play, although there may be talk about strategies to reach goals. In playing games, boys learn to use communication to compete for and maintain status, exert control over others, get attention, and stand out (Messner, 1997a). Specifically, boys' games cultivate four communication rules:

1. Use communication to assert your ideas, opinions, and identity.

2. Use talk to achieve something, such as solving problems or developing strategies.

3. Use communication to attract and maintain others' attention.

4. Use communication to compete for the "talk stage." Make yourself stand out; take attention away from others and get others to pay attention to you.

Alan

I got the message about not letting other guys beat me when I was just 10. Every day on my way home from school, this other boy who was four or five years older would wait for me so that he could beat on me. I got tired of this, so I talked to my dad about it, hoping he'd help me. But he just lit into me some kind of bad. He told me not to ever, ever come to him again saying some other guy was beating up on me. He told me if that guy came after me again, I should fight back and use something to hit him if I had to.

Sure enough, the next day that dude was waiting for me. When he hit me, I picked up the nearest thing—a two-by-four on the ground—and hit him on the head. Well, he had to go to the hospital, but my dad said that was okay because his son had been a man.

These communication rules are consistent with other aspects of masculine socialization that we have already discussed. For instance, notice the emphasis on individuality and competition. Also, we see that these rules accent achievement—doing something, accomplishing a goal. Boys learn they must *do things* to be valued members of the team. Finally, we see the undercurrent of masculinity's emphasis on invulnerability: If your goal is to control and be better than others, you cannot let them know too much about yourself and your weaknesses.

Girls' games. Turning now to girls' games, we find that quite different patterns exist, and they lead to distinctive ways of communicating. Girls tend to play in pairs or in very small groups rather than large ones (Benenson, Del Bianco, Philippoussis, & Apostoleris, 1997). Also, games like house and school do not have preset, clear-cut goals and roles. There is no analogue of the touchdown in playing house, and the roles of daddy and mommy aren't fixed like the roles of linebacker and quarterback.

Because girls' games are not highly structured by external goals and roles, players have to talk among themselves to decide what to do and what roles to play. When playing, young girls spend more time talking than doing anything else—a pattern that is not true of young boys (Goodwin, 1990; Maccoby, 1998). Playing house, for instance, typically begins with a discussion about who is going to be the daddy and who the mommy. The lack of stipulated goals for the games is also important because it tends to cultivate girls' skill in interpersonal processes. The games generally played by girls teach four basic rules for communication:

1. Use communication to create and maintain relationships. The *process* of communication, not its content, is the heart of relationships.

2. Use communication to establish egalitarian relations with others. Don't outdo, criticize, or put down others. If you have to criticize, be gentle.

3. Use communication to include others—bring them into conversations, respond to their ideas.

4. Use communication to show sensitivity to others and relationships.

The typically small size of girls' play groups fosters cooperative discussion and an open-ended process of talking to organize activity, whereas the larger groups in which boys usually play encourage competition and external rules to structure activity (Campbell, 1993). In a study of preschoolers, boys gave orders and attempted to control others, whereas girls were more likely to make requests and cooperate with others (Weiss & Sachs, 1991). In another investigation, 9- to 14-year-old African American girls typically used inclusive and nondirective language, whereas African American boys tended to issue commands and compete for status in their groups (Goodwin, 1990). The conclusion from much research is that girls tend to engage in more affiliative, cooperative play, whereas boys tend to engage in more instrumental and competitive play (Fabes, 1994; Harris, 1998; Leaper, 1991, 1994, 1996). The lessons of children's play are carried forward. The basic rules of communication that many adult women and men employ are refined and elaborated versions of those learned in childhood games (Clark, 1998; Mulac, 1998).

■ Gendered Communication Practices

We will consider features of feminine and masculine speech that have been identified by researchers. We'll also explore some of the complications that arise when people of different genders operate by different rules in conversations with each other.

Feminine speech. People who are socialized in feminine speech communities—many women and some men—tend to regard communication as a primary way to establish and maintain relationships with others. They engage in conversation to share themselves and to learn about others (Johnson, 1996). For feminine people, talk *is* the essence of relationships. Consistent with this primary goal, feminine speech tends to foster connections, support, closeness, and understanding.

Establishing equality between people is important in feminine communication. To achieve symmetry, communicators often match experiences to indicate "You're not alone in how you feel." Typical ways to communicate equality would be saying, "I've felt just like that," or "Something like that happened to me, too, and I felt like you do." Growing out of the quest for equality is a participatory mode of interacting in which communicators respond to and build on each other's ideas in the process of conversing (Hall & Langellier, 1988). Rather than a rigid "You tell your ideas, then I'll tell mine" sequence, feminine speech more characteristically follows an interactive pattern in which different voices interweave to create conversations.

Also characteristic of feminine speech is showing support for others. To demonstrate support, communicators often express understanding and sympathy with a friend's situation or feelings. "Oh, you must feel terrible" communicates that we understand and support how another feels. Related to these first two features is attention to the relationship level of communication (Wood, 1993a, 1993b; Wood & Inman, 1993). You will recall that the relationship level of talk focuses on feelings and on the relationship between communicators rather than on the content of messages. Conversations between feminine people tend to be characterized by many questions that probe for greater understanding of feelings and perceptions surrounding the subject of talk (Beck, 1988). "How did you feel when it occurred?" "How does this fit into the overall relationship?" are probes that help a listener understand a speaker's perspective.

A fourth feature of feminine speech style is conversational "maintenance work" (Beck, 1988; Fishman, 1978). This involves efforts to sustain conversation by inviting others to speak and by prompting them to elaborate their ideas. Questions are often used to include others: "How was your day?" "Did anything interesting happen on your trip?" "Do you have anything to add?" Communication of this sort maintains interaction and opens the conversational door to others.

A fifth quality of feminine speech is responsiveness. A feminine person might make eye contact, nod, or say "Tell me more" or "That's interesting." Responsiveness reflects learned tendencies to care about others and to make them feel valued and included (Chatham-Carpenter & DeFrancisco, 1998; Kemper, 1984). It affirms the other person and encourages elaboration by showing interest in what was said.

A sixth quality of feminine talk is personal, concrete style (Campbell, 1973; Hall & Langellier, 1988). Typical of feminine talk are details, personal disclosures, anecdotes, and concrete reasoning. These features cultivate a personal tone, and they facilitate feelings of closeness by connecting communicators' lives.

A final feature of feminine speech is tentativeness. This may be expressed in a number of forms. Sometimes people use verbal hedges, such as "I kind of feel you may be overreacting." In other situations they qualify statements by saying "I'm probably not the best judge of this, but. . . ." Another way to keep talk provisional is to tag a question onto a statement in a way that invites another to respond: "That was a pretty good movie, wasn't it?" Tentative communication leaves the door open for others to respond and express their opinions.

There has been controversy about tentativeness associated with feminine speech. Robin Lakoff (1975), who first noted that women use more hedges, qualifiers, and tag questions than men, claimed these indicate uncertainty and lack of confidence. Calling women's speech powerless, Lakoff argued that it reflects women's low self-esteem and socialization into subordinate roles. It's important to note that Lakoff's judgment that feminine speech is powerless was based on male speech as the standard. Rather than indicating powerlessness, the use of hedges, qualifiers, and tag questions may reflect desires to keep conversations open and to include others (Mills, 1999; Wood & Lenze, 1991b). You should realize, however, that people outside of feminine speech communities may use masculine standards, as Lakoff did, to interpret tentative speech.

Feminine Communication Style in Politics

Jane Blankenship and Deborah Robson (1995) analyzed the communication of women politicians between 1990 and 1994. They identified five features of feminine political style:

1. Political judgments were based in part on concrete experiences.

2. Communication valued and reflected inclusivity and awareness of relationships among people.

3. Women speakers viewed power as the ability to get things done and empower others.

4. Policy judgments were approached holistically.

5. What are typically regarded as women's issues were moved to the forefront of public discussion.

Masculine speech. Masculine speech communities tend to regard talk as a way to exert control, preserve independence, entertain, and enhance status. Conversation is often seen as an arena for proving oneself and negotiating prestige.

The first feature of masculine speech is establishment of status and control. Masculine speakers do this by asserting their ideas and authority, telling jokes and stories, or challenging others. Equally typical is the tendency to avoid disclosing personal information that might make a man appear weak or vulnerable (Lewis & McCarthy, 1988; Saurer & Eisler, 1990). One way to exhibit knowledge and control is to give advice. For example, a person might say, "The way you should handle that is . . . ," or "Don't let your boss get to you." People socialized in feminine speech communities may interpret someone who gives advice as saying "I know what you should do" or "I would know how to handle that." People socialized in feminine speech communities may perceive such comments as implying that the speaker is superior to the other person.

A second prominent feature of masculine speech is instrumentality—the use of speech to accomplish instrumental objectives. In conversation, this is often expressed through problem-solving efforts to get information, discover facts, and suggest solutions. Conversations between

---

Joanne

My boyfriend is the worst at throwing solutions in my face when I try to talk to him about a problem. I know he cares about me; if he didn't, he wouldn't use up all that energy thinking up solutions for me. But I'm the kind of person who prefers a good ear (and maybe a shoulder) when I have a problem. I would like it so much better if he would forget about solutions and just listen and let me know he hears what's bothering me.

YOU CAN CROSS "CLEAN THE SHOWER" OFF YOUR LIST.

YOU CLEANED IT? I DIDN'T KNOW YOU WERE GOING TO DO THAT.

"I CLEANED THE SCUMMY SHOWER" IS HUSBAND-SPEAK FOR "I LOVE YOU." IT MAY NOT BE AS ROMANTIC, BUT YOU DO GET A CLEAN SHOWER OUT OF THE DEAL.

THAT'S SO SWEET.

Reprinted with special permission from King Features Syndicate.

women and men are often derailed by the lack of agreement on what this informational, instrumental focus means. To many women it feels as if men don't care about their feelings. When a man focuses on the content level of meaning after a woman has disclosed a problem, she may feel he is disregarding her emotions. He, on the other hand, thinks he is supporting her in the way that he has learned to show support—by suggesting how to solve the problem.

A third feature of masculine communication is conversational command. Despite jokes about women's talkativeness, research indicates that, in most contexts, men tend to talk more often and at greater length than women. This tendency, although not present in infancy, is evident in preschoolers (Austin, Salehi, & Leffler, 1987). Compared with girls and women, boys and men talk more frequently and for longer periods of time both in face-to-face conversation and on Usenet and e-mail discussion groups (Aries, 1987; Crowston & Kammeres, 1998). Further, masculine speakers may reroute conversations by using what another says as a jumping-off point for their own topics, or they may interrupt. Although both sexes interrupt, most research suggests that men do it more frequently (Beck, 1988; Johnson, 2000; Mulac, Wiemann, Widenmann, & Gibson, 1988; West & Zimmerman, 1983).

Not only do men interrupt more than women, but they may do so for different reasons. Research indicates that men are more likely to interrupt to control conversation by challenging other speakers or wresting the talk stage from them, whereas women interrupt to indicate interest and respond to others (Anderson & Leaper, 1998; Aries, 1987; Mulac et al., 1988; Stewart et al., 1996). A different explanation is that men generally interrupt more than women because interruptions are considered normal and good-natured within the norms of masculine speech communities (Wood, 1998). Whereas interruptions that reroute conversation might be viewed as impolite and intrusive in feminine speech communities, the outgoing, give-and-take character of masculine speech may render interruptions just part of normal conversation.

Fourth, masculine speech tends to be direct and assertive. Compared with women's, men's language is typically more forceful and authoritative (Murphy & Zorn, 1996; Wood et al., 1997). Tentative forms of speech like hedges and dis-

FYI

Scholarship Versus Popular Psychology

Deborah Tannen (1990a, 1990b, 1995) declares that "communication between men and women can be like cross-cultural communication, prey to a clash of conversational styles (1990b, p. 42). John Gray goes even further, claiming that women and men are so different that it's as though they were from different planets (1992, 1995, 1996a, 1996b, 1998). Both Tannen and Gray have sold millions of books. Should we believe what they say about communication between the sexes?

When trying to determine the worth of their claims, we might first ask about their credentials as experts in communication. Tannen is a linguist who holds a Ph.D. Gray has no graduate degree from an accredited school. Tannen bases her claims on research that she and others have conducted. Gray relies on anecdotes from his personal experience.

Second, we should compare their claims with the findings of sound research. When we do this, we discover gaps between what these popular psychologists tell us and what scholarship documents. Tannen's claims fare better than Gray's. Although Tannen generalizes too broadly from limited and unrepresentative samples, her claims are not wholly without support. Gray, on the other hand, portrays women and men in extreme and dichotomous stereotypes that are not supported by credible research.

If you want to learn about how these popular psychology books measure up to research, read these articles: Goldsmith, D., & Fulfs, P. (1999). "You just don't have the evidence": An analysis of claims and evidence in Deborah Tannen's *You Just Don't Understand*. In M. Roloff (Ed.), *Communication Yearbook*, 22 (pp. 1–49). Thousand Oaks, CA: Sage. Wood, J. T. (2001a). A critical essay on John Gray's portrayals of men, women, and relationships. *Southern Communication Journal, 67,* 201–210.

claimers are used less frequently by men than by women. When another person does not understand or follow masculine rules of communication, however, speech that is absolute and directive may seem to close off conversation and leave no room for others to speak.

Fifth, masculine speech tends to be more abstract than feminine speech. Men frequently speak in general terms that are removed from concrete experiences and distanced from personal feelings (Johnson, 2000; Schaef, 1981; Treichler & Kramarae, 1983). The abstract style typical of many men's speech reflects the public and impersonal contexts in which they often operate and the less personal emphasis in their speech communities. Within public environments, norms for speaking call for theoretical, conceptual, and general thought and communication. Yet within more personal relationships abstract talk sometimes creates barriers to intimacy.

Finally, masculine speech tends to be less emotionally responsive than feminine speech, especially on the relationship level of meaning. Men, more than women, give what are called *minimal response cues* (Parlee, 1979), which are verbalizations such as "yeah" or "umhmm." In interaction with women, who have learned to demonstrate interest more vigorously, minimal response cues may inhibit conversation because they are perceived as indicating lack of involvement (Fishman, 1978; Stewart et al., 1996). Men's conversation also often lacks self-disclosure as well as expressed sympathy and understanding (Lynch & Kilmartin, 1999; Saurer & Eisler, 1990). Within the rules of masculine speech communities, sympathy is a sign of condescension, and the revealing of personal problems is seen as making one vulnerable. Yet within feminine speech communities sympathy and disclosure are understood as demonstrations of equality and support. This creates potential for misunderstanding between women and men.

■ Gender-Based Misinterpretations in Communication

In this final section, we explore what happens in conversations between people from different gender speech communities. We'll consider five particularly recurrent misunderstandings between masculine and feminine individuals.

Showing support. Martha tells George that she is worried about her friend. George gives a minimal response cue, saying only, "Oh." To Martha, this suggests he isn't interested, because women make and expect more of what Deborah Tannen (1986) calls "listening noises" to signal interest. Yet, if George operates according to norms of masculine speech communities, he is probably thinking that, if Martha wants to tell him something, she will. Masculine rules of speech assume people use talk to assert themselves (Bellinger & Gleason, 1982). Even without much encouragement, Martha continues by describing the tension in her friend's marriage and her own desire to help. She says, "I feel so bad for Barbara, and I want to help her, but I don't know what to do." George then says, "It's their problem, not yours. Just butt out." At this, Martha explodes: "Who asked for your advice?" George is now completely confused. He thought Martha wanted advice, so he gave it. She is hurt that George didn't tune into her feelings. Both are frustrated.

The problem is not so much what George and Martha say and don't say. Rather, it's how they interpret each other's communication—actually, how they *misinterpret* it, because they fail to understand that each is operating by different rules of talk. George is respecting Martha's independence by not pushing her to talk. When he thinks she wants advice, he offers it in an effort to help. Martha, on the other hand, wants comfort and a

Jay

Finally I understand this thing that keeps happening between my girlfriend and me. She is always worrying about something or feeling bad about what's happening with one of her friends. I've been trying to be supportive by telling her things like she shouldn't worry, or not to let it get her down, or not to obsess about other people's problems. I was trying to help her feel better. That's what guys do for each other—kind of distract our attention from problems. But Teresa just gets all huffy and angry when I do that. She tells me to stuff my advice and says if I cared about her I would show more concern. Finally, it makes sense. Well, sort of.

connection with George—that's her purpose in talking with him. To her, George's advice seems to dismiss her feelings. He doesn't offer sympathy, because masculine rules for communication define this as condescending. Yet the feminine speech community in which Martha was socialized taught her that giving sympathy is a way to show support.

"Troubles talk." Talk about troubles, or personal problems, is a kind of interaction in which hurt feelings may result from the contrast between most men's and women's rules of communication. Nancy might tell her partner, Craig, that she is feeling down because she did not get a job she wanted. In an effort to be supportive, Craig might respond by saying, "You shouldn't feel bad. Lots of people don't get jobs they want." To Nancy this seems to dismiss her feelings—to belittle them by saying lots of people experience her situation. Yet within masculine speech communities, this is a way of showing respect for another by not assuming that she or he needs sympathy.

Now let's turn the tables and see what happens when Craig feels troubled. When he meets Nancy, Craig is unusually quiet because he feels down about not getting a job offer. Sensing that something is wrong, Nancy tries to show interest by asking, "Are you okay? What's bothering you?" Craig feels she is imposing and trying to get him to show a vulnerability he prefers to keep to himself. Nancy probes further to show she cares. As a result, he feels intruded on and withdraws further. Then Nancy feels shut out.

But perhaps Craig does decide to tell Nancy why he feels down. After hearing about his rejection letter, Nancy says, "I know how you feel. I felt so low when I didn't get that position at Datanet." She is matching experiences to show Craig that she understands his feelings and that he's not alone. According to the communication rules that Craig learned in a masculine speech community, however, Nancy's comment about her own experience is an effort to steal the center stage from him and focus on herself.

The point of the story. Another instance in which feminine and masculine communication rules often clash is in relating experiences. Masculine speech tends to follow a linear pattern, in which major points in a story are presented sequentially to get to the climax. Talk tends to be straightforward without a great many details. The rules of feminine speech, however, call for more detailed, less linear storytelling. Whereas a man is likely to provide rather bare information about what happened, a woman is more likely to embed the information within a larger context of the people

Cathy

When I broke up with Tommy, my dad tried so hard to help me through it. He took me to games and movies, offered to pay for it if I wanted to take horseback riding lessons. He just kept trying to *DO* something to make me feel better. That's how he's always been. If Mom's down about something, he takes her out or buys her flowers or something. It used to really bother me that he won't talk to me about what I'm feeling, but now I understand better what he's doing. I get it that this is his way of showing love and support for me.

involved and other things going on (Wood, 1998, 2000). Women include details, not because they are important at the content level of meaning, but because they matter at the relationship level of meaning. Recounting details is meant to increase involvement between people and to invite a conversational partner to be fully engaged in the situation being described.

Because feminine and masculine rules about details differ, men often find feminine accounts wandering and tedious. Conversely, the masculine style of storytelling may strike women as leaving out all the interesting details. Many a discussion between women and men has ended either with his exasperated demand, "Can't you get to the point?" or with her frustrated question, "Why don't you tell me how you were feeling and what else was going on?" She wants more details than his rules call for; he is interested in fewer details than she has learned to supply.

Relationship talk. "Can we talk about us?" is the opening of innumerable conversations that end in misunderstanding and hurt. In general, men are interested in discussing relationships only if there are particular problems to be addressed. In contrast, women generally find it pleasurable to talk about important relationships even—or perhaps especially—when there are no problems (Acitelli, 1988). The difference here grows out of the fact that masculine speech communities view communication as a means to doing things and solving problems, whereas feminine speech communities regard the *process* of communicating as a primary way to create and sustain relationships. No wonder many men duck when their partners want to "discuss the relationship," and women often feel a relationship is in trouble when their partners don't want to talk about it.

Public speaking. Differences in feminine and masculine communication patterns also surface in public contexts. Historically men have dominated in politics. Thus, it's not surprising that the assertive, dominant, confident masculine style is the standard for public speaking. This male generic standard for public speaking places feminine speakers at a disadvantage in public life. Their style of speaking is judged by a standard that neither reflects nor respects their communication goals and values (Campbell & Jerry, 1988). Women who are effective in politics tend to manage a fine balance in which they are sufficiently feminine to be perceived as acting appropriately for women and sufficiently masculine to be perceived as acting appropriately for politicians. Women such as former Texas governor Ann Richards who are considered effective public speakers manage to combine the traditionally feminine and masculine communication styles (Dow & Tonn, 1993).

These are only five of many situations in which feminine and masculine rules of communication may lead to misinterpretations. Many people find they can improve their relationships by understanding and using both feminine and masculine communication styles. When partners understand how to interpret each other's rules, they are less likely to misread motives. In addition, when they learn to speak the other's language, they become more gratifying conversational partners, and they enhance the quality of their relationships.

SUMMARY

In this chapter we have explored a range of ways in which verbal communication intersects with gender and culture. We first looked at how language reflects and sustains cultural views of masculinity and femininity. By defining, classifying, and evaluating gender, language reinforces social views of men as the standard and as more valuable than women and femininity. From generic male terms to language that demeans and diminishes women, verbal communication is a powerful agent of cultural expression. We also saw, however, that symbolic abilities allow us to think hypothetically and therefore to imagine alternatives to existing meanings. This invites us to examine critically how we define masculinity and femininity in general and our own gender identities in particular.

The second theme of this chapter is that women and men express gendered identities through their communication. Because males and females tend to be socialized into different gender speech communities, they learn different rules for the purposes of communication and ways to indicate support, interest, and involvement. This can lead to misunderstanding, frustration, hurt, and tension between people. Appreciating and respecting the distinctive validity of each style of communication are foundations for better understanding between people. Further, learning to use different styles of communication allows women and men to be more flexible and effective in their interactions with each other.

KEY TERMS

hypothetical thought, 114
male generic language, 105
matriarchal, 109
polarized thinking, 111

speech community, 116
spotlighting, 106
stereotype, 111

DISCUSSION QUESTIONS

1. Read several newspapers. To what extent are women and men represented differently in stories? Do you find that women are described by appearance, marital status, and family life? Are such descriptions pertinent to the news stories in which they are featured?

2. Think about naming, specifically about naming yourself. If you are a woman, how important is it to you to keep your name or take your partner's name if you marry? If you are a man, how much do you expect (or want) your partner to change hers?

3. Think back to your childhood games. Which games did you play? What rules for using talk were implicitly promoted in the games you tended to play? Do you see how engaging in childhood activities may have affected your style of verbal communication?

4. Use the PowerTrac option on your InfoTrac College Edition to read Susan Basow and Kimberly Rubenfeld's article, "Troubles talk: Effects of gender and gender typing," in the February 2003 issue of *Sex Roles*. What does this study show about the relationship between gender and offering sympathy to friends who have problems?

5. The next time you have a conversation in which you feel that gendered rules of talk are creating misunderstandings, try to translate your expectations to the person with whom you are talking. For instance, if you are a woman talking with a man about a problem, he might try to help by offering advice. Instead of being frustrated by his lack of attention to your feelings, try saying to him, "I appreciate your suggestions of what I might do, but I'm not ready to think about how to fix things yet. It would be more helpful to me if you'd help me work through my feelings about this issue." Discuss what happens when you explain what you need or want from others.

6. Use the PowerTrac option on your InfoTrac College Edition to read the 1999 article by Michelle Kirtley and James B. Weaver, III, "Exploring the importance of gender role self-perception on communication style," in *Women's Studies in Communication*. Which predicts communication style better, a person's sex or self-perceived gender?

6

Gendered Nonverbal Communication

We first make our habits, and then our habits make us.
—JOHN DRYDEN

The nonverbal dimension of communication is extensive and important. Scholars estimate that nonverbal behaviors carry from 65% (Birdwhistell, 1970) to 93% (Mehrabian, 1981) of the total meaning of communication. **Nonverbal communication** is all elements of communication other than words themselves. It includes not only gestures and movement, but also inflection, volume, and environmental factors such as space and color. Like language, nonverbal communication is learned through interaction with others. Also like language, nonverbal communication is related to gender and culture in two ways: It expresses cultural meanings of gender, and men and women use nonverbal communication to present ourselves as gendered people. Judith Butler (1990) claims that gender comes into being in our daily performances. In other words, we perform gender by using nonverbal communication that conforms to cultural norms and meanings for femininity or masculinity.

In this chapter we will consider how nonverbal communication reflects and expresses gender. We will identify functions and types of nonverbal communication and then concentrate on gender-related patterns of nonverbal communication.

FUNCTIONS OF NONVERBAL COMMUNICATION

Nonverbal communication supplements verbal communication, regulates interaction, and conveys the bulk of the relationship level of meaning in interaction. In each of these areas, there are some consistent gender differences.

■ To Supplement Verbal Communication

Communication scholars have identified five ways in which nonverbal behaviors supplement verbal messages to shape meanings (Malandro & Barker, 1983). First, nonverbal communication may *repeat* words, as when you say "right" while pointing to the right. Second, we may nonverbally *contradict* a verbal message. For example, the statement "I'm fine" would be contradicted if the person who said it was on the verge of crying. Nonverbal behavior may also *complement* verbal communication by underlining a verbal message. The statement "I never want to see you again" is more forceful if accompanied by a frown and a threatening glare. Fourth, sometimes we use nonverbal behaviors to *replace* verbal ones. Rather than saying "I don't know," you might shrug your shoulders. Finally, nonverbal communication may accent verbal messages, telling us which parts are important. "I love *you*" means something different from "*I* love you" or "I *love* you" because different words are emphasized nonverbally.

■ To Regulate Interaction

Nonverbal communication often regulates interaction. We use body posture, eye contact, and vocal inflection to signal others that we wish to speak or that we are through speaking (Drummond & Hopper, 1993). Whereas women frequently use nonverbal signals to invite others into conversation, men more frequently use them to hold onto the talk stage. For instance, if a man who is talking avoids eye contact with others, they are unlikely to jump into the conversation.

■ To Establish the Relationship Level of Meaning

A final and particularly important function of nonverbal communication is to convey relationship levels of meaning that define relationships between communicators. As Aino Sallinen-Kuparinen (1992) notes, "Nonverbal communication is a relationship language" (p. 163). The overall feeling of relationships is often expressed nonverbally (Burgoon, Buller, Hale, & deTurck, 1988; Burgoon & Le Poire, 1999). Three primary dimensions of relationship-level communication are responsiveness, liking, and power (Mehrabian, 1981), each of which is linked to gender.

Responsiveness. The first dimension of the relationship level of meaning is responsiveness. Nonverbal cues of responsiveness include inflection, eye contact, and attentive body posture that express interest and involvement. Lack of responsiveness may be signaled by yawns or averted eyes. Jon Nussbaum (1992) reports that students learn more from teachers who smile and show responsive body posture and eye contact.

Both women and men display responsiveness, yet they tend to do so in rather distinctive ways. Socialized to be affiliative, many women use nonverbal behaviors to indicate engagement with others, emotional involvement, and empathy. Men, on the other hand, tend to be socialized to focus on status and power, and this is mirrored in their nonverbal responsiveness. More than women do, men use gestures and space to command attention, and vocal inflection and volume to assert their identities and ideas (Major, Schmidlin, & Williams, 1990). Females smile more, maintain more eye contact and direct body orientation, whereas males display, lean forward, and adopt postures congruent with that of the person speaking (Guerrero, 1997).

There are also general differences in how overtly men and women respond to others. Women tend to be more overtly expressive of emotions than men are—a finding reflective of feminine socialization that promotes listening to others and responding to them (Cegela & Sillars, 1989; Ueland, 1992). Many women also show responsiveness by smiling (Burgoon, Buller, & Woodall, 1996), a behavior that says, "I am approachable, interested, friendly," which conforms to cultural ideals of femininity.

Yet gender alone doesn't shape our responsiveness (Hall, 1998). Other aspects of identity, such as race-ethnicity, interact with gender to shape our communication. For instance, Japanese women refrain from smiling in formal or important contexts, including weddings. The norms of Japanese culture define smiling as being not serious (Dresser, 1996). In the United States, African American women generally don't smile as much as Caucasian women. Similarly, attentive eye contact is practiced less by many African American women than by Caucasian women (Halberstadt & Saitta, 1987), reminding us that gender varies across standpoints. In general, if a White woman does not smile and maintain eye contact, others are likely to think she is angry or upset. Conversely, a man who *does* smile a lot and look steadily at others may be suspect.

Women not only tend to display feelings more overtly than men, but they also tend to be more skilled than men at interpreting others' emotions. Researchers report that females exceed males in the capacity to decode nonverbal behaviors and more accurately discern others' emotions (Stewart, Stewart, Friedley, & Cooper, 1996; Hall 1998).

Elaine

I never thought it would be so hard not to smile. When you challenged us in class to go one day without smiling except when we really felt happy, I thought that would be easy. I couldn't do it. I smile when I meet people, I smile when I purchase things, I even smile when someone bumps into me. I never realized how much I smile. What was most interesting about the experiment was how my boyfriend reacted. We got together last night, and I was still working on not smiling. He asked me what was wrong. I told him, nothing. I was being perfectly nice and talkative and everything, but I wasn't smiling all the time like I usually do. He kept asking what was wrong, was I unhappy, had something happened—even was I mad. I pointed out that I was being as friendly as usual. Then he said, yeah, but I wasn't smiling. I told him that I just didn't see anything particular to smile about, and he said it wasn't like me. I talked with several other women in our class, and they had the same experience. I just never realized how automatic smiling is for me.

Krista

I buy the power explanation for women's decoding skill. I know that I learned to do this from my mother. My father is very moody, and you have to know how to read him or there's trouble ahead. I remember, when I was a little girl, my mother would tell me not to ask Daddy for something or not to tell him about things at certain times because he was in a bad mood. I asked her how she knew, and she gave me a blueprint for reading him. She told me when he was mad he fidgeted and mumbled more and that he got real quiet when he was upset. Later she taught me other things like how to tell when he's getting angry about something—his eyebrows twitch. She made it seem like a science, and I guess it was in a way. But she sure knew how to read his moods, and that's how we stayed out of his way when he was on the warpath.

Women's generally greater ability to read nonverbal communication may be explained by biology, social learning and cognitive development (Richmond & McCroskey, 2000), or standpoint. The first explanation of women's generally strong ability to read feelings is sex-related brain differences (Begley, 1995). Both cognitive development and social learning theories explain that, from childhood on, most females are encouraged to be sensitive to others and to relationships. Related to this is women's standpoint as caregivers who often take care of children and sick family members. Women also far outnumber men in the caring professions, such as social work, counseling, nursing, and human resources. Women's involvement in caring gives them a standpoint that prioritizes attending to and caring for others.

Standpoint theory also suggests that women's decoding skill results from their standpoint as subordinate members of society. Those who are oppressed or who have little power learn to interpret others in order to survive (Hall, Halberstadt, & O'Brien, 1997; Henley, 1977; Henley & LaFrance, 1996). Many years ago, Bruno Bettelheim (1943) showed that prisoners in concentration camps learned to interpret their captors' feelings and moods. Bill Puka (1990) also found consistency between the emotional sensitivity typical of women and that of prisoners, slaves, and other oppressed groups. For members of oppressed groups, decoding is a survival skill. Women's decoding skills probably result from a combination of socialization and historic and current power discrepancies between the sexes.

Liking. A second dimension of the relationship level of meaning is liking. We use nonverbal behaviors to signal that we like or dislike others. Nonverbal cues of liking include vocal warmth, standing close to others, touching, and holding eye contact. Because most females are socialized to be nice to others and to form relationships, they tend to employ more nonverbal communication that signals liking than do men (Stewart et al., 1996). For instance, when conversing, two women typically stand or sit closer together than two men, and women, particularly Caucasians, generally engage in more eye contact than men (Cegela & Sillars, 1989; Henley, 1977).

Power or control. The third aspect of the relationship level is power or control. Control issues in conversations include who defines topics, who directs conversation, who interrupts, and who defers. Although many nonverbal behaviors convey control messages, three are especially important: vocal qualities, touch, and use of space. In all three categories, men generally exceed women in nonverbal efforts to exert control. For instance, compared with women, men tend to use greater volume and stronger inflection to highlight their ideas and add to the force of their positions. Men also tend to use touch to assert and reinforce status (Henley & Freeman, 1995; Spain, 1992). In addition, men generally command and use more personal space than women; they take up more space in sitting and standing, a difference not attributable to body size alone. Even at very young ages, boys are taught to seek and command more space than girls (Mills, 1985).

Now that we have seen how nonverbal communication functions to supplement verbal communication, regulate interaction, and define relationships, we are ready to explore how it reflects and expresses cultural definitions of gender.

Forms of Nonverbal Communication

Cultural views of gender are evident in nonverbal messages directed toward males and females. In addition, the nonverbal behaviors encouraged in males and females are distinctive in some respects and function to constitute gendered identities for individuals.

■ Artifacts

Artifacts are personal objects that influence how we see ourselves and express the identity we create for ourselves. Beginning with the pink and blue blankets used in many hospitals, personal objects for children define them as feminine or masculine. Parents send artifactual messages through the toys they give to sons and daughters. Typically, boys are given toys that invite competition and active, rough play, whereas girls are more likely to be given toys that encourage nurturing, domestic activities, and attention to appearances (Caldera, Huston, & O'Brien, 1989; Messner, 2000; Pomerleau, Bolduc, Malcuit, & Cossette, 1990). Despite evidence that sex-typing restricts cognitive and social development (Messner, 2000; Miller, 1987), many parents, especially fathers, tend to discourage interest in toys and activities that they consider inappropriate for a child's sex (Antill, 1987; Lytton & Romney, 1991).

Toy catalogues offer a clear message about cultural meanings attached to the sexes. Even in 2003, as I was writing this book, catalogues for children's toys feature pages titled "For Girls," with play kitchen appliances, makeup and hair accessories, and pink tutu outfits. The pages labeled "For Boys" show soldiers and science equipment, swords and shields, and building sets. Most of the girls' pages are predominantly pink with splashes of other pastel colors, whereas the pages displaying

Dan

I don't care what the experts say about bringing kids up, no son of mine will get any dolls. I think that's just stupid. Boys aren't supposed to play with dolls and stuff like that. I didn't, and I turned out okay. I played with normal guy toys like model planes and cars and erector sets and computers. I did have a G.I. Joe, though. I guess it would be okay with me if my son played with one of them, but no Barbies.

Beth

Women's clothes—that's my pet peeve. I mean, why is it I have to choose between being comfortable and looking nice? Guys don't have to. I'm interviewing for jobs this semester, so I have to wear suits a lot of days, and they make me miserable. The jackets are cut close and don't let me move freely, and the skirts are made to ride up when I sit down. And shoes! They're the pits. To wear nice-looking shoes—ones that look professional— I have to be masochistic. Even in the good lines of shoes, the toes on pumps cramp my toes. There's no way I can walk fast when my body is strapped in a suit and my feet are bound.

items for boys use darker, bolder colors. These catalogues reflect cultural views that girls are pretty, soft, and nurturing, whereas boys are active, adventurous, and aggressive.

Beyond childhood, artifacts continue to manifest and promote cultural views of masculinity and femininity. Although clothing has become less sex distinctive than in former eras (Abdullah, 1999), fashions for women and men still differ. Men's clothes generally are not as colorful or bright as women's, and they are designed to be more functional. Pockets in jackets and trousers allow men to carry wallets, change, keys, and miscellany. The relatively loose fit of men's clothes and the design of men's shoes allow them to move quickly and with assurance. Thus, men's clothing enables activity.

Women's clothing is quite different. Reflecting social expectations of femininity, women's clothing is designed to call attention to women's bodies and to make them maximally attractive to viewers. Form-fitting skirts, clingy materials, and details in design encourage seeing women as decorative objects. Formal women's clothing often has either no pockets or pockets too small to hold wallets and keys without distorting the line of the garment. Further, most women's shoes are designed to flatter legs at the cost of comfort and safety—how fast can you run in two-inch heels?

Other artifacts communicate cultural views of women and men. Advertisements for food, homemaking, and childrearing feature women, reiterating the view of women as homemakers and mothers, and the view of men as uninvolved in parenting. Products associated with heavy work, cars, and outdoor sports feature men (or women in seductive poses who are admiring the strong men). Also, consider the artifacts that women are encouraged to buy to meet the cultural command to be attractive: The cosmetics industry is a multimillion-dollar business in the United States; products to condition, straighten, curl, color, and style hair are similarly thriving. In Chapter 11 on media, we will pursue in greater detail how advertising reinforces social views of women and men.

Some people use artifacts to challenge existing perceptions. For example, some men wear earrings, often to signal support of gays, lesbians, and transgendered and transsexed individuals. Some individuals wear HIV/AIDS tattoos as a means

"I love being a partner Mr. Jenkins! There's just one problem."

From *The Wall Street Journal*—permission, Cartoon Features Syndicate.

of nonverbally resisting the stigma that society attaches to this condition (Brouwer, 1998).

Proximity and Personal Space

In 1968, Edward T. Hall coined the word **proxemics** to refer to space and our use of it. Space is a primary means through which cultures express values and shape patterns of interaction. Early work revealed that different cultures have different norms for how much space people need and how closely they interact. For instance, in Latin American countries, people interact at closer distances than in more reserved societies like the United States (Hall, 1959, 1966; Samovar, Porter, & Stefani, 1998). In some countries, houses for big families are no larger than small apartments in the United States, and the idea of private rooms for individual family members is unheard of.

Proxemics offers keen insight into the relative power and status accorded to various groups in society. Space is a primary means by which a culture designates who is important, who has privilege. In strongly patriarchal societies women are not allowed to own property; thus, they are literally denied space. Only in the mid-1990s did India begin allowing daughters to inherit property from parents.

Consider who gets space in our society. You'll notice that executives have large offices, although there is little functional need for so much room. Secretaries, however, are crowded into cubbyholes that overflow with file cabinets and computers. Generally there is a close correlation between status and the size of a person's

Cross-Cultural Norms for Women's Nonverbal Communication

Imagine that you are a successful American businessperson who travels to Saudi Arabia to negotiate a major deal. Would you expect to have your visa rejected, to be barred from restaurants, and to be ordered to change your dress before attending a business lunch?

That's what happened to Kay Ainsley of Detroit when she went to Saudi Arabia to sell the rights to open Domino's Pizza shops there (Steinberg, 1999). Her business visa was twice rejected, and she was allowed to enter the country only when the Saudi businessman with whom she was meeting intervened with the authorities. Ainsley was asked to change from her conservative business suit into an *abaya,* the long black robe that Saudi women traditionally wear. Trying to get lunch, she discovered that women were not allowed in a sandwich shop, so she had to ask a male colleague to get lunch for her. When Ainsley had successfully negotiated the deal, she found that she was barred from the signing ceremony, and a male colleague had to sign for her.

home, car, office, and so forth. Who gets space and how much space they get indicate power. In fact, both Daphne Spain (1992) and Leslie Weisman (1992) have shown that in the United States proxemics designates lesser status for women and minorities.

Think about the home in which you grew up. Who sat at the head of the table—the place reserved for a leader? In most two-parent, heterosexual families, that position belongs to the man and symbolizes his leadership of the family. Did your father have his own room, space, or chair? Did your mother? Many men have private studies, workshops, or other spaces, but fewer women with families have such spaces. My students initially disagreed with this report and informed me their mothers have spaces. When we discussed this, however, it turned out that most of their mothers' spaces were kitchens and sewing rooms—places where they do things for other people. Students whose mothers had work spaces in the home generally used parts of other rooms (a corner in the living room) or temporary spaces (using the dining-room table for work when it's not needed for meals). Many years ago, Virginia Woolf gave a famous speech entitled "A Room of One's Own," in which she argued that women's ability to engage in creative, independent work is hampered by not having an inviolate space for themselves.

Territoriality is personal space that we don't want others to invade. Yet not everyone's territory is equally respected. People with power tend to have more space than people with lesser power. Those with power also tend to enter the spaces of those with less power, but the converse is not true. In general, men go into women's spaces more than women enter men's spaces and more than men enter other men's spaces.

Gendered Proxemics

Virginia Valian (1998) is a professor of psychology and linguistics who is interested in how gender stereotypes shape perceptions. She conducted an experiment to find out whether college students are equally likely to perceive women and men as leaders. Students were asked to identify the leader in photos of people seated around a conference table. When the people in the photo were all men or all women, students overwhelmingly chose the person at the head of the table as the leader. Students also selected the person at the head of the table as the leader when the photo showed both women and men and a man was seated at the head of the table. However, when both women and men were in the photo and a woman was at the head of the table, students selected the woman at the head as the leader only half the time.

What happens when a person's private territory is invaded? This question has intrigued Judee Burgoon and her colleagues (Burgoon, Buller, Hale, & deTurck, 1988; Burgoon & Hale, 1988; Le Poire, Burgoon, & Parrott, 1992). One response to invasion of our territory is behavior that restores our privacy zone. For instance, if someone moves too close for comfort, you might step back. Similarly, there is the well-known elevator phenomenon in which people are crowded more closely than they like, so everyone looks up or down as if to say "I'm not trying to intrude into your space."

■ Haptics (Touch)

Haptics, or touch, from parents and other adults communicates different messages to boys and girls. Studies of parent-child interaction reveal that parents tend to touch daughters more often and more gently than they do sons (Condry, Condry, & Pogatshnik, 1983). Through social learning, then, girls learn to expect touching from others and to view touching as an affiliative behavior. Boys are more likely to learn to associate touching with control and power and not to expect nurturing touches from others.

Based on these lessons in childhood, women are more likely than men to initiate hugs and touches that express support, affection, and comfort, whereas men more often use touch to direct others, assert power, and express sexual interest (Hall, 1998; Pearson, West, & Turner, 1995). Members of female softball teams exchange more team hugs and hand piles than members of male softball teams, particularly after negative game events (Kneidinger, Maple, & Tross, 2001). Because masculine and feminine meanings of touch may differ, women may perceive men's touch and entry into their space as harassing (Le Poire et al., 1992; Levy & Paludi, 1997).

Roseanne

A few months ago, I was out with this guy I'd been seeing for a while. We weren't serious or anything, but we had gone out a few times. Well, we were at his place listening to music when he started coming on to me. After a while, I told him to stop because I didn't want to go any further. He grinned and pinned my arms back and asked what I was going to do to stop him. Well, I didn't have to, thank goodness, because he didn't really push, but just the same I had to think there really wasn't anything I could have done if he had. That's always there when I'm with a guy—he could overpower me if he wanted to.

Randall

It sounds kind of stupid when we talk about it, but it's true that a guy has to return another guy's stare if he wants to hold his own. It's like a staring contest. Sometimes on a street, another guy will meet my eyes. When I notice, then he's locked into holding the stare, and that means that I have to, too. It's like that old joke about the first one to blink loses. It's kind of dumb, but I'd feel strange not returning another guy's gaze. Like a wimp or something.

Touching behaviors also reflect social norms and the constraints they impose. For example, Laura Guerrero, Joseph DeVito, and Michael Hecht (1999) point out that gay and lesbian couples may not feel free to touch each other in public contexts.

We should also recognize the different degrees of sheer strength men and women in general can exert. Because men are generally larger and stronger than women, they tend to have more physical confidence and to be more willing to use physical force than women (May, 1998a). Some men are unaware of how strong they are, especially in relation to others who are less so.

■ Kinesics (Facial and Body Motion)

Kinesics refers to face and body movements. Women tend to tilt their heads in deferential positions, condense their size, and allow others to invade their spaces. Men, too, tend to enact patterns they were taught by smiling less, using larger gestures, taking more space, and entering others' territories. Western women, particularly Caucasians, also smile more than men. Judee Burgoon and her colleagues (Burgoon et al., 1996) observe that, for women, smiling is a basic interactional behavior, whereas for men it is reserved for expressing emotion. In combination, these gender-differentiated patterns suggest that women's facial and body motions generally signal they are approachable, friendly, and unassuming. Men's facial and body communications, in contrast, tend to indicate they are reserved and in control.

Males are more likely than females to use facial and body movements aggressively in social, business, and other contexts (Kinney, Smith, & Donzella, 2001; Timmers, Fischer, & Manstead, 1998). Male athletes engage in nonverbal confrontations with teammates, whereas female athletes are more likely to talk through tensions than engage in physical confrontations (Sullivan & Short, 2001).

Called by poets the "mirrors of the soul," eyes can express love, anger, fear, interest, challenge—a great range of emotions. Many women have learned to signal interest and involvement by sustaining eye contact, whereas men generally do not sustain eye contact during conversations. An exception to this rule is that men

The man and the woman in these photos are in identical postures. Do you have different perceptions of them based on gendered expectations in our culture?

sometimes use eye contact to challenge others and assert themselves (Pearson, 1985). Men in my classes tell me that they lose face and come across as wimps if they don't return a stare.

Paralanguage

Vocal cues that accompany verbal communication are called **paralanguage.** Although there are some physiological differences in male and female vocal organs (the larynx and pharynx), these do not account fully for differences in women's and men's paralanguage. For instance, the larger, thicker vocal folds of male larynxes do result in lower pitch, but the difference between the average pitch of male speakers and the pitch of female speakers exceeds that explained by physiology.

To understand why women and men tend to have divergent paralanguage, we must once again consider socialization processes. What vocal cues would you expect of someone taught to be deferential and caring? What would you expect of someone taught to be assertive, emotionally reserved, and independent? Your expectations probably closely match identified differences in male and female paralanguage. In general, women use higher pitch, softer volume, and more inflection. To assert themselves and command the conversational stage, men tend to use lower pitch and greater volume.

FYI

Beauty: His and Hers

Q: Isn't it mainly women who have cosmetic surgery?

A: Today, both sexes have cosmetic surgery. Women most often have facial surgeries and fat reduction operations. Men have surgeries to enhance muscles, implant hair, and enlarge penises. Both sexes have cosmetic surgery to make them appear younger.

Q: So what's wrong with having plastic surgery to look better?

A: All of us care about our looks. However, it isn't healthy to have excessive concerns about how we look or unrealistic ideals for appearance. Many plastic surgeons report that prospective patients come to them with pictures of celebrities they want to look like. Others come with pictures of themselves twenty or more years ago and ask to look like they looked then. Even more troublesome are the reasons some people seek cosmetic surgery. Many think others will like them better if they "fix" how they look. They haven't learned to value themselves for qualities more important than physical appearance.

Q: So what's the big deal? Maybe appearance shouldn't matter so much, but if you can afford to have cosmetic surgery, why not do it?

A: There are some risks. Injections to hide wrinkles and smile lines can shrink and distort the face and other areas. Skin resurfacing can cause inflammation and discoloration of skin. Eyelift surgeries can make it difficult or even impossible to close the eyes completely. Scarring sometimes happens, as do pain, nerve damage, and other complications.

A classic study sheds light on cultural stereotypes of men and women (Addington, 1968). A researcher asked participants to judge the personalities of people on the basis of vocal qualities, which he experimentally manipulated. Women with breathy, tense voices were judged to be pretty, feminine, petite, shallow, immature, and unintelligent. Men with throaty, tense voices were judged to be mature, masculine, intelligent, and sophisticated. The researcher concluded that, when women are perceived as feminine, other aspects of the feminine gender stereotype—such as being pretty, immature, and unintelligent—are attributed to them. Perceptions of men as masculine are accompanied by the assumption that they are intelligent and mature.

Wendy

All my life, I've had to live with the "dumb blonde" label. I am blonde, pretty, and petite, and this makes others perceive me as dumb and immature. That's what people always think before they get to know me. They act toward me as if I were dumb, and they don't expect me to be mature. What really gets me is that sometimes I get hooked into their impression of me, and I start *acting* the part of the dumb blonde. Why can't a woman be feminine and smart both?

■ Physical Appearance

We have a perception of how we look and how well our appearance fits—or fails to fit—cultural ideals

FYI

The Quest for the Physical Ideal

Q: How many females and males are preoccupied with achieving ideal bodies?

A: The numbers are increasing for both sexes (Gross, 2000; Morgan, 2002; Pope et. al, 2002). The National Association of Anorexia Nervosa and Associated Disorders estimates that 8 million females and 1 million males suffer from eating disorders. A new disorder is called bigorexia, or the Adonis complex. Men who have this complex perceive their bodies as puny. To change that, they may engage in excessive exercise, and use drugs to bulk up body mass.

Q: Is there any way to get help for eating disorders?

A: Yes. In addition to research cited in this chapter, the following Web sites provide information about symptoms and consequences of eating disorders, personal accounts of living with and recovering from eating disorders, and treatment programs:

 Ability's Bulimia Page: **http://www.ability.org.uk/bulimia.html.**
Pale Reflections: **http://www.pale-reflections.com.**

for femininity and masculinity. Although some men are dissatisfied with their physical appearance (Bordo, 1999; Chaiken & Pliner, 1987; Davison & Birch, 2001), most are not. A 2003 poll (The Man Poll) revealed that 87% of men in America are very or somewhat satisfied with their appearance, and 50% of men don't worry at all about losing their physical attractiveness. Even men who are dissatisfied with their physical appearance tend to compartmentalize their concerns. They may dislike aspects of their appearance, but that seldom affects how they feel about their overall competence and value (Mintz & Betz, 1986). For women, dislike of their bodies often affects overall self-esteem, especially for Caucasian women (American Association of University Women [AAUW], 1991; Beren, Grilo, Hayden, & Wilfley, 1996; Davison & Birch, 2001; Tavris, Meginnis, & Bardari, 2000).

For many girls and women, especially Caucasians, concern about weight starts early. Kirsten Davison and Leann Birch (2001) report that by the age of 5 many girls have negative self-images based on their weight. At least 40% of fourth-grade girls diet and 33% of 13-year-old girls try to lose weight through dieting and other means (Kilbourne, 2004; Nichter, 2000). Pressure to be thin contributes to the epidemic of eating disorders, which affect more than 5 million Americans, a majority of whom are girls and women (Brumberg, 1988; Hicks, 1998a,b). Today an estimated one in four college women has an eating disorder; without treatment, as many as 20% of those with eating disorders may die (Hicks, 1998a,b).

Cultural emphasis on thinness as ideal for women carries a second danger. When they are encouraged to focus so intensely on their bodies, women may give

FYI

Women's Body Ideals and Realities

In the 1950s, the average Miss America weighed 134 pounds. By the early 1980s her average weight had dropped to 117. Today, the average Miss America weighs even less.

In 1962, leading fashion models weighed only 8% less than the average woman in the United States. Thirty years later, in 1992, the highly sought-after fashion models weighed a whopping 25% less than the average woman in the United States. That's a 300% increase in the difference between models and average women ("The Wrong Weight," 1997). In 1998, the average American woman was 5'4" tall, weighed 130, and wore a size 12 dress. Contrast that with the size 0 worn by actress Calista Flockhart (Hicks, 1998a,b).

Given ideals of extreme thinness, it's no wonder that so many women diet. And it's not just women. Girls, too, diet. A 1997 report by researchers at the University of Florida found that 42% of 6- and 7-year-old girls wanted to lose weight. Another study reported that nearly half of the girls surveyed were dieting by age 9 and, on any given day, 25% of girls and women in the United States are dieting.

Nikki

When I was growing up, my mother and grandmother were always on diets. They think being ultra-thin is essential. Four years ago when I came to college, I gained the "freshman 15." When I went home for the summer, my mother and grandmother commented on how much weight I'd gained and how bad I looked. Mother got her doctor to put me on FenPhen, the diet pill. I'd heard it could be dangerous (you've probably read about the lawsuits against it), but I took the pills for two months and lost a lot of weight—more than the 15 pounds I'd gained. Then I started having echoing sounds in my ears. I went to a doctor and he said it was the result of taking FenPhen. The ringing is with me all the time, even though I've quit taking that pill. Being thin is fine, but it's not worth risking your health. I actually feel sorry for my mother and grandmother because they obsess over their weight and never enjoy eating food.

less attention to more important aspects of identity. Historian Joan Brumberg's book, *The Body Project: An Intimate History of American Girls* (1997), claims that, for many young women in America, the body has become an all-consuming project—one that takes precedence over all others. Brumberg says that "girls have moved from basing their identities on good works to good looks" (Winkler, 1997, p. A15).

Awareness of the perils of ultra-thin body ideals for women has motivated some resistance. *Mode* is a women's fashion magazine that challenges the waif look so prevalent in many women's magazines. Debuting in 1997, *Mode* portrays women who are sizes 12, 14, and 16. The full-figured models in *Mode* disprove the idea that only thin women can look good (Navarro, 1998). Emme, a plus-size fashion diva, is 5'11" tall, weighs 190 pounds, and wears a size 14 with style. In 1994, *People* magazine listed Emme as one of the 50 most beautiful people (McDowell, 1998).

Perhaps you are wondering who is most likely to become obsessed with weight. Women who have internalized the culture's views of femininity are

Race and Views of Physical Beauty

What's thin? What's fat? Is weight attractive on women? It turns out that the answers to these questions often depend on the race of the person answering. There is growing evidence that Black and White girls and women view their bodies in different ways and that they have different ideals of feminine beauty.

In a survey of young women in junior high and high school, 90% of White students said they were dissatisfied with their bodies, but 70% of Black students were satisfied with their bodies. Nearly two-thirds of the White students were dieting or had dieted in the past year, whereas fewer Black students dieted or tried to control weight in a sustained way (Ingrassia, 1995).

At early ages, White girls learn that being slender or even thin is considered desirable. When asked to describe a perfectly shaped female, young White women said she would be 5 feet 7 inches tall and weigh 100 to 110 pounds. Young Black women offered more realistic descriptions of the perfect body form: full hips, thick thighs. Young Black women also emphasized that beauty is about more than weight and appearance: It's having the "right attitude." These differences in feminine ideals shed insight on the reasons why anorexia and bulimia are less common among Black girls and women, especially those who are strongly identified with African American culture (Bocella, 2001; Molloy & Herzberger, 1998; Vobejda & Perlstein, 1998).

Thinness is not the only aspect of physical attractiveness that is race related. For years, European American features have been represented as the only standard of female beauty (Edrut, 2000; Finstein, 1993; hooks, 1995; Shandler, 1999). Tyra Banks, Naomi Campbell, and other women of color who are successful models have skin color, hair, and features that are more like those of European Americans than like members of their own ethnic groups.

But change may be coming. In 1997, 20-year-old Alek Wek emerged as one of the hottest international fashion models. She's stolen the scene in Paris, New York, and Milan. Born in Sudan, Wek is 5'11", has dark ebony skin, full lips, a broad nose, and wears her hair closely cropped (Samuels, 1997, p. 68). She represents a traditional African form of beauty.

more susceptible to cultural ideals for women's weight than are androgynous women (Franzoi, 1991; Northrup, 1995). In general, Western Caucasian women are particularly likely to strive to meet unrealistic body ideals. Commenting on the preoccupation with thinness, Moroccan sociologist Fatema Mernissi (2004) states that the size 6 ideal is more oppressive of women than the Muslim veil.

In general, African American women tend to be more satisfied with their bodies, less prone to eating disorders, and less extreme in pursuing unrealistic physical ideals (Henriques, Calhoun, & Cann, 1996; Levinson, Powell, & Steelman, 1986; Powell & Kathn, 1995; Root, 1990; Thomas, 1989; Thomas & James, 1988). Linda

Villarosa (1994) explains that traditional African societies admire full-figured bodies as symbols of wealth and prosperity. African American women who identify strongly with their ethnic heritage are less vulnerable to obsessions with thinness than African American women who leave their communities or who don't have strong Black identities. Adding to Villarosa's explanation are the insights of a Black student from a northern college. In a letter to me, Daneen described the ideology behind the views of physical beauty that she and other Black women in her community learned:

> My family and my African American culture instilled pride in me. I was told that my full lips, round body, and rough hair encompassed the beauty and pride of my history. To want to be skinny or have straight hair or thin lips would be to deny my identity as a Black woman.

Because our culture is increasingly emphasizing men's bodies, more and more men are exercising, working out with weights, and using potentially lethal steroids to develop the muscularity promoted as ideal (Pope, Phillips, & Olivardia, 2002; Seligmann, 1994). One group of men, however, is particularly likely to be concerned about appearance and to develop eating disorders: gay men. Physical appearance is linked more closely to self-worth for gay than straight men, perhaps because gay men, like straight women, want to attract men (Beren et al., 1996; Siever, 1988).

In summary, sex-related differences in nonverbal behavior reflect culturally constructed views of masculinity and femininity. In general, women are more sensitive to nonverbal communication; display more overt interest, attention, and affiliation; constrict themselves physically; are given and use less space; use touch for affiliative purposes but are touched more; and restrict body gestures more than men. Reflecting cultural messages about how to enact masculinity, men tend to use nonverbal communication to signal power and status, to assert themselves and their agenda, to command territories, and to veil their emotions from public display.

CULTURAL VALUES ASSOCIATED WITH GENDERED NONVERBAL COMMUNICATION

Nonverbal behaviors expected of women emphasize communality—building and sustaining relationships and community. Nonverbal behaviors considered appropriate for men emphasize agency, power, achievement, and initiative. How do these prescriptions for feminine and masculine nonverbal communication reflect broad cultural values? We begin by noting that Western society values agency more than communality. In other words, Western culture places higher value on the behaviors associated with masculinity than on those associated with femininity.

The different values assigned to agency and communality were dramatically illustrated in a classic study. A research team (Broverman, Broverman, Clarkson,

Rosenkrantz, & Vogel, 1970) prepared a list of traits that reflected a broad range of human qualities. They then asked 79 male and female psychiatrists, psychologists, and social workers to check the attributes they thought described "normal, healthy women." Next, the clinicians checked traits they associated with "normal, healthy men." Finally, clinicians selected characteristics of "normal, healthy adults." The findings were clear and startling: Normal women were described as dependent, oriented toward relationships, deferential, unassertive, concerned with appearance, submissive, emotional, and uncompetitive. In contrast, clinicians described normal men as independent, aggressive, competitive, more rational than emotional, and ambitious. Associated with normal adults were the same qualities used to describe normal men.

We can draw two conclusions from this study. First, the clinicians perceived stereotypically masculine characteristics as the standard, or norm, for healthy adults. Second, the qualities associated with normal, healthy women were seen as inconsistent with those of normal, healthy adults. The bias favoring masculine qualities continues in Western society (Basow, 1992; McCreary, Newcomb, & Sadava, 1998; Wetherell, 1997; Williams & Best, 1990).

But cultural beliefs are not etched in stone. Instead, they are constructed, sustained, and sometimes altered as members of a society interact in ways that constantly remake social views of gender. We can resist our culture's unequal views of agency and communality if we recognize that different nonverbal styles are simply different—not better or worse, just different. We can also choose not to embody the gendered nonverbal style prescribed for our gender. If we find that social expectations restrict us, we may resist them. In doing so, we act as agents of change who alter cultural understandings of how women and men should and do behave.

■ Respecting Gendered Styles of Nonverbal Communication

What we've learned in this chapter also empowers us to be more effective in our communication and in our interpretation of others' communication. People who have been socialized in masculine speech communities may perceive a woman who defers as less confident of her ideas than a man who advances his views assertively. Similarly, someone socialized in feminine speech communities might view a man as insensitive and domineering if he looks impassive, offers little response to her talk, and promotes his agenda. Yet such judgments reflect the communication rules we have learned, ones that may not apply to others' ways of expressing themselves. If we impose our values on behaviors that emanate from an alternative standpoint that is not guided by the rules we take for granted, then we distort what others mean to communicate. Greater accuracy in interpreting others' nonverbal communication results from understanding and respecting differences in how people use it.

Respecting differences calls on us to suspend judgment based on our own perspectives and to consider more thoughtfully what others mean *in their own terms,* not ours. This might lead you to ask for clarification of intent from conversational partners whose nonverbal communication patterns diverge from yours. For example, it might be constructive to say to someone less facially expressive than you, "I don't know how you're feeling about what I just said, because your face doesn't show any reaction. Could you tell me what you feel?" Conversely, understanding may be enhanced when someone with a masculine, assertive nonverbal style says to his or her more deferential partner, "I'm not sure where you stand, because you seem to be responding to my ideas rather than expressing your own. I'm interested in your opinion." Communicative techniques such as these enable us to show respect for nonverbal differences and, at the same time, to transcend their potential to create misunderstandings.

Understanding and respecting different forms of nonverbal communication require us to make an honest effort to appreciate what another says on his or her own terms. At first this is difficult because we have to get past our own egocentric ways of perceiving the world in order to interpret other people from their standpoints. People who commit to doing this say that it becomes easier with practice.

There's another benefit to learning to understand and respect alternative styles of nonverbal communication. It enhances your personal effectiveness by increasing the range of options you have for communicating with different people in diverse contexts and for varied reasons. Now that you are aware of gendered patterns in nonverbal communication, you may reflect on your own behaviors. Do you fit the patterns associated with your gender? Are you comfortable with your style and the effects it has, or would you like to alter your nonverbal behavior in some respects? By reflecting on your own nonverbal communication, you empower yourself to create consciously a style that reflects the identity you assign to yourself.

SUMMARY

In this chapter we have seen that nonverbal communication expresses cultural views of gender. Social definitions of women as deferential, decorative, and relationship centered are reinforced through nonverbal communication that emphasizes their appearance, limits their space, and defines them as touchable. Views of men as independent, powerful, and in control are reflected in nonverbal behaviors that accord them larger territories and greater normative rights to invade others by entering their space and touching them. Consistent with how nonverbal communication defines men and women are differences in how they use it. Whereas many women embody femininity by speaking softly, condensing themselves, yielding territory, and responding facially, men are likely to command space and volume, defend their turf, and display little facial expression to keep feelings camouflaged.

Recognizing the value of alternative styles of communication, both verbal and nonverbal, enables you to reflect critically on the patterns esteemed in our society and the extent to which different ones are assigned to women and men. In turn, this enables you to resist those social meanings you find unconstructive, to revise your own nonverbal communication to reflect the identity you want, and to work toward changing the values our society assigns to masculine and feminine modes of expression. In doing this, you speak back to society and claim your right to participate in the processes of constructing the meanings of masculinity and femininity and the values assigned to different forms of communication.

KEY TERMS

artifacts, 133
haptics, 137
kinesics, 138
nonverbal communication, 129

paralanguage, 139
proxemics, 135
territoriality, 136

DISCUSSION QUESTIONS

1. Look at the ads in your favorite magazine. What feminine and masculine ideals are reflected in them?

2. Observe people in your classes, in restaurants and stores, and walking around campus. To what extent do you see gendered patterns of nonverbal communication that were identified in this chapter? Do women smile, hold eye contact, and use condensed space more than men? Do men use larger motions and more relaxed posture and command more space than women?

3. Violate one of the expectations for nonverbal communication for your sex. If you are a woman, you might try to go a day without smiling. If you are a man, you might try to smile constantly. Notice how people respond, both what they say and how they react nonverbally.

4. Choose PowerTrac on your InfoTrac College Edition, then select Key Word in the search index. Type "Women and Weight and Magazine Covers." Read the article "Women and Weight: Gendered Messages on Magazine Covers" by Amy Malkin, Kimberlie Wornian, and Joan Chrisler, which was published in a 1999 issue of the journal *Sex Roles*. Are the authors' findings consistent with your experiences? How might symbolic interaction theory (discussed in Chapter 2) explain their findings about the influence of magazine covers and women's feelings about weight?

7 Gendered Family Dynamics

The family is the linchpin of gender, reproducing it from one generation to the next.

—SUSAN MOLLER OKIN

Imagine yourself 10 years in the future. Write a one- or two-paragraph description of a perfect day in the life you want to have 10 years from now. Later in this chapter we'll return to what you've written.

Our experiences during the early years of life profoundly influence who we are. Although we continue to evolve throughout our lives, the foundations of our identities, including gender, are established through communication during the first few years of life. This chapter explores how children learn social views of gender and how the majority of women and men internalize and embody these in their own communication, thereby reproducing social views of gender.

To launch our discussion, we will examine how the self is created through interactions with others. We will then trace how parents' communication teaches children the cultural gender code. Finally, we will consider contemporary college students' views of what it means to be a man or a woman in America today. By understanding the origins and implications of gender roles, you should gain insight into how you became who you are and perhaps how you might continue to create yourself.

ENTERING A GENDERED SOCIETY

According to Mead (1934), we have no self at birth. But we are born into a gendered society that guides us to develop a gendered self. From the pink and blue blankets many hospitals continue to use, to parents' distinctive interactions with sons and daughters, gender messages besiege infants from the moment of birth. As infants and young children interact with family members, peers, and others, they engage in two processes central to developing a personal identity: conceiving the self-as-object and monitoring.

Self-as-Object

As we noted in Chapter 5, humans are able to reflect on themselves. We are able to notice, describe, and evaluate our own activities much as we would those of others. For instance, we say, "I am attractive" or "I am strong." **Self-as-object** is the ability to think about ourselves, to view and respond to ourselves.

At first, others' views of us are external. Gradually, however, we internalize them so that they become key to how we see ourselves. Mead, in fact, insisted that we can *experience self only after experiencing others and their views of us.* The emphasis others place on gender explains why gender is one of the first senses of self that we develop.

Monitoring

Because we can view the self as an object, we are able to monitor ourselves, which means we observe and regulate our attitudes and behaviors. We use symbols, usually language, to define who we are (*son, student, mother, attorney, kind, independent,* and so on).

Mead spoke of *internal dialogues* to indicate that **monitoring** happens inside of us, but it consists of conversations with others whose perspectives we have internalized. As we engage in internal dialogues, we remind ourselves what others have told us we are supposed to think, do, look like, and feel—that is, we tell ourselves what the social codes stipulate as appropriate for our age, sex, and so forth. For instance, a 5-year-old girl might think, "I want to go play in the yard" and then monitor that wish by repeating her mother's words: "Nice girls don't get dirty." The little girl's voice and the mother's voice engage in an internal dialogue through which the child decides what to do. Because we can take ourselves as objects and use social perspectives to monitor ourselves, our personal identity is always, inevitably social—who we are and how we see ourselves is deeply influenced by the family and society of which we are a part.

GENDERING COMMUNICATION IN THE FAMILY

Through overt instruction and subtle, unconscious communication, families contribute in major ways to the formation of gender identity. To understand how families gender children, we will first elaborate the largely unconscious process of internalizing gender, which was introduced in Chapter 2. Second, we will draw on social learning and cognitive development theories to examine more overt ways in which children learn gender in families.

■ Unconscious Processes: Identification and Internalization

The conscious level of human experience does not fully explain human personality, including gender identity. Insight into unobservable yet very important unconscious dynamics comes primarily from psychoanalytic theories, which claim that the core personality is shaped by family relationships in the early years of life.

Sigmund Freud, who lived from 1856 until 1939, is famous for claiming that "anatomy is destiny," by which he meant that biology, particularly the genitals, determines with which parent a child will identify and, thus, how the child's psyche will develop. According to Freud, at an early age children of both sexes focus on the penis. Boys identify with their fathers, who also have penises, whereas girls recognize their similarity with their mothers, who do not have penises. Freud theorized that girls regard their mothers as responsible for their "lack" of penises, whereas boys view their fathers as having the power to castrate them. Both children see the father and the penis as power.

As interesting as Freud's theory is, there has been little empirical support for it, and some studies indicate that at least parts of the theory may not be valid (Basow, 1992; Pleck, 1981; Williams, 1973). Newer psychoanalytic theories reject Freud's assertion that anatomy is destiny and his claim that females experience penis envy.

According to more recent thinkers (Chodorow, 1978, 1989; Goldner, Penn, Sheinberg, & Walker, 1990; Miller, 1986), females do not literally envy the penis. What they may envy is what the penis symbolizes—the privilege and power that our society bestows on males.

Although current psychoanalytic theorists reject some of Freud's ideas, they agree with the basic psychoanalytic view that families are critical to the formation of gender identity. During the earliest stage of life, children of both sexes depend on and identify with the person who takes care of them. Usually this is a woman, often the mother. Thus, children of both sexes usually form their first identification with an adult woman.

Yet common identification with a female does not mean that boys and girls pursue similar developmental paths. Mothers tend to identify with daughters more closely than with sons, and they

Eileen

I don't buy this stuff about penis envy. I've never envied my brother his penis. I remember when we were both little, we took baths together sometimes, and I saw that he was made differently than I was. I thought it looked strange, but I didn't want it myself. But I do remember being jealous of him, or of the freedoms my parents allowed him but not me. They let him go off all day long to play, but I had to stay in the yard unless my mother was with me. He could play rough and get dirty, but I'd get a real fussin' if I did it. I remember wishing I were a boy so that I could do all of the fun things, but I didn't wish I had a penis. Definitely not.

encourage daughters to be connected to them (Apter, 1990; Chodorow, 1989). Mothers are inclined to encourage sons to differentiate from them. Through a variety of verbal and nonverbal communications, mothers fortify identification with daughters and restrain it with sons.

According to psychoanalytic theory, around the age of 3 male development and female development diverge dramatically. You'll recall from cognitive development theory that this is the time at which gender constancy is secured so that children realize their sex is an unchanging, continuous part of their identity. For most girls, development proceeds along the path initially established—identification with the mother. Through concrete, daily interactions with her mother, a daughter continues to crystallize her sense of self within the original primary relationship.

To develop masculine gender identity, however, boys need to lessen the early identification with the mother and focus on identifying with a male. This process is complicated by the fact that fathers are generally less involved in boys' everyday lives and often emotionally remote as well (Banerji, 1998; Keen, 1991; Way, 1998). Many young boys have difficulty finding an adult masculine gender model with whom they can identify; in fact, in the 1990s the number of American households headed by single mothers increased by 25% (Schmitt, 2001).

Because a number of boys lack a strong, personal relationship with the person they are supposed to emulate (Ingrassia, 1993), masculine gender can be elusive and difficult to grasp. This may help explain why boys typically define their masculinity predominantly in negative terms—as not feminine, not like mother. They repress the original identification with mothers and deny feminine tendencies or feelings in themselves. By extension, this may be the source of boys' tendency to devalue the feminine in general ("Ugh, girls are icky"), a pattern not paralleled by girls' views of masculinity. Research suggests that young boys' forceful contempt for anything feminine is a means of assuring themselves that they are truly masculine (Chodorow, 1989; Gaylin, 1992; Kantrowitz & Kalb, 1998; Miller, 1986).

Adrienne

I helped Mom a lot with cooking and cleaning when I was little. I used to really enjoy that because it made me feel like an adult. I remember thinking "I'm just like Mommy" when I'd be cleaning or doing stuff in the kitchen. I wanted to be like her, and doing what she did made me feel we were the same.

Rich

My father left us before I was even a year old, so I didn't know him at all. My mom worked all day and was too tired to date or anything else, so there wasn't a man around. I tried to help Mom, but she'd tell me I didn't have to do this stuff because I was "her little man." I used to watch Mom doing stuff around the house and I'd think, "That's not what I'm supposed to do," but I had a lot of trouble figuring out what it was that I *was* supposed to do. I just knew it wasn't girl stuff. Then I got a Big Brother through a program at school. He was 17, and he spent most every Saturday with me and sometimes some time after school during the week. Michael was great. He'd let me hang out with him, and he'd show me how to do stuff like play ball and use tools to make things. Finally I had a sense of what I was supposed to be like and what I should do. Michael really helped me figure out who I was.

As development continues, girls are given positive rewards for being "Mommy's helper" and interacting with their mothers, and they learn to see the mother as a role model for femininity. Boys, however, are rewarded for roaming away from home to find companions. Boys' social development typically occurs in larger groups with temporary and changing memberships; for many girls, it unfolds within continuing, personal relationships with individuals, including mothers. These different developmental paths encourage boys to become achieving and independent and girls to become nurturing and relationally oriented (Chodorow, 1989; Gilligan, 1982; Miller, 1986). To date there is little research on what happens when men, not women, are primary caregivers. It is possible that male caregivers might encourage a more relational, communal identity in male children because the boys could define themselves within a primary relationship with an adult male.

Nancy Chodorow (1989) theorizes that, because girls develop feminine identity within personal, ongoing relationships, throughout life they continue to seek close relationships and place importance on personal communication with others. Because boys separate from their initial relationship with their mothers to form masculine identities, and because they tend to interact in activity-specific groups with changing members, they learn to define themselves relatively independently of others and to maintain some distance between themselves and others.

It's important to remind ourselves that we are discussing gender, not sex. This means, first, that we are not born with a preference to be independent of or connected to others; we learn it. Second, it means that men and women with masculine inclinations tend to value independence and prefer distance from others. Conversely, women and men with feminine orientations place a premium on relationships and interpersonal closeness.

■ Ego Boundaries

At the same time that we construct our gender identity, we also form **ego boundaries** (Chodorow, 1989; Surrey, 1983). Ego boundaries define the point at which an individual stops and the rest of the world begins. They distinguish the self—more or less distinctly—from everyone and everything else. Because they are linked to gender identity and evolve concurrently with it, masculine and feminine ego boundaries tend to differ. Individuals who develop feminine gender identities, which emphasize interrelatedness with others, tend to have relatively permeable ego boundaries. Because girls do not need to differentiate sharply from their mothers in order to develop a feminine gender identity, they often do not perceive clear-cut or absolute lines between themselves and others.

The relatively permeable ego boundaries associated with femininity may partially explain why many girls and women tend to be empathic—to sense the feelings of those close to them and to experience those feelings almost as their own. It may also explain why women, more than men, sometimes become so involved with others that they neglect their own needs. Finally, this may shed light on the femi-

JUMP START reprinted by permission of United Feature Syndicate, Inc.

nine tendency to feel responsible for others and for situations that are not one's own doing. When the lines between self and other are blurred, it's hard to make a clear distinction between *your* responsibilities and needs and those of others.

Masculine gender identity is premised on differentiating from a female care-giver and defining self as "not like her." It makes sense, then, that masculine indi-viduals tend to have relatively impermeable ego boundaries. They generally have a clear sense of where they stop and others begin, and they are less likely to experi-ence others' feelings as their own. The less permeable ego boundaries that accom-pany a masculine gender identity explain why, later in life, many men keep some distance from others and are less likely than most women to experience others' feelings as their own. People with masculine ego boundaries aren't nec-essarily unconcerned about others. It's more accu-rate to conclude that they generally experience others' feelings as distinct from their own.

After measuring ego boundaries in nearly 1,000 people, Ernest Hartmann (1991) concluded that there are "clear-cut differences between men and women. . . . Overall, women scored significantly thinner than men—thinner by about twenty points, or 8% of the overall score" (p. 117). He also found that women tend to be comfortable feeling connected to others, sensing that their lives are interwoven with those close to them, and they may be uneasy with too much autonomy. Most men, on the other hand, tend to feel secure when autonomy and self-sufficiency are high, and they may feel suffocated in relationships that are extremely close. Permeable ego boundaries may be why women tend to create more emotionally intense same-sex friendships than men (Rubin, 1985;

Vince

My girlfriend is so strange about her friends. Like, the other night I went by her apartment and she was all upset and crying. When I asked her what was wrong, she told me Linda, her best friend, had just been dumped by her boyfriend. I said she acted like it was her who'd broken up, not Linda, and she didn't need to be so upset. She got even more upset and said it felt like her problem too; couldn't I understand what Linda was going through? I said I could, but that *she* wasn't going through it; Linda was. She told me it was the same thing because when you're really close to somebody else you hurt when they hurt. It didn't make sense to me, but maybe this con-cept of ego boundaries is what that's all about.

Schaef, 1981). With other women, they find the kind of intimate, personal connection they value.

Although the early years are important in shaping our identity, they are not absolute determinants of who we will be as adults. Our understanding of gender and of our personal gender identity changes over time as we experience different situations and diverse people who embody alternative versions of masculinity and femininity.

■ Parental Communication About Gender

Among the people who influence our gender identities, parents are especially prominent. Children learn gender roles through the rewards and punishments they receive for various behaviors (social learning theory) and through observing and emulating others (cognitive development theory). Typically, girls are encouraged to be cooperative, helpful, nurturing, and deferential—all qualities consistent with social views of femininity. For boys, rewards are more likely to come for behaving competitively, independently, and assertively (Bruess & Pearson, 1996; Leaper, Anderson, & Sanders, 1998; Leaper, Leve, Strasser, & Schwartz, 1995). In addition, as we learned when we discussed cognitive development theory in Chapter 2, children learn about gender by observing what mothers and fathers do, using parents as models for themselves.

One gender lesson that most children learn through early communication is the relative value placed on males and females. In the United States, sons are preferred, although the preference is less strong than in former eras (Marleau, Saucier, Borgeat, Bernazzani, & David, 1997). In some cultures the preference for males is so strong that female fetuses are often aborted and female infants are sometimes killed after birth (French, 1992; Hegde, 1999a,b; Pollitt, 1999). In other cultures, female and male children are equally valued; in still others, females are more valued (Cronk, 1993; Lepowsky, 1998).

Parents' communication toward sons and daughters often reflects gender stereotypes. In a classic study, researchers found that within just 24 hours of birth, parents responded to their babies in

Mala

Males are favored over females in Indian culture. It is custom for a girl's family to give a dowry to a man who marries the girl to make it worth his while. As a result, many poor families in India kill a newborn baby if it is female and rejoice if the baby is male. When my third sister was born, my great grandmother expressed her disappointment that we had no boys and so many girls.

Bonita

You asked us to think about whether we ever got the message that males are more valued than females. I know I did. I guess I got it in a lot of ways, but one really stands out. I remember when I was 9, my mother was pregnant for the third time. When she went into labor, Daddy took her to the hospital with me and my sister. We all sat in the waiting room while they took Mom down the hall. Later the doctor came in and went to my father. I still remember his exact words. He said, "I'm sorry, Mr. Chavis, it's another girl. Guess you'll have to try again."

terms of gender stereotypes (Rubin, Provenzano, & Luria, 1974). Although male and female babies were matched for size, weight, and level of activity, parents described boys with words like *strong, hardy, big, active,* and *alert.* Parents of equally large, active girls described their daughters with adjectives like *small, dainty, quiet,* and *delicate.* More recent experiments show the persistence of parental gender-stereotypes (Delk, Madden, Livingston, & Ryan, 1986; Stern & Karraker, 1989).

Parents tend to communicate different expectations about achievement to sons and daughters. Middle-class Caucasian mothers in the United States emphasize and encourage achievement more when talking to sons than to daughters (Flanagon, Baker-Ward, & Graham, 1995). Yet Asian and Asian American families tend to encourage high achievement in children of both sexes (Woo, 2001). African American families, particularly those that are working class, tend to encourage greater educational achievement in daughters than in sons (Beal, 1994). Chicano/a families may actively discourage educational achievement in daughters to the point of regarding daughters who attend college as *Chicana falsa*—false Chicanas (Leland & Chambers, 1999).

Parents also convey different messages about assertiveness and aggressiveness to sons and daughters. As children, boys and girls don't differ a great deal with respect to feelings of anger or aggression. Because of gender socialization, however, they learn different ways of expressing those feelings (Butaine & Costenbader, 1997; Deffenbacher & Swaim, 1999; Kivel, 1999). Research shows that parents positively reward verbal and physical aggression in sons and positively reward interpersonal and social skills in daughters (Davis, 1995; Fagot, Hagan, Leinbach, & Kronsberg, 1985; Leaper, Anderson, & Sanders, 1998; Mills, Nazar, & Farrell, 2002). Parents, especially fathers, encourage in children what they perceive to be gender-appropriate behaviors, encouraging sons to be independent and aggressive and daughters to be emotional and gentle (Bryant & Check, 2000; Fivush, Brotman, Buckner, & Goodman, 2000).

In addition to responses to children's behaviors, parents communicate gender expectations through the toys and clothes they give children and the chores they assign to them. A group of researchers surveyed the rooms of 120 boys and girls who were under 2 years old (Pomerleau et al., 1990). They found that girls' rooms had dolls and children's furniture, and the color pink was prominent. Boys' rooms most often were decorated in the colors blue, red, and white, and in them were various vehicles, tools, and sports gear. Although boys and girls themselves show little difference in toy preference during the preschool years, they are often taught to develop gendered preferences. Thus, by age 5 most boys prefer action toys, and most girls prefer dolls (Pereira, 1994).

Many parents actively discourage their children's interest in toys and games that are associated with the other sex (Antill, 1987; Lytton & Romney, 1991). For instance, boys may be persuaded not to play house or cook, and girls may be dissuaded from engaging in vigorous, competitive games. Different types of toys and activities promote distinct kinds of thinking and interaction. More "feminine" toys, such as dolls, encourage quiet, nurturing interaction with another, physical closeness, and verbal communication. More typically "masculine" toys, such as sports equipment and train sets, promote independent or competitive activities that require little verbal interaction. Parents who limit their children's toys to those considered appropriate for one gender limit their children's development of varied ways of thinking and interacting.

Another way parents communicate gender expectations is through the household chores they assign to sons and daughters. As you might expect, domestic duties such as cleaning and cooking are most often designated for girls, and more active chores such as outdoor work, painting, and simple repairs are assigned to boys (Burns & Homel, 1989; Goodnow, 1988; McHale, Bartko, Crouter, & Perry-Jenkins, 1990). There are several implications of delegating different responsibilities to girls and boys. First, like toys, various tasks cultivate particular types of thinking and activity. Domestic chores emphasize taking care of others and taking responsibility for them (cleaning their clothes, cooking for them, and so on), whereas outdoor work and repair jobs encourage independent activity. Domestic chores also tend to occur in small, interior spaces, whereas outside chores are frequently done in open spaces.

In general, boys are more rigidly gender socialized than girls, particularly in Caucasian families (Bardewell, Cochran, & Walker, 1986; Beal, 1994; DeFrancisco & Chatham-Carpenter, 2000; Hale-Benson, 1986). It's much more acceptable for girls to be tomboys than for boys to play house or cuddle dolls. Similarly, it's considered more suitable for girls to be strong than for boys to cry, for girls to act independently than for boys to need others, and for girls to touch and show tenderness toward other girls than for boys to demonstrate closeness to male peers. When it comes to toys, fathers are more insistent on gender-stereotyped toys and activities, especially for sons, than are mothers (Caldera, Huston, & O'Brien, 1989; Fagot & Leinbach, 1987; Lamb, 1986). Overall, boys are more intensively and rigidly pushed to become masculine than girls are to become feminine.

■ Parental Modeling

Another way parents communicate gender is through modeling masculinity, femininity, male–female relationships. For most children, parents are the single most visible, constantly present models of men and women.

As you will recall from Chapter 2, cognitive development theory tells us that, once children have gender constancy, they actively look for role models of their sex and use those models to develop masculine or feminine qualities, behaviors, and so forth. By observing parents, children of heterosexuals gain understanding of the roles socially prescribed for females and males. In heterosexual families that adhere to traditional sex roles, children of both sexes are likely to learn that women are supposed to nurture others, clean, cook, and show emotional sensitivity, and that men are supposed to earn money, make decisions, and be emotionally controlled. Not all families, however, adopt traditional sex roles. Single mothers provide children with a broad model of women's roles. The fact that a large number of African American families are headed by a single mother (Ingrassia, 1993) may explain why African American women, in general, are more self-reliant and assertive than European American women. In two-parent African American families, men are generally more involved with family, especially sons, and with extended kin than are White men (Gaines, 1995).

Parents also model attitudes about gender and physical appearance. Fathers who work out and engage in vigorous physical activities may impart the message that physical strength is masculine. Mothers who make disparaging remarks about their weight or about eating communicate that to be feminine is to be thin. Mothers powerfully influence daughters' body images and attitudes toward food (Davison & Birch, 2001). Nutritionist Debra Waterhouse says, "Our daughters hear us making comments like 'I hate my thighs' or 'I ate like a pig' . . . and that forms their definition of womanhood" ("The Wrong Weight," 1997, p. 7).

One particularly striking example of gender roles that children learn from parents involves mothers' and fathers' involvement in caring for children. Research consistently shows that, in two-parent heterosexual families, mothers invest considerably more time than fathers do in taking care of children (Brush, 1999; F. Deutsch, 2001; Goldstein, 2000). Even when both parents hold full-time jobs outside the home, fewer than one third of male partners do half the child care and homemaking chores (Steil, 2000). Race and economic class seem to interact with gender to influence men's involvement in child care. In general, African American marriages are more egalitarian than Caucasian marriages; both partners have power and both do the work of keeping the home and raising children (McAdoo, 1997). Blue-collar men are more likely than white-collar men to think taking care of the home and children is "woman's work" (Alvesson & Billing, 1997; Deutsch & Saxon, 1998). Middle-class and highly educated men are most likely to be full participants in parenting (Dienhart, 1998; Strauss & Goldberg, 1999).

Even when mothers and fathers actively parent, they tend to engage in different kinds of child care. Mothers do the constant, day-in, day-out activities of feeding, bathing, dressing, supervising, and so forth. Fathers more typically engage in occasional activities and those that are more enjoyable for both children and parents, such as playing games or taking weekly trips to the bagel shop or zoo (Burns & Homel, 1989; Hochschild, 1989). Given

David

We used to wait for Dad to come home, because he'd always spend a half hour or so before dinner playing with us—tossing a ball or working with the trains or whatever. Mom never did that. Now I can see that she was really doing more for us all of the time—fixing our meals, buying us clothes, taking care of our doctor's appointments, and just generally being there for us. Maybe Dad was more special to us because he was around less than Mom. Anyway, he was the one we looked forward to playing with.

this, it's not surprising that many children regard fathers as the preferred play-mates (Thompson & Walker, 1989).

The Different Contributions of Mothers and Fathers

Although both parents play important roles in children's gender development, mothers' and fathers' contributions tend to be different and complementary. Fathers generally help children, especially sons, develop a sense of personal agency —independence, initiative, and achievement. Mothers are more likely to foster competence in relating to others—making connections with others and feeling emotionally secure.

In general, mothers emphasize relationships in their interactions with children. Mothers typically focus on providing comfort, security, and emotional develop-

Fathering: Past, Present, and Future

Throughout most of human history, women and men have lived and worked together with both sexes sharing the responsibilities of providing and caring for families. The Industrial Revolution drew men away from their families and led to a division between public and private spheres of life.

In our time, fatherhood is once again being recognized as a major part of men's lives and as an important relationship for both fathers and children. Typically, father–child interaction has focused on discipline and play, whereas mothers have tended to engage more in caregiving activities with children (Snarey, 1994; Yogman, Cooley, & Kindlon, 1988). Yet, play and discipline are not the only—or necessarily the most important—aspects of father–child relationships. Research (Palm, 1993; Secunda, 1992) indicates that men who are actively involved with their children foster social and emotional development in their sons and daughters. Also, active fathering cultivates personal growth in men (Palm, 1993; Smith, 1995), giving them opportunities to expand their patience, compassion, and nurturing abilities (Greif, 1990; Hanson, 1988).

In a 1996 Princeton survey, men reported increasing commitment to fathering. More than half of the fathers surveyed said that being a parent is more important to them than it was to their fathers. Fully 70% of fathers surveyed said they spend more time with their children than their fathers spent with them (Adler, 1996). Further, in 1999 there were 2.1 million single dads in the United States (Wellington, 1999). Many of these single dads report that parenting is their most important role. Yet they also note that society doesn't always respect men who place parenting ahead of career advancement (Jackson, 1999; Milbank, 1997).

To learn more about groups that support active fathering, visit this Web site:

 American Federation for Fathers: **http://www.acfc.org.**

ment. They engage in more eye contact and face-to-face interaction with children than do fathers. Further, mothers tend to repeat infant daughters' vocalizations more than those of infant sons (Trudeau, 1996), perhaps because of the bond of likeness mothers feel with daughters. More than fathers, mothers tend to play with children at the children's level, which develops children's confidence and security in play.

Fathers typically focus more on playing with than taking care of children (Popenoe, 1996). They tend to engage in play that is physically stimulating and exciting, and they encourage children to develop skills and meet challenges. Fathers, more than mothers, stretch children by urging them to compete, achieve, take risks and move beyond their current level of ability (Stacey, 1996).

Whereas girls generally use both parents as models, boys tend to rely almost exclusively on their fathers or other males (Basow, 1992; Kivel, 1999). Further, the extent to which fathers themselves hold strong gender stereotypes affects the attitudes about gender that children develop. Children of fathers with traditional gender beliefs tend to be conservative and hold rigid gender stereotypes themselves. They also seem to have narrower views of what males and females can do (Fagot & Leinbach, 1989). African American fathers, like European American ones, tend to interact more with their sons than with their daughters (Hyde & Texidor, 1994).

In summary, parents play a major role in shaping children's understandings of gender in general and their own gender in particular. The gender socialization begun in the family is sustained and reinforced by other cultural influences such as media, which we will discuss in later chapters.

THE PERSONAL SIDE OF THE GENDER DRAMA

What does it mean to us as individuals to grow up masculine or feminine in present-day America? To answer this question, we'll translate the research we've considered into personal portraits of becoming gendered in our society.

Growing Up Masculine

What does it mean to be masculine in the United States in the 21st century? To understand the advantages, challenges, and issues of masculinity, let's consider what six college men say. In their commentaries, Pete, Charles, Roger, Ben, Derek, and Brad focus as much on the pressures, expectations, and constraints of manhood as its prerogatives and privileges. In his book *The Male Experience*, James A. Doyle (1997) identifies five themes

Pete

To me, being a man means that I have to be ready to not only get in the rat race, but to win it. I feel a lot of pressure to be really successful, to beat others at whatever I do. If I'm just average at my career, I'll pretty much see myself as a failure.

Charles

Being an African American man means my woman expects me to provide for her and our kids later, but that society thinks I'll run out on them, since everyone thinks Black men desert their families. It means when I walk on campus at night, White women cross the street or hook up with some White guy—whether they know him or not—because they think I'm going to rape them. It means I'm supposed to be tough—all the time. I can get away with being tough and pushing my weight around—women can't do that—but I can't get away with being sensitive or giving in to others. It means I get a better job than my wife, but it means I am supposed to, and I can never not think about providing like she can. It's a mixed bag, which you don't hear a lot about.

Roger

I always assumed I would be the main or only breadwinner for my family, but I'm not so sure I can pull that off today. The economy is really bad. I've had 12 interviews so far and I haven't gotten a single job offer. The idea of supporting my family is really important to my identity. Who am I if I can't earn a good salary?

Ben

What it means to be a man depends totally on whether you're gay or straight. I'm gay—knew that since I was 9 or 10. And being gay is hell for a teenager. Other guys, the straight ones, called me names all through middle school and high school—fag, queer, girlie. It didn't matter that I was big and toned and good at baseball. They totally excluded me because I was gay.

of masculinity, which are woven throughout the commentaries of these six men. We will consider each of these elements of the male role, as well as a sixth that seems to have emerged since Doyle made his analysis.

Don't be female seems to be the most fundamental requirement for manhood. Early in life, most boys learn they must not think, act, or feel like girls and women. Any male who shows sensitivity or vulnerability is likely to be called sissy, crybaby, mama's boy, or wimp (Kantrowitz & Kalb, 1998; Pollack, 2000). The antifemale directive is at least as strong for African American men as for European American men. Like Ben, many gay males discover that straight men consider them unmanly.

The second element of the male role is the command to *be successful*. Men are expected to achieve status in their professions, to "make it." Warren Farrell (1991) writes that men are regarded as "success objects," and their worth as marriage partners, friends, and men is judged by how successful they are at what they do. Training begins early with sports, where winning is stressed (Messner, 2000). Peer groups pressure males to be tough, aggressive, and not feminine (Lobel & Bar, 1997; Ponton, 1997).

As Pete notes in his commentary, the theme of success translates not just into being good at what you do but into being better than others, more powerful than peers, pulling in a bigger salary than your neighbors, and having a more expensive home, car, and so on than your friends. Most men today, like Pete and Roger, think that being a good provider is the primary requirement for manhood —an internalized requirement that appears to cut across lines of race and economic class (Eagly, 1996; Ranson, 2001).

A third injunction for masculinity is to *be aggressive*. Even in childhood, boys are often encouraged to be roughnecks or at least are seldom scolded for being so (Cohen, 1997). They are expected to take stands and not run from confrontations (Nelson, 1994b; Newburger, 1999; Pollack, 2000). Later, sports reinforce early training by emphasizing aggression, violence, and toughness (Messner, 2000). Coaches psych teams up with demands that they "make the other team hurt, hurt, hurt" or "make them bleed." The masculine code tells men to fight, inflict pain on others, endure pain stoically themselves, and win, win, win. Dr. Michael Miller (2003) says that many men don't seek help when they are depressed because their gender identity is "tied up with strength, independence, efficiency, and self-control" (p. 71).

Men's training in aggression may be linked to violence (Gordon, 1988; Kivel, 1999; Messner, 1997a,b), especially violence against women. Because masculine socialization encourages aggression and dominance, some men think they are entitled to dominate women. This belief surfaces in studies of men who rape (Costin & Schwartz, 1987; Scott & Tetreault, 1987) and men who abuse girlfriends and wives (Gelles & Straus, 1988; Wood, 2001b, In press). One study (Thompson, 1991) reports that both college women and men who are violent toward their dates have masculine gender orientations, reminding us again that *gender* and *sex* are not equivalent terms.

A fourth element of the male role is captured in the injunction to *be sexual*. Men should be interested in sex—all the time, anytime. They are expected to have a number of sexual partners; the more partners a man has, the more of a stud he is (Gaylin, 1992; Martin & Hummer, 1989). During rush, a fraternity recently sent out invitations with the notation "B.Y.O.A.", which one of my students translated for me: Bring your own ass. Defining sexual conquest as a cornerstone of masculinity encourages men to view and treat women as sex objects rather than as multidimensional human beings (Brownmiller, 1993; French, 1992; Russell, 1993).

Finally, Doyle says the male sex role demands that men *be self-reliant*. A "real man" doesn't need others, particularly women. He depends on himself, takes care of himself, and relies on nobody. Autonomy is central to social views of manliness. As we noted earlier, male self-development typically begins with differentiation from others, and from infancy most boys are taught to be self-reliant and self-contained (Newburger, 1999; Thompson & Pleck, 1987). Men are expected to be emotionally controlled, not to let feelings control them, and not to need others.

In addition to the five themes of masculinity identified by Doyle, a sixth seems to have emerged. This theme highlights the mixed messages about being men that

Brad

I didn't learn that I had to be a good breadwinner to be a good man. My father was the main breadwinner for our family until I was 10. Then he got laid off his job and he couldn't find another one. Mom moved from part-time to full-time work and became the sole breadwinner for our family, and Dad stayed home with me and my two younger sisters for eight years. From watching my parents, I learned that either person can be the breadwinner and that either can take care of a home and children.

Derek

It's really frustrating to be a man today. My girlfriend wants me to open up and show my feelings and talk about them and stuff like that. But the guys on the team get on my case whenever I show any feelings other than about winning a game. I'm supposed to be sensitive and not. I'm supposed to keep my feelings to myself and not. I'm supposed to open doors for girls and pay for dates but then respect them as equals. A lot of times it feels like a no-win situation.

confront many boys and men today: *Embody and transcend traditional views of masculinity.* In his commentary, Derek expresses his frustration with the paradoxical expectations both to be a "real man" in traditional ways and simultaneously to defy traditional views of men by being sensitive and egalitarian (Kindlon & Thompson, 1999).

For many men today, the primary source of pressure to be conventionally masculine is other men who enforce what psychologist William Pollack (2000) calls the "boy code." Boys and, later, men encourage each other to be silent, tough, and independent and to take risks. Boys and men who don't measure up often face peer shaming ("You're a wuss," "Do you do everything she tells you to do?"). At the same time, many men feel other pressures—often from romantic partners, female friends, and mothers—to be more sensitive and emotionally open and to be a full partner in running a home and raising children. It's hard to be both traditionally male and not traditionally male. Just as women in the 1960s and 1970s were confronted with mixed messages about being traditionally female and not, men today are negotiating new terrain and new ways of defining themselves.

What happens when men don't measure up to the social expectations of manhood? Some counselors believe men's striving to live up to social ideals of masculinity has produced an epidemic of hidden male depression (Kahn, 1997). Terrence Real is a psychotherapist who specializes in treating depressed men. According to Real (1997), male depression is widespread, and so is society's unwillingness to acknowledge it, because it is inconsistent with social views of masculinity. Whereas depressed women suffer the social stigma of having emotional problems, Real says men who admit they are depressed suffer the double stigma of having emotional problems and being unmanly by society's standards.

The first five themes of masculinity clearly reflect gender socialization in early life and lay out a blueprint for what being a man means. Yet we also see a sixth theme that points out and challenges the contradictions in traditional and emerging views of masculinity. Individual men have options for defining and embodying masculinity, and many men are crafting nontraditional identities for themselves. In later chapters, we'll discover examples of ways to revise masculine identity.

Growing Up Feminine

What does it mean to be feminine in the United States in the 21st century? Casual talk and media offer us two quite different versions of modern women. One suggests that women now have it all. They can get jobs that were formerly closed to them and rise to the top levels of their professions; they can have egalitarian marriages with liberated men and raise nonsexist children. At the same time, our culture sends us the quite different message that women may be able to get jobs, but fewer than 20% will actually be given opportunities to advance to the highest levels of professional life. Crime statistics warn us that the incidence of rape is rising, as is battering of women. We discover that married women may have careers, but more than 80% of them still do most of the housework and child care. And media relentlessly carry the message that youth and beauty are women's tickets to success. Prevailing images of women are conflicting and confusing, as the commentaries by Christina, Jeanne, Bernadette, Sharon, and Jana demonstrate. We can identify five themes in current views of femininity and womanhood.

The first theme is that *appearance still counts.* As Christina states, women are still judged by their looks (Greenfield, 2002; Haag, 2000). To be desirable, they are urged to be pretty, slim, and well dressed. The focus on appearance begins in the early years of life, when girls are given dolls and clothes, both of which invite them to attend to appearance. Gift catalogues for children regularly feature makeup kits, adornments for hair, and even wigs so that girls learn early to spend time and effort on looking good. Dolls, like the ever-popular Barbie, come with accessories such as extensive wardrobes so that girls learn that clothes and jewelry are important. Teen magazines for girls are saturated with ads for makeup, diet aids, and hair products. Central to current cultural expectations for women is thinness, which can lead to harmful and sometimes fatal eating disorders (Davies-Popelka, 2000; Pike & Striegel-Moore, 1997). Jeanne's comments show powerfully how tyrannical this expectation can be.

The ideals of feminine appearance are communicated to women when they enter retail stores. Most manikins in stores are size 2, 4, or 6, which does not reflect the size of most normal, real-life women. Social prescriptions for feminine beauty are also made clear by the saleswomen, who are often hired because of their looks, not their experience or skills. Stores that market to young women like to hire people who are young, sexy, and good-looking. According to Antonio Serrano, a former assistant store manager for Abercrombie and Fitch, he and other employees were told by upper management "to approach someone in the mall who we think will look attractive in our store. But if someone came in who had lots of retail experience and not a pretty face, we were told not to hire them at all" (Greenhouse, 2003, p. 10 YT). Elysa Yanowitz, who was a regional sales manager for L'Oreal stores, says she was pressured to hire physically attractive saleswomen and once told to fire a

Christina

I think being a woman means that no matter what else I am or do, I'm not okay if I don't look good. I have to get up an hour earlier than my boyfriend to fix my hair and makeup and dress nice. He rolls out of bed, throws on whatever, and he's ready to go. Girls who do that get really slammed. Sometimes I really wonder what it would feel like to have others judge me for what I am and what I do, not how I look.

Jeanne

Hungry. That's what being a woman means to me. I am hungry all of the time. Either I'm dieting, or I'm throwing up because I ate too much. I am scared to death of being fat, and I'm just not made to be thin. I gain weight just by smelling food. I think about food all the time—wanting it but being afraid to eat, eating but feeling guilty. It's a no-win situation. I'm obsessed, and I know it, but I can't help it. How can I not think about my weight all the time, when every magazine, every movie, every television show I see screams at me that I have to be thin to be desirable?

top-performing employee who was "not hot enough" (Greenhouse, 2003, p. 10 YT). The Equal Employment Opportunity Commission has brought suit against a number of companies for discriminating against people who do not meet the current ideals for attractiveness.

At Abercromie and Fitch, The Gap, and throughout the culture in general, cultural ideals of feminine beauty continue to reflect primarily White standards (Lont, 2001). Women of color may be unable to meet White standards of beauty on the one hand and, on the other, to reject the standards that the culture as a whole prescribes (Garrod, Ward, Robinson, & Kilkenny, 1999; Haag, 2000). In a critique of Blacks' acceptance of White standards of beauty, bell hooks (1994, 1995) describes the color caste system among Blacks whereby lighter skin is considered more desirable. She also points out that some Black children learn early to devalue dark skin, and many Black men regard biracial women as the ideal. In a society as ethnically diverse as ours, we need to question and challenge standards that reflect and respect only the identities of some groups.

A second cultural expectation of women is to *be sensitive and caring.* Women feel pressure to be nice, deferential, and helpful in general, whereas men are not held to the same requirements (Hochschild, 1975, 1979, 1983; Tavris & Baumgartner, 1983). In addition, girls and women are supposed to care about and for others. It's part of their role as defined by the culture. From assuming primary responsibility for young children to taking care of elderly, sick, and disabled relatives, women do the preponderance of hands-on caring (Aronson, 1992; Cancian & Oliker, 2000; Ferguson, 2000). Caring for others is seen as a requirement for femininity.

At the opening of this chapter, I asked you what an ideal day would be like for you 10 years in the future. When psychologist Barbara Kerr (1997, 1999) asks this question of undergraduates in her classes, she reports a striking sex difference in responses. College men tend to describe their perfect day like this:

Is Adolescence a Danger Zone for Girls?

What is it that causes so many confident, happy 8- and 9-year-old girls to lose confidence and self-esteem between the ages of 11 and 14, when boys of the same ages don't experience these losses (Gilligan, Ward, Tayor, & Bardige, 1988; Lally, 1996)?

As girls enter puberty, society, peers, and sometimes family encourage them to focus on pleasing others. Girls are encouraged to lose weight, dress well, and use makeup so that others will find them attractive. They're taught to soften their opinions and to accommodate others, particularly males. One 15-year-old said that if she stood up to males at school and spoke her mind, they immediately called her a "bitch" (Haag, 2000). The bottom line is that, for many girls, adolescence means shifting attention from becoming personally competent to pleasing others. What's at stake is loss of self.

I wake up and get into my car—a really nice, rebuilt '67 Mustang—and then I go to work—I think I'm some kind of manager of a computer firm—and then I go home, and when I get there, my wife is there at the door (she has a really nice figure), she has a drink for me, and she's made a great meal. We watch TV or maybe play with the kids. (p. B7)

Contrast the men's perfect day with this typical description from college women:

I wake up, and my husband and I get in our twin Jettas, and I go to the law firm where I work. Then after work, I go home, and he's pulling up in the driveway at the same time. We go in and have a glass of nice wine, and we make an omelet together and eat by candlelight. Then the nanny brings the children in and we play with them until bedtime. (p. B7)

Note that the typical male scenario features wives who work but who also have drinks and a meal ready for husbands. Fewer and fewer college women see this as an ideal day—or life. Yet, women's fantasy of shared responsibilities for home and family are not likely to be met unless there are major changes in current patterns.

A third persistent theme of femininity is *negative treatment by others*. According to substantial research, this still more or less goes with the territory of being female. Supporting this theme are the differential values our culture attaches to masculinity and femininity. Devaluation of femininity is not only built into cultural views but typically is internalized by individuals, including women. Negative treatment of females begins early and can be especially intense in girls' peer groups (Chesler, 2001; Lamb, 2002; Simmons, 2002; Tavris, 2002). Girls can be highly critical of other girls who are not pretty, thin, and otherwise feminine. Another aspect of negative treatment of women is the violence inflicted on them. They are vulnerable to battering, rape, and other forms of abuse in ways men generally are not (Goldner et al., 1990; Wood, 2001b).

Be superwoman is a fourth theme emerging in cultural expectations of women. Jana's sense of exhilaration at "being able to have it all" is tempered by the realization that the idea that women *can* have it all appears to be transformed into the command that they *must* have it all. It's not enough to be just a homemaker and mother or to just have a career—young women seem to feel they are expected to do it all.

Women students talk with me frequently about the tension they feel in trying to figure out how to

Bernadette

I think expectations of women today are impossible. I read magazines for working women, since I plan to work in business when I graduate. They tell me how to be a good leader, how to make tough decisions and keep others motivated, how to budget my time and advance in an organization. Then in the same magazines there's an article on how to throw a great dinner party with a three-course meal plus appetizers and dessert. Am I supposed to do that after working from 8 to 6 every day? Somehow the husband's role in all of this never gets mentioned. It's all supposed to come together, but I don't see how. It seems to me that a career is a full-time responsibility and so is running a home, yet I get the feeling I'm supposed to do both and keep my cool all the time. I just don't see how.

Sharon

My mother and I talk about women, and she tells me that she's glad she didn't have so many options. She says it was easier for her than it is for me because she knew what she was supposed to do—marry and raise a family—and she didn't have to go through the identity crisis that I do. I see her point, yet I kind of like having alternatives. I know I wouldn't be happy investing my total self in a home and family. I just have to be out doing things in the world. But my best friend really wants to do that. She's marrying a guy who wants that too, so as soon as they've saved enough to be secure, they plan for her to quit work to raise a family. I know someone else who says she just flat out doesn't want to marry. She wants to be a doctor, and she doesn't think she can do that plus take care of a home and family, so she wants to stay single. I don't really know yet if I will or won't have kids, but it's nice to know I can choose to go either way. My mother couldn't.

Jana

I like being a woman today. It's the best time ever to be female, because we can have it all. When I finish my B.A., I plan to go to law school, and then I want to practice. I also want to have a family with two children. My mother couldn't have had the whole package, but I can. I love the freedom of being a woman in this time—there's nothing I can't do.

have a full family life and a successful career. They tell me that they want both careers and families and don't see how they can make it all work. The physical and psychological toll on women who try to do it all is well documented (Coltrane & Adams, 2001; Greenberg, 2001; Orenstein, 2000), and it is growing steadily as women find that changes in the workplace are not paralleled by changes in home life. Perhaps it would be wise to remember that superwoman, like Superman, is a comic-book character, not a viable model for real life. Instead of trying to have it all, some young women aim to have some of it all—some career, some family (Greenberg, 2001; Orenstein, 2000).

A final theme of femininity in the 1990s is one that reflects all the others and the contradictions inherent in them: *There is no single meaning of feminine anymore.* A woman who is assertive and ambitious in a career is likely to meet with approval, disapproval, and curiosity from some people and to be applauded by others. At the same time, a woman who chooses to stay home while her children are young will be criticized by some women and men, envied by others, and respected by still others. This underlines the excitement and possibilities open to women of this era to validate multiple versions of femininity. Perhaps, as Sharon suggests in her commentary, there are many ways to be feminine, and we can respect all of them.

Prevailing themes of femininity in North America reveal both constancy and change. Traditional expectations of attractiveness and caring for others persist, as does the greater likelihood of negative treatment by others. Yet today there are multiple ways to define femininity and womanhood, which may allow women with different talents, interests, and gender orientations to define themselves in diverse ways and to chart life courses that suit them as individuals.

■ Growing Up Outside Conventional Gender Roles

Not every male and female grows up identifying with the gender society prescribes for him or her. For people who do not identify with and embody the prescribed

gender role, growing up is particularly difficult. Gay men are often socially ostracized because they are perceived as feminine, while lesbians arc scorned for being masculine. Social isolation also greets many people who are (or are thought to be) transgendered, as Mike's commentary illustrates. Although statistics tell me that more than one of my students is transgendered, Mike is the only one who volunteered a commentary on what this means.

Many transsexuals and transgendered and intersexed people want "a society free from the constraints of nonconsensual gender" (Bornstein, 1994, p. 111). In other words, they want the freedom to choose the gender and sex that suits them personally and have society accept them as the people they choose to be. Instead, in the United States they find themselves trapped in a society that rigidly pairs males with masculinity and females with femininity. There are no in-between spaces; there is no room for blurring those rigid lines. For people who do not fit the conventional sex and gender roles, it is hard to find role models and equally difficult to find acceptance from family, peers, and society (Berlant & Warner, 1998; Fausto-Sterling, 2000; Feinberg, 1996; Glenn, 2002).

> **Mike**
>
> I have no idea what it means to be a man. I've never felt I was one, never identified with men. As a kid I liked to dress in my mother's clothes until my dad caught me and beat the —— out of me! I still identify more with women, and I think that I was meant to be a woman. Growing up looking like a male but feeling like a female meant that I didn't belong anywhere, didn't fit with anyone. It's better now that I'm in college and have found some people like me, but there was nobody in my rural southern hometown!

SUMMARY

Communication plays a primary role in shaping gender identity. Through interaction with others, we come to understand how society defines masculinity and femininity. Communication encourages gendered identities by transforming us from biological males and females into gendered individuals.

But we need to remember that socialization is not as deterministic as it may seem. Clearly, we are influenced by the expectations of our culture, yet these expectations endure only to the extent that individuals and institutions sustain them. Through our own communication and the ways that we act, we reinforce or challenge existing views of gender. As we do so, we contribute to forming social views that affect the extent to which each of us can define ourselves and live our lives as we choose.

KEY TERMS

ego boundary, 152
monitoring, 149
self-as-object, 149

DISCUSSION QUESTIONS

1. Use InfoTrac's College Edition's EasyTrac option. Type in "Single fathers," then access the 2001 *Time* article, "Father makes two: Unmarried men who raise children are one of the fastest-growing groups in America." How are the challenges of being a single father different from and similar to those of being a single mother?

2. How permeable are your ego boundaries? How do permeable ego boundaries enrich life and relationships? How might they constrain and limit someone? What are the advantages of firm ego boundaries? How might they restrict a person?

3. What kinds of chores did you have, growing up in your family? Were they consistent with social definitions of your gender? Did you help with outside work or activities inside the home? Did you ever resent what you were told to do and what you were told was not your job?

4. How did your parents model masculinity and femininity? Explain how parents (mother, stepmother, father, stepfather) represent what it means to be feminine and masculine. Does your own embodiment of gender reflect their influences?

5. To what extent do the themes of masculinity and femininity discussed in this chapter apply to you and your generation?

8

Gendered Close Relationships

The doors we open and close each day decide the lives we live.

—FLORA WHITTENMORE

erhaps you have found yourself in situations such as those Paige and Mark describe here. For Mark, as for most people socialized into masculinity, the purpose of talking is to address an issue or solve a problem. For Paige, it's incomprehensible that Ed can work on his paper when there is a problem between them. She doesn't realize that working on the paper is Ed's way of coping with his distress about their argument. If Paige and Mark do not figure out that their gendered viewpoints are creating misunderstandings, they will continue to experience frustration in their relationships.

In this chapter we will focus on gender dynamics in close relationships. To begin our discussion, we will consider masculine and feminine ways of experiencing and expressing closeness. Then we'll explore gendered dynamics in friendships and romantic relationships. As we discuss masculine and feminine communication styles, we want not only to understand each one but also to appreciate each on its own terms.

Paige

Honestly, I almost left my boyfriend when we had our first fight after moving in together. It was really a big one about how to be committed to our relationship and also do all the other stuff that we have to do. It was major. And after we'd yelled for a while, there seemed to be nothing else to do—we were just at a stalemate in terms of conflict between what each of us wanted. So Ed walked away, and I sat fuming in the living room. When I finally left the living room, I found him working away on a paper for one of his courses, and I was furious. I couldn't understand how he could concentrate on work when we were so messed up. How in the world could he just put us aside and get on with his work? I felt like it was a really clear message that he wasn't very committed.

Sometimes I just don't know what goes on in Ellen's head. We can have a minor problem—like an issue between us, and it's really not serious stuff. But can we let it go? No way with Ellen. She wants "to talk about it." And I mean talk and talk and talk and talk. There's no end to how long she can talk about stuff that really doesn't matter. I tell her that she's analyzing the relationship to death and I don't want to do that. She insists that we need "to talk things through." Why can't we just have a relationship, instead of always having to talk about it?

THE MEANING OF PERSONAL RELATIONSHIPS

Of the many relationships we form, only a few become really personal. These are the ones that occupy a special place in our lives and affect us deeply. **Personal relationships** are those in which partners depend on each other for various things from affection to material assistance and see each other as irreplaceable. In personal relationships, partners are interdependent. They expect affection, companionship, time, energy, and assistance with the large and small issues in life. Also, partners in personal relationships regard each other as unique individuals. If a casual friend moves or dies, a replacement may be found; if a business associate goes to another company, we can find a new work colleague. When a personal partner leaves or dies, however, the relationship ends, although we may continue to feel connected to the person who is no longer with us. Not all long-term relationships are personal. For instance, you might work with someone or talk to a neighbor for many years without ever feeling that the person is irreplaceable.

■ Gendered Patterns in Personal Relationships

Differences in masculine and feminine orientations to close relationships generally —but not universally—coincide with male and female approaches to relationships. Yet researchers disagree about what the differences mean. Some scholars argue that masculine orientations are inferior to feminine ones, while others think the two styles are different yet equally valid. We'll consider each of these viewpoints.

The male deficit model. Because our society views women as interpersonally sensitive, it is widely assumed that their ways of forming relationships and interacting with others are "the right ways." Sharing the cultural assumption that women are better than men at relating to others, a number of researchers claim that men's style of building and maintaining relationships is inadequate. This view, the **male deficit model,** maintains that men are less skilled in developing and sustaining personal relationships.

The central assumption of the male deficit model is that personal, emotional talk is the hallmark of intimacy. With this assumption in mind, researchers began to study how women and men interact in close relationships. A classic investigation (Caldwell & Peplau, 1982) measured the intimacy of men's and women's same-sex friendships by the amount of intimate information disclosed—a type of communication generally used more by women than by men. Given this measure of intimacy, it is not surprising that the researchers concluded that women were more intimate than men. Findings such as this led to judgments that men's ways of relating are inadequate. Some researchers called men's inexpressiveness "a tragedy of our society" (Balswick & Peek, 1976). These researchers advised men to overcome masculine socialization by getting in touch with their feelings and learning to communicate openly and expressively.

The tendency to privilege women's ways of relating and disparage men's was strengthened by one of the men's movements we discussed in Chapter 4. Male feminists thought that men were emotionally repressed and would be enriched by becoming more aware and expressive of their feelings, and many men worked on developing and expressing emotions more openly in their relationships. In the 1980s the male deficit model prevailed. Researchers claimed that men "feel threatened by intimacy" (Mazur & Olver, 1987, p. 533); that men are "lacking in mutual self-disclosure, shared feelings and other demonstrations of emotional closeness" (Williams, 1985, p. 588); that men suffer from "stunted emotional development" (Balswick, 1988); and that men do not know how to experience or communicate feelings (Aukett, Ritchie, & Mill, 1988).

Much academic and popular sentiment still holds that men are unskilled in expressing emotions and caring. A number of books written in the late 1990s and early part of this century state that personal disclosures are the crux of intimacy, that women have more intimate relationships than men, that boys' friendships lack the emotional depth of girls' friendships, and that males focus on activities to avoid intimacy (Burleson, 1997; Oliker, 2001). The assumption underlying the male deficit model is that emotional expressiveness and personal disclosures are the best ways to create closeness. Gradually, however, a few researchers began to question this assumption, leading to a second interpretation of differences between how men and women, in general, create and experience closeness.

The alternate paths model. The **alternate paths model** agrees with the male deficit model that gendered socialization is the root of differences between women's and men's typical styles of relating. It departs from the deficit model, however, in two important ways. First, the alternate paths model does not presume that men lack feelings or that emotional depth is unimportant in men's lives. Rather, the alternate paths explanation suggests that masculine socialization constrains men's comfort in verbally expressing some feelings and, further, that it limits men's opportunities to practice

Edwin

I don't have any problem being emotionally sensitive or expressing my feelings. I may not go on forever about my feelings, but I know what they are, and I can express them fine. It's just that the way I express my feelings is different from the way most girls I know express their feelings. I'm not dramatic or sentimental or gushy, but I have ways of showing how I feel.

emotional talk. Second, the alternate paths model argues that men *do* express closeness in ways that they value and understand—ways that may differ from women's but are equally valid.

Françoise Cancian (1987, 1989) claims that the ways in which we have learned to think about intimacy are heavily gendered. In Western culture, she suggests, we use a "feminine ruler" to define and measure closeness. She argues that using a specifically feminine ruler (emotional talk) misrepresents masculine modes of caring in the same way that using male standards to measure women's speech misrepresents women's communication. Cancian (1987) states that "there is a distinctive masculine style of love, . . . but it is usually ignored by scholars and the general public" (p. 78).

Influenced by this viewpoint, Scott Swain (1989) studied men's perceptions of their close friendships. He discovered that men develop a closeness "in the doing" —a connection that grows out of doing things together. For men, Swain concluded, engaging in activities is not an avoidance of intimacy but an alternate path to intimacy. Following Swain's lead, other scholars reported that men's friendships are as intimate as women's, but closeness between men generally doesn't primarily grow out of emotional talk and self-disclosure (Clark, 1998; Paul & White, 1990; Sherrod, 1989). For many men, like Paige's boyfriend, talking about problems may be less effective than diversionary activities to relieve stress (Riessman, 1990; Tavris, 1992).

Recent research provides further insight into gendered communication in close relationships. In a study of how men and women communicate support, Daena Goldsmith and Susan Dun (1997) found that women tend to engage in both emotional and instrumental forms of communication. Similarly, Françoise Cancian and Stacey Oliker (2000) found that women friends enjoy doing things together and helping each other out. In general, most men engage in less explicit emotional communication, yet most men do experience and express emotions in a range of ways (Chapman & Hendler, 1999).

The sex of the person needing support may be as important as the sex of the person offering support. Communication scholars Jerold Hale, Rachael Tighe, and Paul Mongeau (1997) report that women typically engage in more sensitive comforting messages than men do. However, both sexes are more overtly sensitive and feeling when trying to comfort women than when trying to comfort men. Further, men offer more sensitive comforting communication in response to major stresses, whereas women tend to provide sensitive comfort for both major stresses and daily events.

From this research we may conclude that males less often express their feelings in feminine ways, just as women less frequently express theirs in masculine ways. This suggests some men may find that intimate talk doesn't make them feel close, just as some women find instrumental demonstrations of commitment unsatisfying. If so, then becoming "bilingual" is a necessity for healthy relationships. As we explore women's and men's communication in friendships and romantic commitments, remember that there may be different but equally valuable ways of creating and expressing closeness. The goal is to understand and learn from each orientation.

GENDERED STYLES OF FRIENDSHIP

Let's begin by noting that there are many similarities between women's and men's friendships. Both sexes value close friends and invest in them (Reis, 1998). Also, both sexes engage in instrumental and expressive modes of building and expressing closeness, although they vary in the degree to which they use each (Berscheid, Snyder, & Omoto, 1989; Duck & Wright, 1993; Jones, 1991; Umberson, Chen, House, Hopkins, & Slaten, 1996). Against the backdrop of commonalities in the genders' approaches to friendship, there are some differences in how women and men typically—but not invariably—build friendships and interact within them.

As early as 1982, Paul Wright pointed to interaction style as a key difference between women's and men's friendships. He noted that women tend to engage each other face to face, whereas men usually interact side by side. By this, Wright meant that women are more likely than men to communicate directly and verbally with each other to share themselves and their feelings. Men more typically engage in activities with friends. Wright suggested that the crux of friendship differs between the sexes: For men, it tends to be doing things together; for women, being and talking together is the essence. Wright's research gives us a foundation for exploring the qualities of friendship between women, between men, and between men and women.

■ Women's Friendships: Closeness in Dialogue

Across races and ethnicities, women use talk to build and enrich friendships (Veniegas & Peplau, 1997; Winbush, 2000; Yildirim, 1997). They share their personal feelings, experiences, fears, and problems in order to know and be known by each other. In addition, women talk about their daily lives and activities. By sharing details of lives, women feel intimately connected to one another. To capture the quality of women's friendships, Caroline Becker (1987) describes them as "an evolving dialogue" through which initially separate worlds are woven together into a common one. The common world of women friends grows out of ongoing communication that is the crux of closeness between women.

Women friends want to know each other in depth. To achieve this, they talk about personal feelings and disclose intimate information (Buhrke & Fuqua, 1987; Johnson, 1996; Oliker, 1989; Reisman, 1990; Walker, 2004). They are each other's confidantes, sharing personal vulnerabilities and inner feelings. Consistent with gender socialization, communication between women friends also tends to be expressive and supportive (Maccoby, 1998; Wright & Scanlon, 1991). The more

Janice

One of the worst things about being female is not having permission to be selfish or jealous or *not* to care about a friend. Usually, I'm pretty nice; I feel good for my friends when good things happen to them, and I want to support them when things aren't going well. But sometimes I don't feel that way. Like right now, all my friends and I are interviewing for jobs, and my best friend just got a great offer. I've had 23 interviews and no job offers so far. I felt good for Sally, but I also felt jealous. I couldn't talk about this with her, because I'm not supposed to feel jealous or to be selfish like this. It's just not allowed, so my friends and I have to hide those feelings.

permeable ego boundaries encouraged by feminine socialization cultivate abilities to empathize and feel emotionally connected.

Because women are socialized to be attentive, emotionally supportive, and caring, certain problems may arise in their friendships. It is difficult for many women to deal with feelings of envy and competition toward friends. It is not that women don't experience envy and competitiveness but rather that they think it's wrong to have such feelings, because they aren't consistent with cultural prescriptions for femininity. Many women also find it difficult to override socialization's message that they are supposed to be constantly available and caring. Thus, when women lack the time or energy required to nurture others, they may feel guilty (Eichenbaum & Orbach, 1983; Miller, 1986). The responsiveness and caring typical of women's friendships both enrich and constrain people socialized into feminine rules of relating.

Another quality of communication between women friends is explicit talk about their relationship. The friendship itself and the dynamics between women are matters of interest and discussion (Winstead, 1986). It is not unusual for women to state affection explicitly or to discuss tensions within a friendship. The ability to recognize and talk about problems allows women to monitor and improve their friendships.

A final quality typical of women's friendships is breadth. With close friends, women tend not to restrict their disclosures to specific areas but invite each other into many aspects of their lives. Because women talk in detail about varied aspects of their lives, women friends often know each other in complex and layered ways (Buhrke & Fuqua, 1987; Wright & Scanlon, 1991).

In summary, women's friendships tend to develop out of the central role accorded to communication, which fosters disclosure, expressiveness, depth and breadth of knowledge, and attentiveness to the evolving nature of the relationship. Many women feel deeply connected to friends even when they are not physically together.

■ Men's Friendships: Closeness in the Doing

Like women, men value friendships and count on friends to be there for them. However, activities rather than conversation are the center of most men's friendships. Beginning in childhood, friendships between males often revolve around shared activities, particularly sports. Scott Swain's (1989) phrase "closeness in the doing" captures the way many men build friendships. More than two-thirds of the men in Swain's study described activities other than talking as the most meaningful times with friends. Engaging in sports, watching games, and doing other things together cultivate camaraderie and closeness between men. Whereas women tend to look for confidantes in friends, men more typically seek companions (Inman, 1996). Many men perceive talking as only one way—and not necessarily the best one—to build closeness with friends (Monsour, 1992; Paul & White, 1990; Swain, 1989; Walker, 2004; Wood & Inman, 1993).

Growing out of the emphasis on activities is a second feature of men's friendships: an instrumental focus. Many men like to do things for people they care about (Cancian, 1987; Sherrod, 1989); their friendships involve instrumental reciprocity. For example, one helps the other repair his car, and the other provides computer skills—an exchange of favors that allows each man to hold his own while showing he cares about the other. The masculine inclination toward instrumentality also surfaces in how men help each other through rough times. Rather than engaging in explicit, expressive conversation about problems as women often do, men are more likely to help by suggesting diversionary activities that take the friend's mind off troubles (Cancian, 1987; Riessman, 1990; Tavris, 1992).

Keith

My best friend and I almost never sit and just talk. Mainly we do things together, like go places or shoot hoops or watch games on TV. When we do talk, we talk about what we have done or plan to do or what's happening in our lives, but we don't say much about how we feel. I don't think we need to. You can say a lot without words.

Lee

I don't know what girls get out of sitting around talking about problems all the time. What a downer. When something bad happens to me, like I blow a test or break up with a girl, the last thing I want is to talk about it. I already feel bad enough. What I want is something to distract me from how lousy I feel. That's where having buddies really matters. They know you feel bad and help you out by taking you out drinking or starting a pickup game or something that gets your mind off the problems. They give you breathing room and some escape from troubles; girls just wallow in troubles.

The masculine emphasis on doing things together may explain why men's friendships are less likely than women's to last if one friend moves away. According to Mary Rohlfing (1995), women friends can sustain their closeness through phone calls, letters, and electronic mail. It's more difficult to shoot hoops or have jam sessions with someone who lives miles away.

Third, men's friendships often involve "covert intimacy" (Swain, 1989). Male friends tend to signal affection by teasing, friendly competition, and playful punches and backslaps. Most males learn very early in life that physical displays of affection between men are prohibited except in specific situations such as sports (Hunter & Mallon, 2000). According to Kory Floyd (1995, 1996a, 1996b, 1997a, 1997b), both women and men consider overt expressions of affection important, yet men are likely to restrict them to opposite-sex relationships, whereas women employ them in both same-sex and opposite-sex relationships. Compared to

Reprinted with special permission from King Features Syndicate.

women friends, says Floyd, men "simply communicate affection in different, more 'covert' ways so as to avoid the possible ridicule that more overt expression might invite" (1997b, p. 78).

Finally, men's friendships are often, although not always, restricted in scope. Men tend to have different friends for various spheres of interest (Buhrke & Fuqua, 1987; Wright & Scanlon, 1991). Thus, Jim might play racquetball with Mike, work on cars with Clay, and go to games with Rubin. Because men tend to focus friendships on particular activities, they may not share as many dimensions of their lives with friends as women typically do. Overall, then, men's friendships involve shared activities, instrumental demonstrations of affection, covert intimacy, and defined spheres of interaction.

In summary, distinctive communication tendencies characterize many men's and women's same-sex friendships. Women tend to see closeness as sharing themselves and their lives through personal communication. Men more typically create closeness by sharing particular activities and interests and by doing things with and for others. Describing these gender differences, Lillian Rubin (1985) writes that men tend to bond nonverbally through sharing experiences, whereas women typically become intimate through communicating verbally.

■ Friendships Between Women and Men

Friendships between the sexes pose unique challenges and offer special opportunities for growth. Because our culture so heavily emphasizes gender, it is difficult for women and men not to see each other in sexual terms (Bingham, 1996; Johnson, Stockdale, & Saal, 1991). Even when cross-sex friends are not sexually involved, an undertone of sexuality often permeates their friendship.

Another tension in friendships between women and men arises from sex-segregated socialization. Beginning in childhood, males and females are often separated (Cohen, 1997; Monsour, 2002). We have Boy Scouts and Girl Scouts, rather than Scouts, and many athletic teams are still sex segregated. As boys and girls interact with same-sex peers, they learn the norms of gendered speech communities. Different understandings of how communication works create potential for misunderstanding and awkwardness in mixed-sex friendships of African Americans as well as Caucasians (Gary, 1987).

Despite these difficulties, many women and men do form friendships with each other and find them rewarding (West, Anderson, & Duck, 1996). In mixed-sex friendships, each partner has something unique to offer as the expert in particular areas. For many women, a primary benefit of friendships with men is companionship that is less emotionally intense than that with women friends. For men, an especially valued benefit of closeness with women is access to emotional and expressive support, which tends to be less overtly communicated in friendships between men.

> **Raul**
>
> Last year I got to be close friends with a girl who was in one of my classes. I felt I could tell her things I wouldn't tell my guy friends. She was always willing to listen and empathize with my problems, and she never put me down if I felt bad or hurt or anything. I always felt better about whatever was wrong after I talked with her, because she was so accepting and supportive, and in later situations she never threw up weaknesses I revealed.

Men say they receive more emotional support and therapeutic release with women than with men friends. Women also say they receive more support from women than from men friends (Reisman, 1990; Werking, 1997). In cross-sex friendships men generally talk more and get more attention, response, and support than they offer. A majority of both sexes report that friendships with women are closer and more satisfying than those with men (Buhrke & Fuqua, 1987; Werking, 1997). This may explain why both sexes tend to seek women friends in times of stress and why both women and men are generally more comfortable self-disclosing to women than to men (Buhrke & Fuqua, 1987; Rubin, 1985).

GENDERED ROMANTIC RELATIONSHIPS

Nowhere are gendered roles as salient as in heterosexual romantic relationships. The cultural script for romance is well known to most of us (Alksnis, Desmarais, & Wood, 1996; Rose & Frieze, 1989):

- Feminine women and masculine men are desirable.

- Men should initiate, plan, and direct most activities in a relationship.

- Women should facilitate conversation, generally defer to men, but control sexual behavior.

- Men should excel in status and earning money, and women should assume primary responsibility for the relationship, the home, and the children.

■ Developing Romantic Intimacy

Personal ads offer insight into what heterosexual men and women seek in romantic partners. Ads written by men looking for women often place priority on stereotypically feminine physical qualities, using words such as *attractive, slender, petite,* and *sexy*. Women's ads for male partners frequently emphasize status and success and include words such as *secure, ambitious, professional,* and *successful* (S. Davis, 1990; Smith, Waldorf, & Trembath, 1990). In reality as in personal ads, women's and men's views of desirable partners often reflect cultural gender expectations—success in males and beauty in females (Stewart, Stinnett, & Rosenfeld, 2000).

The conventional heterosexual dating script calls for men to take the initiative. Although many people claim they don't accept this pattern, research shows that most heterosexuals still conform to it (Cochran & Peplau, 1985; Ickes, 1993; Riessman, 1990). However, there are exceptions to compliance with cultural scripts. Androgynous individuals, who break from rigid cultural definitions of masculinity and femininity, behave in more flexible, less stereotypical ways (DeLucia, 1987). And there is less role playing between gay men and even less between lesbian women (Kurdek & Schmitt, 1986b, 1986c, 1987; Patterson, 2000; Rutter & Schwartz, 1996).

Is one gender more romantic than the other? Contrary to folklore, research indicates that men tend to fall in love faster and harder than women. They tend to be more active, impulsive, sexualized, and game-playing than women, whose styles of loving are more pragmatic and friendship focused (Bierhoff, 1996; Cancian, 1987; Hendrick & Hendrick, 1986, 1996; Riessman, 1990). For instance, men may see love as taking trips to romantic places, spontaneously making love, and surprising their partners. Women more typically think of extended conversations, sharing deep feelings, and physical contact that isn't necessarily sexual. Reflecting these same gendered patterns, lesbians tend to date for a while before becoming sexual, whereas gay men are more likely to have sex early in their relationships (Scrivner, 1997).

Women are more likely than men to focus on relationship dynamics—a pattern that holds regardless of sexual orientation (Eldridge & Gilbert, 1990; Kurdek & Schmitt, 1986c; Patterson, 2000; Wood, 1993e). Lesbian partners tend to take mutual responsibility for nurturing and supporting relationships. Gay couples, on the other hand, are least likely to have a partner who focuses on nurturing the dyad and provides emotional leadership (Kurdek & Schmitt, 1986b; Patterson, 2000; Wood, 1993e).

> ### *Gina*
>
> I consider myself a very independent, untraditional woman. I plan a career in law, and I am very assertive. But when it comes to dating relationships, I fall into some really conventional patterns. I think a woman should be able to call a guy she likes and ask him out, but I can't bring myself to do that. I also kind of expect guys to pay for dates, at least until a relationship gets serious, even though I think it's more fair to split expenses. I expect the guy I'm with to make plans and decisions about a date, and I expect myself to be more interpersonally sensitive. I guess some of the old roles do persist.

Enduring heterosexual love relationships, in general, continue to reflect traditional gender roles endorsed by the culture (Riessman, 1990; Wood, 1993a). Men tend to be perceived as the head of the family and the major breadwinner; women tend to assume primary responsibility for domestic labor and child care; and men tend to have greater power. African American relationships tend to be more egalitarian and less defined by rigid gender roles than those of European Americans (McAdoo, 1997).

Because gender distinctions are less salient, many gay and lesbian relationships do not follow the roles typical of heterosexual couples. Both gay and lesbian commitments resemble best-friend relationships with the added dimensions of sexuality and romance. Following the best-friends model, long-term lesbian relationships tend to be monogamous and high in emotionality, disclosure, and support, and partners have the most equality of all types of relationships (Eldridge & Gilbert, 1990; Huston & Schwartz, 1996; Kurdek & Schmitt, 1986c; Murphy, 1997). Gay couples, in general, place less emphasis on monogamy (and are more tolerant of extra-relationship sexual involvements) and greater emphasis on independence and power (Kurdek & Schmitt, 1986b; Wood, 1993e).

■ Engaging in Committed Relationships

Gendered orientations influence four primary dimensions of long-term love relationships: modes of expressing care, needs for autonomy and connection, responsibility for relational maintenance, and power. As we will discover, these dynamics are influenced by the distinctive styles and priorities emphasized by masculine and feminine socialization.

Gendered modes of expressing affection. As we have seen, the masculine mode of expressing affection is instrumental and activity-focused, whereas the feminine mode is expressive and talk-focused. Anne Wilson Schaef (1981) notes that "women are often hurt in relationships with men because they totally expose their beings and do not receive respect and exposure in return" (p. 150). Conversely, some men feel resentful or intruded on when women push them to be emotionally expressive.

For many women, ongoing conversation about feelings and daily activities is a primary way to express and enrich personal relationships. The masculine speech communities in which most men are socialized, however, regard the primary reasons to talk as solving problems and achieving goals.

Phil

What does my girlfriend want? That's all I want to know. She says, if I really loved her, I'd want to be together and talk all the time. I tell her all I do for her. I fix her car when it's broken; I give her rides to places; I helped her move last semester. We've talked about marriage, and I plan to take care of her then, too. I will work all day and overtime to give her a good home and to provide for our family. But she says, "Don't tell me what you *do* for me," like *do* is a bad word. Now, why would I do all this stuff if I didn't love her? Just tell me that.

Thus, unless there is a problem, men often find talking about a relationship unnecessary, whereas many women feel that ongoing talk keeps problems from developing. Generally, men are more likely to express caring by doing things for and with their partners. Thus, the different genders may not recognize each other's ways of communicating care.

More feminine or androgynous ways of expressing care are valued by both sexes. Research shows that both men and women are more satisfied with partners who are willing to engage in intimate self-disclosure, give emotionally supportive responses, and express their own feelings clearly (Ickes, 1993; Lamke, Sollie, Durbin, & Fitzpatrick, 1994). Yet most of us also count on traditionally masculine modes of caring —we feel cherished when a romantic partner does things for us and wants to do things with us. In Western culture, however, we're less likely to define masculine, instrumental behaviors as demonstrations of intimacy and caring.

The cultural bias favoring feminine modes of expressing love is illustrated by a classic study (Wills, Weiss, & Patterson, 1974). The researchers wanted to know how husbands' shows of affection affected wives' feelings. To find out, they instructed husbands to engage in different degrees of affectionate behavior toward their wives, and then the wives' responses were measured. When one wife showed no indication of receiving affection, the researchers called the husband to see if he had followed instructions. Somewhat irately, the husband said he certainly had— that he had thoroughly washed his wife's car. Not only did his wife not experience this as affection, but the researchers themselves concluded he had "confused" instrumental with affectionate behaviors. Doing something helpful was entirely disregarded as a valid way to express affection! This exemplifies the cultural bias toward feminine views of loving. It also illustrates a misunderstanding that plagues many heterosexual love relationships.

Gay and lesbian couples tend to have more understandings in common about how to communicate affection. Gay men, like their heterosexual counterparts, tend to engage in limited emotional and intimate dialogue and do not talk constantly about their relationship. Lesbians, on the other hand, generally share responsibility for taking care of a relationship and build the most expressive and nurturing communication climates of any type of couple (Kirkpatrick, 1989; Patterson, 2000; Wood, 1993e). Lesbian partners' mutual attentiveness to nurturing and emotional openness may explain why lesbians report more satisfaction with their romantic relationships than gays or heterosexuals do (Eldridge & Gilbert, 1990; Kurdek & Schmitt, 1986c).

Sharon

Most of this course has been a review of stuff I already knew, but the unit on how men and women show they love each other was news to me. I'm always fussing at my boyfriend for not showing me he cares. I tell him he takes me for granted and if he really loved me he'd want to talk more about personal, deep stuff inside him. But he bought me a book I'd been wanting, and a couple of weeks ago he spent a whole day fixing my car because he was worried about whether it was safe for me—I thought of that when we talked about the guy in the experiment who washed his wife's car. I guess he has been showing he cares for me, but I haven't been seeing it.

Gendered preferences for autonomy and connection. Autonomy and connection are two basic needs of all humans (Baxter, 1990; Scarf, 1987; Wood, 1995). We all need to feel that we have both personal freedom and meaningful interrelatedness with others. Yet gender influences how much of these we want. Masculine individuals tend to want greater autonomy and less connection than feminine people, whose relative priorities are generally reversed. We all want some autonomy and some connection, yet the proportionate weights that feminine and masculine people assign to each generally differ.

Desires for different degrees of autonomy and connection frequently generate friction in close relationships. Many couples are familiar with a pattern called "demand–withdraw" (Christensen & Heavey, 1990; James, 1989). In this pattern one partner feels distant and tries to close the distance by engaging in personal, intimate talk, and the other partner withdraws from a degree of closeness that stifles his or her need for autonomy. The more one demands talk, the more the other withdraws; the more one withdraws from interaction, the more the other demands talk and time together. Both men and women are likely to withdraw when partners demand or request change; however, the intensity of withdrawal is greater when a woman requests change in a man than when a man requests change in a woman (Sagrestano, Heavey, & Christensen, 1998). Socialized toward independence, masculine individuals tend to be more comfortable when they have some distance from others, whereas feminine people tend to be more comfortable with close connections (Wood, 1993a). Ironically, the very thing that creates closeness for one partner impedes it for the other.

More hurtful than the demand-withdraw pattern itself, however, are partners' tendencies to interpret each other according to rules that don't apply to the other's behavior. For instance, to think that a man who wants time alone doesn't care for his partner or value a relationship is to interpret his withdrawal according to a feminine rule. Similarly, to perceive a woman who wants intimate conversation as intrusive is to judge her by masculine standards. Although the demand–withdraw pattern may persist in relationships, we can eliminate the poison of misinterpretation by respecting different needs for autonomy and connection (Bergner & Bergner, 1990).

Gendered responsibility for relational health. Lesbian couples tend to share responsibility for their relationships. Because most lesbians, like most heterosexual women, learn feminine ways of thinking and acting, both partners tend to be sensitive to interpersonal dynamics and interested in

> ### Hal
>
> My former girlfriend definitely wanted more connection than I was comfortable with. When we first started dating, we would call each other and talk on the phone for hours on end. After a while, though, I wasn't interested in long talks unless there was something important to say. But she kept calling and wanting to talk about all kinds of trivial things. I would have rather gone out, done something, gone somewhere, but she was happiest just talking on the phone or sitting around talking in person.

When Focusing on Feelings Makes Us Feel Bad

In general, women pay more attention to feelings than men do. This allows women to be in touch with their emotions and to work through feelings.

But there may be a down side. Research shows that women generally have a greater tendency than men to brood about bad feelings, a tendency that seems to result from positive reinforcements (social learning theory) for focusing on feelings and seeing other girls and women model emotional reflection (cognitive development theory). Excessive brooding can lead women to get stuck in unhappy feelings and to spiral downward emotionally into depression (Nolen-Hoeksema, 2003; Shea, 1998).

After more than 10 years of studying women's tendency to brood excessively, Susan Nolen-Hoeksema (2003) suggests that, to avoid getting stuck in unhappy feelings, women might go somewhere, do something, focus thoughts elsewhere. In other words, instrumental—typically masculine—coping strategies may be helpful.

talking about their relationship and working through problems in it (Kirkpatrick, 1989; Schwartz & Rutter, 1998; Wood, 1993e).

Against the standard set by lesbians, heterosexual couples do not fare as well in distributing responsibility for relational health. In heterosexual relationships, both men and women tend to assume that women have primary responsibility for keeping relationships on track (Miller, 1986; Ragsdale, 1996; Stafford, Dutton, & Haas, 2000). Two scholars (Thompson & Walker, 1989) summarize much research in this area, concluding that wives "have more responsibility than their husbands for monitoring the relationship, confronting disagreeable issues, setting the tone of conversation, and moving toward resolution when conflict is high" (p. 849).

Shannon

I don't think I should be *the* one to take care of my marriage or children. I think that Vince and I should do that equally. But what I *think* and what I *feel* are different things. I feel I should be the one the kids count on. I feel I should take care of Vince and our home. The feelings are not so much from Vince as from me. I expect myself to be a caretaker. I hope the next generation of women doesn't feel as compelled to be caretakers as I and my peers do.

The expectation that one person should take care of relationships burdens one partner with the responsibility of keeping a relationship satisfying. In addition, it is difficult for one person to meet this responsibility if a partner does not acknowledge and work on matters that jeopardize relational health. The partner who is expected to safeguard the relationship may be perceived as a nag by the one who fails to recognize problems until they become very serious (Tavris, 1992). Not surprisingly, research shows that the highest levels of couple satisfaction exist when both partners share responsibility for the relationship (Gunter & Gunter, 1990; Peterson, Baucom, Elliott, & Farr, 1989).

Gendered power dynamics. As one might predict, problems fostered by believing that men should be more powerful are absent in lesbian relationships. On the other hand, in some gay relationships partners constantly compete for status and dominance (Kurdek & Schmitt, 1986a, 1986b; Rutter & Schwartz, 1996). Tensions about power often center on partners' earnings. A majority of women and men still believe that men should be the primary or sole breadwinner (Loscocco, 1997; Risman & Godwin, 2001). In a *Newsweek* poll (Tyre & McGinn, 2003), 41% of Americans said that it is better for everyone if men achieve outside the home and the women take care of families, and 25% of those polled said it was unacceptable for women to be the major breadwinners.

The belief that men should be the primary breadwinners doesn't match reality for the 30.7% of married, two-worker households in which the woman earns more than the man (Tyre & McGinn, 2003). Among African Americans, the trend toward greater achievement by women is evident from adolescence: 13.5% of Black women drop out of high school, while 17% of Black men do; 35% of Black women attend college, whereas 25% of Black men do; 24% of Black women have managerial and professional jobs, while 17% of Black men do (Bell & Komo, 2001; Hacker, 2003a,b; Samuels, 2003). Donna Franklin, author of *What's Love Got To Do With It?* (2001), reports that Black men often resent wives who earn more than they do. Concurring, Michael Eric Dyson (2003) says that many Black men feel threatened by successful Black women, particularly if those women are their partners. Franklin (2001) thinks this contributes to the fact that divorce rates for Blacks have quadrupled since 1960.

People who adhere to traditional views of gender in relationships where the woman earns more are likely to experience a decrease in both self-esteem and marital satisfaction (Anderson & Leslie, 1991; Steil & Weltman, 1991). How well couples adapt to the man's earning less than the woman depends a great deal on the examples set by their parents. Men whose fathers were actively involved in home life, sometimes as the primary homemaker, tend to see homemaking as compatible with masculinity (Schneider & Stevenson, 1999). Women and men who had mothers who were successful in the paid labor force tend to see a woman's career success as consistent with femininity (Cose, 2003; Hattery, 2000; Schneider & Stevenson, 1999; Tyre & McGinn, 2003).

Aikau

My mother works all day at her job. She also cooks all of the meals for the family, does all of the housework, and takes care of my younger brother and sister. When my mother goes out of town on business, she fixes all of the family meals and freezes them before she leaves. She also arranges for day care and cleans very thoroughly before she leaves. My father expects this of her, and she expects it of herself.

Ernest

As a male who was reared by a single mother, I see women differently from most of the White men I know. I and a lot of Blacks see women as our equals more than most White men do. We treat the women in our lives with a lot more respect than middle-class White males. Men who were raised by a single mother understand women and their plight better than most White men. We know we and Black women are in it together.

Reprinted with special permission from King Features Syndicate.

In heterosexual relationships, the belief that men have more power than women is also reflected in the distribution of labor in the home. Although the vast majority of heterosexual families today have two wage earners, the housework and the care of children, parents, and other relatives continue to be done primarily by women (Delamont, 2001; Gerson, 2004; Jena, 1999; Maushart, 2001; Nussbaum, 1992; Risman & Godwin, 2001). Dubbing this the "second shift," sociologist Arlie Hochschild (Hochschild with Machung, 2003) reports that the majority of wives employed outside of their homes have a **second-shift** job in the home. In dual-worker heterosexual families, women spend an average of 27 hours each week on homemaking and child care, whereas men spend an average of 16 hours; women are doing about 65% of the work involved in family life (Goldstein, 2000; Johnson, 2002). In stark contrast to women's juggling of their paid work and the second shift, the amount of housework and child care that husbands do weekly has risen by only 4 hours (from 12 to 16) since 1965 (Johnson, 2002).

Not only do women work more than men at home, but the work they do is generally more taxing and less gratifying. For instance, whereas many of the contributions men typically make are sporadic, variable, and flexible in timing (for example, mowing the lawn), the tasks women typically do are repetitive, routine, and constrained by deadlines. Women are also more likely to do multiple tasks simultaneously—for example, helping a child with homework while preparing dinner. Whereas mothers tend to be constantly on duty, fathers more typically volunteer for irregular and fun child-care activities such as trips to the zoo.

Another way in which women's contributions to home life are greater is in terms of **psychological responsibility**—the responsibility for remembering, planning, and making sure things get done (Hochschild with Machung, 2003). For instance, partners may agree to share responsibility for tak-

Gloria

I'm a mother and a professional and a part-time student, but I am not the only one who takes care of my home and family. That's a shared responsibility in our home. My daughter and son each cook dinner one night a week, and they switch off on chores like laundry and vacuuming. My husband and I share the other chores 50–50. Children don't resist a fair division of labor if their parents model it and show that it's expected of them.

FYI

Balancing Fatherhood and Professional Life

Today many American men want to spend more time with their families, particularly their children. The trend toward greater involvement with children is particularly strong among educated, middle-class men (Straus & Goldberg, 1999).

Fathers' desires, however, are often at odds with professional norms and social prescriptions for masculinity. Men who want to spend more time with families may be at a disadvantage in the workplace because their supervisors don't expect or approve of men who want to balance family and work life (Grover, 1999; Silverstein & Auerbach, 1999).

The increasing number of men who resist being full-time workers and absentee fathers may push businesses and organizations to alter attitudes about men as well as specific policies such as those regarding parental leave.

ing children to doctors and dentists, but typically the woman is expected to remember when various inoculations are due, to schedule appointments, to notice when the child needs attention, and to keep track of whose turn it is to take the child. Similarly, partners may share responsibility for preparing meals, but women usually take on the associated responsibilities of planning menus, keeping an inventory of food and cooking supplies, making shopping lists, and going to the grocery store. All of this planning and organization is a psychological responsibility that is often not counted in couples' agreements for sharing the work of a family.

The consequences of women's second shift are substantial. Women who do most of the homemaking and child-care tasks are often extremely stressed, fatigued, and susceptible to illness (Hochschild with Machung, 2003; Jena, 1999). Similar stress has been found in single fathers who work a second shift (Ranson, 2001). Frustration, resentment, and conflict are also likely when only one person in a partnership bears the double responsibilities of jobs inside and outside the home (Kluwer, Heesink, & Vliert, 1996; Knudson-Martin & Mahoney, 1996). In addition, the inequity of the arrangement is a primary source of relationship dissatisfaction and instability. Marital stability is more closely tied to equitable divisions of housework and child care than to a couple's income. The roughly 20% of heterosexual couples who share equally in running a home and raising children are the most satisfied (F. Deutsch, 2001).

Another clue to power dynamics is whose preferences prevail when partners differ. Research on marriages consistently finds that both partners perceive that husbands' preferences count more than those of wives on everything from how often to have sex to who does the housework (Paul & White, 1990; Schneider & Gould, 1987; Thompson & Walker, 1989). Further, we know that masculine individuals (whether female or male) tend to use more unilateral strategies to engage

Two careers plus children may be too much! Many two-worker families find they can't fulfill all of their responsibilities at home and in the workplace. One solution is to hire someone else to take care of the home, an option increasingly chosen by many dual-earner families. For the many people who want to minimize the cost of hiring full-time help for the home, the cheapest domestic labor is women from underdeveloped countries who will work for a fraction of the cost that Americans will (Honolagneu-Sotelo, 2001).

That solves one problem but creates another. Each year millions of women leave Mexico, the Philippines, and other relatively poor countries to become maids and nannies for well-to-do families in the United States. Poor countries become even poorer as women migrate to the United States to work here rather than in their home countries. The result is a "care deficit" in countries that already have too few resources (Ehrenreich & Hochschild, 2002).

in and to avoid conflicts (Stafford et al., 2000). Feminine individuals more typically defer or compromise to reduce tension, and they employ indirect strategies when they do engage in conflict (Howard, Blumstein, & Schwartz, 1986; Miller, 1986; Mulac, 1998; White, 1989).

More than feminine or androgynous persons, individuals with masculine identities tend to minimize problems or to exit when conflict arises, thus enacting the masculine tendency to maintain independence and protect the self. Feminine persons, in contrast, tend to initiate discussion of problems and stand by in times of trouble (Rusbult, 1987; Stafford et al., 2000). As you might expect, the tension between masculine and feminine ways of exerting influence is less pronounced in lesbian relationships, where equality is particularly high. For gay partners, power struggles are especially common and are sometimes a continual backdrop for the relationship (Kurdek & Schmitt, 1986b).

Finally, gendered power dynamics underlie violence and abuse, which are means of exercising dominance over others. We will cover the topic of violence in detail in Chapter 12, but we also need to acknowledge here that intimate partner violence is one manifestation of gendered power dynamics in romantic relationships. Not confined to any single group, violence cuts across race, ethnic, and class lines. Researchers estimate that at least 28% and possibly as many as 50% of women suffer physical abuse from partners, and even more suffer psychological abuse (Wood, 2001b).

Violence is inflicted primarily by men, most of whom have been socialized into masculine identities (Pastore & Maguire, 2001). In the United States, every 12 to 18 seconds a woman is beaten by a man; four women each day are reported beaten to death; and women are 600% more likely to be brutalized by an intimate than are

FYI

The Verdict on Moms Who Work Outside the Home

Should mothers work outside the home when they have young children? For years we've had no solid evidence for an informed answer to that question—until now. In 1999 psychology professor Elizabeth Harvey released the findings of an exhaustive study that compared children of stay-at-home moms with those of moms who worked outside the home during the first one to three years of the children's lives. She studied more than 5,000 children over a 12-year period, testing them for everything from academic achievement to self-esteem.

The answer? It's a draw, says Harvey. She found virtually no differences between the two groups of children. Summarizing her study, she says, "The results suggest that both being at home and working outside the home are good options" (Sheehan, 1999, p. 1A). Which option is better depends on a host of factors, including the family's economic resources, the particular child's personality and needs, and the mother's (or father's) interest in staying home versus working outside the home.

men (Wood, 2001b). Cross-cultural research indicates that partner abuse, like rape, is lowest in societies that have ideologies of sexual equality; it is most frequent in cultures that are stratified by sex and believe in male dominance of women (Levinson, 1989).

Convincing evidence that violence is connected more closely to gender than to sex comes from a study by Edwin Thompson (1991). Based on reports from 336 undergraduates, Thompson found a high degree of violence in dating relationships. Sex alone, however, did not explain the violence. Thompson discovered that violence is linked to gender, with abusers—both male and female—being more masculine and less feminine in their gender orientation. This led Thompson to conclude that physical aggression is associated with traditionally masculine emphasis on control, domination, and power.

We've seen that personal relationships reflect the expectations and orientations encouraged by feminine and masculine socialization. Gender differences surface in partners' expressions and experiences of caring, preferences for autonomy and connection, the distribution of responsibility for maintaining relationships, and power dynamics.

SUMMARY

Gendered ideas continue to shape friendships and romantic relationships. Yet, today many people feel that traditional gender roles aren't satisfying or realistic. As people discover the limits and disadvantages of traditional gender roles, they are experimenting with new ways to form and sustain relationships and their own identities within those relationships. For instance, some men choose to be stay-at-home dads because they find greater fulfillment in nurturing a family than in pursuing a career in the paid labor force. Some women discover that they are more effective and more fulfilled by work outside of the home than by work inside it. And many people balance home and paid work in ways that transcend traditional roles. Examples such as these remind us that we can edit cultural scripts, using our own lives to craft alternative visions of women, men, and relationships.

KEY TERMS

alternate paths model, 171

male deficit model, 170

personal relationships, 170

psychological responsibility, 184

second shift, 184

DISCUSSION QUESTIONS

1. Use PowerTrac on your InfoTrac College Edition to read Saijo Mauno and Ulla Kinnunen's 2001 article, "Perceived job insecurity among dual-earner couples: Do its antecedents vary according to gender, economic sector, and the measure used?" in the *Journal of Occupational and Organizational Psychology.* Summarize the findings of this study and their consistency with gendered patterns discussed in this chapter.

2. Reread the quote on the opening page of this chapter. How could you apply this quote to the idea of building and sustaining personal relationships?

3. To what extent do you agree with the male deficit and alternate paths models of closeness? How does the model you accept affect your behaviors and interpretations of others?

4. Keep experimenting with expanding your personal repertoire. If you have relied primarily on talk to build closeness, see what happens when you do things with friends. Do you experience "closeness in the doing"? If your friendships have tended to grow out of shared activities, check out what happens if you talk with friends without some activity to structure time.

5. Do you see gendered patterns of interaction in your romantic relationships? Does knowing about gender-linked patterns regarding these issues affect how you interpret what happens in your own relationships?

9

Gendered Education:
Communication in Schools

The mind has exactly the same power as the hands;
not merely to grasp the world, but to change it.

—COLIN WILSON

chools are powerful agents of gender socialization. In addition to educating us in subject areas, schools teach us about the roles and status that are open to different people, including ourselves. The roles of males and females in schools and the ways male and female students are treated teach us how social systems work and which people have more and less status within them.

Historically and today, schools reflect society's understandings of gender. In the first centuries of America's life, women were excluded from higher education because it was believed they were too fragile to withstand the rigors of serious study. Further, thinking at that time cautioned that exposure to higher education might "unsex" women, since an educated woman was "unnatural" (Gordon, 1998). The few women who pursued education beyond high school generally attended finishing schools, which taught them how to be good wives, mothers, and homemakers.

In the United States today, women and men have relatively equal access to education. Even so, many schools continue to have unequal views of and expectations of women and men. From preschool through graduate programs, educational institutions reproduce and encourage gendered identities and ambitions. Although it is not the intended purpose of education, schools provide powerful lessons in gender.

In addition to the explicit curriculum, schools have a **hidden curriculum** (Lee & Gropper, 1974) that reflects gender stereotypes and sustains gender inequities by giving less attention and encouragement to female and minority students than to white male students. This hidden curriculum is taught through the organization of schools, curricular content, and communication inside and outside of classrooms. As we explore these three dimensions of the hidden curriculum, we will probe how they shape our personal and professional lives.

FYI

A Short History of Gendered Education in America

Throughout America's history, schools have echoed cultural views of gender (Gordon, 1998; Minnich, 1998). In America's earliest years, most women did not pursue education beyond high school. The few who did attended finishing schools, where they learned traditional skills such as sewing and cleaning. In the 1800s some female academies were established to train women as nurses or teachers, two professions considered appropriate for women.

The Morrill Act of 1862 established coeducational state universities and land grant colleges to educate women and men in liberal arts and practical skills. Practical education for men included agriculture and mechanics, while practical education for women was home economics. By 1870 30% of U.S. colleges enrolled students of both sexes. In 1920 fully 70% of U.S. higher education institutions enrolled women and men. The Progressive Education Movement in the 1920s and 1930s led to development of women's colleges that stressed intellectual development, personal independence, and creativity, emphases not offered to women at most coeducational institutions.

Throughout most of America's history, many colleges practiced various types of sex discrimination. For instance, for years Stanford had a quota system that accepted three males for every one female. Even in the 1960s many schools accepted only women applicants who were better qualified than male applicants. With passage of Title IX of the Education Act Amendments in 1972, all educational institutions that receive federal funds are required to treat boys and girls, men and women, equally. Only since the 1980s have roughly equal numbers of women and men attended colleges and universities in the United States (Mayberry, 1996).

THE ORGANIZATION OF SCHOOLS

As we have noted in previous chapters, cultural life is organized so that certain practices, roles, and ways of behaving seem natural, right, and just "the way things are." As we participate in cultural institutions, most of us come to see as natural the prevailing order they embody. Among the organizations that embody and perpetuate the social order, schools are particularly important.

■ Gendered Hierarchies in Schools

The organization of schools communicates strong messages about relationships between gender and status. Think about your elementary and high schools. Who were the teachers? Who were the principals? Who were the aides, cafeteria workers, and secretaries? In elementary schools nearly 85% of teachers are female, but 96% of superintendents and assistant superintendents are male (Maume, 1999). Further, at higher levels of education, where the position of teacher has more status, the number of women decreases (AAUW, 1998; Spade, 2001).

School athletics also are typically organized so that more males than females have positions of high status and authority. Before passage of **Title IX,** which mandated equal sporting opportunities for the sexes, more than 90% of coaches of women's sports were women. Ironically, today fewer women's sports are coached by women, and all Division I colleges pay male coaches more than women coaches

Title IX: Fiction and Fact

Although Title IX has been around for a good while, it is still widely misunderstood. Check your understanding of Title IX (Suggs, 1999, 2000, 2003a,b; Messner, 2002; Neinas, 2002; Zimbalist, 2000).

Fiction: Title IX is binding on all schools in the United States.

Fact: Title IX is binding only on schools that accept federal funds.

Fiction: Title IX bans sex discrimination only in athletics.

Fact: Title IX bans sex discrimination of all sorts in federally supported schools. This applies to academics as well as athletics.

Fiction: Title IX has reduced opportunities for male college athletes.

Fact: Since the passage of Title IX, college men's sports opportunities have actually increased. In 1997–1998, there were 203,686 male athletes and 135,110 female athletes playing college sports.

Fiction: To comply with Title IX, most Division 1 colleges have dropped male athletes.

Fact: Only 38 Division 1 colleges have dropped more than 10% of male athletes, whereas 165 Division 1 colleges have added more than 10% male athletes.

Fiction: Because of Title IX, colleges that receive federal funds provide fully equal support to women's and men's sports.

Fact: Compared to male athletes, female athletes receive fewer scholarship dollars and their teams get fewer dollars for recruiting and operating teams. Salaries for coaches of women's sports are 1/4 to 1/3 of the salaries paid to coaches of male sports.

Fiction: Most Americans don't support Title IX.

Fact: In a 2000 poll, 79% of Americans said that they approve of Title IX. Support for Title IX didn't vary much by sex. 79% of women and 73% of men supported it.

Reprinted by special permission from King Features Syndicate.

(Suggs, 1999, 2003a,b; Zimbalist, 2000). Male athletes also receive more support than female athletes.

■ Gendered Career Aspirations

As students see males more often in positions of authority, they begin to form ideas about career options for themselves. Students are more likely to think that both women and men can be principals if they have had a woman principal than if they have had a man principal (Paradise & Wall, 1986). Because more males than females are principals, the organization of schools teaches that it's "normal" for men to hold positions of status and authority. The predominance of female teachers in elementary schools also perpetuates the gender stereotype that women—and not men—are responsible for young children (Oyler, Jennings, & Lozada, 2001).

At higher levels, gendered school organization continues to affect perceptions of career opportunities and appropriate roles for women and men. At colleges and universities, faculty are predominantly male, especially at the highest ranks. Nationwide, only about one-third of permanent faculty in higher education are female (Wilson, 2001). The racial imbalance is even more dramatic than the gender imbalance: 85% of full-time faculty in higher education are White (Wilson, 2001).

Schooling also reproduces gender stereotypes by not encouraging boys and men to develop traditionally feminine skills such as caring for others and by not encouraging males to enter traditionally feminine fields (Bailey & Campbell, 1999; Stewart, 1998). Nel Noddings is a distinguished education professor at Stanford University, where she has devoted her career to the practice and philosophy of education. In a recent book (2002), Noddings argues that education at all levels should prepare both males and females not only to have careers outside of the home but also to be responsible, caring family members. Noddings's ideal is schools that teach not only science, history, and math, but also how to care for others and build a satisfying family life.

FYI

Gender Stratification in Higher Education

Following is a summary of findings from the U.S. Department of Education's recent survey of full-time faculty and instructional staff in institutions of higher education (Wilson, 2001).

Type of Institution	Men	Women
All Institutions	63.7	36.3
Public Research	70.5	29.5
Private Research	73.9	26.1
Public Doctoral	66.7	33.3
Private Doctoral	63.6	36.4
Public Comprehensive	61.7	38.3
Private Comprehensive	63.3	36.7
Private Liberal Arts	62.2	37.8
Public 2-year	50.1	49.9

■ Unequal Role Models for Male and Female Students

In higher education, women make up 36% of all faculty (up from 23% in 1974–1975) but only 19% of faculty at the rank of full professor. Across the United States, women are presidents of only 20% of colleges, mostly smaller schools and community colleges (Lively, 2000). Because so few women and minority faculty members exist, they are overburdened with a disproportionate number of requests for committee service and advising (Phillips, Gouran, Kuehn, & Wood, 1993; Welch, 1992).

Research documents a relationship between the presence of women and minority faculty and the career aspirations of minority and women students. Women students' levels of ambition and self-confidence are highest in women's high schools (Lee & Marks, 1990) and colleges (Rice & Hemmings, 1988; Tidball, 1989), where women hold nearly all positions of status and authority.

Scarlett

I always liked science. Right from the first grade, it was my favorite subject. The older I got, though, the more I felt odd in my science classes. Especially in college after the required courses, I felt odd. Sometimes I was the only woman in a class. I was majoring in early education and just took science electives for fun. That changed when I had a woman professor in a course about unsolved problems in biology. She was really good and so was the course, but to me the main thing was seeing a woman teaching science. That's when I decided to change my major and become a science teacher.

FYI

Is Separate Equal in Education?

In October 1992, a federal appeals court ruled that single-sex education is justifiable because it results in greater student learning. Yet, that ruling didn't end the controversy over single-sex education. Proponents of women's schools claim that women receive better educations in all-female institutions. The facts on graduates of women's schools are persuasive: Although women's colleges produce fewer than 5% of all female college graduates, 25% of all women who are on boards of Fortune 500 companies and 50% of women in Congress graduated from women's colleges. When the Citadel was all male, its graduation rate was 70%—much higher than the 48% national average (AAUW, 2001; Beck & Biddle, 1995; Leslie, 1998).

But single-sex education also has critics. Maggie Ford, president of the American Association of University Women, argues that sex-segregated education isn't the answer to gender inequities in schools. She says that a better solution is to make sure that teachers in all schools treat *all* students equally so that males and females have the same educational opportunities and support.

Then there's the case of Heather Sue Mercer, who decided separate wasn't equal on the football team (Suggs, 2001). In August of 1994, Mercer enrolled in Duke after an all-state career as a kicker and asked to be a walk-on player for the school's football team. The coach, Fred Goldsmith, agreed to let her try out. Although her tryout didn't go well, Mercer persisted. She went to practices and games in the role of manager and went through winter conditioning. That spring, she scored a winning field goal in an intersquad game, and Coach Goldsmith told reporters she was on the team. However, Goldsmith refused to let Mercer attend summer preseason camp and, in a telephone conversation, he said Mercer should enter beauty pageants instead of playing football. Later, he formally dismissed her from the team and refused to let her participate in winter conditioning. Mercer hired a lawyer and sued. A jury awarded her two million dollars. Duke appealed the decision. The original decision against Duke was upheld, and Duke was also ordered to pay Mercer's attorney fees—nearly $400,000.

Similarly, African American faculty serve as role models who influence the likelihood that African American students will pursue further education and careers (Freiberg, 1991; Lee & Marks, 1990). White male students have the advantage of multiple role models whose presence communicates that it's appropriate for men to pursue high-status careers.

Persistent gender inequities might lead you to think single-sex education is a good idea. Although it has some benefits (Riechmann, 1996), not everyone favors it. David Sadker (Sadker & Sadker, 1994), a professor of education at American University, has two reservations about sex-segregated education. First, he notes, it diverts attention from identifying and solving the problems that make coeducational schools inequitable. Second, he says, single-sex schools aren't available to everyone.

Nearly all single-sex schools are private and charge tuitions that most families can't afford. Thus, although single-sex schools may benefit girls from well-to-do families, they won't do much to help the majority of female students (Nelson, 1996).

CURRICULUM CONTENT

The content of the curriculum is a second aspect of the hidden curriculum. In the 1970s researchers began to examine educational content to determine what it communicates about women and men. For more than 30 years, reports have documented pervasive and persistent gender stereotyping in instructional materials.

The White Male Standard

Readers in elementary school perpetuate gender stereotypes in several ways. First, they represent White males as standard by overrepresenting men and underrepresenting women. Misrepresentation of the sexes was first discovered in a classic investigation conducted in 1972 (Women on Words and Images, 1972). Entitling their study "Dick and Jane as Victims," the researchers reported that, in the 2,760 stories examined, there were approximately three males for every female. In biographies, males outnumbered females by an even higher percentage—approximately six to one. When males are the focus of the majority of stories and men are more worthy of biographies than women, students of both sexes are taught that males are both standard and important.

Perhaps you are thinking that "Dick and Jane as Victims" is interesting but irrelevant to education today. The same idea occurred to two communication scholars (Purcell & Stewart, 1990), so they replicated the 1972 study. They found that, although the numbers of male and female characters are more nearly equal now, other sex stereotypes persist. Males are still featured in two-thirds of the pictures and photographs in books. Perhaps more important, the researchers found that both sexes were portrayed in sex-stereotyped ways: Females were shown depending on males to help and rescue them; males were portrayed as engaging in more adventurous activities than females, and males continue to be depicted in a wider range of careers. A related study of elementary readers found that male characters are more visible, more active, and more involved in areas of life that are considered important in our society (Tetenbaum & Pearson, 1989). Other research confirms the persistence of gender biases in textbooks:

- In elementary reading books, there are twice as many male as female characters (Witt, 1996).

- High school chemistry texts have a three-to-one ratio of male to female images (Balzer & Simonis, 1991).

- High school history texts feature four times as many photos of men as women (Sadker & Sadker, 1994).

- In top-selling college psychology texts, males significantly outnumber females as authors and reviewers as well as in the examples in the books (Peterson & Kroner, 1992).

The male standard bias in our society is further reflected in theories taught in schools. For instance, prominent theories of human moral and cognitive development are based on research that relied exclusively on male subjects. Thus, the ways in which males develop morally were universalized to members of both sexes (Gilligan, 1982; Wood & Lenze, 1991b). As we learned in earlier chapters, however, many males and females are socialized in different contexts and in ways that lead to distinctly different cognitive and moral orientations. In general, feminine socialization prioritizes caring for others and responding to their needs, whereas masculine socialization emphasizes being fair to others and respecting their rights. Not surprisingly, when women were measured by a theory that excluded their experiences, they were judged to be less mature than men, on whom the theory is based.

By representing male moral development as standard, instruction misrepresents the range and forms of human morality. Until recently, science textbooks routinely described the process of human reproduction in ways that glaringly reflect social views of women and men: The active sperm "invade" the passively waiting egg. When scientists proved that the egg is also very active in the process, many science books revised their description of the process (Hammonds, 1998).

■ Gender-Stereotyped Representations of Women

Although curriculum content is less biased than in the past, gender stereotypes persist. Consider how history is taught and which people are emphasized. Accounts of wars, for instance, focus on battles and military leaders. Seldom noted are the contributions of women both on the battlefields and at home. Who kept families intact and food on the table while men fought? Who manufactured supplies for troops on the front? Chronicles of important events such as the civil rights movement focus on male leaders' speeches and press conferences and obscure the ways in which women contributed to the movements. We are taught about the leadership of Stokely Carmichael, Malcolm X, and the Reverend Martin Luther King, Jr., but most of us didn't learn about Ella Baker's pivotal work in organizing neighborhoods in support of civil rights.

The few women who are highlighted in curricula tend to fall into two categories. First, there are women who fit traditional stereotypes of women. For example, most of us learned that Betsy Ross sewed the first American flag. A second group of women highlighted in curricula distinguished themselves on men's terms and in masculine contexts. Mother Jones, for example, was a powerful organizer for unions. Women in this category tend to be represented as exceptional cases—as atypical of women in general. This implies that most women can't do what these few notable ones did (Spitzack & Carter, 1987). Women such as Ella Baker who achieve impact in other ways and other settings remain hidden (Spitzack & Carter, 1987).

Women and their experiences and perspectives are similarly neglected in other academic disciplines. For instance, Karlyn Campbell (1991) notes that women are significantly underrepresented in public address anthologies and public speaking textbooks. She argues that, in omitting women's speeches and women speakers, the field has undermined the goal of public speaking courses, which is to empower students to speak. Women, she observes, are not empowered when their courses teach them that only men and masculine ways of speaking merit study.

The male bias in curricular materials is further detected in the practice of defining historical epochs by their effects on men (usually powerful White men) while neglecting their impact on the lives of women. For instance, the Renaissance is taught as a period of rebirth and progress in human life when, in fact, it reduced the status and opportunities of most women (Kelly-Gadol, 1977).

As in other areas we have discussed, sexism in education intersects with other forms of discrimination: racism, classism, and heterosexism (Carty, 1992). Not just any males are presented as the standard: White, heterosexual, able-bodied, middle- and upper-class men are depicted as the norm. How often have you studied important people who were lesbian or gay? How frequently did you learn about the lives and contributions of economically disadvantaged people? Have you learned about Black women and men in journalism, Asian women and men in music, Hispanic scientists, or gifted African writers? Along with women, Blacks and other minorities are neglected in education, where the reference point has been and remains White males.

Dorothy Smith (2004) is an internationally recognized scholar in sociology. Her research and experiences as an educator convince her that schools teach a key gender lesson: who has agency. According to Smith, because of gender inequities in curricula "some students learn that their own voices have authority, that they count and should be heard; others learn their lack. Some learn that they belong to groups that have agency in society and that they can count on being recognized" (p. 285).

Gender-biased curricular material diminishes education. When students learn primarily or only about men and their experiences and accomplishments, they may come to believe that men matter more than women (Gastil, 1990; Hamilton, 1991; Switzer, 1990). This deprives all students of knowledge about women's contributions to culture and

Teresa

When I went home over break, I was telling my daddy about this class, and he got all upset when I started explaining the distortions in education. He started ranting that education was being ruined by a bunch of misguided liberals who are putting political correctness before truth. So I said to him that it's just a matter of *whose* politics are in control. It seems to me that it was pretty political to write books in the first place that ignored what a lot of women and minorities did, but that kind of political correctness is consistent with my father's values.

about areas of life in which, historically, women have predominated. On a more personal level, gender biases in instructional content encourage men to see themselves as able to fulfill high ambitions and affect the course of events, and discourage women from those self-perceptions (AAUW, 1998; Spade, 2001).

COMMUNICATION INSIDE AND OUTSIDE THE CLASSROOM

A third dimension of the hidden curriculum consists of communication that devalues women and feminine ways of learning and expressing knowledge.

■ Not Taking Women Students Seriously

In a classic essay titled "Taking Women Students Seriously," Adrienne Rich (1979) called attention to the fact that men routinely are treated as serious students, whereas women sometimes are not. Teachers often praise female students for their appearance, personalities, and nurturing inclinations, whereas their academic abilities and achievements receive little notice or encouragement (Brandt, 1994; Marshall & Reihart, 1997). When professors show interest in men's ideas and encourage them to work further but do not give the same support to women students, the clear message is that males are more academically serious—and worthwhile.

Compounding this are differences in how academic advisors and faculty mentors counsel male and female students. More time, effort, and mentoring typically are given to males than to females (Hall & Sandler, 1984; Sandler, Silverberg, & Hall, 1996). Women are sometimes discouraged from pursuing challenging careers and pointed toward less demanding careers. Further, as we noted earlier, the limited number of women in positions of authority in education reduces the likelihood that female students will find role models who could mentor them (Marshall, 1996).

Sexual harassment is a particularly reprehensible form of devaluing women students. Indicative of the overall lack of regard for women as students and persons, sexual harassment is widespread on college campuses (Haag, 2000). Women faculty and staff report being sexually harassed by male colleagues and administrators (Kreps, 1992; Wood, 1992b). Women students from elementary school to college report that some males routinely jeer, make lewd suggestions, and touch them without invitation or consent (Haag, 2000; Murnen & Smolak, 2000).

Bailey

It's so unfair how professors treat women. I'm a serious student, and I plan a business career, but my professors have never asked me about my career plans. Even when I bring the subject up, all I get is really superficial stuff—like they really don't want to talk to me. One of my boyfriend's teachers invited him to have coffee and talk about graduate school. My boyfriend didn't even have to ask! They spent over an hour just talking about what he would do after undergraduate school. And my grades are better than his!

Sexual discrimination and harassment are not confined to peer interactions. Some faculty treat women students in gender-stereotyped ways. Ranging from compliments on appearance instead of academic work to offers of higher grades for sexual favors, these actions make women students' sex more salient than their intellectual abilities and aspirations. In treating women as sexual objects, such actions tell women students that they are not taken seriously as members of an intellectual community.

■ Unequal Attention to Male and Female Students

From preschool through graduate education, many teachers pay more attention to male students. Further, teachers often give male students greater reinforcement than they give female students (Sadker & Sadker, 1994; Sandler, Silverberg, & Hall, 1996).

Gender biases in teachers' communication. Teachers' communication with students often reinforces gender stereotypes. Whereas teachers praise males for academic interest and achievement, they offer more support to female students for being quiet and compliant (Lister, 1997; Sadker & Sadker, 1986). This pattern was first noticed in elementary classrooms, but later research shows that it continues throughout all levels of education (Hall with Sandler, 1982; Sandler & Hall, 1986; Sandler et al., 1996).

More than two decades ago, a pioneering study (Hall with Sandler, 1982) called attention to verbal and nonverbal communication of teachers that gives less recognition and encouragement to female students than to male students. That investigation identified the following communication behaviors of teachers—both male and female—devaluing female students:

- Teachers are more likely to know the names of male than female students.

- Teachers maintain more eye contact and more attentive postures when talking to male students than when addressing female students.

- Teachers ask more challenging questions of male students.

- Teachers give longer and more significant verbal and nonverbal responses to males' comments than to those of females. When male students cannot respond to a question, they tend to be given additional time along with encouragement and coaching until they come up with a good answer; when female students do not answer correctly, instructors frequently move on.

- Teachers call on male students more often.

- Teachers are more willing to make time and to devote longer periods of time to confer with male students than with female students.

FYI

Gendered Education Around the Globe

A major study by Population Action International found significant differences in the education of males and females in 50 countries (Sharpe, 1994). The gender gap is greatest in sub-Saharan Africa, North Africa, South Asia, and the Middle East. In India, for example, 33 million fewer girls than boys attend school. The worst education for girls is in Chad, where the average adult woman has less than a month of education.

Women in the United States have the most years of school, 12.4 years on average. Yet the education of women in the United States ranked only sixth in the survey because fewer women than men attend high schools in this country. Ahead of the United States in the overall educational index were Belgium, France, Canada, Finland, and Norway.

- Teachers interrupt, ignore, or dismiss female students' contributions more often than those of male students.

- Teachers extend and pursue comments by male students more than those of female students.

You may be thinking that a 20-year-old study is irrelevant to what's happening in schools today. Unfortunately, that's not true. Research shows that teachers continue to engage in a range of behaviors that take male students more seriously than female students (Jones, Evans, Byrd, & Campbell, 2000; Marshall & Reihart, 1997; Sadker & Sadker, 1986; Sandler, 2004; Sandler et al., 1996). In 1992 the American Association of University Women Educational Foundation commissioned a comprehensive review of 1,331 studies of gender and educational practices. The result was a report titled "How Schools Shortchange Girls" ("Sexism in the Schoolhouse," 1992), in which evidence was amassed showing that female students continue to receive less attention, encouragement, and serious regard than their male peers.

Not coincidentally, this report also found that "girls enter first grade with the same [as] or better skills and ambitions [than] boys. But, all too often, by the time they finish high school, 'their doubts have crowded out their dreams'" ("Sexism in the Schoolhouse," 1992, p. 62). The evidence of this study led to the conclusion that the hidden curriculum creates a downward intellectual mobility cycle in which "girls are less likely to reach their potential than boys" (p. 62). The reasons for this pattern seem to lie in the cumulative effects of communication that devalues women students.

Another way some teachers reinforce traditional gender roles is by encouraging gender-stereotypical behaviors in male and female students. Consistent with cultural views of femininity, teachers typically reward female students for being quiet,

In their book, *Educated in Romance*, Dorothy Holland and Margaret Eisenhart (1992) ask why so many young women who enter college with strong preparation and ambitious career goals wind up radically downsizing their ambitions during their college years.

The authors spent 10 years studying women in college, many of whom moved from high career goals into a **culture of romance** in which being attractive to men became more important than academics and career preparation. Holland and Eisenhart concluded that two forces propel college women into the culture of romance. First, many women in college become discouraged by barriers to their academic achievement such as required readings and class discussions that emphasize important men and men's achievements and give little or no attention to important women and their achievements. Another barrier to college women in this study was seeing their professors treat male students with greater respect and interest than they treated female students. The second factor propelling college women into the culture of romance is intense peer pressure that emphasizes being attractive to men as more important than anything else women can do. It's a one-two punch: First, many college women discover that they and their career goals aren't taken seriously at college; then they turn to the culture of romance, which promises them a different kind of success.

obedient, and cooperative. Equally consistent with cultural views of masculinity, teachers often reward male students for accomplishments, assertion, and dominance in classrooms (Jones et al., 2000; Sadker & Sadker, 1986; Sandler, 2004). Whereas teachers tend to accept answers that boys shout out, they routinely reprimand female students for "speaking out of turn." This communicates to students that boys are expected to assert themselves, whereas girls are supposed to be quiet and polite.

Teacher expectations are particularly striking in their effects on African American students. When they begin school, African American girls tend to be active, ambitious, and independent—results of their familial socialization—but teachers encourage them to be less assertive and autonomous. By age 10, these girls have often learned that independence and achievement are not rewarded. Some teachers also communicate low expectations of African American males. More than their White peers, African American males are disproportionately targets of teacher disapproval and unfavorable treatment (Adams & Singh, 1998; Ferguson, 2004; Murray, 1996). Even when actual behaviors don't differ according to students' race, some teachers perceive African American males as more disruptive and less intellectually able than White males or females of either race (Ross & Jackson, 1991). When these attitudes infect the everyday life of schools, it's small wonder that African American males drop out in higher numbers than White males or females of any race.

FYI

Gendered Technology Education

Even cyberspace seems gendered! From elementary school through college, boys and men in the United States use computers more and enjoy them more than girls and women (Whitley, 1997). Initially this difference was explained as a result of males' greater aptitude for technology. However, that explanation lost credibility when researchers discovered that other cultures don't show the same pattern—across cultures, males do not have more positive attitudes toward computers or greater skill in using computers (Brosnan & Lee, 1998; Huppert, Yaacoby, & Lazarowitz, 1998).

So what might explain the differences in the United States? A likely contributor to gender differences is software. Much of the educational software features aggressive action, loud noises, and competitive activity, which is more appealing to males than to females. Research shows that many female students are bored by competitive, high-action educational software (Schiebinger, 1999). Female students are more interested in software oriented toward words and mysteries (Kafai, 1999; Schiebinger, 1999).

Are there differences in male and female teachers' expectations and behaviors? At least at higher education levels, there seem to be rather consistent differences. Compared with their male counterparts, female university and college professors are more likely to recognize females' contributions and intellectual talents and are more generous in giving them academic and career advice. In general, female students participate more actively and more equally with their male peers in classes taught by women than in those instructed by men. Research also indicates that differences in teachers parallel those found in parents, with male teachers tending to have stronger, more rigid gender stereotypes than female teachers (Weiler, 1988).

Communication among peers. The power of peer pressure is no myth. Once children begin interacting with other children, peers exercise strong influence on gender attitudes and identities. Acceptance by peers is higher when children conform to gender stereotypes (Maccoby, 1998; Reay, 2001), and this is especially true for boys (Messner, 2001). Males are much more insistent that boys do boy things than females are that girls do girl things, which continues the more rigid gender socialization that families give to boys than girls.

Looking back on your own experiences, you can probably confirm that it is less acceptable for boys to engage in feminine activities than for girls to engage in masculine ones. Most young girls play rough sports, but most young boys don't play house. Those who do are likely to hear the cardinal insult for a young boy: "You're a sissy!" Peers communicate gender expectations for aggressiveness and passivity, although once again there is greater acceptance of girls who deviate from feminine prescriptions for passivity than for boys who don't measure up to the rules for

FYI

Girl Culture(s)

At early ages girls teach one another about different kinds of femininities—different options for being a girl. And the options have different status among girls. A recent study (Reay, 2001) revealed that girls in primary schools recognize four clear types of girls and evaluate them differently:

- **Nice girls** follow the rules of traditional femininity—they are polite and quiet and deferential to males. Girls regard them as having no attitude.

- **Girlie girls** flirt with boys, write love letters to boys, and focus much more on boys than on girl peers.

- **Spice girls** celebrate girl power, don't defer to boys, and give priority to time with girl peers.

- **Tomboys** play sports with boys and try to be like boys.

Although girls tend to give the highest status to spice girls, teachers don't. Teachers regard them as too assertive, unfeminine, and, to quote one teacher, "real bitches."

masculinity ("How Boys and Girls Teach," 1992; Maccoby & Jacklin, 1987). Peers make it quite clear that boys are supposed to act like boys, which means above all that they must not show any signs of femininity. Once again, this reinforces the cultural message that masculine is more valuable than feminine: Boys may not act feminine, but girls may act masculine.

Male bonding that begins during adolescence reinforces masculine identification in most boys (Gaylin, 1992; Kerr, 1999; Messner, 2001; Rubin, 1985; Wood & Inman, 1993). At the same time, female bonding reinforces feminine identity in most girls (Greenfield, 2002; Reay, 2001). Because peer acceptance is extremely important in the first two decades of life, fitting in with school friends and chums is a cornerstone of esteem. Thus, children and adolescents generally do what is necessary to gain the approval and acceptance of their peers. This is a source of considerable frustration to many parents, who try to eliminate stereotypes in how they raise their children, only to find that peers quickly and effectively undo their efforts.

Masculine teaching practices. Teaching practices also disadvantage women students by favoring a classroom climate more conducive to masculine modes of learning and achievement. In Chapter 5 we discussed how gendered speech communities encourage distinctive ways of communicating. In general, males learn to use talk to assert themselves and compete, whereas females use talk to include others and build cooperative relationships. In line with the lessons of gendered speech communities, research shows that female students are more comfortable and perform better in classrooms that are interactive and that encourage collaborative learning (Seymour, 1995). With this in mind, consider what kind of classroom climate would foster learning and involvement for each gender.

The expected and rewarded patterns of classroom participation are more consistent with masculine than feminine ways of communicating (Gabriel & Smithson, 1990; Hall & Sandler, 1982, 1984; "Sexism in the Schoolhouse," 1992; Wood & Lenze, 1991a). From grade school to graduate school, classroom climates typically emphasize assertion, competition, and individual initiative. Students are encouraged to compete with one another in class discussions, performances, and tests. Further, assignments emphasize individual efforts and seldom allow for collaborative work. Assertion and self-confidence are more rewarded than collaboration and questioning. People who have learned to use communication to build relationships and collaborate with others find it uncomfortable to compete, to assert themselves over others, and to speak in absolute terms that don't invite others to participate. This may explain why many women students in coeducational institutions speak up less often in classrooms.

The effects of instruction favoring one gender's communication style are linked to the sex of students and teachers. In 1983, Paula Treichler and Cheris Kramarae reported on an experimental class that used styles of interaction and learning primarily reflective of feminine speech communities: discussion, group projects, interactive teaching and learning, cooperative review sessions, and interaction in which students collaborate rather than compete with one another. Women students particularly responded to this learning environment; men in the class at first found it uncomfortable but came to realize it had distinctive values and enlarged their learning. Later research (Crawford & MacLeod, 1990; Statham, Richardson, & Cook, 1991) indicates that women college faculty tend to encourage more participatory classroom climates than do male instructors. Not surprisingly, in classroom environments that are inclusive and invite collaboration, women students take more active roles, participating in relative equity with their male peers. These findings suggest that women, like men, excel in settings that favor and affirm their ways of thinking and communicating. By implication, the ideal instructional style might blend masculine and feminine modes of communicating, which would enable all students to participate comfortably some of the time and stretch all students to supplement their styles of interacting by learning additional ones.

The difference between the instructional styles in which each sex flourishes is one of the issues fueling the controversy about women in military training schools (Beck & Biddle, 1995). Formerly all-male South Carolina's Citadel and the Virginia

Military Institute were known for lack of privacy, harsh discipline, and punitive treatment, and for encouraging competitiveness and unflinching fortitude. But the all-female Virginia Women's Institute for Leadership and South Carolina's Institute for Leadership at Converse College, just 200 miles away from the Citadel, have a very different style of training. These schools rely on positive reinforcement and nurturing to develop women's leadership ability. Recent court rulings have made it illegal for military schools supported by taxpayers to remain all male or all female. The challenge now is for these schools to develop instructional styles that benefit both sexes equally.

The hidden curriculum makes schools more hospitable to males, particularly White heterosexual males, than to females. Although some of the issues we have noted here appear small, together they work to disempower women students. Although each specific form of gender inequity in education might seem minor, the *cumulative* impact can be overwhelming in communicating constantly that women and feminine modes of communicating and learning are less valued, less respected, and less able than men and masculine modes of communicating and learning.

Certainly not all women students are derailed by gender biases that permeate education. Probably you know some women students who are very successful academically; perhaps you are one yourself. It's also likely that you have been in classes where teachers didn't favor male students and perhaps were even biased toward female students. The gender inequities in education we have discussed, like other gender patterns, have predictable *general* consequences for women and men as groups. This doesn't mean some individual women and men aren't exceptions. Clearly, some are. Those who are may not accept limiting social views of gender, or they may be able to overcome the general biases that operate in schools, or they personally may not have experienced gender bias in their educations. But exceptions to the rule don't negate the rule—the general patterns that make schools more hospitable to boys and men than to girls and women. The point is that no student—woman or man—should have to work against the odds to gain an education. Learning should be equally accessible to all.

SUMMARY

In this chapter we have gone beneath the surface of education to examine the hidden curriculum, which creates unequal educational opportunities for women and men. The hidden curriculum consists of three elements. First, in mirroring the gender stratification of society, educational institutions reproduce the idea that men and masculinity are superior. Second, curriculum content devalues women by inadequately representing women and their experiences, contributions, perspectives, and contexts. In so doing, it represents men and male experiences as the norm, or standard, and women and their experiences as marginal and unimportant. Third, communication in schools contributes to gendered education by giving male students greater attention, respect, and recognition than are given to female students. In combination, these three elements reproduce gender inequities in schools, making education a process that generally empowers men more than women.

Noteworthy trends, such as those we have discussed, indicate that many educators are becoming more aware of the hidden curriculum and the covert, subtle ways in which it creates inequitable learning climates for males and females. Further, increasing numbers of teachers are reading articles on gender sensitivity and attending workshops that help them discover subtle biases in their own instruction. It is also encouraging to see the wealth of materials being written by scholars to provide resources for those who wish to include women's contributions and perspectives along with those of men to make educational content representative of the range and diversity of people who compose and participate in cultural life.

Finally, we should realize that many students actively challenge sexism, racism, and heterosexism in education. Many students, including a number of men, are taking courses in women's studies and African American studies to enrich the breadth of their education. Further, they often use what they learn in those classes to call attention to racial, gender, and sexual orientation biases in other courses they take. After taking my course in gender and communication, students sometimes report back to me that they have used what they learned in our course to challenge sexism in other classes. For instance, one man told me he had asked a professor to stop using male generic language, and the professor stopped. Another student said she had used her knowledge to intervene in a class where males interrupted females and where the professor paid more attention to male students' comments. Whenever a woman was interrupted, she would say, "I'd like to hear what Jane was saying"; whenever a woman student's ideas were dismissed, she would find a way to credit the woman in her own comments: "I think Mary had a good point when she said . . . and I'd like to extend it." Students are powerful agents of change and a major force in charting the future of education.

KEY TERMS

culture of romance, 201
hidden curriculum, 189
Title IX, 191

DISCUSSION QUESTIONS

1. Reread the FYI on Educated in Romance on page 201. To what extent is there a "culture of romance" on your campus?

2. Use the PowerTrac option in your InfoTrac College Edition to read Verne Bacharach, Alfred Baumeister, and Michael Furr's 2003 article, "Racial and gender science achievement gaps in secondary education," published in the *Journal of Genetic Psychology.* What factors do the authors cite as contributing to the differences between races and sexes?

3. Examine one or more of the textbooks used in other courses you are taking this term. To what extent do you find they include gender inequities?

4. Notice gendered patterns of communication in your classes. Do teachers call on male and female students equally? Do they respond with equivalent interest and encouragement to students of both sexes?

5. Think about your experiences as a student. In elementary and secondary school, what did your teachers praise about you and your work? What did they criticize? Are your experiences consistent with patterns identified in this chapter?

10

Gendered Organizational Communication

Pick battles big enough to matter, small enough to win.
—JONATHAN KOZOL

What do you see as the major challenges to getting a job and advancing in your career? If you are like most people, your answers differ according to your sex. When men and women were asked to identify barriers to their success in careers, 17% of women and 1% of men named sexual discrimination and harassment, 23% of women and 11% of men named prejudices of colleagues, and 14% of women and 6% of men named inflexible work patterns and schedules (Wajcman, 1998).

As we will see in this chapter, women's expectations of greater career barriers are well founded. We'll begin by discussing gender stereotypes that affect how women and men are perceived and treated in the workplace. Next, we'll examine gendered dynamics in formal and informal networks and see how these can result in inequitable treatment of women and men. Finally, we'll consider ways to redress sex and gender discrimination in organizations.

GENDERED STEREOTYPES IN THE WORKPLACE

The people who make up organizations have views of women and men, femininity and masculinity. Some of these views are gender stereotypes—broad generalizations about women and men that may or may not be accurate. Stereotypes of women and men affect how others perceive and treat them in professional contexts.

◼ Stereotypes of Women

Women in the work force are often classified according to one of four roles, each of which reflects a deeply gendered stereotype: sex object, mother, child, or iron maiden (Aries, 1998; Jamieson, 1995; Kanter, 1977; Wood & Conrad, 1983)

Sex object. This stereotype defines women in terms of their sex or sexuality. Frequently, it is expressed in expectations that a woman's appearance and actions will conform to cultural views of femininity; one example occurred in the summer of 1990, when an airline fired a woman ticket agent for not wearing makeup. The woman sued on the grounds of sex discrimination, claiming that makeup was not required of male employees and was irrelevant to her job performance. Even though she won the case, the incident dramatically illustrates the institutional expectation that women should be attractive.

Here is a recent example of defining women by their sexuality and appearance. As this book was going to press, the premiere Bolshoi Theatre fired Anastasia Volochkova, one of Russia's best-known ballerinas. The reason? She was "too fat." Volochkova is at least 5'7" tall (reports vary) and weighs 109 pounds (Kishkovsky, 2003).

Regarding women as sex objects contributes to sexual harassment, which at least 50% of the female work force has experienced (Rundblad, 2001). Stereotyping and harassing women are particularly prevalent in the military (Bourg & Segal, 2001) as exemplified by the Tailhook scandal in 1991, in which male military personnel mauled, violated, and verbally harassed female personnel. Incidents such as Tailhook reflect the continuing tendency to perceive and treat women as sex objects in the workplace.

The sex-object stereotype is also used to define and harass gay men and lesbians. Like heterosexual women, gays and lesbians are often perceived primarily in terms of their sexuality and their conformity—or lack of conformity—to conventional gender roles.

Mother. In institutional life, the stereotype of women as mothers has both figurative and literal forms. The figurative version of this stereotype is expressed when others expect women employees to take care of the "emotional labor" for everyone—to smile, exchange pleasantries, prepare coffee and snacks, and listen to, support, and help others (Basinger, 2001; Bellas, 2001; Cahill & Sias, 1997; Fritz, 1997).

> ### *Charlotte*
>
> I know the mother role all too well. Before coming back to college, I worked as an adjuster for an insurance company. In my office, there were 11 men and one other woman, Anne. I'll bet there weren't more than 10 days in the three years I worked there that one of the guys didn't come in to talk with me or Anne about some personal problem. Sometimes they wanted a lot of time and sympathy; sometimes they just wanted a few minutes, but always it was Anne and me they came to— never one of the guys. What really burns is that they went to each other to consult about professional matters, but they never came to Anne and me about those. They treated us like mothers, not colleagues.

Stereotyping women as mothers is the basis of job segregation by gender, a subtle and pervasive form of discrimination. Approximately three-fourths of women in the paid labor force work in service, clerical, or support positions (Matthaei, 1998). Although 60% of the U.S. work force is female, only 11.9% of the corporate officers of America's 500 largest companies are women (Armas, 2000; Erkut, 2001; Hoffman, 1998). The jobs to which women tend to be relegated generally have the least prestige and the lowest salaries. Gender and race intersect to influence job segregation; African American women are more often expected to fill mothering jobs than European American women are (Matthaei, 1998; Segal & Zellner, 1992).

The woman-as-mother stereotype also has a literal form. Women employees who have or plan to have children are often perceived as "not serious professionals" (Ashcraft, 1999; Jorgenson, 2000; Trethewey, 2000). The mother stereotype can become a self-fulfilling prophecy. For instance, if a manager doesn't offer a new assignment to Janet Thomas because he assumes she is preoccupied with her children, then Ms. Thomas is deprived of experience relevant to advancement. Later, when the manager is looking for someone with a background and experience in a certain area, he notes that Ms. Thomas is not qualified and attributes this to her motherhood.

Child. A third stereotype that is sometimes imposed on women defines them as children or pets—cute but not to be taken seriously. This stereotype reflects a view of women as less mature, less competent, and less capable of making decisions than men are. Stereotyping women as children often masquerades as "protecting" women. A few years ago, a company tried to bar all female employees of childbearing age from working in positions that exposed them to lead, because such exposure may affect fetuses. (It may also affect males' reproductive capacities, but men were not restricted from these jobs.) Regardless of whether the women planned to have children, the company insisted on "protecting" them from the dangers of these jobs (which, incidentally, were higher-paying jobs in that company). The policy was struck down when a court ruled that a company could not act as the parent of women employees, who are adults and capable of assessing risks and making their own choices.

One argument against allowing women in combat is that they should be protected from the gruesome realities of war. This is ironic, as women have been involved in and killed in every war fought by our nation. "Protecting" women from challenging work often excludes them from experiences that lead to promotion and raises, as well as from the personal development that comes with new challenges. Within the military, for instance, combat duty is virtually essential for advancement to the highest levels.

Stereotyping women as sex objects, mothers, and children contributes to the disparity between women's and men's earnings—a disparity that is not explained by qualifications, level of education, amount of experience, or performance (Aaronson & Hartmann, 1998; Henry, 2002; Steinberg, 2001). Consider examples

FYI

Gendered Wages

In 1963 the U.S. Congress passed the Equal Pay Act. At the time, women earned 59 cents for every dollar men earned. Today, women earn 86 cents for every dollar men earn. But averages don't tell the whole story. Women in the top 20% of the workforce have made most of the gains, while women in the lower half are paid about what they were 30 years ago. And women in the work force who are mothers are paid even less than women who do not have children (Crittenden, 2001).

Why does the wage gap persist? The President's Council of Economic Advisors reports that the difference between men's and women's pay isn't accounted for by training, experience, or type of occupation. After adjusting for these factors, a 12% difference remains that can be explained only by discriminatory attitudes and practices.

Might discrimination decrease when today's college students enter the workforce? Don't count on it. In an experiment, students were given money and told to negotiate with another player how much they would keep and how much they had to give to the other player. Both men and women made lower offers when the other player was a woman. ("She's a Woman," 2001).

of salaries of men and women in equivalent positions (U.S. Bureau of Labor Statistics, 2000):

Occupation	Mean Weekly Salary for Men	Mean Weekly Salary for Women
Financial manager	$1,154	$703
Physician	$1,364	$852
Attorney	$1,340	$974
College faculty	$1,038	$859
Computer operator	$ 610	$485
Bus driver	$ 498	$384
Insurance Adjuster	$ 660	$501

Iron maiden. If a woman manages not to be classified according to one of the three stereotypes we've discussed, she may be defined by a fourth. A female professional who is independent, ambitious, directive, competitive, and sometimes tough may be labeled an "iron maiden" (Garlick, Dixon, & Allen, 1992). An example of this occurred in 1990, when Ann Hopkins sued the accounting firm of Price Waterhouse for sex discrimination (Hopkins, 2001; Hopkins & Walsh, 1996). Ms. Hopkins brought in more money in new accounts than any of her 87 male peers, yet 47 of the men were made partner, whereas Ms. Hopkins was not. Describing Hopkins as "authoritative" and "too tough," executives told her that, if she wanted to be promoted, she should look and act more feminine.

FYI

Bully Broads

What's a business to do when one of its managers is a bully? That depends on whether the manager is a man or a woman. According to Jean Hollands (2001), a Silicon Valley executive coach, nobody likes a bully, but a man can get away with being one, whereas a woman can't. Bullying behaviors, such as demanding results and yelling at subordinates whose work is poor, are tolerated in men because they are consistent with cultural views that men are aggressive. The same behaviors are inconsistent with cultural views of femininity, so women who bully subordinates tend to be judged as ineffective.

The solution, says Hollands, is anti-assertiveness training that teaches managerial women to be more feminine. Her company, Growth and Leadership Center, offers "Bully Broad" programs that teach women managers to act nurturing, friendly, tentative, and deferential. Hollands coaches women to stutter, wear ruffles, smile, soften their voices, use self-deprecating humor, and cry—yes, cry, because it has tactical value for women, says Hollands. So far, Bully Broads has coached clients sent by premier companies such as Intel, Cisco Systems, Hewlett-Packard, Sun Microsystems, and Lockheed-Martin.

I met with Ann Hopkins to discuss her case. In our conversation, she recalled that a senior man in the firm had advised her to fix her hair and wear more jewelry (2001). Ms. Hopkins was promoted after a federal district court ruled that she was the target of gender stereotyping, which is a form of sex discrimination and therefore illegal. Yet many women who face discrimination lack the funds or confidence to fight for their rights.

These four stereotypes define women as undesirable employees. Women are viewed as incompetent (sex object, child), as able only to support others (mother), or as unacceptably unfeminine. Each stereotype discounts women as workers; each defines women in terms of sex and gender instead of job qualifications and performance. Explaining how they escaped these stereotypes, successful career women report that they were very careful not to be unfeminine yet simultaneously not to act "too much like women" (Nadesan & Trethewey, 2000).

■ Stereotypes of Men

Within institutional settings men are also stereotyped. Like stereotypes of women, those applied to men reflect cultural views of masculinity and men's roles. Three stereotypes of men are particularly prevalent in organizations: sturdy oaks, fighters, and breadwinners.

Sturdy oak. The sturdy oak is a self-sufficient pillar of strength who is never weak or reliant on others. In politics, we see dramatic examples of the extent to which men are expected to be sturdy oaks. Ronald Reagan ran for election and governed as a man's man, catapulting his role in Western movies into political life. One of George H. Bush's greatest handicaps as both a candidate and a president was that he was perceived as whining, leaning on others, and not his own man. The stereotype of the sturdy oak can hinder men in professional contexts. If others communicate that they think it is unmanly to admit doubts or ask for help, male workers may rule out consulting others for advice or assistance. One result can be decision making that is faulty because of lack of important input.

Fighter. Cultural stereotypes also cast men as fighters—brave warriors who go to battle, whether literally in war or metaphorically in professional life. Childhood training to be aggressive, to "give 'em hell," and to win at all costs translates into professional expectations to beat the competition. There is no room for being less than fully committed to the cause (your country, team, or company), less than aggressive, less than eager for combat, or less than ruthless in defeating the competition.

Because fighters are not supposed to take time from work for family, men who do so risk disapproval from co-workers. Although more than half of the men working outside the home would like to spend more time with their families (Klerman & Leibowitz, 1999; Schellhardt, 1997; Worley & Vannoy, 2001), many organizations disapprove of men who ask for time off to be with their families (Rapoport, Bailyn, Kolb, & Fletcher, 1998).

Breadwinner. Perhaps no other stereotype so strongly defines men in our society as that of breadwinner. Being the primary or sole breadwinner for a family is central to how our society judges men, as well as how many men judge themselves. Men who tie their identity and worth to earning power are in danger in an uncertain economy where job security is not assured. Also, as we saw in Chapter 8, an increasing number of women in two-earner families earn larger salaries than their partners do. Psychiatrist Willard Gaylin (1992) reports that most men who commit suicide do so because of business failures.

The accuracy of the stereotypes we have discussed is not supported by research on real women and men in the work force. Decades of intensive study show that women are effective as workers and managers (Aries, 1998; Deal & Stevenson, 1998; Williams, 2000). Research also demonstrates that stereotypes of fighters, sturdy oaks, and breadwinners don't fit all men in the work force (Eyer, 1992; Rapoport et al., 1998). Both women and men can be nurturing and supportive, and both can be ambitious and tough.

MASCULINE NORMS IN PROFESSIONAL LIFE

Because men historically have dominated institutional life, masculine norms infuse the workplace. Masculine norms establish expectations for professional communication and lead to three misperceptions that affect employment and advancement.

■ Misperception 1: Think Manager–Think Male

Within many organizations there is a pervasive mindset that management scholars call the "think manager–think male" phenomenon (Schein, 2001). Equating *male* with *manager* in the workplace poses a major barrier to women's advancement. The ability to manage and lead is widely associated with communication traits that are cultivated more in masculine speech communities than in feminine ones— assertiveness, independence, competitiveness, and confidence. To the extent that women engage in traditionally feminine communication, they may be neither recognized as leaders nor marked for advancement in settings where masculine standards prevail.

Comparisons of women and men in the same professional roles show that women of most races are more likely than men to base career choices on the desire to help others (Fletcher, 1999; Murrell, Frieze, & Frost, 1991; Woody, 1992). Women are also more likely than men to engage in caring, personal communication on the job (Lunneborg, 1990; Otten, 1995). For instance, female physicians tend to be more compassionate and patient centered than male physicians, and female attorneys tend to be more concerned with clients' feelings than are male attorneys (Gilligan & Pollack, 1988; Rosener, 1990).

Similar differences have been found between the managerial styles of women and men. Women leaders tend to prefer collaborative, participative communication that enables others (Aries, 1987; Helgesen, 1990; Rosener, 1990). Men, in general, engage in more directive, unilateral communication, which is consistent with communication patterns in masculine speech communities (Eagly & Karau, 1991).

Does this mean that women are less professional and less able to lead than men? Not according to research. Subordinates judge male and female leaders to be equally effective, and judge both masculine and feminine styles of communication to be important in leaders (Eagly & Johnson, 1990; Fletcher, Jordan, & Miller, 2000; Natalle, 1996). The most effective leadership style appears to incorporate both relationship-building and instrumental qualities (Cann & Siegfried, 1990; Fletcher, 1999).

Tara

When I first started working, I tried to act like the men at my level. I was pleasant to people, but I didn't talk with co-workers about my life or their lives. I did my work, led my team with firm, directive communication, and stressed results. When I had my first performance review, I got great marks on achieving tasks, but there was serious criticism of "my attitude." A number of people—both my peers and staff I supervised—complained that I was unfriendly or cold. People criticized me for not caring about them and their lives. I pointed out to my supervisor that nobody made those complaints about men, and she told me that I couldn't act like a man if I wanted to succeed in business.

There's one further insight to add. Men and women may be judged differently for enacting the *same* communication. This fact highlights the importance of distinguishing between how women and men *actually* behave and how others *perceive* them. If communication is perceived through gender stereotypes, then women and men may need to communicate differently to be equally effective. Because cultural views link femininity to friendly and supportive behavior, women who use assertive and instrumental communication may be branded "iron maidens" (Aries, 1998; Bradley, 1981; Butler & Geis, 1990). Co-workers who hold gender stereotypes may negatively evaluate women—but not men—who communicate assertively and who demand results. Thus, it may well be that women and men who communicate similarly may be judged very differently based on the gendered expectations of their co-workers (Deal & Stevenson, 1998; Rudman, 1998).

■ Misperception 2: Communication Styles Don't Change

Earlier chapters in this book demonstrated that our communication styles are learned. Feminine speech communities encourage communicating to create and sustain interpersonal connections and respond to others, whereas masculine speech communities emphasize communicating to assert independence and status. But are we bound forever by what we learned in childhood? Can we change our communication styles?

To answer this question we return to standpoint theory, which states that our ways of knowing and communicating are influenced by our contexts. Yet standpoint theory also claims that, as our contexts change, so will our ways of thinking and communicating. If this is true, then as women enter into positions requiring forms of communication not fostered by feminine socialization, they should become proficient in new skills. Similarly, as men interact with co-workers who use feminine communication styles, men should develop skills in collaboration and support.

Support for standpoint theory's claim comes from research showing that both men and women develop new communication skills that are needed for effectiveness on the job (Aries, 1998; Downey et al., 1998; Hochschild, 1975; Kaye & Applegate, 1990; McGowen & Hart, 1990). All of us can develop communication skills when we find ourselves in positions that require abilities not emphasized in our early socialization.

Nate

Dad died when I was 11, and up until then Mom had been gentle and not demanding. But then she had to go to work to support us. She took a job in a factory in our town, and she was so good at her work she got promoted to supervisor in a couple of years. I watched her become more independent, more sure of herself, and more willing to lay down the law to me and my sisters. Before, she would let us get away with just about anything, but she became stricter and more willing to enforce her rules. I also saw changes in how she dealt with others, like salesmen. She used to let them push her around, but that was history after she went to work. She became a stronger person in a lot of ways.

■ Misperception 3: Men and Women Can't Work Together

Because our culture defines women and men as opposites, some people believe that the sexes cannot work well together. This idea that we work best with "our own kind" has been used to justify the exclusion of minorities, lesbians, and gay men from professions.

Research does not support the idea that men and women don't work well together. Mixed-sex groups may enhance the quality of decision making (Cleveland, Stockdale, & Murphy, 2000). People who use feminine communication to support others and build team cohesion are complemented by people who use masculine communication to focus on the task and ensure efficiency. Effective groups need both kinds of communication.

GENDERED PATTERNS IN ORGANIZATIONS

Organizations have both formal and informal practices. Formal practices include policies regarding leaves, work schedules, performance reviews, who reports to whom, who authorizes and evaluates whom, and so on.

Informal practices include normative behaviors and understandings that are not covered by explicit policies: what is required to be on the fast track, gossiping and exchanging information, advising, mentoring, and so forth. As we will see, both formal and informal networks often entail gendered dynamics.

■ Formal Practices

Leave policies. In 1993, the Family and Medical Leave Act (FMLA) was passed so that employees could take time off to care for newborns, newly adopted children, or sick family members. The act, however, doesn't cover all workers. Only companies with 50 or more workers are required to grant family leaves, and some employees can be exempted from leave. Some individual states, however, do require companies with as few as 25 employees to grant family and medical leave (Bernstein, 1999). Further, FMLA does not require that companies pay workers who take leaves; therefore many workers cannot afford family leave even if they qualify for it.

The FMLA is not a complete solution. It covers only about 46 percent of workers in the private sector (Stafford, 2003). Unpaid leave is feasible only for well-paid professionals, leaving the majority of workers without a safety net ("Child Care," 1992; Cowell, 1992; Okin, 1989; Quinn, 2000). When time must be taken for families, it is usually a woman who takes it. Most fathers are reluctant to take family leave because they know doing so would lead co-workers and supervisors to take them less seriously as professionals (Adler, 1996). The view of women as mothers combines with the stereotype of men as breadwinners to create a situation in which it is exceedingly difficult for men to become full partners in raising children.

The language of leave policies also poses another dilemma. When companies name only maternity, paternity, or parental leaves, they exclude leaves to care for disabled or dying parents. As the human life span increases, a growing number of older citizens will need some assistance. How can children care for parents when leave policies don't acknowledge this need? The fact that generous parental and family leave policies are working in other countries—every industrialized nation except America has a national policy—provides reason to think they could work here also (Crittenden, 2001; Gerson, 1986; Hewlett, 1986, 1991; Okin, 1989).

Work schedules. Another way in which organizational rules affect men and women employees stems from rigid working schedules generally mandated. Increasingly, the 9-to-5 model of the workday is giving way to the expectation that 7 or 8 A.M. to

FYI

The Derailed Daddy Track

In fall 1993, Houston Oilers tackle David Williams learned a very expensive lesson: that men who put families above work get little support. Williams missed a game to be with his wife when she gave birth. He was fined a hefty $125,000 for his absence (Rubin, 1994). Like Williams, many men who take family time encounter resistance at work. Part of the reason for resistance is that many senior executives are men who grew up in an era when the norm was for professional men's wives to be full-time homemakers and mothers. The standpoint of the old guard makes it difficult for them to understand younger men who want to share family responsibilities. This problem showed up when John Kostouros asked for a parenting leave. His boss told him, "I can't figure why a grown man would want to be with his baby" (Rubin, 1994, p. 19A).

Despite resistance, many men want to be actively involved in their families. Nearly equal numbers of women and men who work outside of the home say balancing work and family is a major priority in their lives—74% of men and 78% of women (Gerson, 1994, 1998; Shellenbarger, 1997).

FYI

Maternity Leave Around the World

	Minimum Weeks Guaranteed	Percent Salary
Sweden *	51	90
France	16–38	84
Italy	20	80
Britain	18	90
Canada	15	60
Germany	14	100
Japan	14	60
Netherlands	7	100
United States	None	None

* For both parents combined.
Source: Child care. (1992, August 10). *Fortune*, pp. 50–54.

7 or 8 P.M. is normal for "really committed professionals." Obviously, this model—or even the 9-to-5 one—does not accommodate family needs (Williams, 2000). Even if parents can afford day care, children are sometimes too sick to attend; sometimes arrangements fall through, making it necessary for a parent to take responsibility for child care. Women are more likely than men to take time off to care for children, which reflects and reinforces gendered assumptions that women put families first and men put careers first.

> **Joan**
>
> I'm a single mother, and it's really hard to be that and a worker too. It's not fair that women so often have to sacrifice career advancement because businesses won't create more flexible work hours. When my daughter was young, I had to use my lunch hour to pick her up from preschool. Often I had to ask a neighbor of the day-care provider to stay with her until the preschool opened because I had to attend early morning meetings.

Research shows that providing more leave and flexible working hours frequently saves employers money. Most businesses find it less expensive to grant leaves than to replace employees (Walt, 1997). Further, many businesses have found that family-friendly policies enable them to recruit and keep talented workers they would otherwise lose (Quinn, 2000).

■ Informal Practices

In addition to formal policies, organizations operate with a number of informal, unwritten understandings that can make or break careers. Through

FYI

The Report Card on Family-Friendly Policies

The bipartisan Commission on Family and Medical Leave studied what happened in the workplace in the three years following passage of the Family and Medical Leave Act (Meckler, 1996). Other researchers have also studied the effects of family-friendly practices in the workplace (Worley & Vannoy, 2001). Among the findings:

■ Fewer than 4% of eligible workers took family leaves.

■ Ninety percent of employers surveyed reported little or no increase in costs as a result of the Family and Medical Leave Act.

■ More than 86% of employers said the Family and Medical Leave Act did not affect business productivity.

An increasing number of employers are providing family-friendly policies beyond the Family and Medical Leave Act. These policies include child-care subsidies, flexible work hours, on-site day care, and coverage of child-care costs during business travel.

a range of normative practices, some organizations emphasize gender differences, define one sex or gender as standard, or extend different opportunities to women and to men.

Unwelcoming environments for women. In Chapter 9 we identified a range of ways in which some schools marginalize and devalue women students. A similar pattern occurs in organizations that include language and behavior that are more familiar and comfortable to male employees than to female ones (Cheney, Christensen, Zorn, & Ganesh, 2004).

A key contributor to organizational climates in which some women feel devalued is language that emphasizes men's experiences and interests. Pervading most workplaces are terms taken from sports (*hit a home run, huddle on strategy, ballpark figures, second-string player, come up with a game plan, be a team player, line up, score a touchdown*), sexuality (*hit on a person, he has balls, he is a real prick, screw the competition; get into a pissing contest; stick it to them;* calling women employees "hon" or referring to women generally in sexual ways), and the military (*battle plan, mount a campaign, strategy, plan of attack, under fire, get the big guns*). Intentional or not, language related to sports, sexuality, and the military binds men into a masculine community in which some women feel unwelcome (Messner, 2001).

Even today, there is often resistance—and occasionally outright hostility—to women who enter fields in which men predominate (Palmer & Lee, 1990;

". . . And just when did 'our people' become 'our guys' . . . ?"

Schroedel, 1990; Strine, 1992). Women may be given unrewarding assignments, isolated from key networks of people and information, and treated stereotypically as sex objects, mothers, or children. Each of these techniques contributes to a communication climate that defines women as "not real members of the team." Sexual harassment further devalues women's professional abilities and highlights their sex, which complicates women's work lives in ways men seldom experience (Morin & Rosenfeld, 1998; Strine, 1992; Taylor & Conrad, 1992; Wood, 1993d, 1993f).

Tangia

Where I used to work, the boss was always dropping in on the men who held positions at my level, but he never dropped in to talk with any of the women at that level. He also had a habit of introducing males in our division to visitors from the main office, but he never introduced women to them. It was like there was a closed loop and we weren't part of it.

The informal network. Relationships among colleagues are important in creating a sense of fit and providing access to essential information that may not come through formal channels. Because men have predominated in the workplace, most informal networks are largely or exclusively male, giving rise to the term *old boy network*. Hiring and promotion decisions are often made through informal communication within these networks. For example, while golfing, Bob tells Nathan about a job candidate; over drinks, Ed tells Joel about an impressive trainee, so that trainee stands out later when Ed selects people for an important assignment; Mike talks with Ben, John, and Frank about his new marketing plan, so when Mike introduces it formally in a meeting, he has support lined up. Informal communication networks are vital to professional success.

Women tend to be less involved than men in informal networks. They often feel out of place because of their minority status. When only one or two women are in a company or at a particular level, they stand out (Kanter, 1977; O'Leary & Ickovics, 1991). Only when a group reaches about 30% does it have critical mass, that is, sufficient size not to be marginalized (Rowling, 2002). A sense of difference also is experienced by people of color when they enter predominantly White organizations. Co-workers' behaviors often compound women's and minority people's feeling of being different. When a woman enters an all-male group, men sometimes intensify masculine behaviors, talking more loudly, crudely, and perhaps profanely in what is probably an unconscious male bonding process (Kanter, 1977). Similarly, Mary Strine (1992) has shown that sexual harassment in the workplace, in addition to violating women, sends the message that "you are not wanted here." In the face of communication that defines them as outsiders, women may avoid informal networks and thus lose out on a key source of information and support.

Mentoring relationships. A **mentor** is a senior colleague who assists a junior employee in building a career. A mentor is at least helpful and sometimes indispensable to career advancement. Women and minorities are less likely to have mentors than White men are.

Several factors account for the low number of women and minority people who have the benefit of mentors. First, the numbers game works against them. The paucity of women and minorities in senior positions means that there are few who might counsel new female and/or minority employees. Research indicates that African American women are the least likely of all groups to be mentored (Morrison & Von Glinow, 1990). Men are sometimes reluctant to mentor young women for a variety of reasons: They may fear gossip about sexual relations; they may assume that women are less serious than men about careers; or they may feel less comfortable with women than with men. This pattern perpetuates the status quo, in which White men get more help in climbing the corporate ladder than women and minorities.

In an effort to compensate for the lack of networks and mentors available in existing organizations, some professional women have formed their own networks in which women share ideas, contacts, strategies for advancement, and information.

Reggie

I've tried to get into the informal network at my job, but I'm the only Black guy there. After I first started work, when I saw a group of the White men standing around talking, I would go over to join them. One of two things happened: Either they stopped talking and the group broke up, or they kept talking but made no effort to include me, nor even to acknowledge I'd joined them. I don't think they meant to dis me, but they sure communicated that I wasn't one of them. Now I just do my work and don't try to be one of them.

In addition to furnishing information, these networks provide women with support and a sense of fit with other professionals like them. As men and women become accustomed to interacting as colleagues, they may become more comfortable mentoring one another and forming sex-integrated communication networks.

Glass ceilings and walls. Finally, we consider what has been called the **glass ceiling**, an invisible barrier that limits the advancement of women and minorities. In 1991, *U.S. News and World Report*'s lead business story concerned the glass ceiling that blocks women's progress in professions ("Trouble at the Top," 1991). Labeling her report the "glass ceiling initiative," Labor Secretary Lynn Martin revealed that gender discrimination pervades the workplace, particularly at the upper levels.

Since publication of that report over a decade ago, other research has confirmed the persistence of glass ceilings that limit women's careers (Armas, 2000; Ekrut, 2001; Valian, 1998). Most often, women's progress is impeded by subtle discrimination that limits their opportunities. It might be the stereotype of women as mothers that leads an executive to assume that a working mother would not be interested in a major new assignment that could advance her career. It might be seeing a woman in sexual terms so that her competence is overlooked. It might be misinterpreting an inclusive, collaborative style of communication as indicating lack of initiative. All of these stereotypes and misperceptions pose subtle barriers —a glass ceiling that keeps women out of the executive suite.

But glass ceilings may be only part of the problem. As a 1992 report ("Study Says Women Face Glass Walls," 1992, p. B2) first noted, "If the ceiling doesn't stop today's working woman, the walls will." The term **glass walls** is a metaphor for sex segregation on the job, in which women are placed in positions that require traditionally feminine skills (assistant, clerical, counseling, human relations). Typically, such jobs do not include a career ladder on which doing well at one level allows advancement to the next. In essence, many of the positions that

---

FYI

Microinequities

Microinequities are pervasive and subtle forms of discrimination. These are verbal comments and behaviors that devalue members of a group but are not specific violations of laws prohibiting discrimination. Examples are speaking to male colleagues but not speaking to female ones, asking only a male worker to fill in as supervisor when the supervisor has to be away from the office, and not telling women workers what they need to do to improve job performance and qualify for promotions. Mary Rowe (1990) reports that, although microinequities don't cross the line of illegal actions, they have negative impact on morale, job performance, and opportunities for promotion and training.

---

women are encouraged to take have no advancement paths (Hoffman, 1998; Wharton, 2004).

Recognizing that subtle, unintentional discrimination is no more acceptable than overt prejudice, some companies are taking steps to break through glass ceilings and walls. Du Pont, for example, has initiated a rotation policy that moves women and men employees through different jobs so that all employees have opportunities to learn about the company and qualify for advancement ("Study Says Women Face Glass Walls," 1992, p. B2). This is a model of institutional effort to accommodate diverse workers and in the process enlarge the pool of talent available to organizations.

EFFORTS TO REDRESS GENDERED INEQUITY IN INSTITUTIONS

A desire to correct discrimination based on sex and gender as well as other factors has led to four efforts to end discrimination: equal opportunity, affirmative action, quotas and goals, and diversity training. Understanding the methods of redressing inequities and how they differ is important so that we can evaluate arguments for and against them and decide our own positions. Although this chapter focuses specifically on the workplace, these four remedies apply to both professional and educational settings, the two contexts in which efforts to end discrimination have been most pronounced.

▓ Equal Opportunity Laws

Laws prohibiting discrimination began with the landmark *Brown v. Board of Education* case in 1954, in which the U.S. Supreme Court overturned the "separate but equal" doctrine that allowed separate educational systems for White and Black citizens.

Following *Brown v. Board of Education,* a number of laws were passed in the 1950s and 1960s to prohibit discrimination against individuals who belong to groups that historically have faced discrimination. Two primary examples of **equal opportunity laws** are Title VII of the Civil Rights Act of 1964, which prohibits discrimination in employment on the basis of race, color, religion, sex, or national origin, and the 1972 Title IX, which forbids discrimination in educational programs that receive federal aid. Although Title IX is considered the primary federal law regarding discrimination on the basis of sex, it is not the only one. Others are Title IV of the 1964 Civil Rights Act, the Women's Educational Equity Act of 1974 and 1978, an amendment to the 1976 Vocational Education Act, and laws pertaining to specific institutes and foundations.

Equal opportunity laws focus on discrimination against *individuals.* In other words, complaints filed with the Equal Employment Opportunity Commission

(EEOC) must claim that a particular person suffered discrimination because of sex, race, or other criteria named in laws (Public Agenda Foundation, 1990). Equal opportunity does not ask whether a group (for example, women or Hispanics) is underrepresented or is treated inequitably. Instead, it is concerned solely with discrimination against individuals. Equal opportunity is assessed on a case-by-case basis.

Further, the equal opportunity strategy focuses on *present* practices; historical patterns of discrimination are irrelevant. For example, a university with a record of denying admission to women is not subject to suit unless a particular individual can prove she personally and currently suffered discrimination on the basis of her sex. Governmental obligation extends only to ensuring equality of opportunity in the present. It makes no attempt to address the impact of historical patterns of discrimination.

The scope of Title IX was weakened in 1984 when the Supreme Court narrowed its application from whole institutions to specific programs and activities that receive federal money. Despite laws, discrimination against women persists in educational settings. In Chapter 9 we saw that curricular materials, school organization, and educational processes unequally benefit women and men.

■ Affirmative Action Policies

President Lyndon Johnson used his 1965 commencement address at Howard University to inaugurate a new strategy for combating discrimination. Saying that recent passage of civil rights legislation was important but insufficient to end discrimination, Johnson called for policies that addressed the weight of historical prejudice. He said, "You do not take a person who for years has been hobbled by chains and liberate him, bring him to the starting line of a race, and then say, 'you are free to compete with all the others.'" Johnson went on to argue that equality of opportunity, which is the guarantee of civil rights legislation, must be matched with equality in results. To do this, he claimed, there must be measures to compensate for historical patterns of discrimination against groups as well as subtle forms of discrimination such as institutional racism and sexism.

Affirmative action is based on three key ideas (Public Agenda Foundation, 1990). First, because discrimination has systematically restricted the opportunities of *groups* of people, remedies must apply to entire groups, not just to individuals. Second, there must be *preferential treatment* for members of groups that have suffered discrimination, to compensate for the legacy of discrimination. Third, the effectiveness of remedies is judged by *results,* not intent. If a law does not result in a greater presence of women and minorities, then it is ineffective in producing equality.

The goal of affirmative action is to increase the representation, in education and in the workplace, of available and qualified women, minorities, and other historically marginalized groups. Some people think that aiming for greater numbers of women and minorities in companies and academic programs results in excluding better-qualified White males. Yet the claim that affirmative action deprives Whites of admission to schools is challenged by a recent study by William Bowen, president of the Mellon Foundation and former president of Princeton, and Derek Bok, former president of Harvard University (1998). After analyzing grades, SAT scores, and other data for 93,000 students of all races, Bowen and Bok found that eliminating affirmative action would raise Whites' chances of admission by a mere 1.5%.

Many people do not realize that affirmative action includes two important limitations. First, the goal is to increase the number of *qualified* members of historically marginalized groups; there is no pressure to admit, hire, or promote women and minorities who lack necessary qualifications. Affirmative action policies also recognize the *limited availability* of qualified people from historically underrepresented groups. Because of long-standing discriminatory practices, fewer women and minorities may be qualified for certain jobs and academic programs. Affirmative action attempts only to increase the number of qualified members of minority groups commensurate with their availability.

To understand how affirmative action policies work, it's important to distinguish between *qualified* and *best qualified*. Consider an example: Jane Evans and John Powell are the final two candidates for the single remaining opening in a medical school that requires a 3.2 undergraduate grade point average and a score of 1200 on the medical aptitude exam. Jane's undergraduate average is 3.4, whereas John's is 3.6. On the entrance exam, she scores 1290, and he scores 1300. Although his qualifications are slightly better than hers, both individuals clearly meet the school's requirements; both are adequately qualified. In such a case, affirmative action would require admitting Jane instead of John because she meets the qualifications and does so despite historical patterns that discourage women from studying sciences and math.

Affirmative action attempts to compensate for the effects of a legacy of bias by giving slight preference to individuals whose qualification was achieved despite obstacles and discrimination. For this reason, in every case in which the Supreme Court has upheld affirmative action, there has been what Justice O'Connor calls "a fixed time period within which it would operate" (Schmidt, 2003, p. A33). Affirmative action also recognizes the importance of critical mass, which we discussed earlier in this chapter. Only when groups that have been historically excluded achieve critical mass are individual members of those groups perceived as individuals, not representatives of their groups.

Since affirmative action began, U.S. courts have wrestled with the question of how much admission and hiring practices should take into account applicants' membership in particular group categories (sex and race, for example). Consistently the courts have ruled that increasing diversity is an important social goal, which makes it appropriate to consider factors such as race and sex (Gose, 2001). Diversity is considered especially important in educational institutions because they have a special responsibility to prepare leaders for the future and to prepare all

Doug

I think I speak for a lot of White guys when I say that affirmative action is unfair. It's nothing but race discrimination against Whites. I am working just as hard to earn my degree as women or minorities on campus. Why should I be at a disadvantage when it comes to getting a job? That's just unfair.

Sheretta

I get so ripped off when I hear White guys badmouth affirmative action. They don't know what they're talking about. They speak totally from their self-interest and their ignorance. The first thing they say is that qualified White men are losing jobs to unqualified Blacks. That's not true. Affirmative action doesn't require (or even suggest) that a job should go to an unqualified person, even if the individual is a green lesbian from Istanbul! Another thing White guys say a lot is that they didn't hold Blacks down in the past, so they shouldn't be penalized today. To that I'd like to say they sure as hell don't mind taking a heap of advantages they didn't earn, like good schools and clothes and financial support. Do they think they earned those things? How do they think their daddies and granddaddies earned them? I'll tell you how: off the labor of Black people that they were holding back, that's how.

students to work in a world that includes people of various races, religions, sexes, sexual orientations, and so forth (Schmidt, 2003; Will, 2003).

Extensive polling reveals that substantial majorities of students and faculty think they benefit educationally from ethnic and racial diversity on their campuses (Schmidt, 2001). Further, an Associated Press poll showed that 51% of Americans think affirmative action programs are necessary to overcome discrimination, 53% think affirmative action should be continued, and only 8% think America is very close to eliminating discrimination (Rives, 2003).

Ever since affirmative action policies were enacted, public debate about them has been vigorous. Yet until recently there has been little hard evidence about the effects of affirmative action. That changed with a 1997 study that compared the careers of 356 students admitted to medical schools under affirmative action with a matched sample of students admitted using standard admission criteria (Dreier & Freer, 1997). On a 4.0 grading scale, the mean GPA of the affirmative action students was 3.06 compared with a 3.5 mean average for students who did not receive special consideration for admission. Students admitted under affirmative action had lower grades during their first years in medical school, but graduation rates were very similar: Ninety-four percent of the affirmative action students graduated, and 97% of the regularly admitted students graduated. Evaluations of the graduates years later showed that members of the two groups did equally well in their residencies and became equally qualified physicians. Further, Black men who graduated from selective schools were more likely than their White peers to become civic and community leaders (Bowen & Bok, 1998).

In 2003 the Supreme Court again considered the constitutionality of affirmative action. The court heard two cases, both involving the University of Michigan. One case was brought by students who were denied admission to the University of Michigan as undergraduates. These students argued that it was unfair that minority students were given 20 of the 150 points needed for admission. The Court agreed, ruling that set points or percentages cannot be given solely on the basis of race. Chief Justice William Rehnquist explained the ruling this way: "The automatic distribution of 20 points has the effect of making the factor of race decisive for virtually every minimally qualified underrepresented minority applicant" ("In Their Words," 2003, p. 5A). In other words, race may be *a* factor in admissions decisions, but it cannot be *the* deciding factor.

The second case challenged the University of Michigan's Law School for admitting minority applicants who had less impressive qualifications than White applicants who were not admitted. The Law School did not award a set number of points to minority applicants. Instead, it judged every application on its individual, overall merit, and it gave consideration to race as well as other factors. The Law School justified this practice by saying it allowed the School to have a critical mass of minority students, which is distinct from having a rigid quota. The Court ruled that this is constitutional. Explaining the majority opinion, Justice Sandra Day O'Connor said that, "universities occupy a special niche in our constitutional tradition. . . . the Law School has a compelling interest in a diverse student body. . . . It is necessary that the path to leadership be visibly open to talented and qualified individuals of every race and ethnicity" ("In Their Words," 2003, p. 5A).

▪ Quotas and Goals

Quotas. Perhaps the most controversial effort to redress discrimination is **quotas.** Building on affirmative action's focus on results, a quota specifies that a number or percentage of women or minorities must be admitted, hired, or promoted. For instance, a company might stipulate that 30% of promotions must go to women. A binding quota requires a specified number or percentage of women regardless of circumstances such as merit. If there are not enough qualified women to meet the 30% quota, then women who lack qualifications must be promoted.

A famous case relevant to quotas was brought in 1978 when Alan Bakke sued the University of California at Davis's medical school for rejecting him, a White

When Quotas Raise Questions—and When They Don't

Some people say it's unfair to reserve places for women and minorities. They argue that all applicants should be evaluated on individual merit and not be given special favors because they belong to some group. It's interesting that questions aren't raised about a long-standing quota system that has benefited White and male students (Marble, 1994; Schmidt, 1998). Many, if not most, universities have legacy policies, which accord preferential consideration to the children of alumnae and alumni. At Harvard, for example, 44% of the class that entered in 1992 were admitted under the quota for legacies.

male, in favor of less-qualified minority applicants. Bakke won his case on the grounds that he had been a victim of "reverse discrimination" because the University of California at Davis violated his Fourteenth Amendment right to equal protection under the law. However, the Court did not outlaw the use of race as one factor in admissions decisions. It only ruled that schools may not set aside specific numbers of spaces for minorities. In other words, the Court allowed race to be a factor as long as it didn't result in a rigid quota. This view prevailed again in 2003 when the Supreme Court ruled that race can be one factor in admissions decisions, but no factor, including race, can be set as a quota or given a set advantage such as points added to admission profiles.

Nicola

The quota system is the only thing that can work. The laws aren't enforced, so they don't help, and affirmative action is just a bunch of talk. I've watched both my parents discriminated against all of their lives just because of their skin color. All the laws and pledges of affirmative action haven't done a damned thing to change that. Quotas cut through all of the crap of intentions and pledges and say point-blank there will be so many African Americans in this company or this school or whatever. That's the only way change is ever going to happen. And when I hear White dudes whining about how quotas are unfair to them, I want to throw up. They know *nothing* about unfair.

Tyrone

I resent the way so many people at this school assume that any minority student is here only because of affirmative action or quotas. I've heard people say that if it weren't for racial quotas, there wouldn't be anyone here who isn't White. One of my suitemates even said to my face once that since he hadn't had a quota to get him in here, *he* had to bust his butt to get into this school. I asked him what his SAT score was. He said 1080. I told him mine was 1164; then I walked out.

Goals. Goals are different from quotas, although the two are frequently confused. A goal states an institution's intention to achieve representation of minorities or women. For instance, a company could establish the goal of awarding 30% of its promotions to women by the year 2007. But goals do not require results. If the company awarded only 13% of its promotions to women by 2007, there would be no penalty; the company could simply announce that its new goal was to award 30% of its promotions to women by the year 2015. The effectiveness of goals depends on the commitment of those charged to pursue them. For this reason, groups that have been victims of discrimination are often skeptical of goals as serious efforts to increase equity.

Ironically, both quotas and goals can work *against* women and minorities. They can be used to limit the numbers of women and minorities in schools and organizations. The numbers specified by quotas and goals can be interpreted as a maximum number of women and minorities rather than a minimum. In our example, the 30% number could be used to keep more than 30% of promotions from going to women, even if 40% of qualified applicants were women. Departments may hire an African American or woman scholar and then cease to consider other female and minority applicants for future openings—they've met their quota by employing one.

Goals and quotas can work against women and minorities in a second way. When goals or quotas are in effect, members of institutions may assume that women and minorities got in only because of their sex or race. When this happens, individual women and people of color are not regarded as capable members of the school, business, or trade. Regardless of their qualifications, women and minorities may be perceived as not deserving admission, hiring, or promotion.

Diversity Training

A final remedy for persistent discrimination is diversity training, which includes workshops and materials that increase awareness of and respect for differences that arise from distinct standpoints. This strategy assumes that many people are unaware of biases against women and minorities. If lack of awareness is the problem, then a promising solution is to make people conscious of practices that inadvertently devalue and marginalize women and to teach them how to avoid unconscious discrimination.

Implementing this solution requires developing programs that inform educators and professionals of subtle biases and introduce them to alternative styles of behaving and interpreting others. For instance, faculty and staff at some colleges and universities attend workshops that teach them to recognize communication and course content that excludes or devalues women and people of color (Mickelson & Smith, 1998; Wood & Lenze, 1991b). In addition, participants are introduced to methods of making their classrooms more inclusive and equitable for people of color and women.

Of course, not everyone cares about inequities, and many people are unwilling to make changes, especially changes that may limit some of their own privileges. Thus, an important drawback of gender sensitivity programs is that they require the personal commitment and interest of administrators and participants.

SUMMARY

In this chapter we have considered a variety of ways in which institutional life intersects with cultural understandings of gender and communication. Cultural views of masculinity and femininity seep into the formal and informal life of organizations.

Yet what exists today will not necessarily exist in the years ahead. You and your peers will make up and define the workplace of the future. One of the most pressing challenges for your generation is to remake our institutions to correspond to the lives of today's men and women. By recognizing and challenging inequities and the stereotypes behind them, you have the opportunity to contribute to changes that improve the conditions in which we all live and work.

KEY TERMS

affirmative action, 224
equal opportunity laws, 223
glass ceiling, 222
glass walls, 222

goals, 228
mentor, 221
quotas, 227

DISCUSSION QUESTIONS

1. What do you perceive as the greatest barriers to equal participation in the paid labor force? What means of overcoming these barriers can you identify?

2. Have you observed instances of classifying women or men according to the sex stereotypes identified in this chapter? How are these stereotypes imposed on workers? How do people respond when they are classified according to a stereotype?

3. Use your InfoTrac College Edition's PowerTrac to access Herman Auginis and Christine Henle's 2001 article, "Effects of nonverbal behaviors on perceptions of female employees' power bases," in the *Journal of Social Psychology*. How did participants in this research judge identical behaviors enacted by women and men?

4. Interview some people involved in careers to discover how important networks are. To what extent do women and men professionals report that they are equally welcomed into informal networks in their organizations and fields?

5. Now that you understand distinctions among equal opportunity laws, affirmative action, goals, quotas, and sensitivity training, how do you evaluate each?

11 Gendered Media

Reality is wrong. Dreams are for real.

—TUPAK SHAKUR

Bruce Willis plays a sensitive psychologist in *The Sixth Sense;* a devoted husband and father in *The Story of Us;* a decisive, confident, aggressive businessman in *Armageddon,* and an authoritarian, cold-blooded general in *The Siege.* Julia Roberts portrays a flighty, flirty woman who is waiting for the right man in *Runaway Bride;* a successful movie star who longs for a man who loves her in *Notting Hill;* and a smart, assertive, sexy investigator in *Erin Brockovich.*

How would you describe the roles played by Willis and Roberts? How do these roles depart from established views of gender? How do they reinforce traditional views of gender? These examples, as well as others we'll discuss in this chapter, illustrate two key points about gender and contemporary media. First, today's media offer us both traditional and nontraditional portraits of gender. Today major actors embody established gender stereotypes: men as aggressive, independent, and violent; women as sexy, dependent and domestic. At the same time, media offer us gender portraits that depart from traditional stereotypes: men as sensitive and nurturing; women as assertive and independent.

The second key point is more subtle. Beneath the new images of women and men lie some very traditional gender stereotypes. Erin Brockovich can defy traditional views of femininity by being assertive and independent as long as she also embodies traditional ideals of femininity by being sexy. Elizabeth Corday on *ER* was acceptable as a brilliant surgeon as long as she was also in a committed relationship with Mark Green. Ainsley Hayes appeared as a strong, independent-thinking attorney on *The West Wing,* but viewers also called her "the blonde Republican sex kitten." The Powerpuff girls are smart and strong yet also very soft and nurturing. Bruce Willis can be gentle because he is clearly very masculine in traditional ways. Tony Soprano can be sensitive, but he's also a mobster who doesn't hesitate to kill. Jed Bartlet is a kind, caring man, but as the president of the United States, he's also the most powerful man in the world. What at first appear to be radically different images of women and men are still entwined with some very familiar, very traditional images.

Media offer a fascinating stage on which different, sometimes contradictory images of gender are played out. In this chapter we explore how contemporary media represent gender. We first establish the significance of media in contemporary Western culture and identify basic themes in media portrayals of women, men, and relationships between the sexes. Next, we examine media's role as gatekeeper of information on news related to gender. Finally we examine some key implications of media portrayals of men, women, and gender.

MEDIA SATURATION OF CULTURAL LIFE

Stephani

I don't think the media influence who I am or what I do. I mean, sure, I watch a lot of shows and movies and read magazines like *Cosmo* and *Self,* but I think for myself. I like to see new styles of clothes and hair and makeup and then I try them out for myself. That doesn't make me a dupe of the media.

Fred

I don't think my generation is very critical of media. Whatever it shows, we try to copy. Look at the "yard" [jail yard] look that everyone's wearing now, with jeans falling off our butts. We saw rap stars wearing jeans that way, and now we're all doing it. I remember when I was a kid and *Charlie's Angels* was on TV and Farrah Fawcett was so hot. My mom got the Farrah hairdo. So did a lot of her friends. Now the girls I know are copying Britney or Ally or whoever is hot at the moment.

Media pervade our lives. We watch television and go to films. While driving or biking, we take in an endless procession of billboards that advertise various products, services, people, and companies. Magazines abound, and each one is full of stories that offer us images of men and women and their relationships. Advertisements, which make up nearly half of some magazines, tell us what products we need if we are to meet cultural expectations of women and men. Newspapers, news programming, and talk shows shape our perspectives on contemporary issues. Popular advice books and gothic novels are best-sellers; pornographic print and visual media are increasingly popular.

Many people think they are immune to media influences. In fact, surveys show that almost everyone thinks media affect others but not themselves (Kilbourne, 1999; Schutzman, 1999). However, scholars who study media say most people rely on media to craft their opinions, identities, and lives (Calvert, 1999; Croteau & Hoynes, 1999). Joanna Wyn and Rob White (1997) assert that "media not only represent youth, but actively shape the experience and meaning of youth" (p. 20). In her book *Fast Forward: Growing Up in the Shadow of Holly-*

wood (1997), Loren Greenfield claims that, because most adults and young people grew up in a media-saturated world, they believe in the importance of image and use media images to construct their identities and relationships.

Media scholar Douglas Kellner (1995) argues that we live in a media culture whose "images, sounds and spectacles help produce the fabric of everyday life, dominating leisure time, shaping political views and social behavior, and providing the materials out of which people forge their very identities" (p. 1). Kellner also explicitly ties the impact of media culture to gender when he notes that media culture provides us with "models of what it means to be male or female" (p. 1). From newspapers to MTV, media shape our understandings of gender. By presenting us with images of women, men, and relationships, media suggest who we should be personally as women and men.

GENDERED THEMES IN MEDIA

What models of gender do media offer us? Three themes predominate. First, women and minorities are underrepresented. Second, men and women are portrayed primarily in stereotypical ways that reflect and sustain conventional views of gender. Third, depictions of relationships between men and women emphasize traditional gender roles and unequal power between men and women.

■ Underrepresentation of Women and Minorities

Media consistently underrepresent women and minorities. Whether it is prime-time television, children's programming, or newscasts, males outnumber females. A recent study of Sunday-morning news programs reported that only 10% of guests are women, and female guests were given less time to talk than males (Jenkins, 2003). Although in reality women outnumber men, media (mis)representations tempt us to believe the opposite.

Minorities are even less visible than women. Members of minority groups appear in supporting roles, and they are likely to be shown in predominantly White cultures with their own racial culture and values obscured (Holtzman, 2000; Merritt, 2000; Rhodes, 1995). Black characters are scarce and often stereotyped as subordinate, bad, or exotic. Ellen Seiter (1995), a professor of telecommunications, notes that, in Saturday-morning commercials on children's TV, Whites outnumber Blacks; speaking roles are reserved almost entirely for Whites; and Blacks usually appear on the sides of the screen, whereas Whites appear on the screen's center.

David Evans (1993) criticizes television for stereotyping Black males as athletes and entertainers. These roles, writes Evans, mislead young Black male viewers into thinking success "is only a dribble or dance step away" (p. 10) and obscure other, more realistic ambitions. African Americans are also underrepresented in news programming. Sixty percent of news stories on Blacks portray them negatively, and reports of crimes in which Blacks are accused are less likely to include prodefense sound bites than are reports of crimes in which Whites are accused (Entman, 1994; Meyers, 1997). Hispanics and Asians are nearly absent on prime-time television, and when they are presented, it is usually as villains or criminals (Holtzman, 2000).

Also underrepresented is the single fastest-growing group of Americans—older people, the majority of whom are women. In contrast to demographic realities, media consistently show few older women, probably because cultural ideals of femininity center on youth and beauty. Further, elderly individuals are frequently portrayed as sick, dependent, fumbling, and passive—images that don't fit many older citizens.

■ Portrayals of Men and Women

Media most often represent boys and men as active, adventurous, powerful, sexually aggressive, and largely uninvolved in human relationships, and represent girls and women as young, thin, beautiful, passive, dependent, and often incompetent. Although these remain the dominant gender images, media also present alternative, less traditional images of men and women, masculinity and femininity.

Portrayals of men. The majority of men on prime-time television are independent, aggressive, and in charge. Television programming for all ages disproportionately depicts men, particularly White heterosexual men, as serious, confident,

FYI

The Resurgence of the Military Man

Have you noticed the resurgence of wartime movies and, with them, the popularity of the traditional military man? Film critic Michael Medved (2000) has. He thinks Americans are renewing their admiration of the military man—in his most traditional form. In the wake of Vietnam, many Americans were disillusioned with war and military values, including the macho man embodied by John Wayne in *Sands of Iwo Jima,* which was produced in 1949.

Now, half a century later, we're getting updated but not really different military stories and military heroes. *Gladiator* exemplifies the most traditional military values—courage, strength, decisiveness, and honor. The same is true of *Rules of Engagement,* in which a court-martial leads to an embrace of the military warrior's code. Reflecting on what this means, Medved says, "The John Wayne military image may become an icon again. . . . The comeback of the military personality may also connect with a reborn interest in manliness in general."

competent, and powerful. Popular films such as *Fight Club, Armageddon,* and *Gladiator* exalt extreme stereotypes of masculinity: hard, tough, independent, sexually aggressive, unafraid, violent, totally in control of all emotions, and—above all—in no way feminine. The same stereotypical images of men dominate in popular magazines (Currie, 1998; Kolbe & Albanese, 1997). Jackson Katz and his colleagues (Katz, Earp, & Jhally, 1999) claim that media teach boys and men that being a "real man" means being powerful and in control.

Equally interesting is how males are *not* typically portrayed. They are seldom shown nurturing others or doing housework. With the notable exception of the 1983 film *Mr. Mom* (Vavrus, 2002), media tend to portray men as incompetent at homemaking, cooking, and child care. Television and magazines present ads for cooking and cleaning supplies that caricature men as incompetent klutzes in the kitchen and no better at taking care of children (Gates, 2000; Pendergast, 2000; Vigorito & Curry, 1998). Although children's books sometimes depict women engaged in activities outside the home, there has been little parallel effort to show men involved in home life. When someone is shown taking care of a child or doing housework, it is usually a woman, not a man.

Media often represent men in home situations as lazy dolts who care only about beer, cars, and sports (Kilbourne, 1999). A good example of this

Kaleb

What burns me up is those programs and commercials that show men as absolute idiots. One of the worst is that one where the mother gets sick and the kids and husband just fall apart without her to fix meals and do laundry. Give me a break. Most guys can do the basic stuff just as well as women, and I'm tired of seeing them made into jokes anytime they enter a nursery or kitchen.

negative portrayal of men is a commercial that opens with a woman leaving for work with her husband dressed in grungy clothes and slouching on the sofa, remote control in his hand. She tells him that the only thing she needs him to do that day is to open an Ameritrade account. Viewers see the man watching TV, eating junk food, and napping throughout the day. He is awakened by the sound of his wife's car in the garage. Quickly, he dashes to the computer and has opened the Ameritrade account by the time she walks in the door. The man is portrayed as a lazy, irresponsible child who must be made to behave by his wife.

Yet traditional representations of men are not the whole story. In *When a Man Loves a Woman,* Andy Garcia plays a man who is both sensitive and sexy, both nurturing and assertive. During the course of *As Good As It Gets,* Jack Nicholson's character is transformed from a homophobic, sexist, egocentric jerk into a more compassionate man who takes care of others. In *Nobody's Fool* Paul Newman plays a man who embodies both traditional and nontraditional masculinity. He is independent, largely self-reliant, interested in women, and a bit of a rogue. At the same time, he takes care of many people—his family of choice—and doesn't need to dominate others.

Contradictory images of masculinity are also embodied by rock and rap artists and their music. Some rappers uphold very traditional images of men, women, and relationships even as they claim to be alternatives to the mainstream. For instance, Eminem raps about violent, homophobic men who dominate and harm women, 50 Cent trades on his criminal past, and Nelly imitates gangsters with his gold tooth and yard fashions. At the same time, an LL Cool J video features a gospel choir and portraits of young children. In his video "Retrospect for Life," 25-year-old Common shows a young, pregnant Black woman who faces single motherhood until the father returns to stay with her. What accounts for the change? In an interview with *Newsweek*'s Veronica Chambers, Common said, "A lot of my friends were getting turned off to hip-hop music because we were growing up" (Chambers, 1998, p. 66). LL Cool J, who had children with a woman to whom he wasn't married, offered a different answer: "I went to see my kids and my son asked me, 'Daddy, are you going to marry Mommy?' That was deep to listen to. That told me he was yearning for a family" (Chambers, 1998, p. 67). Snoop Doggy Dogg and Coolio soon followed LL Cool J to the altar.

Portrayals of women. Although media sometimes present women in nontraditional roles or with nontraditional qualities, most media images reflect long-established cultural stereotypes of women and femininity. The feminine ideal is young and thin, preoccupied with men and children, and enmeshed in relationships or housework (Crane, 1999; Holtzman, 2000). Traditional views of femininity even find their way into news shows, where female newscasters are young, attractive, and less outspoken than males (Craft, 1988; Jenkins, 2003; Sanders & Rock, 1988).

Wanted: News Anchor for CNN. Qualifications: Female, Blonde, Young, and Gorgeous; No Journalistic or News Experience Needed.

In 2001, as part of revamping its *Headline News,* CNN decided to hire a new anchor. Did they look for veteran journalists or people who had experience working with the news? No. Instead, they hired Andrea Thompson, best known for her role as a detective on *NYPD Blue* if not for her erotic appearances in films such as *Jag* and *A Gun, a Car, a Blonde* (Levesque, 2001). Although Thompson never completed high school, she's confident viewers will accept her as a news anchor, despite what she refers to as "creative decisions" about her artistic career (Stroup, 2001). In an effort to become qualified after CNN hired her, Thompson worked with KRQE-TV in Albuquerque to learn how to write broadcast copy and do stand-up work in front of cameras. Hiring Thompson for her appearance was an example of media's long-standing tendency to favor very young, very attractive women and to use them to decorate news (Halper, 2001).

From children's programming, in which a majority of female characters typically spend their time watching males do things (Thompson & Zerbinos, 1995, 1997), to MTV, which routinely pictures men dominating women, who enjoy it (Jhally & Katz, 2001), media repeat the cultural view of women as dependent, ornamental objects who exist to look good, please men, care for children, and be sexually desirable and available. Current popular magazines aimed at women provide better coverage than women's magazines of a decade ago on issues such as managing money, social projects, and obtaining credit. However, they also continue to advise women how to look better, lose weight, appeal to men, cook nice meals, maintain relationships, keep the home clean, and care for families (Kuczynski, 2001; Rapping, 1994).

Media have created two opposing images of women: good and bad. These polar opposites are often juxtaposed to dramatize differences in the consequences that befall good and bad women. Good women are pretty, deferential, faithful, and focused on home and family. Subordinate to men, they are usually cast as victims, angels, martyrs, and loyal helpmates.

But aren't we seeing some images of good women who don't fit the old stereotypes? For instance, in the *Charlie's Angels* films, three very smart, aggressive women are portrayed positively,

Jill

I hate reading magazines or watching TV anymore. All they tell me is what's wrong with me and what I should do to fix it. I think my butt is too big; my roommate has decided hers is too little. Doesn't anybody have a butt that is right? Same for breasts. I wonder if I should have breast enlargement surgery. It sounds stupid, but I keep thinking that I would look better and be more popular. I pluck my eyebrows and wax my legs and streak my hair. I wonder if it will ever be okay for women to look like they really look!

Regina

The ad that just kills me is the one where a woman is cleaning her carpet with whatever product is being advertised—something you sprinkle on your rug and then vacuum up. This woman is dancing around with her vacuum and seems deliriously happy—like this is what she most loves to do in the world. We may do cleaning, but only a total bimbo would get ecstatic about it. That ad makes women look silly and stupid and trivial.

and *Titanic* features Rose, a woman who takes charge of her life. If we look more closely at these allegedly nontraditional images of women, we see that a desirable woman can be strong and successful if and only if she also meets traditional stereotypes of femininity—that is, if she is beautiful, compassionate, and identified with one or more men (Simonton, 1995). The women in *Charlie's Angels* are very sexy and are often shown partially nude—dancing in underwear, wrapped in bath towels, and exposing cleavage even as they engage in fights. They fight the movie's villains in leather outfits and high heels and never break a sweat. In *Titanic* Rose becomes a powerful character, but initially she is very passive—engaged to a man she doesn't love, going on a cruise her mother has forced on her. Rose gains personal power and voice only when Jack brings her alive with his attentions. In today's media, even as women seem to depart from the "good woman" image, many continue to embody it.

Media also offer us the "evil sister of the good homebody" image. Versions of this image are the witch, bitch, whore, or iron maiden. Exemplifying the evil woman is Glenn Close's role in *Fatal Attraction*. Elisabeth Shue plays a call girl in 1995's *Leaving Las Vegas,* and Sharon Stone appears as an alcoholic in *Casino* in the same year. Four years later, in 1999, Sharon Stone plays Gloria, a "bad woman" (an ex-mistress and ex-convict) who develops maternal inclinations toward an orphan and thereby is transformed into a "good woman." In children's literature, we encounter witches and mean stepmothers as bad women and beautiful, passive females like Snow White and Sleeping Beauty as good women.

In the 1990s more women were featured as strong main characters on primetime television (Seplow, 1996). CBS's popular *Chicago Hope* featured Christine Lahti as Dr. Kathryn Austin, a brilliant cardiac surgeon who was chief of staff and then chief of surgery. Women portrayed top officers on NBC's *Law & Order* and Fox's *New York Undercover.* This trend continued with women in strong roles on *The Practice, The X-Files, The West Wing,* and *ER* (Liner, 2001). It's interesting to note that networks rejected *Any Day Now* for eight years. Networks repeatedly told Nancy Miller, the writer and producer, that they would be interested in airing the series if she changed the two main characters from girls to boys (Jenkins, 2003).

The criteria for the good woman have been challenged in some recent films and TV shows. For instance, Camryn Manheim on *The Practice* is considerably heavier than social ideals of femininity prescribe. The character of Dr. Melfi on *The Sopranos* is middle aged and not especially thin or sexy. Princess Fiona in *Shrek* is an overweight, green ogre who never changes into a beautiful princess. *Sailor Moon* is a popular children's show in which a female lead character gets involved in amazing adventures (Leaper, 2000). And Marina, the lead character in Disney's *Sinbad,*

"**N**obody invades Earth without a fight!" declares Blossom as she, Bubbles, and Buttercup prepare to fight aliens. Meet the Powerpuff Girls, one of the hot new hits on the Cartoon Network. Their show attracts a 2 million-plus audience; the Powerpuff Girls CD was a hit on both children's and college charts; and Powerpuff Girls costumes are huge favorites for Halloween. Craig McCracken, who created the Powerpuff Girls, says he liked the contrast between traditional images of cute girls and the nontraditional image of tough, powerful women (Rosenfeld, 2001). And these aren't the one-stereotype-fits-all kind of gals. Each one has a unique identity. Red-headed Blossom is the leader. Bubbles is blonde and silly. And Buttercup is the tough, quick-tempered fighter who likes to hit first and ask questions later. Together they fight all the dangers that threaten their home of Townsville, while offering images of girls that combine nurturing and aggression, giggling and fighting, independence and taking care of others.

decides not to marry the prince. Instead, she chooses the adventurous life of sailing the seas, becoming a pirate, and saving her crew and ship from sirens. The runaway hit *Crouching Tiger, Hidden Dragon* tells the story of Jen Yu, a strong woman who resists the marriage that has been arranged for her. Jen Yu fights fiercely, never needs to be rescued, and calls her own shots. Although Jen Yu, like Thelma and Louise, goes over a cliff to avoid being controlled by others, she is nonetheless a strong, self-made character. When director Ang Lee accepted the Golden Globe Award in 2001 for this film, he said he had modeled his female characters after "my wife, who is the strongest person I know." Susan Sarandon portrays women who are strong, serious, capable, and not particularly young or beautiful. Recently, women warriors have become popular in shows such as *Xena, Dark Angel, Buffy the Vampire Slayer, Alias,* and *Witchblade.*

At the same time that some women are being portrayed in nontraditional ways, other portrayals of women reproduce highly traditional images and roles. For instance, with the exception of Dr. Melfi, the women on *The Sopranos* are dependent on men, and their primary identity is that of sex object. Tony Soprano and other men on the show have wives and mistresses, and a favorite gathering place for the men on the show is Ba Da Bing, a strip club. In a bow to traditional views of femininity, the women members of the Soprano family aren't allowed to work in the family business.

Perhaps the most interesting trend in media is combining traditional and nontraditional images of gender in a single character. For instance, Erin Brockovich meets the conventional feminine image of sexiness, but she defies prevailing expectations of femininity by refusing to put her children ahead of her own goals. On *Star Trek: Voyager,* Captain Katherine Janeway transcended traditional views of women by commanding a spaceship while also conforming to established images of femininity by referring to the crew as "a family." Jack in *Titanic* is traditionally masculine in his adventurous spirit and independence, yet he is also nurturing and gentle. In *Saving Private Ryan*, Tom Hanks's character fulfills dominant views of masculinity by being a soldier and engaging in the violence of war; at the same time, he disputes conventional views of masculinity by showing nurturance and tenderness.

Images of Relationships Between Men and Women

Four themes in media reflect and promote traditional images of relations between the sexes. Yet, occasionally media challenge traditional views of male-female relationships.

Women's dependence/Men's independence. Media continue to portray women as domestic and dependent on powerful, independent men. Although this portrayal is dominant, it is no longer the only image of male–female relationships.

Consider first the prevalence of depictions of girls and women as dependent and boys and men as independent. Disney's award-winning animated film *The Little Mermaid* vividly embodies females' dependence on males for identity. In this feature film, the mermaid quite literally gives up her identity as a mermaid in order to be with her human lover. Similarly, Disney's *The Lion King* features female lions that depend on a male lion to save them, and the heroine of *Pocahontas* is portrayed as a beautiful, sexy maiden rather than the brave young Native American girl she actually was.

Sugar and Spice, Snakes and Snails

Advertisers seem to think the old nursery rhyme is right. Communication scholars Fern Johnson and Karen Young (2002) analyzed television ads aimed at children. They found:

- Boys were targeted for toys involving action or violence (Electronic Karate Fighters, War Planets), whereas girls were targeted for toys involving caretaking (Take Care of Me Twins, Tea Bunnies) and fashion (Fingernail Fun Salon Set).

- Ads targeting boys emphasized action, competition, destruction, and control, whereas ads targeting girls emphasized feelings and nurturing.

- Power words were prevalent in ads that targeted boys and absent in ads that targeted girls.

Women as well as minorities are still more often cast in supporting roles than leading ones in both children's shows and their commercials. The vast majority of MTV portrays females as taking care of others and waiting for men's rescue or attention, whereas males are shown ignoring, exploiting, or directing women (Jhally & Katz, 2001). Some male gangsta rappers refer to women as "bitches" and "hos" (whores), terms that invite disrespect and violence toward women. News programs hosted by male and female teams routinely cast the female as deferential to the male (Craft, 1988; Sanders & Rock, 1988). Similarly, Blacks are unlikely to be represented as experts on topics other than Black affairs (Entman, 1994), and Blacks are still too often cast in racially stereotyped roles (Kern-Foxworth, 1994; Merritt, 2000). In commercials, men are usually shown positioned above women, and women are more frequently pictured in varying degrees of undress (Crane, 1999). Such nonverbal cues represent men as powerful and women as vulnerable and submissive.

In a brief departure from this pattern in the 1970s, films and television responded to the second wave of feminism by showing women who were independent but not hard, embittered, or without close relationships. Films such as *Alice Doesn't Live Here Anymore*, *Up the Sandbox*, *The Turning Point*, *Diary of a Mad Housewife*, and *An Unmarried Woman* offered realistic portraits of women who sought and found their own voices independent of men's. *My Brilliant Career* particularly embodies this focus by telling the story of a woman who chooses work over marriage. During this period, television followed suit, offering viewers prime-time fare such as *Maude* and *The Mary Tyler Moore Show*, which starred women who were able and achieving in their own rights (Dow, 1996). *One Day at a Time*, which premiered in 1974, was the first prime-time program about a divorced woman.

By the 1980s, however, traditionally gendered images of heterosexual relationships resurged as the backlash movement against feminism gained strength. Film fare in the 1980s and 1990s included *Pretty Woman*, in which a prostitute becomes a good woman when she captures the heart and brings out the tender side of a stereotypically powerful, rich man. Meanwhile, the film *Tie Me Up, Tie Me Down* trivializes abuse of women and celebrates women's dependence on men with a story of a woman who is bound by a man and colludes in sustaining her bondage. The series *Crossing Delancey* showed professionally accomplished Amy Irving talked into believing she needs a man to be complete, a theme reprised by Cher in *Moonstruck*.

Continuing into the present era, the campaign to restore traditional gender roles is obvious in magazines, which have reinvigorated their focus on women's role as the helpmate and supporter of husbands and families. Even magazines such as *Working Woman* and *Savvy*, which are aimed at professional women, show a renewed attention to appearance and dress, along with articles on career topics. The same is true of magazines for preadolescent and adolescent girls (Kuczynski, 2001).

Recently we've seen a few challenges of the traditional depiction of relations between the sexes. In the children's show *Dexter's Laboratory,* a little boy is a genius in his basement laboratory. However, his big sister usually outsmarts him. Captain Janeway on *Star Trek: Voyager* was in charge of all the men and women on her spaceship. A number of women play strong characters on shows such as *ER, Law & Order, X-Files,* and *NYPD Blue.* In departing from the predominant media images of women as dependent on men and subservient to them, these views of gendered relationships offer us new possibilities for individual identity and interpersonal interaction.

Women's incompetence/Men's authority. A second still-prevalent theme in media representations of relationships is men as the competent authorities who save women from their incompetence. Children's literature vividly implements this motif by portraying females who are rescued by males. Sleeping Beauty's resurrection depends on Prince Charming's kiss. The same theme appears in highly popular gothic romance novels and soap operas for adults.

One of the most pervasive ways in which media define males as authorities is in commercials. Women are routinely shown anguishing over dirty floors and bathroom fixtures only to be relieved of their distress when Mr. Clean shows up to tell them how to keep their homes spotless. Even when commercials are aimed at women and are selling products intended for them, 90% of the time a man's voice is used to explain the value of what is being sold (Basow, 1992; Bretl & Cantor, 1988). Using male **voice-overs** reinforces the cultural view that men are authorities and women depend on men to tell them what to do. Men are also portrayed as authorities in newspapers—more than two-thirds of cited sources are male (Zoch & Turk, 1998).

As with other stereotypes, this one is being challenged. The children's film *Sinbad* tells the story of a young woman who decides not to marry a prince. Instead, she follows her heart to sail the seas and becomes a pirate. Jen Yu in *Crouching Tiger, Hidden Dragon* takes care of herself instead of waiting for a man to rescue her. The same is true of Queen Amidala in *Star Wars–Episode I,* and of Buffy, Abigail Bartlet on *The West Wing,* and Eleanor Frutt on *The Practice.* As we see alternative images of women and men, we gain freedom to imagine and create ourselves as we choose.

Women as primary caregivers/Men as breadwinners. A third perennial theme in media is that women are caregivers and men are breadwinners. Since the 1980s, in fact, this gendered arrangement has been broadcast with renewed vigor. Media portrayals of career women often give little or no attention to their career activities. Although these characters have titles such as lawyer or doctor, they are shown predominantly in their roles as homemakers, mothers, and wives. In the popular sitcom, *Ally McBeal,* we saw Ally mainly outside of the courtroom and immersed in very traditional feminine roles and activities such as needing a man ("I feel empty without a man."), obsessed with her appearance ("I'm nothing without my face.") (Heywood, 1998).

Magazines play a key role in promoting appearance and pleasing others as foci of women's lives (Kuczynski, 2001; Peirce, 1990). Advertising tells women how to be "me, only better" by coloring their hair; how to lose weight and get rid of wrinkles so "you'll still be attractive to him"; and how to prepare gourmet meals so "he's always glad to come home." The ads and articles emphasize that women need to change themselves to be adequate—they need to fix, improve, repair, rejuvenate, disguise, and correct some or all parts of themselves. Beneath these ads is the warning that, if a woman fails to look good and please her man, he might leave (Kang, 1997; Kilbourne, 1999; Lont, 1995).

There is a second, less obvious way in which ads contribute to stereotypes of women as focused on others and men as focused on work. Sometimes advertisers control the *content* of magazines. In exchange for placing an ad, a company sometimes receives **complementary copy**—one or more articles that increase the market appeal of its product (Turner, 1998). A soup company that places an ad might be given a three-page story on how to prepare meals using that brand of soup; an ad for hair-coloring products might be accompanied by interviews with famous women who dye their hair.

Women's roles in the home and men's roles outside of it are reinforced by newspapers and news programming. Both emphasize men's independent activities and, in fact, define news almost entirely as stories about and by men. Stories about men focus on work and on their achievements (Luebke, 1989), reiterating the cultural message that men are supposed to *do,* to perform. Meanwhile, the few stories about women tend to emphasize their roles as wives, mothers, and homemakers. Even stories about women who are in the news because of achievements and professional activities typically mention marriage, family life, and other aspects of women's traditional roles. For example, when Margaret Thatcher became prime minister of England, newspapers repeatedly referred to her as "a housewife," a label that ignored her long and active role in politics (Romaine, 1999).

Women as victims and sex objects/Men as aggressors. A final theme in media's representations of relationships is that women continue to be portrayed as sex objects. In this representation, the very qualities women are encouraged to develop (beauty, sexiness, passivity, and powerlessness) in order to meet cultural ideals of femininity contribute to objectifying and dehumanizing them (Jhally & Katz, 2001). Also, the qualities that men are urged to exemplify (aggressiveness, sexuality, and strength) are the same qualities that are linked to abuse of women (Messner, 2001; Wood, 2001b).

Prevalent in media of all types are images of desirable men as aggressive and dominant and of desirable women as young, pretty, sexual, and helpless (Kang, 1997). Advertising directed at men often links products with hypermasculinity and violence. For example, leading brands of condoms bear the names of ancient warriors (Trojans) and kings (Rameses). Super-athlete Michael Jordan advertises Hanes underwear for men. Other athletes are used to advertise yogurt, deodorant, and light beers—if a star athlete will eat yogurt and drink light beer, these products must be manly (Katz, 1995).

Whereas men are seldom pictured nude or even partially unclothed, women habitually are (Ansen & Bunn, 1995). Advertisements for makeup, cologne, shampoo, and clothes often show women attracting men because they used the products to make themselves irresistible. Perhaps you've seen the commercial for a particular shampoo. First we see an attorney in a courtroom. When the judge says the word "urge," she goes into a highly eroticized fantasy in which buff men shampoo her hair with the product. The message is that, even in a professional context, a woman is basically sexual. That message is reinforced by on-air comments that demean women's professionalism and emphasize their sexuality. For example, the *New York Post* referred to foreign correspondent Christiane Amanpour as a "war slut," and the *Wall Street Journal* criticized her choice of clothing; the *Wall Street Journal* had earlier criticized CNN's Paula Zahn's hairstyle (Jenkins, 2003). Whether praising women who are young, pretty, and fashionable or criticizing women who don't meet those ideals, media emphasize attractiveness as the primary criterion of femininity (Holtzman, 2000).

Portrayals of women as sex objects and of men as sexual aggressors are common in music videos and other programming. Typically, MTV portrays females dancing provocatively in scanty or revealing clothing. Frequently, men are seen coercing women into sexual activities or physically abusing them. Male dominance and sexual exploitation of women are themes in virtually all R- and X-rated films (Cowan, Lee, Levy, & Snyder, 1988; Cowan & O'Brien, 1990). Horror movies, especially slasher films, portray women as distressed, helpless, passive victims (Clover, 1995). In carrying to extremes long-standing cultural views of masculinity as aggressive and femininity as passive, these portrayals encourage us to see violence as sexy (Arnold, 2001; Clover, 1995; Jhally & Katz, 2001; Russell, 1993).

One of the more interesting variations on the stereotype of woman as sex object comes from some women's fashion subcultures and some women musical artists. In the video game "Tomb Raider," Lara Croft is a digitally voluptuous, sexy female who carries and uses weapons. In combining conventional femininity (sexuality) and masculinity (weapons and violence), she challenges sex/gender dualities and personifies erotic fantasies that merge female sexuality and power. Punk subculture also disputes and disrupts traditional views of femininity; women wear ripped

Madonna

Who is Madonna? Whatever else she may be, she is a lightning rod for views of women, femininity, and power relations between the sexes. She has been called

a feminine icon	a brilliant artist
an immoral opportunist	a gender politician
a knowing virgin	resistant to conventional views of women
a pervert	consistent with conventional views of women
a feminist	a purveyor of soft porn
a whore	an embodiment of female-defined sexuality

Maybe she's all of these and more. She's presented herself as a material girl, traditionally feminine, erotically charged, a submissive victim of male aggression, a dominatrix, a mother, and . . . stay tuned, because it's a good bet that she will continue to reinvent herself. Madonna flaunts her sexuality, radically and repeatedly changes her identity, inverts and subverts any stable notion of femininity (Arnold, 2001). In so doing, she insists that women who are ultrafeminine and ultra-sexy are both intimidating and seductive. Sheila Whiteley (2000), professor of popular music, says the key to how people see Madonna is whether they perceive her work as ironic. If you see her videos, music, and films as ironic, you see her as deliberately playing with and disrupting conventional notions of femininity, including the dichotomy of "good girls" and "bad girls." If you don't view her work as ironic—if you regard it more literally—you're likely to regard her as reproducing entrenched views of women as sex objects. Perhaps the question is whether Madonna flirts with the camera or manipulates it or both.

fishnet tops and combat boots and use makeup and hairstyles to create a garish, unnatural look that mocks traditional views of women even as it plays with them (Arnold, 2001; Whiteley, 2000). And then there's Madonna, who uses, abuses, and changes all the rules!

Gangsta rap also carries messages about relationships between women and men. According to Leonard Pitts, Jr., an African American music critic, "There's something vile and evil moving beneath the surface of this music. Something that hates you. And shames me" (1993, p. 7E). C. Delores Tucker, chair of the National Political Congress of Black Women (NPCBW) has pressured record companies to stop distributing gangsta rap that uses street language to applaud drug use, impersonal sex, rape, and murder. She says that the lyrics of gangsta rap "teach African American men how to mistreat African American women. For our women to accept this is nothing short of mental and spiritual contamination" (cited in Ransom, 1993, p. A6). Scholar and social critic bell hooks (1994) urges African American women to speak out against the violence toward women that is glorified in much gangsta rap.

BIAS IN NEWS COVERAGE

As gatekeepers of information, newspapers and news programs shape our perceptions by deciding which stories to feature, how to represent issues and events, and how to depict women and men. By selectively regulating what we see, media influence how we perceive movements about gender and gender itself.

■ Bias in Reporting on Women's Movements

Beginning with the second wave of U.S. feminism in the 1960s, media have consistently misrepresented the goals, activities, and members of women's movements. In the early days of radical feminism, media portrayed feminists as man-hating, bra-burning extremists. In fact, the famous bra-burning didn't happen but was reported by a journalist who misunderstood the facts (Dow, 2003). In the early 1970s an editor at *Newsday* gave these instructions to a reporter he assigned to research and write a story on the women's movement (Faludi, 1991): "Get out there and find an authority who'll say it's all a crock of shit" (pp. 75–76). Little wonder that the story that later appeared reported that the women's movement was a minor ripple without validity or support.

One of the most famous—or infamous—media stunts of the 1980s was an example of the backlash movement against feminism, which consistently received more favorable press than the women's movement itself. The cover story in the June 21, 1986, issue of *Newsweek* was about the so-called "man shortage." With dramatic charts showing that chances for marrying plunge precipitously as women age, *Newsweek* proclaimed that, after age 40, a woman was more likely to be killed by a terrorist than to marry. Behind the headlines, the facts were shaky. The predictions of women's opportunities to marry were based on a study that was discredited and withdrawn from publication. Did the flaws in the study and its withdrawal get headlines? No way. When the U.S. Census Bureau's figures disproved the bogus report, *Newsweek* relegated that information to a mere two paragraphs in a minor column (Faludi, 1991).

> ### Louise
>
> Talk about biased coverage. Last year a group of us went to Washington, D.C., for a pro-choice march. The turnout was fabulous and showed that a lot of women support freedom to choose what happens to our bodies. But was it given coverage? It got less than one minute on the nightly news that night, but a big business deal got over two minutes, and an athlete's decision to switch teams was the newsmaker interview that night. The march didn't even make the first section in some papers. If you just tuned in the news, you could think the whole march never happened. In fact, my mother and father told me they'd heard nothing about it when I got home.

Another incident illustrative of media's distortion of feminism came in 1989, when Felice Schwartz, a management consultant, published an article in the prestigious *Harvard Business Review*. In that article, she argued that women who want to have children cost businesses too much money and should be placed on a separate track in which they do not get the opportunities for advancement that go to men and women who are career oriented. Dubbing this "the **mommy track**," newspapers and magazines cited Schwartz's article as proof that women's place really is in the home and that they are lesser players in professional life. Once again, though, facts to support the claim were flimsy. Schwartz's article was speculative, as was her opinion that most women would willingly trade promotions and opportunities for more time with their families. Schwartz later retracted her advocacy of the mommy track, saying she had erred in claiming that women were more expensive as employees than men. Her retraction, however, got little coverage, because Schwartz's revised point of view did not support the media's bias regarding women's roles. Because there was virtually no coverage of Schwartz's retraction, many people read only the first article and continue to believe it.

■ Bias in Reporting Gender Issues

Media reports of gender issues are often biased. Communication scholars Lauren Danner and Susan Walsh (1999) analyzed newspaper coverage of the United Nations Fourth World Conference on Women and discovered that barely one-fourth of the stories focused on substantive issues at the conference. The majority

FYI

Day Care = Aggression in Children. Read All About It!

In April 2001, newspapers all over the country carried headlines such as "Day Care Causes Aggression in Children." The articles that followed the headlines were about a study of the effects of day care on children. The study was particularly noteworthy because it took place over ten years, included more than 1,000 children in ten different locations, and was conducted by researchers at the highly respected National Institute of Child Health and Human Development. The finding that media highlighted was that 17% of kindergarten-aged children who spent thirty or more hours in day care each week were highly aggressive. News accounts went on to note than only 6% of children who spent fewer than ten hours weekly in day care were highly aggressive.

Media coverage invited the conclusion that women should be stay-at-home moms. But several of the researchers who conducted the study say their research doesn't support that conclusion. They say the news reports misrepresented their investigation by distorting some findings and choosing not to report findings that don't support the idea that stay-at-home moms are best for children (Garrison, 2001; Goodman, 2001). What did the media leave out in its gatekeeping? For starters:

- Children who were in quality day care had better-developed language and cognitive skills than children who spent little or no time in day care.

- Fully 83% of children who spent thirty or more hours a week in day care were *not* highly aggressive, so the majority didn't show the effect announced by the headline.

- The researchers who conducted the study reported that the 17% of children who were labeled "highly aggressive" were in the upper range of "normal."

- The researchers stated that the proportion of aggressive children who spend thirty or more hours a week in day care is equivalent to the proportion of the overall population that is highly aggressive.

- Many young children who aren't in day care don't have opportunities to play—or fight—with peers. They might be judged more aggressive if they interacted with peers.

- The research report states that family interactions are a greater influence on children's behavior than hours spent in day care.

- And, by the way, why were fathers never mentioned in the reports? Do no fathers take care of children? Do only mothers influence children?

of coverage emphasized conflicts among women at the conference (referred to as "bickering"), conferees' appearances (criticized for "letting themselves go" and having no sense of style), and feminism as the root problem for women. Further, most stories were placed in the inside pages or lifestyle sections—a location that would never be considered for stories on other United Nations conferences.

Coverage of other gender issues reflect media biases. Two instances of bending events to fit gender stereotypes occurred during the 1990 Gulf War. Throughout the war, newspapers and magazines featured melodramatic pictures of children watching mothers go to war, while talk shows asked the question "Should a woman leave her baby to go to war?" (Flanders, 1990). Surely this is a reasonable question to ask about any parent, but it was rarely applied to fathers. In focusing on women's roles as mothers, the media implied that women—good women—don't leave their children. The media also suggested that fathers were not able to take care of children while mothers were overseas.

> ### Thelma
>
> I was very interested in how the media covered the story about Jessica Lynch. Some stories on TV and in the paper showed her as a courageous soldier. But a lot of stories focused on her winning the Miss Congeniality title in her hometown and on her being rescued by men. Obviously, she was *both* a brave fighter and rescued, but some news stories emphasized the latter more.

A second gender issue relating to the Gulf War surfaced when an American woman in the military, along with several men, was taken as a prisoner of war. Rather than presenting this as straightforward news, however, media focused on her femininity rather than her military role. Newspapers showing photographs of all POWs featured the males in military uniform and the female in a glamour shot from her school yearbook. Public attention focused, as the media directed it to, on the possibility of sexual assault of women POWs, thereby reinforcing images of women as sex objects. Only a year later, we learned of the Tailhook scandal, in which numerous male naval personnel sexually harassed female personnel. This made it clear that women are at least as likely to suffer sexual assault from male peers in the service as from enemies who capture them.

The media's role as gatekeeper is as powerful as we allow it to be. If we want to have informed perspectives and opinions, we must exercise critical thinking about news reports. Too often media misinform us about issues that affect our lives and perceptions.

IMPLICATIONS OF MEDIA REPRESENTATIONS OF GENDER

Media potentially hamper our understandings of ourselves as women and men in three ways. First, media perpetuate unrealistic ideals of women and men. Second, media pathologize the bodies of men and especially of women, prompting us to consider normal physical qualities and functions as abnormal and requiring corrective measures. Third, media contribute significantly to normalizing violence against women, making it possible for men to believe they are entitled to abuse women or force them to engage in sex, and making it possible for women to consider such violations acceptable.

◼ Fostering Unrealistic and Limited Gender Ideals

Many of the images dispensed by media are unrealistic. Most men are not as strong, bold, and successful as the males on the screen. Few women are as slender, gorgeous, and well dressed as stars and models, whose photographs are air-brushed and retouched to create their artificial beauty. Most people will not reach executive positions by the age of 30, and those who do are unlikely to be as glamorous, stress free, and joyous as the atypical few featured in magazines like *Savvy, Business Week, Fortune,* and *Working Woman.* Further, no woman who is healthy can avoid turning 40, the age at which women virtually disappear from media. The relationships depicted in media also defy realistic possibilities, because most of us will encounter problems that cannot be solved in thirty minutes (minus time for commercial interruptions), and most of us will not be able to pursue a demanding career and still be as relaxed and available to family and friends as media characters are.

You might think that, because we all know the difference between fantasy and reality, we don't accept media images as models for our own lives and identities. Research, however, suggests that the unrealistic ideals in popular media do influence how we feel about ourselves and our relationships. Recent anthropological research suggests that media are very powerful in shaping—or distorting—body images. For centuries the people of Fiji were a food-loving society. People enjoyed eating and considered fleshy bodies attractive in both women and men. In fact, when someone seemed to be losing weight, acquaintances would chide her or him for "going thin." All of that changed in 1995 when television stations in Fiji began broadcasting American programs such as *Melrose Place, Seinfeld,* and *Beverly Hills 90210.* Within three years, an astonishing number of Fijian women began dieting and developing eating disorders. When asked why they were trying to lose weight, young Fijian women cited characters such as Amanda (Heather Locklear) on *Melrose Place* as their model (Becker & Burwell, 1999; Becker, Burwell, Gilman, Herzog, & Hamburg, 2002; Goodman, 1999).

Commercial television appears to promote sex stereotypes in children and adolescents (Leaper, 2000; Morgan, 1987), especially in working-class families (Nikken & Peeters, 1988). Children who watch television have more stereotyped views of the sexes. In one study, when television was introduced into communities that had not had television, the children's beliefs became more sex typed (Kimball, 1986). On the other hand, viewing television that presents nonstereotypical portrayals of males and females tends to decrease, not fortify, sex stereotypes (Rosenwasser, Lingenfelter, & Harrington, 1989).

The effects of media are not limited to childhood. Radio is a major influence on adolescents, whose average listening time is five hours a day—slightly less for Caucasians and slightly more for African Americans, especially African American females (Brown, Childers, Bauman, & Koch, 1990). Although most popular music reflects sex stereotypes (Lont, 1990, 2001), this is less true of work composed and/or sung by some contemporary women artists such as Lauryn Hill, Melissa Etheridge, Tori Amos, Lorrie Morgan, and Ani DiFranco.

Media images of relationships contribute to unrealistic expectations (Steele, 1999). MTV's and rock music's emphasis on eroticism and sublime sex is linked to an expectation of sexual perfection in real relationships. Further, research shows that readers of self-help books tend to have less realistic ideals for relationships than do nonreaders of such books. Consequently, those who read self-help books experience more frustration and disappointment than is typical when their relationships fail to meet the ideals promoted by media (Shapiro & Kroeger, 1991).

Unrealistic images of what we and our relationships should be promote dissatisfaction with our relationships and ourselves, as well as feelings of inadequacy, which may lead people to have cosmetic surgery or develop eating disorders (Cooper, 1998; Mazzarella & Pecora, 1999; Posavac, Posavac, & Posavac, 1998). When we are constantly besieged with impossible images of how women and men should look, feel, act, and be, it's difficult not to feel inadequate. If we use media as a reference point for what is normal and desirable, we may find ourselves constantly feeling that we and our relationships are inferior by comparison.

▨ Pathologizing the Human Body

Media encourage us to perceive normal bodies and normal physical functions as problems. It's understandable to wish we weighed a little more or less, had better-developed muscles, and never had pimples or cramps. What is not reasonable, however, is to regard normal, functional bodies as unacceptable. Yet this is precisely the perception cultivated by the predominant media portrayals of women and men.

Media not only encourage us to measure ourselves against artificial standards but also to see normal bodies and normal bodily functions as pathologies (Kilbourne, 2004). A good example is the media's construction of premenstrual syndrome (PMS). Historically, PMS was not construed as a problem. In fact, in earlier eras very few women were affected by PMS (Parlee, 1973, 1987). After World War II, when women were no longer needed in the work force, opinion changed, and the term *premenstrual tension* was coined (Greene & Dalton, 1953) and used to support the idea that women were inferior employees. In 1964, only one article on PMS appeared; from 1988 to 1989, a total of 425 were published (Tavris, 1992). Drug companies funded research and publicity because selling PMS meant selling their remedies for the newly created problem. Facts aside, many people believe that PMS is pervasive and makes women unfit for leadership.

Menopause is similarly pathologized. Books and articles describe menopause "in terms of deprivation, deficiency, loss, shedding, and sloughing" (Tavris, 1992, p. 159), language that defines a normal process as negative. The cover of the May 25, 1992, *Newsweek* featured a drawing of a tree in the shape of a woman's head.

The tree was stripped of all leaves. Across the picture was the cover-story headline "Menopause." From first glance, menopause was equated with being lifeless and desolate. The article focused primarily on the problems and losses of menopause. Only toward the end did readers find reports from anthropologists whose cross-cultural research reveals that in many cultures menopause is not an issue or is viewed positively. Women in Mayan villages and on the Greek island of Evia don't report hot flashes and depression, symptoms often associated with menopause in Western societies ("Menopause," 1992). Because Western countries stigmatize menopause as "the end of womanhood," Western women are likely to feel negatively about the cessation of menstruation (Greer, 1992).

Media also pathologize normal male bodies. No longer is it good enough to be healthy and active. The bodybuilding trend has created unrealistic ideals for masculine bodies. Today, abuse of steroids is an increasing problem among men. Surveys show that about 18% of male high school athletes use anabolic steroids (Angier, 1999). Although media's idealization of extreme musculature and strength is not the only cause of steroid use, we should not dismiss the influence of portrayals of muscle-bound men as ideal. Media's increasing glorification of unrealistic male bodies is reflected in action toys marketed to young boys. Since the G.I. Joe doll was introduced in 1964, each new version of the doll has been more muscular and more sharply cut than its predecessor.

Changes in men's sexual vigor are also represented as problems to be solved. In recent years, Viagra has become a blockbuster drug, making millions for the company that can solve "the problem." The problem, of course, is constructed; rather than accepting changes in male sexual interest and activity as normal, media encourage us to see them as problems that can be solved by taking Viagra.

Advertising is very effective in convincing us that we need products to solve problems we are unaware of until some public relations campaign persuades us that something natural about us is really unnatural and unacceptable. Media have convinced millions of U.S. women that what every medical source considers "normal body weight" is really abnormal and cause for severe dieting (Mazzarella & Pecora, 1999; Rogers, 1999; Wolf, 1991). Similarly, gray hair, which naturally develops with age, is now something all of us, especially women, are encouraged to cover up (Sharkey, 1993). Facial lines, which indicate that a person has lived a life and accumulated experiences, now can be removed so that we look younger—a prime goal in a culture that glorifies youth (Bordo, 1999; Greer, 1992; Gilman, 1999).

Body hair is another interesting case of media's convincing us that something normal is really abnormal. In 1915, a sustained marketing campaign informed women that underarm hair was unsightly and socially incorrect. (The campaign against leg hair came later.) *Harper's Bazaar,* an upscale magazine, launched the crusade against underarm hair with a photograph of a woman whose raised arms revealed clean-shaven armpits. Underneath the photograph was this caption: "Summer dress and modern dancing combine to make necessary the removal of objectionable hair" (Adams, 1991). By 1922, razors and depilatories were firmly ensconced in middle America, as evidenced by their inclusion in the women's section of the Sears & Roebuck catalogue.

Media efforts to pathologize natural physiology can be very serious. As we have seen in previous chapters, the emphasis on excessive thinness contributes to severe and potentially lethal dieting and eating disorders, especially in Caucasian women. Nonetheless, most of the top female models are skeletal. Female models are significantly thinner than average, healthy women. Seeing the super-skinny models as the ideal, one in five college women deliberately eats less food than is required for adequate daily nutrition (Finstein, 1993). Women who diet excessively are trying to force their bodies to fit a socially constructed ideal that is unrealistic and unhealthy. Dangers—including heart attack, stroke, and liver disease—also exist for men who use steroids in an effort to meet the ideal masculine form promoted by media (Angier, 1999).

Many women's natural breast size exceeded the cultural ideal in the 1960s, when thin, angular bodies were represented as ideal. Thus, breast reduction surgeries increased. By the 1980s, cultural standards had changed to define large breasts as the feminine ideal. Consequently, breast augmentation surgeries accelerated, and fully 80% of implants were for cosmetic reasons. In an effort to meet the cultural standards for beautiful bodies, many women endured and continue to endure surgery that sometimes leads to disfigurement and loss of sensation.

Christi

When I used to diet, I remember thinking that I was in control. I believed what all the ads said about taking charge of myself, exerting control. But I was totally *not* in control. The advertisers and the companies making diet products were in control. So was society with the idea that "you can't be too thin" and that it's more important for girls to look good (read thin) than to feel good (read not hungry). Society and its views of women were in control, not me. I was totally a puppet who was just doing what they told me to do.

FYI

Fixing the Pathologized Body

Obsession with having—or creating—the perfect body is at an all-time high (Bordo, 1999; Gerhart, 1999; Gilman, 1999). In 1998 teenagers had more than 25,000 cosmetic surgeries. This is almost a 100% increase over the number of cosmetic surgeries performed in 1992. Nearly 2,000 teenage females had breast implants, and another 1,645 had liposuction. But one London doctor bucked the trend. In 2001 he refused to perform breast enhancement on a 16-year-old female. He told the insistent parents that she was too young and her breasts were not fully developed. The parents stated that "the operation would give their daughter greater confidence and remove any 'hangups' she felt about her body" ("Doctor," 2001, p. 18A).

Signe Wilkinson, Cartoonist and Writers Syndicate/cartoonweb.com.

In their book *Measuring Up,* Laurie Shields and Dawn Heinecken (2001) argue that advertising encourages us to measure up to impossible ideals. When we fail, as inevitably we must, we feel bad about our bodies and ourselves. Accepting media messages about our bodies and ourselves, however, is not inevitable: We can reflect on the messages and resist those that are inappropriate or harmful.

■ Normalizing Violence Toward Women

Violence is so pervasive in modern life that all of Chapter 12 is devoted to examining it. Yet it would be irresponsible not to mention violence in the context of media. The average 18-year-old has watched a stunning 19,000 hours of television and has seen 200,000 acts of violence, including 40,000 murders (Zuckerman, 1993).

Although it would be naïve to claim that media *cause* violence, there is mounting evidence that violence in media contributes to increasing male violence in real life. From *Die Hard, Rambo,* and *Fight Club* to violent video games, media teach children to perceive violence as part of normal social life (Dietz, 1998; Jhally & Katz, 2001). Children who watch a lot of television violence in their early years are more likely to commit violent crimes as adults (Zuckerman, 1993). Many popular video games feature intense and graphic violence (Dietz, 1998;

> ### *Miriam*
>
> My kids are so much more violent than I was or than my friends were when we were young, and I think the violence they see on television is a big part of the reason. When I caught my 3-year-old trying to hit our dog, he told me that he'd seen that on a cartoon show —a cartoon show! I try to screen what my children watch, but it's getting so there are very few programs that don't include violence. How can kids think it is anything but normal when they see it every day?

Goldstein, 1998); the most violent are marketed more to boys and men than to girls and women (Casell & Jenkins, 1998; Kafai, 1999).

Particularly noteworthy is the extent to which violence against women occurs in movies, television (including children's programming), rock music, and music videos. Viewing habits may influence real-life behavior. Research also shows that, after watching sexually explicit films that degrade women (not just sexually explicit films), men become more dominant toward women with whom they interact (Mulac, Jansma, & Linz, 2003). When we continually see violence in media, we may come to view it as commonplace, normal, and increasingly acceptable as part of ordinary life.

Is Censorship the Answer?

Should we ban violent, homophobic, sexist music and films that celebrate violence against women? Even those who are most outraged by the objectification and sexism of media seldom advocate censorship. The U.S. Constitution provides strong protections of freedom of speech, and for good reason. The problem with censoring is that somebody decides what all of us can watch, hear, see. Who has the right to make this decision for all of us? A better answer may be to demand that media offer us multiple, diverse images of women and men. Instead of banning what we don't like, perhaps we work to enlarge the range of ways in which people and relationships are portrayed (Clemetson & Samuels, 2000).

SUMMARY

From children's cartoons to pornography, media influence how we perceive men and women in general and ourselves and others in particular. Media also shape our views of what's normal and right in relationships between women and men. The historical trend of emphasizing gender-stereotyped roles and images continues today; yet it is sometimes challenged by alternative images of women, men, and relationships. For the most part, however, media representations that on the surface don't seem to conform to gender stereotypes do reflect traditional views of women and men on a deeper level. Media representations of gender foster unrealistic gender ideals in men and women, encourage us to pathologize normal human bodies and functions, and normalize violence against women.

Understanding the overt and subtle gender messages in media empowers us to be more critical consumers. As individuals, parents, and citizens, we have opportunities and responsibilities to criticize media representations that demean men and women and that contribute to attitudes that harm us and our relationships.

FYI

Learning More, Taking Action

If you want to learn more about gender and media, or if you want to become active in working against media that devalue women and celebrate violence, visit these Web sites:

 Media Watch: **http://www.mediawatch.com;** the National Coalition on Television Violence: **http://www.nctvv.org.**

Another excellent site for getting informed and taking action is About-Face, which is devoted to media literacy about gender and self-esteem. Among About-Face's features is an ever-changing list of "Top Ten Offenders," which features ads that destructively stereotype women and men and, in some cases, condone violence toward women. About-Face provides the addresses of companies featured in each ad so you can contact the companies directly to express your response. Access About-Face through

 http://www.mediawatch.com.

KEY TERMS

complementary copy, 243
mommy track, 247
voice-over, 242

DISCUSSION QUESTIONS

1. Sign on to InfoTrac College Edition. Select PowerTrac, select Author Index, then type: "Helene Shugart." Read her 2003 article, "She shoots, he scores: Mediated constructions of contemporary female athletes in coverage of the 1999 U.S. Women's Soccer Team," which appeared in the *Western Journal of Communication.* What does Shugart mean when she claims that strategies of sexualizing female athletes are more subtle today than in the past?

2. Watch children's programming on Saturday morning. Are male characters more prominent than female characters? Are there differences in the activities of male and female characters? How do you think commercial children's programming influences children's ideas about gender?

3. Use InfoTrac College Edition's PowerTrac to access the 1999 article by Adrian Furnham and Twiggy Mak, "Sex role stereotyping in television commercials: A review and comparison of fourteen studies done on five continents over 25 years." Do the authors report that sex-role stereotyping varies across the cultures studied? What roles and activities in advertising are generally associated with males and females?

4. Watch morning and evening news programming. What kinds of stories do male and female reporters and newscasters present? Are there differences in story content? Are there differences in the communication styles of male and female newscasters?

5. Bring advertisements from magazines to class and discuss the images of women, men, and relationships in them. Are these healthy? What are your options as a reader and a consumer?

12

Gendered Power and Violence

The world is a dangerous place to live, not because of the people who are evil, but because of the people who don't do anything about it.

—ALBERT EINSTEIN

Gendered violence is pervasive. Currently, it's estimated that every 12 seconds in the United States a woman is battered by an intimate, and each day ten women die from violence committed by intimates (Hasenauer, 1997; May, 1998a). Many more women are battered and killed by intimates, but their cases are unreported or are mislabeled as accidental injuries and deaths. In the United States, every five minutes a woman reports a rape, and the FBI estimates that only 36% of rapes are reported. In the time it has taken you to read this far in the chapter, at least one woman has been raped and at least two have been beaten by a friend, lover, or family member.

This chapter focuses on the distressing topic of gendered violence. In advance, I caution you that I found it difficult to research and write this chapter, and you may find it upsetting to read. Yet if we wish to lessen gendered violence, we must first understand the many forms it takes and the ways in which cultures condone or implicitly support it. In the pages that follow, we'll discuss the nature and extent of gendered violence and identify social structures, practices, and attitudes that underlie it. To close the chapter, we'll consider how we can use our voices to diminish violence in our lives.

THE SOCIAL CONSTRUCTION OF GENDERED VIOLENCE

Gendered violence is not the result of individual attitudes or pathologies. Isolated incidents of violence may occur because of unique personal and situational fac-

Facts About Violence

- The FBI reported that, in 2000, rates declined for most violent crimes, such as murder and robbery; rates for forcible rape increased.

- Twenty-five percent of American women will be victims of rape in their lifetimes.

- Over 140 million women around the world have had genital surgery to comply with cultural traditions.

- Intimate partner violence is the leading cause of injury for U.S. women between the ages of 15 and 44.

- Thousands of women in India have been burned to death so that their husbands could remarry and collect new dowries.

- Thirty to 50% of women students and 75% of women workers have been sexually harassed.

tors, but such factors don't begin to explain violence that is pervasive and disproportionately inflicted on certain groups. Widespread violence exists only if a society allows or endorses it. In other words, the epidemic of gendered violence reflects cultural values and social definitions of femininity, masculinity, and relationships between women and men.

Media bombard us with violent images, especially acts of violence against women. Family members often encourage a battered woman to stay with her partner for the sake of the children. Many police officers are reluctant to interfere in intimate partner violence, and judges often fail to impose substantial sentences on batterers. From families to courtrooms, many institutions in our culture communicate that violence against women is not a serious offense.

Social acceptance of domination of and violence toward women is not new. As you learned in previous chapters, in the United States women originally were regarded as the property of men—of their fathers or husbands. During the early years of U.S. history, wife beating and other abuses of women were legal (Deed, 1998; Wriggins, 1998; Zinn, 1995). Although first-wave feminists managed to get most states to establish laws against wife beating, the laws were weakly and inconsistently enforced (Kramarae, 1992).

Gendered violence exists around the world. Because it is a global problem, we will discuss its occurrence both in developing nations and in developed countries. My students sometimes ask why they need to learn about dowry deaths in India or genital surgery in Africa. "It's not relevant to me," they claim. But these practices *are* relevant to all of us because we belong to a world that is larger than our own country.

T HE MANY FACES OF GENDERED VIOLENCE

What comes to mind when you hear terms such as *gendered violence* and *sexual violence*? Most people think of rape, battering, and perhaps sexual harassment. That trilogy of abuses, however, doesn't include all the forms gendered violence takes. The term **gendered violence** refers to physical, verbal, emotional, sexual, and visual brutality that is inflicted disproportionately or exclusively on members of one sex. In the following pages we'll discuss six types of gendered violence.

▧ Gender Intimidation

Gender intimidation occurs when members of one sex are treated in ways that make them feel humiliated, unsafe, or inferior because of their sex (Kramarae, 1992). Probably all of us feel unsafe at times. Gender intimidation, however, exists when members of one sex have reason to feel more vulnerable than members of the other sex.

Gender intimidation includes lewd remarks and requests shouted at women as they walk on streets or on campuses. A number of women students at my university often take longer, less direct routes around campus to avoid workmen who assault them with sexual comments and suggestions. They feel unsafe and uncomfortable in areas where others can violate them with verbal propositions, comments, and evaluations.

Gender intimidation also occurs when space is invaded and individuals are forced to tolerate unwelcome sexual conduct. The brothers of one fraternity had a ritual in which they broke into the dining room of a sorority at dinnertime. While one fraternity brother delivered a vivid speech on Freud's theory of penis envy, another brother demonstrated masturbation with an artificial penis (Lyman, 1987). On another campus, a group of men arranged themselves into two lines on each side of one of the main paths to classrooms. Women who passed through the lines were subjected to hearing the men rate their attractiveness and sexual desirability. A Dartmouth fraternity printed and distributed sex newsletters that gave detailed accounts of sexual activities between brothers and female students and gave the names of some women who were described as "loose" and "guaranteed hookups" (Hoover, 2001, p. A36). The newsletters promised a future issue that would provide "patented date rape techniques" (p. A35). When deans on the campus were informed of the newsletters, the fraternity's charter was revoked.

Tim

I think gay bashing is a kind of gender intimidation. I've been a victim of insults and really gross remarks just because I'm gay. I'll be just walking along minding my own business, and someone will shout "fag" at me or even come at me screaming, "We don't want any queers around here." When I go into bathrooms on campus I usually see gay-bashing graffiti. I have to tolerate these hassles strictly because I'm gay. That makes it gender intimidation.

When crime statistics tell us that one in four women will be raped in her lifetime, there's reason for a woman to be wary, even afraid, of going out alone. Even when there is no specific wish to go somewhere or do something, the knowledge that it would be dangerous to go out alone restricts women. Michael Kaufman (1995) says that it is unfair that "compared to women we [men] are free to walk the streets at night" (p. 15).

> ### Sharon
>
> I'm not what you'd call a timid person, but I am scared to go out alone at night. Last year one of the girls in my suite was raped when she was walking to the library. She's not the only one—just the only one I know personally. Every week I read stories about women who are assaulted and raped just because they're out alone.

■ Sexual Assault

Sexual assault is sexual activity that occurs without the informed consent of at least one of the persons involved. Rape is one type of sexual assault, but it isn't the only one. In fact, what *rape* means isn't as clear-cut as you might think. In many states, first-degree rape is limited to forced vaginal intercourse. This means that forced anal and oral intercourse are not considered first-degree rape. It also means that the group of boys who repeatedly thrust a broomstick into the vagina of a retarded girl were not prosecuted for rape. A man who is forced to have sex with another man has not been raped, according to laws that define rape as vaginal intercourse.

Sexual assault includes rape and other forced sexual activities with strangers; sex that is coerced by "friends" or dates, forced sex in marriage, incest, and sexual activities with children. In other words, sexual assault occurs whenever one person doesn't consent to sexual activity or is unable to give **informed consent.** Informed consent can be given only by an adult who has normal mental abilities and whose judgment is not impaired by circumstances, including use of alcohol or other drugs. Informed consent cannot be given by children, so the sexual abuse of at least

Defining Rape

The meaning of *rape* is not the same in all cultures or in any culture over time. Consider these facts (Beyer, 2001; Brownmiller, 1975; Kelly & Radford, 1998).

- United States laws originally classified rape as a property crime for which offenders had to compensate the father or husband of the victim.

- According to Bolivian laws, rape can be committed only if the victim is both a virgin and under the age of legal consent.

- Before a Pakistani woman can bring charges of rape, she must have four male witnesses.

Kendall

My father started doing things to me when I was 5 years old—maybe even before that, but that's as far back as I remember. At first he would come into my bedroom when Mom wasn't home and touch me in private places. When I was 12, he raped me the first time, and he made me promise to keep it our secret. I kept "our secret" until about two years ago, when the shame overwhelmed me and began to interfere with my schoolwork. Now I'm in counseling to get my life on track.

Killian

The first week I was on campus, I went to a fraternity mixer and had too much to drink. I never drank at home, so I didn't know what alcohol could do. I passed out, and when I woke up the next morning, I was in a guy's room—he wasn't even my date—and naked in bed and bleeding. That was rape.

Clarence

I don't believe that a man can rape his wife or girlfriend. Maybe it's rape if a guy wants sex and a woman he doesn't know well doesn't, and he forces her. But a guy has a right to have sex in a relationship that is established. All this talk about date rape and marital rape is baloney. No woman I'm going with had better believe that baloney.

33% and perhaps as many as 66% of children, both boys and girls, under age 18 is sexual assault (Clutter, 1990; Haugaard, 2000; Trexler, 1997). Whenever sex occurs without informed consent, it is sexual assault.

Rape is increasing in the United States. In the last decade the overall rate of violent crimes in the United States has declined, but rates of rape have increased (Jhally & Katz, 2001; "Violent Crime's Era of Decline," 2001). The FBI states that rape is the single most underreported violent crime in the United States (Fuentes, 1998). At least 20% of women in the United States have been sexually assaulted (Tjaden & Thoennes, 2000), and many of them were assaulted before reaching age 18 (Fuentes, 1998). More than half of women in college report that they have been coerced into some type of unwanted sex (Ullman, Karabatsos, & Koss, 1999). Not confined to assaults between strangers, rape occurs with tragic frequency between dates and acquaintances. More than 75% of rapes are committed by men who know their victims (Fuentes, 1998; Wriggins, 1998).

Research indicates that one reason for the prevalence of rape is that a substantial number of men regard forced sex as acceptable. In one study, a shocking 50% of college men reported that they had coerced, manipulated, or pressured a woman to have sex or had had sex with a woman after getting her drunk. As many as 1 out of 12 men at some colleges admitted engaging in behaviors that met the legal definition of rape or attempted rape (Koss, Gidycz, & Wisniewski, 1987). In a study of 520 undergraduate students, Grace Kim and Michael Roloff (1999) found that both women and men tend not to judge forced intercourse as rape if it occurs with an acquaintance or friend and is not violent. This may reflect a "rape script" (Kahn & Mathie, 1994; Livingston & Testa, 2000; Truman, Tokar, & Fischer, 1996), which is the belief—conscious or unconscious—that dates and friends can't rape because rape is a violent act imposed by a stranger. Many victims of rape are also reluctant to prosecute because they fear they will be judged negatively or because their families fear social disapproval if rape is reported (Zaharlick, 2000).

Rape is not confined to civilian contexts. A 1996 report based on congressional hearings estimated that between 60,000 and 200,000 women in the military have been sexually assaulted by American servicemen. Lawrence Korb, former president Reagan's assistant secretary of defense, acknowledges that the government and military services have "treated military women like prostitutes" (Moniz & Pardue, 1996, p. 22A). Women in the military are sexually assaulted by men in the military at twice the rate of civilian women (Quindlen, 2003). The 2002–2003 sexual assault scandal at the Air Force Academy revealed that male cadets raped female cadets with horrifying frequency and that investigations and punishment were rare (Quindlen, 2003).

> ## Belinda
>
> I don't know why guys think that because you have sex sometimes, you have to do it whenever they want. Once when my boyfriend wanted to mess around, I wasn't in the mood so I said no, but he wouldn't take that for an answer. He kept insisting and then tried to force me. I screamed to get him to stop, and he was furious. He still doesn't get it that having a relationship doesn't mean he has an automatic right to sex whenever it suits him. It's my body, after all.

Although rape involves sex, it isn't motivated primarily by sexual desire. Instead, rape is an act of aggression that is designed to humiliate and dominate another person (Jhally & Katz, 2001; Scully, 1990; South & Felson, 1990). This

FYI

Myths and Facts About Rape

Myth	Fact
Rape is is motivated by sexual urges.	Rape is an aggressive act used to dominate another person.
Most rapes occur between strangers.	More than 75% of rapes are committed by a person known to the victim.
Most rapists are African American men, and most victims are European American women.	More than three-fourths of all rapes occur within races, not between races.
False reports of rapes are frequent.	False reports of rapes constitute only 2% of all reported rapes.
The way a woman dresses affects the likelihood she will be raped.	Most rapes are planned in advance without knowledge of how the victim will dress.

FYI

Comfort Women

In 1942, Pak Kumjoo was a happy 17-year-old. Then officials in her hometown of Hamun, Korea, complied with orders from the Japanese to recruit women for factory work to help in the war effort. When Korean officials sent Pak and other young women to the Japanese, the women were not given factory jobs. Instead, they were taken to "comfort stations," where they were forced to have sex with 20 to 30 soldiers a day. Japanese Lieutenant-General Okamura Yasuji recruited "comfort women" to put a stop to raping by Japanese troops stationed in China (Berndt, 1997; Horn, 1997).

The comfort women—many of whom were torn from their families in their early teens— suffered profound abuse. The repeated and sometimes brutal rapes caused some of them to become sterile. Those who became pregnant were given injections of teramycin, which caused their bodies to swell and usually induced abortions. Many were beaten, sustaining permanent scars and injuries. Many committed suicide.

After the war, the Japanese government denied it had forced women to work at comfort stations. In 1991, however, three Korean women sued the Japanese government for having forced them to serve as comfort women. In 1992, Professor Yoshimi Yoshiaki at Chuo University found wartime documents that confirmed that Japanese forces had operated comfort stations. In 1995 the Japanese government acknowledged it had forced women to serve in comfort stations and provided some compensation to them.

explains why rape is one way in which male prison inmates brutalize one another and establish a power hierarchy.

Sexual assault includes forced prostitution, also called sexual slavery. During World War II, the Japanese forced countless women to be "comfort women" for Japanese soldiers. They were compelled to have sex with any and all Japanese soldiers who wanted them. Even today, in countries such as the Philippines and Thailand, some women are kidnapped and forced to be prostitutes (Barry, 1998b; French, 1992).

■ Intimate Partner Violence

At least 28% and possibly as many as 50% of women suffer **intimate partner violence,** which is physical, mental, emotional, verbal, or economic power used by one partner against the other partner in a romantic relationship (Jackman, 2003; May, 1998a; Murphy-Milano, 1996). National surveys report that nearly 25% of women and 30% of men regard violence as a normal and even positive part of marriage (Jacobson & Gottman, 1998), which suggests substantial acceptance of marital violence in our culture (Jones, 1994, 1998a, 1998b; Wood, 2001b). Intimate partner violence is also on the rise in dating relationships, including those of very young people (Capaldi, Shortt, & Crosby, 2003; Wolfe & Feiring, 2000). In a comprehensive study of dating violence, 20% of girls between the ages of 14 and 18 reported they had been hit, slapped, shoved, or forced to have sex by a date (Goode, 2001).

Increasingly, stalking is recognized as a form of intimate partner violence. Stalking is repeated, intrusive behavior that is uninvited and unwanted, that seems obsessive, and that makes the target afraid or concerned for her or his safety. In research done in 2000 on college campuses, 13% of women students and 2% of male students reported having been stalked during the previous year (Brownstein, 2000). About half of female victims are stalked by ex-partners and another 25% by men they have dated at least once (Meloy, 1998; Orion, 1997; Spitzberg, Nicastro, & Cousins, 1998).

Intimate partner violence is inflicted primarily by men and primarily on women. Twenty-six percent of all female murder victims in 1995 were killed by husbands or boyfriends, whereas only 3% of male murder victims were killed by wives or girlfriends (Frieze & Davis, 2000; Hammer, 2002; "Women Usually Attacked," 1996). Sex is, however, less important than gender in explaining intimate partner violence. A study of 336 undergraduates showed that both men and women who abused their partners had strong masculine gender orientations (Thompson, 1991). The use of violence to control others is linked to masculinity (Messner, 2001; Wood, in press).

Intimate partner violence typically follows a cyclical pattern (Jacobson & Gottman, 1998). In the first stage, the batterer experiences mounting tension. Perhaps the individual has problems at work or feels insecure or frustrated. As tension mounts, verbal and emotional abuse may occur. In the second stage, there is a violent explosion involving physical assault—kicking, beating, throwing the victim against a wall, cutting, or shooting. The third stage in the cycle of abuse is called remorse because the batterer typically acts ashamed, apologizes, and promises never to do it again. In the fourth stage, the honeymoon phase, the abuser acts lovingly and often brings gifts to the

Paula

The worst thing I ever went through was being stalked by my ex-boyfriend. We'd dated for about a year when I broke up with him. He was so jealous—wouldn't let me go out with friends or anything, so I just decided to end the relationship. But he didn't want it to end. He followed me around campus, showed up at movies when I was out with other guys, and called at all hours of the night. Sometimes he would tell me he loved me and beg to get back together; other times he would threaten me. I finally called the police, and that put an end to his terrorism.

Brice

Growing up, I saw my father shove Mom around whenever he was having a rough time at work. Sometimes it was more than shoving—he would actually hit her. Always the next day, he would be Mr. Nice, and things would go along fine for a while until he got upset about something else; then it would start all over again. I hated him because of what he did to Mother, and I swore I would never be like him. But last year when I was going through a really rough time, the girl I was dating kept nagging me, and I hauled off and hit her. I never thought I could do that.

FYI

The Cycle of Intimate Partner Violence

Stage 1: Tension builds, and the abusive partner blames the other for problems or for not being supportive. Typically, the abuser begins psychological battering with insults, threats, taunts, and intimidation. Victims, especially in chronically abusive relationships, learn to spot cues and to be extremely compliant and to not do anything to annoy the partner. This seldom helps, because the abuser is looking for an excuse to relieve frustration by exerting power over another.

Stage 1
Tension

Stage 2
Explosion

Stage 3
Remorse

Stage 4
Honeymoon

Stage 2: An explosion occurs. Tension erupts into physical violence. The abuser may wait until the victim is relaxing or even asleep and then attack. Often victims require hospital care. Sometimes they are pregnant and miscarry.

Stage 3: The abuser appears contrite and remorseful. The abuser may apologize to the victim and typically promises it will never happen again. The victim sees the "good person" inside and remembers what led to commitment or marriage.

Stage 4: This is the honeymoon phase. The abuser acts courtly and loving. The victim becomes convinced the abuse was an aberration that will not recur—even if it has repeatedly. And then the whole cycle begins anew.

For information, write to the National Coalition Against Domestic Violence, Department P, Post Office Box 18749, Denver, CO 80218-0749.

battered partner. The apologies of stage 3 and the loving acts of stage 4 often convince victims to stay with abusive partners. Thus, the cycle continues.

Brice's experience, in his commentary on page 265, is not unusual. There is a strong relationship between growing up in a family with one or more abusive adults and becoming an abuser (Ingrassia & Beck, 1994; Wood, in press). In our families of origin, we learn what is normal and allowable in relationships between men and women. What we learn in families, however, need not be the blueprint for our lives. We can choose not to repeat destructive patterns that we observed in our families.

Are women always the victims and men always the perpetrators of violence in intimate relationships? No—both women and men can be victims and abusers. Some men are abused by their wives or girlfriends, but they keep silent because they fear others will question their manhood (Lucal, 1995; McFarlane & Wilson,

2000; Mignon, 1998). Richard Gelles ("Husbands Are Battered," 1994) estimates that, cumulatively, about 100,000 men have been battered by women partners. As horrible as that statistic is, it pales beside the fact that each year at least 2 million women in the United States are beaten by their partners (White & Bondurant, 1996; Wood, 2001b).

There are general differences, however, in the frequency, motivation, and type of violence committed by women and men. Men commit 90% of documented acts of intimate partner violence in the United States (Pastore & Maguire, 2001). Men and women also differ in the severity of violence they inflict on others. Abusive women most often verbally abuse or push, slap, or shove partners. In contrast, abusive men are more likely to commit brutal, sometimes deadly, assaults (Frieze & Davis, 2000). Although both sexes may engage in violence, men are far more likely to inflict serious injuries; women are seven times more likely than men to suffer moderate to severe physical injury at the hands of an intimate ("Husbands Are Battered," 1994).

In comparing women's and men's abusive tendencies, we should also consider differences in motives. Many women engage in violent acts in self-defense. They slap a partner who has beaten them or throw an object at a partner who has slugged them (Jacobson & Gottman, 1998). Women generally aggress only when they can't resolve issues through strategies prescribed for women, such as crying, talking with friends, and turning anger inward. For most women, physical aggression toward others is a method of last resort when all else has failed (Campbell, 1993; O'Connell, 1995).

Gendered Violence Is a Men's Issue

In a chapter that discusses men's violence toward women, it's easy to forget that most men are not violent toward women. These men have a stake in speaking out against men who are and in challenging social views that link violence and masculinity. Sut Jhally and Jackson Katz (2001, p. 31) put it this way:

> The majority of men are in fact nonviolent. . . . The silence of nonviolent men in the face of other men's violence is a key factor that allows masculinity to be coded in narrow and destructive ways. . . . What we have to do now is offer more resources to these men—the majority—in order to help them intervene in male culture in a productive fashion . . . to become, in the words of Pearl Jam's Eddie Vedder, "better men."

To learn more about men who are committed to stopping men's violence, visit this Web site:

 http://menstoppingviolence.org.

FYI

Myths and Facts About Violence Between Intimates

Myth	Fact
Victims of battering can just leave the abusive relationship.	Many victims of battering have nowhere to go and no means of supporting themselves and their children.
Abuse of intimates often stops on its own.	Abuse of intimates seldom stops without intervention or other radical measures.
Abuse is confined primarily to the working and poverty classes.	Abuse occurs in relationships between members of the upper and middle classes as well as members of the working and poverty classes.
Victims of battering would be safer if they left abusive relationships.	Victims of battering are more likely to be murdered by abusive partners if they try to leave.

Men who inflict violence on others are generally motivated by reasons different from those that motivate women to be violent. Many use physical aggression to gain or sustain self-esteem, to win the respect of others, and to maintain control over people and situations. Among children aged 4 to 7, girls aggress to protect themselves and their property, whereas boys aggress to dominate others and increase their status (Bordo, 1998). As boys become men, they are most likely to resort to violence when they feel they need to prove their toughness or feel they need to gain control (May, 1998a; Messner, 2001; Wood, in press). These patterns are consistent with the social prescriptions for gender that we have discussed throughout this book.

■ Sexual Harassment

In 1991, law professor Anita Hill testified that Clarence Thomas, then a nominee for the Supreme Court, had sexually harassed her years earlier when she worked with him. The Hill–Thomas hearings raised public awareness about **sexual harassment,** which is unwelcome verbal or nonverbal behavior of a sexual nature that links academic or professional standing or success to sexual favors or that interferes with work or learning.

Prior to the 1970s, the term *sexual harassment* was not used (Wise & Stanley, 1987). Our language gave victims no socially recognized way to label what happened to them as wrong and unacceptable. Once sexual harassment was named, those who were targets of it had a way to define their experience and demand institutional and legal redress. Although women are the predominant targets and men the predominant harassers, the Supreme Court has recognized that either sex can be the target or the perpetrator. Men who file charges of sexual harassment usually cite other men as the harassers (Talbot, 2002). Men bring approximately 14% of all sexual harassment charges (Stockdale, Visio, & Batra, 1999; Abelson, 2001). Two broad categories of sexual harassment are widely recognized today.

Quid pro quo. **Quid pro quo harassment** is the actual or threatened use of professional or academic rewards and/or punishments to gain sexual compliance from a subordinate or student. *Quid pro quo* is a Latin phrase that means "this for that." For instance, a professor might promise a student a good grade in exchange for a date, or a manager might offer a subordinate a promotion in exchange for sex. Quid pro quo harassment may also involve punishing someone for not providing sexual favors. For example, a manager might withhold an earned raise from an employee who refuses to have sex.

Hostile environment. In 1986 the courts recognized a second type of sexual harassment, one at least as common as quid pro quo. **Hostile environment harassment** is unwelcome conduct of a sexual nature that interferes with a person's ability to perform a job or gain an education and/or that creates a hostile, intimidating, or offensive working environment because of sexualized conduct (Bordo, 1997; Paetzold & O'Leary-Kelly, 1993). Both women and men have brought suits for hostile environment sexual harassment. In one recent case, a jury awarded $3.75 million to a male prison guard whose employer did nothing to stop a female co-worker who harassed him by calling his home, following him at work, and making repeated sexual comments and invitations to him ("Sexually Harassed Male," 1999). Hostile environment sexual harassment may involve making lewd remarks, using language that demeans one sex, hanging pinups, and circulating rumors about an individual's real or speculated sexual activities.

I sometimes consult with attorneys who are trying sexual harassment cases. In one instance, a woman sued her former supervisor for subjecting her to continuous comments about her body and questions about her sexual activities. The supervisor's constant sexualized communication interfered with the woman's ability to concentrate on her job and to feel safe in her work environment. In another case on which I consulted, the first woman in a region was appointed high school principal. On her first day in her high school, a male faculty member told her, "We're renaming the school Hen-House High because you're principal." Another male faculty member said, "Having a woman in charge is like a cancer on our school." A subscription to *Playboy* was anonymously given to her by faculty members. These and

Same-Sex Harassment Recognized by Supreme Court

In the spring of 1998 the U.S. Supreme Court unanimously ruled that federal law protects employees from being sexually harassed by people of their own sex in the workplace. In explaining the court's opinion, Justice Antonin Scalia said that sexual harassment laws should address the conduct itself, not the sex or motivation of the individuals involved. Within the intent of Title VII of the Civil Rights Act of 1964, stated Scalia, equal protection exists for victims of both heterosexual and homosexual harassment.

other incidents formed a pattern of abusive conduct of a sexual nature that undercut the principal's authority and created a climate that was offensive to her and other women in the school.

A hostile environment is created by a pattern of behavior. A single action, even if it is unwelcome and inappropriate, is unlikely to meet the legal standard for sexual harassment. Instead, there must be a pervasive pattern of unwelcome conduct of a sexual nature (Bingham, 1996). This standard ensures that isolated misconduct, which might be deliberate or inadvertent, doesn't result in excessive penalties.

Whose perspective counts? Perhaps you are thinking that people may differ in what they consider offensive. Research shows that women and men, in general, differ in how they perceive sexist comments and jokes in the workplace. Many men regard such acts as harmless or as friendly flattery of women. In contrast, many women perceive such acts as demeaning or as abuses of power (Levy & Paludi, 1997). Men who harass are also likely to see themselves as embodying the masculine role by pursuing women and initiating interest in sexual activity (Kurth, Spiller, & Travis, 2000).

The courts have struggled with the question of whose perspective counts since sexual harassment cases first appeared on trial dockets. Within Western legal traditions, the convention for judging behavior has been the "reasonable man" standard; for example, to determine whether a homeowner who shot a burglar behaved appropriately, the court would ask, "What would a reasonable man do if someone broke into his home?"

The reasonable man standard prevailed in early sexual harassment cases. For example, in *Rabidue v. Osceola Refining Company* (1986), the majority opinion of the 6th Circuit Court was that behavior that might offend many women was "an everyday occurrence . . . [that] is natural, acceptable, and part of the fabric of society's morality" (Pollack, 1990, p. 65). In *Rabidue*, male perceptions were declared to be the standard for social conduct. Dissenting from the majority opinion in *Rabidue*, Judge Damon Keith asserted that differences in the conditions of women's and men's lives may lead them to perceive events in distinct ways and, specifically, to find different behaviors intimidating and offensive (Forell, 1993). Although Judge Keith's opinion was the minority in *Rabidue*, he inaugurated judicial awareness of the reasonable woman standard.

A few years after *Rabidue*, courts dealt with the question of whether pinups in public areas of a workplace create an offensive working environment. In this case, the judge ruled that, although nude and near-nude photos of women might not offend a reasonable man, they could well offend a reasonable woman (Tiffs & VanOsdol, 1991). Since that ruling, the reasonable woman standard has been used to judge sexual harassment in a number of cases (Farrell & Matthews, 2000). This legal criterion draws on the logic of standpoint theory, which we discussed in Chapter 2.

Regardless of which standard is used, the law insists on the criterion of reasonableness. This provides a safeguard against highly individualistic perceptions. Courts assess whether perceptions of behaviors as harassing are warranted in light of commonly held perceptions of particular behaviors (Sandler, 1996).

▪ Genital Surgery

Some people have never heard of genital surgery (also called genital mutilation). Of those who have, many think it is an ancient procedure that is no longer practiced. Yet genital surgery is practiced in many parts of the world today (Dreifus, 2000; Gruenbaum, 2001). Estimates are that more than 140 million women have had genital surgery (Jones, 2000). In this section, we'll discuss forms of genital surgery and their consequences. I'll warn you in advance that you may find the pages that follow very disturbing. It isn't possible to discuss this topic in a way that isn't distressing.

Male circumcision. **Male circumcision** is the removal of the sheath, or prepuce, of the penis. In many countries, including the United States, male babies are routinely circumcised shortly after birth. The rationale for male circumcision is that it makes it easier to keep the penis clean and reduces the likelihood of infections. Medical research, however, has not demonstrated any clear health advantages of male circumcision. Thus, this procedure may endure because of tradition, not sound scientific evidence.

Sunna. The word *sunna* comes from the Arabic word for "religious duty" (Trangsrud, 1994) and is a form of female genital surgery practiced in parts of Africa, the Middle East, India, Malaysia, and Indonesia (Hosken, 1992). This procedure involves removing both the sheath and the tip of the clitoris. Although you might think sunna and male circumcision are equivalent, they are different in severity and consequence. Removal of the foreskin of a penis doesn't preclude a man's sexual pleasure, but removal of the prepuce and tip of the clitoris usually leaves a woman unable to experience sexual excitement or orgasm. Sunna also has greater potential for medical complications.

Excision or clitoridectomy. A second type of female genital surgery is excision or **clitoridectomy,** which involves removal of the entire clitoris and parts of the labia minora. This operation greatly diminishes women's ability to experience sexual pleasure, so it is thought to reduce the likelihood that a woman will be sexually active before marriage or unfaithful after marriage. Of lesser concern to those who endorse the practice is that it often has medical complications and increases pain and danger in childbirth.

It might surprise you to learn that clitoridectomies were performed in the United States and Europe in the 19th and 20th centuries. In the United States, some physicians also removed women's ovaries in the belief that eliminating all sources of women's sexual sensation would "cure" masturbation and prevent nymphomania, not to mention orgasm, which was considered an "ailment" that good women didn't have (Dreifus, 2000; Lightfoot-Klein, 1989; Spitz, 1952). Reminding us again of the power of social constructions of gender, views that women should be sexually "pure" were, and still are, used to justify the mutilation of women.

Infibulation. The most radical form of genital surgery is **infibulation.** In this operation, the clitoris and labia minora are removed. Next, the flesh of the labia majora is scraped raw and sewn together to form a hood over the vagina, with a small opening left for urination and menstruation (Toubia, 1994). When a female who has been infibulated marries, an opening is cut to permit intercourse. Sometimes the opening is deliberately made extremely small to increase male sexual pleasure, although it makes intercourse painful to women. The Arabic term for infibulation is *adlat el rujal,* which means "men's circumcision," because it is designed to increase men's sexual pleasure. Husbands may order their wives resewn when they go on journeys or to prevent pregnancy.

This technique seems to have been first used by ancient Upper Egyptians who fastened a clasp (fibula) through the large genital lips of slave women to keep them from having children, which would interfere with their work. Today, infibulation is practiced primarily in some Muslim and West African societies that regard the procedure as a rite of passage that transforms young girls into virgins, an identity based on having undergone infibulation and not on having refrained from sexual intercourse (Van der Kwaak, 1992). After giving birth or losing a husband, some women recapture their status as virgins by being reinfibulated (Slack, 1988).

Women who have been infibulated report that the process is excruciatingly painful (Finnerty, 1999; Ziv, 1997). A woman from Somalia who was infibulated at the age of 6 reported that four women held her down and a razor blade was used to amputate her clitoris and all of her vaginal lips. Then thorns were used to close the wound, and her legs were bound together from her heels to her thighs. As in this case, genital surgery is seldom conducted in sterile settings with anesthesia and precise surgical instruments. It is usually performed by people who have little or no medical training. They work in unsanitary conditions, often using dirty, imprecise implements, including shards of glass, rusty razors, and lids of tin cans (Trangsrud, 1994). The immediate consequences may include excruciating pain, hemorrhage, tetanus, gangrene, blood poisoning, and fractured bones from the force needed to hold girls down during the operation. Long-term consequences include sterility, agonizing pain during intercourse, increased difficulty in delivering babies, permanent incontinence, and stillbirths of babies who cannot emerge through birth canals that have been scarred and deformed by genital operations (Oakley, 2002).

Suchuna

I know American college students cannot understand our ways. In Africa, we do not call it mutilation. We call it the custom. My friends here ask why mothers let this be done to their daughters. It is because men will not marry women who do not follow the custom. A mother who doesn't have the custom for her daughter dooms the daughter to being a social outcast and unmarriageable.

To many people, the idea of genital surgery seems barbaric and unjustifiable. Yet that opinion reflects a standpoint that differs from the standpoint of members of cultures whose traditions include female genital surgery. Within these societies, genital surgery ensures a woman's social status, and girls who have not undergone genital surgery are often ridiculed and made to feel unclean. Dr. Nahid Toubia (1993), one of the international authorities on female genital surgery, says a young girl who had not been infibulated told him that she felt ashamed in front of her friends who had been infibulated, and that her friends refused to let her touch them because she was unclean.

FYI

Defining Human Rights

Fauziya Kasinga grew up in Togo, Ghana. Unlike most men in Togo, Fauziya's father was progressive. He didn't believe in polygamy, forced marriage, or denying education to women. He also refused to let any of his five daughters be circumcised as was the custom in Togo. But when her father died, Fauziya was scheduled for genital surgery. She managed to escape and came to the United States, where she asked for asylum on the grounds that she would be subjected to genital mutilation if she returned home.

The judge who heard her case concluded that her story was "unbelievable" and that Fauziya was not credible. Her case was investigated and then supported by Amnesty International and other human rights groups. On appeal, she was granted asylum—the first time the United States acknowledged that forced genital surgery is a violation of human rights (Goodman, 1996; Kassindja, 1998). This landmark decision defined abuses based on gender as equal to those based on race, religion, or politics.

Changing Customs

Senegal, Togo, and five other African countries have recently banned clitoridectomy (Pollitt, 1999), although the ban is still unevenly enforced. Waris Dirie, who suffered genital mutilation at 5 years old, fled Somalia and became the United Nations special ambassador on female genital mutilation (Dirie, 1998). Dirie says Westerners should not try to change African customs—changes must come from within the countries themselves. She believes female genital mutilation is coming to an end in Africa: "I've heard the chief of a village say, 'We know it is wrong and we've got to stop it'" (Finnerty, 1999, p. 22).

Consider another example of cultural traditions that changed only when members of the culture resisted them. In China for centuries women's feet were bound. Yet this practice was eliminated in a mere 17 years (1895–1912) in urban China when progressive Chinese citizens launched an education campaign against foot binding. Also critical to ending the practice was the formation of associations of fathers who refused to bind their daughters' feet and prohibited their sons from marrying women whose feet had been bound (Lorber, 1997). When enough fathers made these commitments, it affected marriage patterns and made women with unbound feet attractive as marriage partners.

When we acknowledge religious and cultural traditions that uphold the practice of altering female genitalia, we realize it would be ineffective to try to legislate changes without first understanding cultural traditions and providing education about alternative ways to honor traditions (Gruenbaum, 2001; Trangsrud, 1994).

Even though we should be hesitant to apply the standards of our culture to the practices of other cultures, troubling questions about genital surgery cannot be ignored. We have to realize that genital surgery increases a woman's status in societies that endorse this practice. Yet we also must ask why this painful and dangerous procedure is needed for a woman to have status. We should also recognize the gender inequity that exists when men don't have to suffer genital surgery to gain status.

■ Gender-Based Murder

Consider two facts: (1) When both sexes are given adequate care, more females than males survive; and (2) in many countries today, men substantially outnumber women. How can both of these facts be true? According to Amartya Sen (1999), "inequality between women and men afflicts—and sometimes prematurely ends —the lives of millions of women" (p. 15).

One way to reduce the number of women is to selectively abort female fetuses, a common practice in some countries today (Pollitt, 1999). If a female child is born, cultures that don't value females condone female infanticide, the active or passive killing of female children. Active female infanticide is sometimes practiced by smothering a newborn female or drowning her in a bucket of water kept by the birthing bed. More passive methods of female infanticide include feeding girl babies little or nothing and denying them essential medical care (Hegde, 1999a, 1999b).

Women who survive to adulthood aren't necessarily safe. **Femicide** is the killing of women. In many places, including India, Pakistan, Albania, Mexico, and United Arab Emirates, adult women disappear or are killed. Governments do little to investigate cases of women who are found dead or who simply disappear (Lydersen, 2003). Femicide also takes the form of dowry deaths, or bride burnings. Some groups in India still follow the custom in which a woman's parents give a sum of money or other goods to the bridegroom when he marries their daughter. After the marriage, the new husband sometimes makes additional demands for payments from the bride's parents. If the demands aren't met, the husband's family may hold the bride near the cooking stove until her sari catches fire and she burns to death. The husband is then free to get another wife and another dowry. Hundreds of thousands of women have been victims of bride burning, which the culture has condoned by not investigating cases in which women "accidentally" burn to death (French, 1992).

From abortions of female fetuses to killing of female babies to femicide, females around the world are being murdered daily. These practices are dramatic evidence of the devaluation of girls, women, and femininity. By now, the body count produced by these values is in the millions and still growing.

Throughout this book we have seen that what is considered acceptable or normal is a matter of social negotiation and communication in a culture. Years ago it was considered normal for women not to have the right to vote or pursue higher education and careers. It was also considered normal for women to be men's property and for men to control everything from women's living conditions to decisions about medical procedures performed on women. Today, in some countries genital mutilation, female infanticide, and femicide are regarded as normal. In the next section of this chapter, we will identify social processes that allow or encourage gendered violence.

THE SOCIAL FOUNDATIONS OF GENDERED VIOLENCE

We can't understand gendered violence by analyzing only individual motives. Although particular individuals commit violent acts and should be held responsible for them, we have to consider causes beyond individual psychology and circumstances. To unravel cultural forces that cultivate tolerance for violence toward women, we will consider how media, institutions, and language normalize gendered violence.

■ The Normalization of Violence in Media

There is fairly convincing evidence that exposure to sexual violence in media is linked to increased tolerance, or even approval, of violence in actual relationships (Cuklanz, 1996; May, 1998a, p. B7). As we noted in Chapter 11, violence is customary—not unusual—in films, on MTV and television programs, and in popular music. Violence is also wired into video games, which many children and adolescents play for hours each day. One video popular with 10- to 14-year-olds is "Carnal Sins," which is extremely violent. Gangsta rap includes lyrics that refer to women as "hos" (whores) and "bitches" and glorify killing for sport. Some critics of gangsta rap have suggested that it reflects the pathological lifestyle and values of many young Black males. Yet this analysis fails to recognize that the musicians and the lyrics they compose exist in and are accepted by larger social systems. In other words, gangsta rap reflects a widespread and deeply ensconced cultural ideology that esteems violence (Dyson, 1995, 1996).

bell hooks (1994) strongly denounces the misogyny, sexism, and violence of gangsta rap, but she does not make the mistake of thinking it reflects values that are distinctive of Black youth culture. Although hooks acknowledges that "black male sexism is real and a serious problem in our communities" (p. 118), she also points out that a lot of White people produce, market, and listen to gangsta rap. Addressing Black women like herself, hooks says it's wrong to believe they must support violence and sexism "under the guise of standing by our men. If black men are betraying us through acts of male violence, we save ourselves and the race by resisting" (p. 123).

Research on **pornography** further confirms the link between exposure to portrayals of violence in media and willingness to engage in or accept violence in real relationships (Russell, 1993). Before we discuss this research, however, it's important to distinguish pornography from **erotica**. Pornography is not simply sexually explicit material. Rather, it is material that favorably shows subordination and degradation of individuals by presenting sadistic behaviors as pleasurable, pain as enjoyable, and forced sex as positive. Erotica, on the other hand, depicts consensual activities that are desired by and pleasurable to all parties. Erotic material doesn't seem to cultivate violence in relationships, whereas pornographic media are linked to violence between intimates (Donnerstein, Linz, & Penrod, 1987; MacKinnon, 1987).

Pornography is a multibillion-dollar business in the United States. Pornographic videos account for 50% to 60% of all videos selected (Fox-Genovese, 1991). One study of pornographic films found that more than 80% of X-rated films included scenes in which one or more men dominate and exploit one or more women; 75% of these films portray physical aggression against women, and 50% explicitly depict rape (Cowan et al., 1988). A number of researchers report that repeated exposure to sexual violence may lead viewers to see it as acceptable and enticing (Demare, Briere, & Lips, 1988; Donnerstein et al., 1987; Jhally & Katz,

2001). Confirming this is the finding that the single best predictor of the frequency of rape in society is the ease of access to pornographic materials that glorify violence against women (Baron & Straus, 1989).

■ The Normalization of Violence by Institutions

There is growing consensus that many of the basic structures and institutional practices of Western culture tolerate or uphold violence, especially violence toward women. They do this in a variety of ways such as refusing to interfere in domestic disputes, advising victims not to prosecute batterers, and encouraging women to fulfill social prescriptions for femininity by standing by their men.

Family. One of the most important institutions shaping cultural consciousness, including perspectives on violence, is the family (Noddings, 2002). In families where violence exists, parents may teach daughters to expect it. In a recent study I conducted, one woman explained why she stayed with a man who physically and sexually brutalized her: "Once when I told my mama that Gerald was sometimes mean, she said that all men are and that's just how they are—that all of them have bad spells—that's what Mama called them—and sometimes you just have to overlook those" (Wood, 2001b, p. 254). Many parents still encourage girls to be physically reserved, sensitive to relationships, and deferential to others. Boys are encouraged to be physically aggressive and to control others. The combination of these two gender scripts lays the groundwork for men to be sexually aggressive and for women to defer or tolerate abuse from men (Messner, 2001). A man who internalizes social prescriptions for masculinity may regard it as appropriate to dominate and inflict violence on women. Some men who engage in abuse justify their violence by saying their partners deserved it, their partners provoked them, or they had to use force to get what they were entitled to have (Christopher & McQuaid, 1998; Stamp & Sabourin, 1995; Wood, in press).

Tolerance of intimate partner violence is greater in cultures that emphasize family cohesiveness and masculine superiority in families. Hilda Burgos-Ocasio (2000) reports that intimate partner violence among Hispanics is "not only condoned, but also encouraged by the culture" (p. 129), and Anahid Kulwicki (2000) has found that many women and men of Arab ancestry accept the cultural norm that men have a right to abuse women and that women should tolerate abuse and remain loyal. Some African American women don't report intimate partner violence because family cohesiveness is culturally important and because they don't want to fuel negative stereotypes of their race (Winbush, 2000).

When masculine socialization is extreme, it can promote appalling violence, such as that engaged in by members of the Spur Posse, a group of high school athletes in a California suburb who established status by the number of sexual encounters they could score and the disdain with which they treated the women with whom they had sex. Although some parents of the Spur Posse members were upset when they learned of their sons' exploits, other parents weren't. One father remarked, "Nothing my boy did was anything that any red-blooded American boy wouldn't do at his age" (Quindlen, 1994, p. A23).

A more recent incident of mob violence against women was the wilding in Central Park at the National Puerto Rican Day Parade on June 11, 2000. Four or five dozen men groped and stripped at least 47 women while yelling "Get that bitch" and "You know you want it" (Campo-Flores & Rosenberg, 2000). Over 900 police officers were on duty in the park at the time, but they were unresponsive to pleas for help. In response to public outcry, within a week Mayor Rudy Giuliani promised an intense inquiry into police response, and 17 men were arrested. One of the men arrested shrugged off what he and others did to women, saying that it was "an innocent water fight that got out of hand" (Cloud, 2000, p. 32). The June 26 issue of *Time* included a two-page story on the Central Park wilding. The same issue gave five pages to coverage of an architect and seven pages to an article on television voyeurism.

Law enforcement. Families are not the only social institution that upholds tolerance of violence. Some law-enforcement officers also reflect and sustain cultural acceptance of violence. Police officers are often reluctant to intervene in violence in families. As two reporters noted, "Bluntly put, cops hate domestic calls" (Ingrassia & Beck, 1994, p. 31). Some police officers regard domestic cases as less important than "real crime."

When they fail to treat abusers harshly, the courts also communicate that violence against women is not serious. According to Albert Hunt (1994), most spouse abusers receive lenient treatment in U.S. courts. In 1991, Juanita Leonard testified in divorce court that her husband, Sugar Ray Leonard, had repeatedly hit her, thrown her around, and harassed her in front of their children. The world-famous boxer denied none of his wife's claims. He did, however, say his violence was a private matter between him and his wife, a view that the court found credible (Nelson, 1994a).

Another highly publicized case was that of O.J. Simpson and Nicole Brown Simpson (Bordo, 1997). After Nicole Brown Simpson was found murdered, O.J. Simpson was accused of her murder. He tried to flee but was caught and brought to trial. Reports on the trial dominated headlines and television news for months. Although there was some evidence suggesting that O.J. might have committed the murder, the jury found him not guilty, and he was released. This was not the first time O.J. had been suspected of violence toward Nicole. In 1989, when they were still married, police entered the Simpsons' home and found Nicole Brown Simpson badly beaten and fearful for her life. The officers accepted O.J.'s statement that he and his wife were involved in "a family matter . . . we can handle it" (Hunt, 1994). Judge Ronald Schoenberg didn't sentence repeated abuser O.J. Simpson to any prison time or even counseling. Another case, this one in New Hampshire in 1993, involved a man who smashed his partner's face so badly that she needed 17 stitches. Acknowledging that the man had battered the woman, the judge nonetheless ruled, "I can't conclude that it was completely unprovoked" (Hunt, 1994). Judgments such as this one communicate dramatically that it is acceptable to batter women. In so doing, they perpetuate violence against women and the values that underlie it.

Based on interviews with 80 survivors of violence at the hands of intimates, James West (1995) reported that women who are abused by partners often face strong social pressure to stay in relationships. West found that some judges, prosecutors, and other officers of the courts advise victims of battering to return home, not to press charges, or to "work things out." These messages from people in powerful institutional positions communicate that abuse of women is unimportant in the eyes of the law and society.

Counseling. Compounding the legal system's contribution to normalizing violence against women is the advice given by some clergy and lay counselors to victims of violence. They may urge women to return to their battering partners in order to "be a good wife," "keep the family together," and "not be selfish" (West, 1995). The commentary by Jenni is not from a student but from a battered woman (West, 1995, p. 129). Jenni describes what happened after she turned to her church for help when her husband beat her and the priest advised her to return home.

Some institutions also perpetuate violence against women by suggesting that women are wrong to object to brutality and harassment. In her studies of responses to women who have been sexually harassed, Robin Clair (1994) found that victims' protests are often dismissed ("You misunderstood"), trivialized ("Don't make a mountain out of a molehill"), or defined as inappropriate ("All the guys around here do that"). Each of these responses defines the victim, not the sexual harasser, as wrong or at fault. By routinely treating sexual harassment and other forms of violence toward women as unimportant, institutions sustain a cultural ideology that licenses violence toward women.

Language. Another cultural practice that reflects and sustains tolerance of violence is language.

Jenni

I said, "I can't [go home]. What am I supposed to do if he's cheating on me and hits me?" He [the priest] said, "You should forgive him." And I said, "What if he continues to do it?" Then he said, "You should pray that he'll stop." I said, "I'm sorry, I'm sorry, I've waited for a long time for him to stop and he hasn't and I'm not going back." Then he told me that I was very selfish and all I cared about was myself and what I was doing.

Geneva

When I was a sophomore, an instructor in my chemistry class tried to hit on me. He asked me to come to his office to discuss my work. But when I got there, he started touching me and asking if I'd go out with him. I don't remember what I said, but I got out of there as fast as I could. When I went to the chair of the department, he told me I was overreacting to "a misunderstanding." My advisor said the same thing, so I finally figured I must be wrong to think it was such a big deal. I quit going to the class because I wanted to avoid the instructor, so I failed. No big deal, right?

Throughout this book and especially this chapter, we've noted ways in which communication reflects and sustains cultural views of gender and gender-related behavior, including violence. Much of the language used to describe violence between intimates conceals the brutality of what happens. Why do newspapers and news programs use inappropriately gentle terms such as *domestic dispute* or *spousal conflict* to camouflage acts such as smashing women's faces with fists and hammers, slashing women with knives, and breaking bones by throwing or stomping on women (Lamb, 1991, 1999)? James West (1995) notes that the term *domestic violence* "provides an image of the violence in a family as somehow less severe than violence between strangers" (p. 140).

Commonly used language about gendered violence also obscures moral responsibility. Terms such as *spousal conflict* and *family problems* distort reality by representing the issue as one for which partners share culpability. Responsibility for violence is also diminished by passive language that fails to name aggressors—for example, "The battery occurred on Sunday," "Women are abused frequently," or "Many women are beaten." The horror of intimate partner violence is also diminished when the language of love is used to describe physical abuse. Media accounts of battering of women often include phrases such as "He loved her too much," "She was the victim of love," and "It was love that went too far" (Jones, 1994; Meyers, 1994, 1997).

It's clear that many of our cultural institutions reflect and sustain the acceptance of violence as normal. It would be nice to believe that individuals don't necessarily share institutional views that violence is acceptable. If that were true, however, during O.J.'s frantic attempt to elude capture, why did drivers on the Los Angeles freeway stop their cars to let him pass, all the while chanting "Go, O.J., go"? They cheered a known wife batterer and an accused murderer in his flight from justice.

Cultural acceptance of gendered violence is supported—subtly and overtly, deliberately and inadvertently—by a number of social practices and institutions. Compelling evidence of the cultural foundations of gendered violence comes from cross-cultural studies that reveal pronounced differences among societies in the frequency of rape and other violations of women. Rape is most common in societies that embrace ideologies of male toughness and that disrespect women and nature (Basow, 1992; Coltrane, 1996, 1998; Sanday, 1986; Wriggins, 1998). On the other hand, rape is rare in cultures where women have rights equal to those of men and in cultures that value nurturance and harmony with nature (Griffin, 1981; Sanday, 1986). Of 95 tribal societies studied, approximately one-half have virtually no rape (West Sumatra, for example) (Basow, 1992; Griffin, 1981). The existence of societies in which rape and other forms of gendered violence are rare demonstrates that violence against women is not innate in male sexuality and acceptance of violence is not inevitable. Attitudes toward gendered violence reflect particular cultural ideologies that can be transformed.

RESISTING GENDERED VIOLENCE: WHERE DO WE GO FROM HERE?

I suspect that this chapter has been as distressing for you to read as it was for me to research and write. However, mere distress about the extent of gendered violence will not lessen it. We must ask how we can be agents of change who resist gendered violence and who compel revisions in cultural attitudes toward it.

Personal Efforts to Reduce Gendered Violence

Each of us can do a great deal to lessen gendered violence. The most basic personal choice is to decide that you will not engage in or tolerate violence in your relationships. You can also make conscious choices about the language you use to speak about gendered violence. You can heighten others' awareness of the extent and brutality of violence against women by selecting words that accurately represent the ugliness and inhumanity of violent actions. An extension of this is to speak out against violence. If a woman you know verbally abuses her boyfriend, you can either remain silent or let her know that you think what she's doing is wrong. You can also speak against others who violate or threaten to violate women. You may be able to intervene in some situations to prevent violence.

There are other ways you personally can take a stand against gendered violence. You might volunteer to work with battered women or women who have been raped. Most campuses and communities have a number of women's groups that offer outreach programs to educate citizens about violence toward women. Men on many campuses work to get other men involved in combating violence toward women. Becoming a community educator is one way to be an active agent of change. You can also make a personal statement by writing or calling in to object to magazine stories, radio programs, and televisions shows that present violence as normal or acceptable.

You can use your voice to resist gendered violence by supporting friends and acquaintances who are victims of violence. For too many years, people have looked away from sexual harassment and violence between intimates. We've pretended not to see bruises, not to notice on-the-job harassment. If you suspect that a friend or colleague is experiencing

Denny

Cindy and I were at a bar, and it was pretty late, and most folks had been drinking for hours. I overheard a group of guys talking about this one girl who had danced with lots of the men during the evening. One of the guys said he bet she'd had enough to drink that she wouldn't be able to put up much of a fight. The other guys agreed and then started talking about who would take the next dance and move her outside. I kind of eased my beer down on the bar and went over to dance with the girl. When the song ended, I guided her back to where Cindy was, and we just kind of hung out with her until closing time. I saw *The Accused,* so I knew what could happen in a bar with guys who'd been drinking.

violence, don't assume "it's none of my business." It *is* your business. Speaking up to support someone who is being harmed is a concrete way to use your voice to reduce the violence in our world.

If you are a parent or plan to be one, you can make a difference by teaching your children that nobody has a right to touch them in a violent or sexual way without their permission. And all children should learn that it is not appropriate or acceptable to be violent toward others or to coerce others into sexual activities.

■ Social Efforts to Reduce Gendered Violence

We must also change cultural practices and structures. Here, too, there are many ways to be an agent of change. Some universities now offer an interdisciplinary minor in Violence Studies that allows students to prepare for careers that help reduce violence (Reisberg, 1999). You can also vote for bonds and tax increases to underwrite more education and counseling. If you have skills as an educator or administrator, you may be able to help design and implement educational programs. In Wai'anae, Hawaii, women developed Peace Education, a two-week curriculum that helps students learn nonviolent ways to manage anger and frustration (French, 1992).

In India a group of women formed *Vimochana,* an organization that helps battered women get legal assistance. In addition to responding to the symptoms of violence (battered women), *Vimochana* tackles the structural causes of it by organizing consciousness-raising groups that help women work together to redefine battering and dowry murders as unacceptable. Groups patterned after *Vimochana* could erode the foundations of gendered violence in other countries, including the United States.

You can also get involved with international efforts to reduce violence toward women. Many organizations work against violence, and they welcome volunteers and financial support. For example, Southeast Asian women formed *Saheli,* which protests dowry deaths. *Saheli* was successful in getting a law passed that requires thorough investigation of any "accidental death" of a woman during the

The Bandit Queen of India

Phoolan Devi was born into Dalit, a low caste of boat rowers in India. At 11, she was married to a man twenty years her senior who was chosen by her parents. Her husband beat her, and later, while under detention, Devi was raped. Instead of accepting this as the fate of women in her society, Devi rebelled. She took up a gun and formed a gang that killed men who harmed women. In 1983 she turned herself in in exchange for the government's promise of an eight-year jail sentence. Devi was jailed without trial for 11 years, then released without comment in 1994. Within a year of her release, women elected her to federal parliament (Schmetzer, 1997).

She became a very powerful advocate for women in India. To her followers, she was the reincarnation of Kali, a Hindu goddess, and a symbol of women's rights in a country that historically has not recognized that women have rights. In 2001, at the age of 38, Devi was gunned down in India by Sher Singh Rana, a 22-year-old student.

first seven years of marriage (French, 1992). Chilean women are risking imprisonment and death to demand that *desaparecidos,* "disappeared women," be returned. In Afghanistan courageous women quietly worked for women's rights, even under the oppressive Taliban rule (Herlinger, 2001). Groups such as these could use support, both personal and financial, from women and men in less hazardous circumstances.

SUMMARY

In this chapter we've examined forms of gendered violence and some of the ways in which communication sustains and normalizes violence, especially violence toward women. It is painful to think about the topics in this chapter. Yet the distress that you and I feel in dealing with these issues pales in contrast to the agony felt by women around the world who are victims of unspeakable violations.

We do not have to accept the current state of affairs. We can do much to reduce gendered violence in our personal lives and to contribute to broader changes in the social structures and practices that sustain cultural acceptance of gendered violence. All that is required is to decide you will assume an active role in improving the world.

We need to work together to provide safe refuges for victims of violence and to provide counseling to both victims and abusers. In addition, we need to develop educational programs that teach very young children that violence toward others is unacceptable. These and other changes in social structures and practices can reform cultural attitudes toward gendered violence. The changes will not be easy, but they are possible. Continuing to live with pervasive and relentless violence is not acceptable.

KEY TERMS

clitoridectomy, 272
erotica, 276
femicide, 275
gender intimidation, 260
gendered violence, 260
hostile environment harassment, 269
infibulation, 272
informed consent, 261

intimate partner violence, 264
male circumcision, 271
pornography, 276
quid pro quo harassment, 269
sexual assault, 261
sexual harassment, 268
sunna, 271

DISCUSSION QUESTIONS

1. What are the values and shortcomings of the various legal standards for judging sexual harassment? Do you support the reasonable man standard, reasonable woman standard, or another standard? How is this issue linked to our discussion of generic language?

2. How we should perceive and respond to genital mutilation is more complex than it might first seem. Would Western efforts to end clitoridectomies and infibulations result in unmutilated women being outcasts who could never marry? (Reread Suchuna's commentary on page 273.) Is it ethnocentric to condemn practices that differ from those in our own culture? Do we have any right to impose our values on people of different standpoints? On the other hand, is it moral to do nothing when human beings are being maimed (following custom) and killed?

3. Use PowerTrac, select Author Index, then type "Kimberly Davis." Read her May 2003 article, "Dying for love: The epidemic of domestic abuse," which appeared in *Ebony.* How does Davis support her claim that intimate partner violence is greater in African American relationships than European American ones?

4. To understand how sexual harassment affects individuals, read the stories of people who have personally experienced it. The fall 1992 issue of the *Journal of Applied Communication Research* includes a special symposium that features the stories of survivors of sexual harassment.

5. Use PowerTrac to read my 1999 article, "'That wasn't the real him!': Women's dissociation of violence from the men who enact it," which appeared in *Qualitative Research Reports.* How might feminine socialization contribute to my finding that many abused women claim that their partners weren't really themselves when they inflicted violence?

Epilogue
Looking Backward, Looking Forward

If you don't like something, change it.

—MAYA ANGELOU

The cultural conversation about gender is ongoing. It is carried on in living rooms, legislative chambers, classrooms, church groups, zines, barbershops, newspapers, personal relationships, and boardrooms. It is a conversation in which we all participate; each generation adds new themes to the overall dialogue. Even though this book is ending, what you've learned about communication, gender, and culture will affect your personal future and your participation in collective life. In this epilogue, we'll look backward at changes that have occurred and look forward to choices that are open to us in the years ahead.

Throughout this book we've seen that society communicates gendered expectations that affect the rights, roles, and opportunities available to each of us. Yet we are not only receivers of cultural communication about gender. We also shape our culture's views of men and women. We fortify or resist prevailing views as we enact our own gendered identities and as we respond to the communication and identities of others.

A central theme of *Gendered Lives* is that current views of gender are not the only possible ones or necessarily the best ones. In this book I've invited you to think critically about current views of gender and to challenge those that limit our individual and collective lives. You and others of your generation will revise what gender means to you and to society. Given the profound impact of gender on personal and social life, this is no small responsibility.

You have inherited opportunities and definitions of gender that were crafted by the generations that preceded you. Women and some men in the 1800s and early 1900s changed laws and the Constitution to give women basic rights. My generation challenged restrictive definitions of women and men and social practices that limited the opportunities available to both sexes. We devoted much of our energy to identifying gender inequities and fighting to change economic, political, professional, and social subordination of women. The legacy of our efforts is substantial, and it has altered the educational, social, professional, and legal rights that are available to you.

Your generation faces its own challenges, and you will need to define different priorities from those that motivated previous generations. Framing the issues of your era is a growing awareness of how the interaction of communication, gender, and culture privileges some people and oppresses others. All around us are inequities—some glaringly obvious, others more subtle. In shaping the future, your generation will decide how to respond to social practices that produce differences in the quality of life and opportunities available to various groups in our culture. We'll review changes that have been made in the areas covered in this book and ask what issues invite our attention in the years ahead.

WOMEN'S AND MEN'S MOVEMENTS

Women's and men's movements have been a major influence on social views of gender. Here we have seen remarkable developments, and additional ones promise to emerge in the coming years.

Feminism

NOW is more than 30 years old, and it has accomplished major changes in the material, political, and social conditions of some women's lives. But liberal feminism isn't the only branch of the women's movement. Challenges to that branch's preeminence have come from other groups, especially multiracial feminists and third-wave feminists. The past ten years have been a stage on which different, sometimes competing views and visions of women have been played out.

Will liberal feminism continue to be the dominant branch of women's movements? Some criticisms of second-wave liberal feminism come from the antifeminist, or backlash movement. Danielle Crittenden (1999), for example, argues that liberal feminism duped women into thinking that they could have jobs as well as families and told them men would desire them even if they had gray hair and wrinkles. Another backlash writer, Wendy Shalit (1999), claims that liberal feminism corrupted women, making them immodest and self-centered. She advises women to return to traditional, conservative principles of womanhood.

A very different criticism of second-wave liberal feminism is that it did not go far enough and that a feminism for the new millennium must be broader and more inclusive, more respectful of differences among people and the diverse conditions of their lives. This seems to be a major impulse propelling the third wave of feminism in the United States. In the coming years, we will see and be part of the conversation about where feminism is and should be heading.

■ Men's Movements

Since the 1980s increasing numbers of men have become involved in exploring masculinity and men's issues. There has been an explosion of books on men and the ways in which culture shapes masculinity (Heller, 1993; May, 1998a). At the same time, we've seen the emergence of a number of men's movements that reflect widely different views of who men are and should be. Some movements seek to reinscribe highly traditional masculine identities. Other branches of men's movements seek alliances with feminism and work to redefine manhood.

> ### Taft
>
> I wonder if it's possible that we'll see a movement for gender equality that involves a lot of men and women. It seems to me that it would be good for us to work together instead of in separate movements. After all, a lot of the issues men face have to do with women and vice versa. Couldn't we get a lot more accomplished by talking with each other and combining forces to work for change?

How will men's movements evolve in the years ahead? Will one of the current movements eclipse others to become dominant, as liberal feminism did in the second wave? Will the movements converge in ways that allow a unified men's movement or a joint women's and men's movement that works together (Stoltenberg, 1995)? Will entirely new men's movements emerge to offer still other views of masculinity? The next 10 to 20 years may be pivotal for men if they, like many women did in the 1960s and 1970s, work together to define their interests, needs, and problems and to build organizations that can change gender ideologies that hamper their lives.

COMMUNICATION

Today we have a heightened awareness of differences in how women and men generally communicate, as well as a greater understanding of the distinctive strengths of each style. As our knowledge of gender-linked communication and its effects has grown, many women have become more assertive, and many men have become more responsive.

In recent decades, women have challenged inequities based on sex and gender. Many women are no longer willing to accept harassment on the job and in schools. Women also advocate government support of family life, continued protection of women's rights to reproductive choice, and equal access to education for all children.

We've also seen changes in men's communication patterns. During the 1992 and 1996 presidential campaigns, candidate Bill Clinton consistently relied on an interactive, conversational mode of communication that historically has been considered feminine. He resisted the traditional format of debates, which had relied on sequential speeches by individual candidates. Instead, he favored an open format that allowed him to interact directly with citizens by letting them pose questions that he would answer. In blending assertion and responsiveness, confidence and openness, and power and sensitivity, Bill Clinton altered stereotypes of how successful men communicate.

Beyond the political realm, many men today are engaging in collaborative, responsive communication with colleagues and friends. Men are also showing that it is possible to combine tenderness and toughness, as exemplified by firefighters who rescued people from the twin towers after the terrorist attack in 2001. These men demonstrated very traditional masculine strength and courage, and they also cried publicly, unafraid to express the depths of their pain.

Looking ahead, how will women's and men's communication continue to evolve? Will more men demonstrate that a man can be simultaneously sensitive and strong? Will more women show us that assertiveness and compassion are compatible? Will advertising and pop culture offer us more realistic, healthier images of women, men, and relationships? As your generation experiments with styles of interaction that depart from rigid sex stereotypes, you will redefine the range of human communication considered appropriate for both sexes.

GENDER IN PERSONAL RELATIONSHIPS

Among the changes achieved in personal relationships during recent decades, three stand out. First, marital rape, date rape, and acquaintance rape have been named as crimes. This gives victims of these crimes a socially recognized vocabulary for seeking justice. Second, divorce laws have been rewritten in many states so that nonfinancial investments in marriage are better recognized and accommodated in property settlements. This change is pivotal because it means that contributions to relationships, family life, and support of another's public career are legally recognized as having value. Third, many men and women of previous generations pioneered new forms of friendship and committed romantic relationships that are more equitable partnerships than those of their parents (Maccoby, 1990; Schwartz, 1994; Schwartz & Rutter, 1998). Yet there is much work still to be done in remaking our close relationships so that they are workable in the present era.

We have been much more successful in moving toward equality in the public realm than in the private realm of home and family. The second shift exemplifies gender inequity in personal relationships. It is neither fair nor loving when one partner in a dual-worker family assumes the majority of domestic and child-care responsibilities. Although some men today are doing more inside the home than their fathers did, it's still the case that most men in dual-worker relationships don't assume a full share of responsibilities. After years of studying marriages, Barbara Risman and Sandra Godwin conclude that marriage represents "a stalled revolution" (2001, p. 139). The second wave of feminism's aim to revolutionize gender relations stalled at the front door of home and family life.

You will make choices in your private relationships that reject or enact a commitment to equity. What kind of family responsibilities will you assume, and what will you expect of your partner? If you are a man, will you contribute equally to cleaning, cooking, and child care, including the repetitive tasks of bathing, feeding, and transporting children? If you are a woman, will you be more assertive than many members of the current generation of women in insisting on equity in home life? You will answer these questions not with statements of intent but in daily practices through which you reinforce or reconfigure existing cultural patterns.

Will your generation find ways to overcome the divisiveness that too often poisons relationships between women and men? Recent decades have tended to portray women's interests as opposed to those of men, and gains in women's opportunities as losses for men. Perhaps your generation will redefine issues so that they are not seen as win–lose. Your voice will fuel or defuse divisions between women and men. Will you find ways to collaborate in creating relationships that are fair and satisfying to men and women? Can we begin to discover what is common to us—the needs we share, the dreams we have—without erasing what is unique about us as individuals?

GENDER IN EDUCATION

Within educational contexts, we have seen some significant changes in gender and communication. At the same time, there is still much to be done if we wish our schools to empower all students equally.

Most basic among changes in this area are new laws that make it illegal for federally funded schools to discriminate on the basis of sex or gender. Other changes of note include growth in female faculty members and the rising number of women in formerly masculine majors, such as science, and in graduate and professional schools.

Another major change is expansion of the curriculum over the past two decades to include the study of gender, both in its own right and as it interacts with sexual orientation, race, and class. This enhances students' opportunities to learn how gender is involved deeply in history, sociology, psychology, literature, and other areas formerly defined as independent of gender.

Yet educational contexts need further reform if they are to provide equal opportunity to all students. It's evident that a hidden curriculum is still part of schools when a report in the mid-1990s confirms that gender-biased educational practices identified in the early 1980s still exist in classrooms across the country. Research on gendered dimensions of education has also shown us that boys and men can be disadvantaged when they are not encouraged to develop collaborative, cooperative modes of interacting with others. Further evidence of continuing gender discrimination lies in the gap between salaries of women and men faculty with equivalent experience, records, and seniority.

Will the coming years bring further progress in eradicating gender discrimination in educational settings? If you continue your education, will you speak out against educational practices that disadvantage women? If you have children, will your daughters get as much intellectual encouragement and attention as your sons? Will you be active in making this happen, for instance, by learning where candidates for school boards stand on gender equity issues? Will you perhaps run for such a position yourself so that you can work more directly toward gender equity in education?

GENDER IN INSTITUTIONAL SETTINGS

Although women have gained entry into professional and public life, the majority of women have been excluded from top positions of leadership and power. Elections in the past ten years have increased the number of minorities and women in the U.S. Congress. In addition, many companies have learned that they benefit by including people with varied backgrounds and perspectives at all levels of their organizations. As it becomes clear that organizations are likely to benefit from diversity, they are making stronger efforts to identify and dismantle subtle barriers that have limited the professional growth of women and minorities (Worley & Vannoy, 2001).

Yet laws against sex and gender discrimination in hiring have had little impact on the more informal structures that govern promotion and advancement. For instance, the Pregnancy Discrimination Act, passed in 1978, makes it illegal to discriminate against pregnant women. Nonetheless, women in increasing numbers report that they are discriminated against when they become pregnant. They suddenly receive a bad evaluation after years of positive ones, or their jobs are filled or eliminated during a pregnancy leave (Noble, 1993). Discrimination against pregnant women creates grave inequities for the 85% of women likely to become pregnant at some point in their lives.

Despite passage of the 1993 Family and Medical Leave Act, we still have no national policy that guarantees *all* workers leaves to care for newborns and newly adopted children or for partners, parents, children, or other relatives who need care. Unlike *every other* developed country in the world, the United States has not designed government and business so that women and men can be both involved professionals and responsible members of families.

You will have opportunities to influence society to create policies and laws that make it possible for both women and men to do well-paid work and be actively involved in their families. Do you plan to take a voice on public issues such as laws to ensure family leave policies for men and women who work outside the home? Do you plan to make commitments within your personal relationships that lead to greater gender equity than traditional norms for relationships have? In the places you work, will you speak out for policies that provide equitable opportunities, working environments, and rewards for women and men on the job? In influencing government and business policies regarding families, your generation will play a critical role in redesigning institutional practices that have an impact on every citizen.

Gendered Media

Media are particularly visible indicators of shifting views of gender. We've seen changes in how media represent women and men, as well as the continuation of traditionally gendered portrayals. In the years to come, media will continue to redraft images of gender.

In recent years we have seen substantial shifts in the kinds of roles available to women and men. Although there is still a preponderance of traditionally sex-typed roles, those are no longer the only ones. A number of recent films and television programs include characters who step outside of narrowly defined, conventional roles. So we see some female characters who are strong as well as sensitive and some male characters who are sensitive as well as strong.

Other changes of note in media include the increase in women's music and companies like Redwood and Ladyslipper that produce music by and for women. Women artists such as Sarah McLachlan, Beyoncé, and Lauryn Hill give voice to experiences, values, and aesthetic forms that are not characteristically represented by males or by women singing lyrics written by men from a mainstream masculine perspective. New women artists increasingly are attracting audiences of both men and women.

In recent years children's films, too, have offered us some new visions of women and men, for example, *Mulan*, Disney's animated film about a Chinese girl who disguises herself as a man and helps China fend off the invading Huns. Film critics Corie Brown and Laura Shapiro (1998) point out that what sets *Mulan* apart from most female characters in children's films is that "she doesn't look like a Barbie doll, she doesn't dream about a prince, and she certainly doesn't hang around waiting to be rescued. The conflict that drives her is about honor, not romance" (pp. 64–65). *Shrek* offers children a similar departure from the classic beautiful-princess-rescued-by-handsome-powerful-prince storyline. How will viewing films such as *Mulan* and *Shrek* affect children's views of what girls and boys can do and become?

What images of women and men will media show in the future? In this area, a number of issues merit the attention of your generation. Consider advertising. Beauty and youth are still represented as the ideal of femininity (Greer, 1992; Kilbourne, 2004; Rakow, 1992; Schwichtenberg, 1989). In addition, ads for men in magazines such as *Esquire* continue to promote images of sturdy oaks and aggressive, successful men as the epitome of masculinity.

Edwina

I really hope my generation does get away from images of the one way to be a man or a woman. It just doesn't make sense for all of us to be the same, when clearly we're not. I say let Madonna do her thing, and let Hillary do hers, and maybe both are okay. Why does one of them have to be wrong? Why isn't it all right to be a full-time homemaker, or a full-time working mother, or not a mother at all? Why is only one choice considered "the right one"? I really hope my generation can put a little elastic into views of women and men.

Chris

I believe my generation can really make a difference, and I want to be part of that. I am angry about the limitations society tries to impose on men and women, and I want to get actively involved in changing them. Too many people are apathetic; they assume that others will fight for needed changes or that change is impossible. I don't want to be that way. I may be just one grain of sand, but every grain counts in forming a beach.

New and emerging communication technologies raise unique questions about gendered interaction. In chat rooms, individuals often misrepresent their sex or don't identify it. Sexually harassing messages on the Internet are frequent. Similarly, flamings, or offensive aspersions, often include overtly sexist and racist slurs. Your generation will shape the norms that govern communication on the Internet and the World Wide Web. What will you do to guide conversations through new media?

Today, media offer us wildly varying images of women. Madonna's book, *Sex,* took to new extremes her efforts to explode any stable definition of women (Schwichtenberg, 1992). She insists there is no one definition of women, and women need not embody any single image. In contrast to Madonna are other visible images of women. For instance, Hillary Rodham Clinton broke decades of tradition when she set up her office in the West Wing of the White House, where policymakers work. Historically, First Ladies have operated from the East Wing.

Oprah Winfrey is a very different woman in the media spotlight. While conforming to some traditional views of women (caring, sensitive), she defies other views by speaking out on social issues and refusing to diet in order to be slim. In contrast to women such as Hillary Clinton and Oprah Winfrey, Laura Bush has adopted a low public profile. She has received less media criticism than her predecessor, perhaps because she conforms to conservative views of women.

As we begin the 21st century, how will you and your peers redraw cultural images of men and women? Historically, efforts to change views of women and men have resulted in pitting one vision of manhood or womanhood against another. Should men be strong or sensitive? Should women be traditional home-makers or fast-track careerists? Is the ideal first lady embodied by Hillary Rodham Clinton or Laura Bush, or can it be either? Creating polar views of women and men does little to expand options, and it promotes divisiveness. Your generation has the opportunity to lead us away from oppositional images and to recognize and affirm multiple versions of sex and gender.

GENDER AND VIOLENCE

Also on your generation's agenda is further work to identify and eliminate crimes of violence, of which women are disproportionately the victims worldwide. From activities that demean and violate women to battering, incest, rape, and gendered murder, there is a long and shameful list of crimes of violence that diminish all of us. Carl Fox, the district attorney in my county, told me that juries are reluctant to convict a man of rape when the victim knew him and had been friendly with him. In short, rape is still widely considered assault by a stranger. This means that knowing a person functionally negates a woman's right to say no and have her refusal respected by our legal system.

Another important area in which views of gendered violence have changed and will change further is sexual harassment. In recent years, much progress has been made in creating laws and institutional policies that condemn sexual harass-ment and levy penalties for its commission. Yet inequities persist. Men who are sexually harassed are sometimes ridiculed, a response that reflects cultural views that men should be strong and self-sufficient. There is still too much willingness to excuse sexual harassment because of "extenuating circumstances." When charges of sexual harassment forced Bob Packwood of Oregon to resign from the Senate in 1995, he claimed that his problems with alcohol were responsible but that he personally wasn't. Where do we draw the line regarding personal responsi-bility for actions?

CREATING THE FUTURE

The future is open. You and others in your generation will decide what it is. Your choices—in personal, social, and professional life—will contribute to defining gender in the years ahead and to how our society deals with the range of people it comprises.

Defining Masculinity and Femininity

Are you satisfied with the views of masculinity that are emphasized today? If you are a man, how will you define masculinity for yourself? What will your actions say about what it means to be a man? How will they shape others' views of manhood? If you are a woman, what will you value in and expect of men? If you have children, will you define active fathering as integral to masculinity? Will you assume a fair share of responsibility for housework and child care? You may also want to consider the traditional relationship between violence and manhood. Like all social views, this one can be changed, but only if you and others take a role in renouncing violence as part of what it means to be a man (Kirby & Krone, 2002).

The connection between masculinity and being a breadwinner will also need rethinking as an increasing number of men of your generation have partners who earn higher salaries, prestige, and public position. If your view of manhood remains tied to status and power, this will create enormous tension in your relationships and your identity. Through your personal and collective choices, your generation will author its own vision of manhood, one that has the potential to revise and enlarge how women and men view masculinity.

Are you comfortable with current cultural views of femininity? If you are a woman, how do you define femininity for yourself? How does your embodiment of femininity affect others' views of what women are and can be? If you are a man, are you comfortable with existing views of women? What will you expect of and value in women? As a man or woman, will you work to discourage unhealthy images that encourage women to starve themselves or to seek breast surgery in order to meet cultural standards? You have the capacity to resist cultural images of women. As a woman, the femininity that you embody in your personal identity will contribute to the diversity in images of women that is available to everyone. As women and men, you can affect what society expects of and admires in women and men.

Remaking Ourselves

Freedom . . . is characterized by a constantly renewed obligation to remake the Self, which designates the free being.

Source: Sartre, J. P. (1966). *Being and nothingness: An essay in phenomenological ontology* (pp. 34–35). New York: Citadel.

■ Responding to Differences

Growing out of what we have discussed is perhaps the most urgent challenge for your generation: enlarging recognition and respect for differences that include and go beyond differences between men and women. Diversity can be a source of strength or divisiveness, and you will choose which one it comes to mean in the future. Will you respect men who give up careers to be homemakers and primary parents *and* men who find their fulfillment in intense entrepreneurial ventures? Will you encourage your sons and daughters to be caring *and* strong? Understand that your real answers to these questions will be found not in what you say but in how you live your life. There is a saying that "those who talk the talk should also walk the walk." We should practice what we say we believe. In living out answers to these questions, you will define your views of women, men, and differences.

Also relevant to the issue of defining differences is the ongoing debate about whether women and men really are different and, by implication, whether they should be treated differently. How we resolve this question profoundly affects our material lives, particularly in terms of legal rights and institutional policies. For example, our courts are currently hearing cases in which one attorney argues for equal treatment of women and opposing counsel argues for special treatment that is responsive to women's distinct nature. A specific example is pregnancy: Should it be defined as a uniquely female condition that requires special provisions, or should pregnancy be classified as one of many temporary human medical conditions?

As your generation transforms social meanings of women, men, and differences, you will simultaneously influence our collective vision of who we are as a culture. Our country has always included people of varied gender identities, sexual orientations, socioeconomic classes, and races. Yet our language and the dominant cultural ideology advocate a single cultural ideal that some people embody more fully than others. Within this perspective, differences are matters of better and worse, and we are encouraged to use a single standard to evaluate ourselves and others. Historically, of course, the White, middle-class, heterosexual male has been that standard.

The belief in the value of a single cultural ideal is reflected in the melting-pot metaphor that has long been used to describe North America. We have encouraged people to erase their differences and become alike—to assimilate into a single culture based on a single denominator. The painful divisions in our society suggest that the melting pot is an inappropriate ideal for us. It no longer works—if indeed it ever did.

Perhaps it is time to abandon the melting-pot metaphor and inaugurate a new one that acclaims difference as valuable and desirable, one that remakes the cultural ideal to include all citizens instead of trying to remake diverse citizens to fit a single, noninclusive ideal. Maybe your generation will discard the melting-pot metaphor and embrace a different one that recognizes commonality without obliterating real and valuable differences among people. To create a new vision, we must realize that we participate in a common world, yet each of us experiences it somewhat differently from standpoints shaped by intersections among gender, race, class, and sexual orientation. What sort of metaphor might capture this as our national character?

In her history of the second wave of feminism in North America, Flora Davis (1991) uses the metaphor of a salad bowl to describe our society. Davis argues that a salad consists of many different ingredients that retain their individual tastes, textures, and colors and at the same time contribute to a whole that is more complex, interesting, and enjoyable than the individual parts or some fusion of those parts. The Reverend Jesse Jackson offered the compelling metaphor of our nation as a family quilt made up of patches of various colors and design. Another metaphor is that of a collage, in which distinct patterns stand out in their individual integrity while simultaneously contributing to the character and complexity of the whole. If your generation is able to affirm diversity in women and men as well as in race, class, ethnicity, sexuality, and sexual orientation, then you will have inaugurated a bold new theme in the cultural conversation—one with the potential to make our society richer and more equitable for all. That is a responsibility and an opportunity that belongs to each of you.

■ Taking a Voice

Men and women like you will be key players in the next stage of the cultural conversation about gender. You cannot evade participation or the responsibilities it entails. Just as speaking out against discrimination is a choice, so too is silence. You can't avoid influence; instead, you only have the option of deciding what influence you will exert and how and where you will do it.

There are multiple ways in which you can influence our cultural views of gender and gender-related issues. In his study of how people respond to toxic chemical disasters, Michael Reich (1991) identified three ways in which citizens affect public awareness, public policy, and redress for victims of chemical disasters. Translating his ideas to our concern with gender, we can identify three forms of influence on cultural views of gender: direct power, agenda setting, and voice.

Direct power is the ability to make others do what they would not do on their own. If you become an executive or own a company, you will have many opportunities to exercise direct power. For instance, you may be able to establish policies that affect family leave, work schedules, and criteria for promotion. Parents exercise direct power when they allow or don't allow children to play with particular toys or to engage in various kinds of activities. Teachers exercise direct power when they assign readings and projects. And citizens exercise direct power when they enter politics, cast votes, and lobby legislators on gender-related issues.

A second form of power is gatekeeping or agenda setting. As we saw in Chapter 11, newspaper editors and television producers set agendas when they decide what stories to cover and how to represent the issues and people involved in those stories. If you pursue a career in advertising, public relations, popular music, or journalism, you will have opportunities to shape the public agenda. You can also participate in agenda setting by writing letters to editors or calling into talk shows to state your opinions and to get issues on the public agenda. Likewise, you can engage in agenda setting in your professional and social relationships by putting on the table issues that operate covertly to sustain gender inequities.

The third way to exercise power is through voice—communicating with others and engaging in everyday acts of resistance and principled stances. One example of the power of voice is adopting a traitorous identity, which we discussed in Chapter 4. Other examples of voice come from third-wave feminists who challenge sexist attitudes and practices in everyday life. They challenge the supervisor who calls female employees "hon" or "sweetheart"; they refuse to diet excessively to meet unhealthful standards for their bodies; they speak up in classes to challenge racist, sexist, and homophobic comments; they participate in protests and rallies; and they use their voices to challenge inequities and to introduce new perspectives in everyday conversations with friends, co-workers, and acquaintances.

Our capacity for influence is large because society is a human creation that we continuously remake through communication in private and public settings. Your voice will join those of others to shape the meaning of gender and the concrete realities of being men and women in the coming years. You will also influence attitudes toward diversity, either by reinscribing the view that differences are divisive or by affirming them as a source of individual and collective strength. What gender and culture will mean in the future is up to you. In your personal and social relationships, professional interactions, and civic activities, you will create and communicate visions of who we can be and how we can live.

> *You must be the change that you wish to see in the world.*
>
> —MAHATMA GANDHI

DISCUSSION QUESTIONS

1. What do you see as the future of women's and men's movements? Do you think one branch will come to predominate in each movement? Will new kinds of movements emerge?

2. What do current diverse visions of women and men imply about cultural views of femininity and masculinity? Do you find the range of images of women and men exciting, empowering, frustrating?

3. If you could write the script, how would you define masculinity and femininity in the year 2020? Ideally, what would each gender be like? Or would there be no need for two

distinct genders? Or would there be more than two? If gender is a linchpin of culture, then changing gender changes culture. How would the ideals you have in mind affect the character of social life?

4. The textbook closes by discussing metaphors for the United States that might replace the melting-pot metaphor. Do you like the alternatives suggested here: a family quilt, a salad bowl, or a collage? Can you come up with other metaphors that simultaneously represent diversity and commonality among members of our society?

affirmative action Collective term for policies that go beyond equal opportunity laws to redress discrimination. Assumes that historical patterns of discrimination against groups of people justify the preferential treatment of members of those groups; focuses on results, not on the intent of efforts to redress inequities; and attempts to increase the number of qualified members of minorities in education and the workplace, commensurate with their availability.

alternate paths model A relationship theory according to which masculine and feminine ways of creating and expressing closeness are different from each other and equally valid.

androgyny A psychological, as distinct from biological, sex-type. Androgynous people tend to identify with and enact qualities socially ascribed to both women and men.

antifeminism A movement opposing any measures that advance women's equality, status, rights, or opportunities; also called the *backlash movement*.

antisuffrage movement A movement that aimed to prevent women from gaining the right to vote in the United States. Opposition to women's suffrage was evident as early as 1848 but had become formalized in organizations by 1911.

artifacts Personal objects that influence how we see ourselves and how we express our identities.

backlash movement A counter-movement that seeks to repudiate and contain feminism by arguing two contradictory claims: (1) that women have never had it so good, so there is no longer any need for feminism; and (2) that feminism has caused serious problems in women's lives and family relationships. Also called *antifeminism*.

biological theory The theory that biological characteristics of the sexes are the basis of gender differences in thinking, communicating, feeling, and other functions.

clitoridectomy Removal of the entire clitoris. Part or all of the labia minora may also be removed. Also called *excision*.

cognitive development theory A developmental theory, according to which children participate in defining their genders by acting on internal motivations to be competent, which lead them to seek out gender models that help them to sculpt their own femininity or masculinity.

communication A dynamic, systemic process in which meanings are created and reflected in and through humans' interactions with symbols.

complementary copy An article or section of writing about an advertiser's product or service that is placed in a magazine by the publisher at no cost to the advertiser, to increase the market appeal of the product or service.

content level of meaning The literal meaning of communication. Content-level meanings are the formal, or denotative, meanings of messages.

cultural feminism The viewpoint that women and men differ in fundamental ways, including biology, and that, in general, women and men have distinct standpoints that foster different experiences, perspectives, skills, and knowledge (for instance, nurturance in women and independence in men). Also called *structural* or *difference feminism*.

culture The structures and practices, especially those relating to communication, through which a particular social order is produced and reproduced by legitimizing certain values, expectations, meanings, and patterns of behavior.

culture of romance The notion prevalent among today's youth that success, for women, lies in attracting men rather than in pursuing ambitious careers.

ecofeminism A movement that integrates the intellectual and political bases of feminist theorizing with ecological philosophy. The specific oppression of women is seen as a particular instance of a larger ideology that esteems violence and domination of women, children, animals, and the earth.

ego boundary Psychologically, the point at which an individual stops and the rest of the world begins; an individual's sense of the line between her or his self and others. Ego boundaries range from permeable (a sense of self that includes others and their issues, problems, and so on) to rigid (a sense of self as completely distinct from others).

equal opportunity laws Laws that prohibit discrimination on the basis of race, color, religion, sex, or national origin. Equal opportunity laws seek to protect *individual* members of groups that have been targets of discrimination; they redress only current discrimination, not historical bias.

erotica Depictions of sexual activities that are agreed to and enjoyed by the parties participating in the activities.

essentializing The reduction of a phenomenon to its essential characteristics, which are generally presumed to be innate and/or unchangeable. To essentialize the sexes is to imply that all women are alike in basic respects, that all men are alike in basic respects, and that the two sexes are distinct from each other because of fundamental, essential qualities.

excision See *clitoridectomy*.

father hunger A term from the mythopoetic men's movement; men's yearning to be close to other men and to build deep, enduring bonds with them. Based on the mythopoetic belief that most young boys have distant relationships with the primary man in their lives—the father—and that the hunger for meaningful contact with men, of which they were deprived in youth, continues throughout life.

femicide The killing of women.

Free Men A branch of the men's movement that seeks to restore the traditional image of men by celebrating and encouraging competitive, independent, and rugged qualities in men.

gender A social, symbolic construction that expresses the meanings a society confers on biological sex. Gender varies across cultures, over time within any given society, and in relation to the other gender.

gender constancy A person's understanding, which usually develops by 3 years of age, that her or his sex is relatively fixed and unchanging.

gender intimidation The treatment of members of one sex in ways that make them feel humiliated, unsafe, or inferior because of their sex.

gendered violence Physical, verbal, emotional, sexual, or visual brutality inflicted disproportionately or exclusively on members of one sex. Includes gender intimidation, sexual assault, violence between intimates, sexual harassment, genital mutilation, and gender-based murder.

glass ceiling An invisible barrier, made up of subtle, often unconscious prejudices and stereotypes, that limits the opportunities and advancement of women and minorities.

glass walls A metaphor for sex segregation on the job. Glass walls exist when members of a group, such as women, are placed in positions based on stereotypes of that group. Typically, such positions do not entail advancement ladders.

goals Statements of intent for the representation of women and minorities. Goals do not require results, nor do they require measures for increasing the number of women and minorities hired by or admitted into institutions.

haptics Touch as a form of nonverbal communication.

hermaphrodite A person whose internal and external genitalia are inconsistent.

hidden curriculum In educational institutions, the organization, content, and teaching styles that reflect gender stereotypes and sustain gender inequities by marginalizing and devaluing female and minority students.

hostile environment harassment Conduct of a sexual nature that interferes with a person's ability to perform a job or gain an education and/or that creates a hostile, intimidating, or offensive working environment.

hypothetical thought Conceiving of things that do not exist.

infibulation Removal of the clitoris and labia minora and subsequent joining of the lips of the labia majora.

informed consent Consent given by an adult with normal mental abilities whose judgment is not impaired by circumstances, including alcohol or other drugs.

intersexed Having both male and female biological sexual characteristics.

intimate partner violence Physical, mental, emotional, verbal, or economic power used by one partner against the other partner in a romantic relationship.

kinesics Facial and body movements; one type of nonverbal communication.

lesbian feminists Feminists whose sexual preference is women, who define themselves as woman identified and committed to fighting for legal rights for all woman-identified women.

liberal feminism (also called *equality feminism, middle-class feminism,* and *White feminism*) Liberal feminism, as distinct from structural feminism, maintains that women and men are alike in important respects and that women should have the same economic, political, professional, and civic opportunities and rights as men. NOW is the best-known organization representing liberal feminism.

male circumcision Removal of the sheath, or prepuce, of the penis.

male deficit model A relationship theory, according to which men are deficient in forming and participating in close relationships; most men's ways of experiencing and expressing closeness are not simply different from, but inferior to, those of women.

male feminists Men who believe that women and men are alike in important respects and that the sexes should enjoy the same privileges, rights, opportunities, and status in society. Male feminists join liberal women feminists in fighting for equitable treatment of women. In addition, many male feminists seek to rid themselves of what they regard as toxic masculinity promoted in men by socialization and to develop sensitivities more typically inculcated in women. Also called *pro-feminist men.*

male generic language Words and phrases that are claimed to refer to both women and men yet are denotatively masculine; for example *man* to refer to all human beings.

masculinist A category of men's movement that sees men as oppressed and seeks to preserve men's freedom from women and femininization.

matriarchal Of or pertaining to matriarchy; literally "rule by the mothers." The term *matriarchy* is generally used to refer to systems of ideology, social structures, and practices that are created by women and reflect the values, priorities, and views of women as a group.

mentor A senior colleague who helps a junior employee build a career.

Mentors in Violence Prevention (MVP). A male antiviolence program that educates men about socialization that links masculinity to violence and aggression; motivates men to reject violence in themselves and other men.

microinequities Verbal comments and behaviors that devalue members of a group but do not violate antidiscrimination laws; can affect morale, job performance, and career advancement.

Million Man March A branch of the men's movement that began with a march in Washington, DC, in 1995, in which Black men atoned for sins and committed themselves to spiritual transformation and political action. Annual marches were also held in later years.

Million Woman March A grassroots gathering of African American women, launched in Philadelphia in 1997 to celebrate and foster solidarity among Black women.

mommy track Informal term for the practice of placing women on a separate career path that limits their career opportunities and advancement.

monitoring The process of observing and regulating our own attitudes and behaviors; possible because humans can reflect on themselves from others' perspectives (self-as-object).

multiracial feminism A branch of the women's movement concerned with race and the racial oppression of women.

mythopoetic movement A branch of the men's movement headed by poet Robert Bly. Mythopoetics believe that men need to rediscover their distinctively masculine modes of feeling, which are rooted largely in myth.

nonverbal communication All elements of communication other than words themselves. Estimated to carry 65% to 93% of the total meaning of communication; includes visual, vocal, environmental, and physical aspects of interaction.

paralanguage Vocal cues that accompany verbal communication, such as accent, volume, and inflection.

patriarchal Of or pertaining to patriarchy; literally "rule by the fathers." The term *patriarchy* generally refers to systems of ideology, social structures, and practices, created by men, that reflect the values, priorities, and views of men as a group.

personal relationships Connections in which partners are interdependent, consider each other irreplaceable, and they are strongly and specifically connected to each other as unique individuals.

physical appearance Aspects of personal appearance; often evaluated according to cultural standards.

polarized thinking Conceiving things as opposites, e.g., good or bad, right or wrong.

pornography Materials that vividly depict the subordination and degradation of a person; for example, sadistic assault presented as pleasurable. Pornography does not feature activities involving mutual agreement and mutual benefit; distinct from *erotica*.

power feminism A movement that emerged in the 1990s as a reaction to feminist emphasis on women's oppression. Urges women to take the power that is theirs and not to see themselves as victims of men or society.

Promise Keepers Begun in 1990, a Christian branch of the men's movement that calls men together to pray and commit to Christ-centered living.

proxemics Space and the human use of space, including personal territories.

psychodynamic theory The theory that family relationships, especially between mother and child during the formative years of life, have a pivotal and continuing impact on the development of self, particularly gender identity.

psychological responsibility The responsibility to remember, plan, think ahead, organize, and so forth. In most heterosexual relationships, even when physical labor is divided between partners, women assume greater psychological responsibility for the home and children.

quid pro quo harassment Actual or threatened use of professional or academic rewards and/or punishments to gain sexual compliance from a subordinate or student.

quota A particular number or percentage of women and/or minorities who must be admitted to schools, hired in certain positions, or promoted to certain levels in institutions.

radical feminism A branch of feminism that grew out of New Left politics and demanded the same attention to women's oppression as New Left organizations gave to racial oppression and other ideological issues. Radical feminists pioneered revolutionary communication techniques such as consciousness raising, leaderless group discussion, and guerrilla theater.

relationship level of meaning The nonliteral meaning of communication. Expresses how a speaker sees the relationship between self and other. May provide cues about how to interpret the literal meaning of a message, for instance, as a joke.

revalorists Feminists who focus on valuing traditionally feminine skills, activities, and perspectives and their contributions to personal, interpersonal, and cultural life.

role Social definitions of expected behaviors and the values associated with them; internalized by individuals in the process of socialization.

second shift The work of homemaking and child care performed by a member of a dual-worker family after and in addition to the job in the paid labor force.

self-as-object The ability to reflect on the self from the standpoint of others. Because humans are able to take others' perspectives, their views of self are necessarily social.

separatists Feminist groups who believe that, because patriarchal culture cannot be changed or reformed, women who find it oppressive must create and live in their own women-centered communities separate from the larger culture.

sex A personal quality determined by biological and genetic characteristics. *Male, female, man,* and *woman* indicate sex.

sexual assault Sexual activity to which at least one participant has not given informed consent.

sexual harassment Unwelcome conduct of a sexual nature.

social learning theory Theory that individuals learn to be masculine and feminine (among other things) by observing and imitating others and by reacting to the rewards and punishments others give in response to imitative behaviors.

speech community A group of people who share assumptions regarding how, when, and why to communicate and how to interpret others' communication.

spotlighting Highlighting a person's sex rather than other, more relevant characteristics; for example, the headline, "Woman Elected Mayor."

standpoint theory Focuses on the influence of gender, race, class, and other social categories on circumstances of people's lives, especially their social positions and the kinds of experiences fostered within those positions.

stereotype A broad generalization about an entire class of phenomena, based on some knowledge of limited aspects of certain members of the class.

structural feminism. See *cultural feminism.*

sunna Also called *female circumcision;* genital mutilation involving removal of the sheath and tip of the clitoris.

symbolic interactionism The theory that individuals develop self-identity and an understanding of social life, values, and codes of conduct through communicative interactions with others in a society.

territoriality An aspect of proxemics; the sense of personal space that one does not want others to invade.

theory A way to describe, explain, and predict relationships among phenomena.

third-wave feminism An emergent movement asserting that feminism for the current era is not just an extension of second-wave feminism. Aims (1) to be inclusive of diverse peoples; (2) to use personal life and personal action for political impact; and (3) to work to build coalitions with other groups that struggle against oppression.

Title IX The section of the Educational Amendment of 1972 that makes it illegal for schools that accept federal funds to discriminate on the basis of sex.

traitorous identity A group member's criticism of particular attitudes and actions—for example, sexist jokes—that are accepted and normative within the group.

voice-over A technique used in audio-visual media, particularly television commercials; over the action on the screen, viewers hear a voice that makes claims about the product, gives advice, or explains the action.

White Ribbon Campaign (WRC). An international group of men who work to end men's violence against women.

womanists A group of women who define their identity and goals as reflecting both race and gender oppression. The womanist movement arose out of dissatisfaction with mainstream feminism's focus on White, middle-class women and their interests.

women's rights movement From the mid-1800s to the 1920s, a movement that focused on gaining basic rights for women, such as the rights to vote, to pursue higher education, and to enter professions.

REFERENCES

Aaronson, S., & Hartmann, H. (1998). Wage gap. In W. Mankiller, G. Mink, M. Navarro, B. Smith, & G. Steinem (Eds.), *The reader's companion to U.S. women's history* (pp. 615–616). Boston: Houghton Mifflin.

Abdullah, H. (1999, January 22). Gender roles, new rules. *Raleigh News and Observer,* pp. E1, E3.

Abelson, R. (2001, June 10). More men taking same-sex harassment charges to EEOC. *Raleigh News and Observer,* p. 8A.

Acitelli, L. (1988). When spouses talk to each other about their relationship. *Journal of Social and Personal Relationships, 5,* 185–199.

Adams, C. (1991, April). The straight dope. *Triangle Comic Review,* p. 26.

Adams, C., & Singh, K. (1998). Direct and indirect effects of school learning variables on the academic achievement of African-American 10th graders. *Journal of Negro Education, 67,* 48–65.

Addington, D. W. (1968). The relationship of selected vocal characteristics to personality perceptions. *Speech Monographs, 35,* 492–503.

Adler, J. (1996, June 17). Building a better dad. *Newsweek,* 58–64.

Adler, J., with Duignan-Cabrera, A., & Gordon, J. (1991, June 24). Drums, sweat and tears. *Newsweek,* 46–54.

Adler, L. L. (1991). *Women in cross-cultural perspective.* Westport, CT: Praeger.

Adler, T. (1989, June). Early sex hormone exposure studied. *APA Monitor,* p. 9.

Adler, T. (1990, January). Differences explored in gays and straights. *APA Monitor,* p. 27.

Alexander, G., & Hines, M. (1994). Gender labels and play styles: Their relative contributions to children's selection of playmates. *Child Development, 65,* 869–879.

Ali, L., & Gordon, D. (2001, July 23). We still want our MTV. *Newsweek,* pp. 50–53.

Alksnis, C., Desmarais, S., & Wood, E. (1996). Gender differences in scripts for different types of dates. *Sex Roles, 34,* 321–339.

Allen, K. (1999, May 24). Third wave versus second wave. Retrieved from http://www.io.com/~wwwave/

Allis, S. (1990, Fall). What do men really want? *Time,* pp. 80–82.

Allman, W. F. (1993, July 26). The biology-behavior continuum. *U.S. News and World Reports,* pp. 6–7.

Almaguer, T. (1993). Chicano men: A cartography of homosexual identity and behavior. In H. Abelove, M. Barale, & D. Halperin (Eds.), *The lesbian and gay studies reader* (pp. 255–273). London: Routledge.

Alvesson, M., & Billing, Y. (1998). *Understanding gender and organization.* Thousand Oaks, CA: Sage.

American Association of University Women (AAUW). (1991). *Shortchanging girls, shortchanging America.* Washington, DC: Greenberg-Lake Analysis Group.

American Association of University Women (AAUW). (1995). *How schools shortchange girls: The AAUW report.* New York: Marlowe.

American Association of University Women (AAUW). (1998). *Gender gaps: Where schools still fail our children.* Washington, DC: American Association of University Women Educational Foundation.

American Association of University Women (AAUW). (2001). *Beyond the "gender wars": A conversation about girls,* boys, and education. Washington, DC: American Association of University Women Educational Foundation.

American Heritage dictionary of the English language (1992). Boston: Houghton Mifflin.

Andelin, H. (1975). *Fascinating womanhood.* New York: Bantam.

Anderson, E. A., & Leslie, L. A. (1991). Coping with employment and family stress: Employment arrangement and gender differences. *Sex Roles, 24,* 223–237.

Anderson, K., & Leaper, C. (1998). Metaanalyses of gender effects on conversational interruption: Who, what, when, where, and how. *Sex Roles, 39,* 225–252.

Andrews, C. (2003). "Raising our boys to be violent: The role of normative masculinity in the perpetuation of men's violence." Unpublished Honors Thesis, University of North Carolina at Chapel Hill.

Angier, N. (1995, November 19). Where woman was, there gal shall be. *New York Times,* p. 2E.

Angier, N. (1999, March 27). Not your average Joe: Dangers of the superman ideal. *Fairbanks Daily News-Miner,* p. C-1.

Ansen, D., & Bunn, A. (1995, September 18). Goodbye to the kids' stuff. *Newsweek,* pp. 74–76.

Antill, J. K. (1987). Parents' beliefs and values about sex roles, sex differences, and sexuality: Their sources and implications. In P. Shaver & C. Hendrick (Eds.), *Sex and gender* (pp. 294–328). Newbury Park, CA: Sage.

Anzaldúa, G. (1999). *Borderlands/la frontera: The new mestiza.* San Francisco: Spinsters/Aunt Lute.

Anzaldúa, G. (2002, October 11). Beyond traditional notions of identity. *Chronicle of Higher Education,* pp. B11–B13.

Anzaldúa, G., & Keating, A. (Eds.). (2002). *This bridge called home.* New York: Routledge.

Apter, T. (1990). *Altered loves: Mothers and daughters in adolescence.* New York: St. Martin's.

Aptheker, B. (1998). Cultural feminism. In W. Mankiller, G. Mink, M. Navarro, B. Smith, & G. Steinem (Eds.), *The reader's companion to U.S. women's history* (pp. 205–206). New York: Houghton Mifflin.

Aries, E. (1987). Gender and communication. In P. Shaver & C. Hendrick (Eds.), *Sex and gender* (pp. 149–176). Newbury Park, CA: Sage.

Aries, E. (1998). Gender differences in interaction. In D. Canary & K. Dindia (Eds.), *Sex differences and similarities in interaction: Critical essays and empirical investigations* (pp. 65–81). Mahwah, NJ: Erlbaum.

Aries, E. J., & Johnson, F. L. (1983). Close friendship in adulthood: Conversational content between same-sex friends. *Sex Roles, 9,* 1183–1196.

Armas, G. (2000, April 24). Gender equality at work improving, statistics show. *Raleigh News and Observer,* p. 4A.

Arnold, R. (2001). *Fashion, desire and anxiety: Image and morality in the 20th century.* New Brunswick, NJ: Rutgers University Press.

Aronson, J. (1992). Women's sense of responsibility for the care of old people: "But who else is going to do it?" *Gender and Society,* 6, 8–29.

Ashcraft, K. (1999). Managing maternity leave: A qualitative analysis of temporary executive succession. *Administrative Science Quarterly, 44,* 240–280.

Aukett, R., Ritchie, J., & Mill, K. (1988). Gender differences in friendship patterns. *Sex Roles, 19,* 57–66.

Austin, A. M. B., Salehi, M., & Leffler, A. (1987). Gender and developmental differences in children's conversations. *Sex Roles, 16,* 497–510.

Avery, S. (1999, November 19). Whatever happened to the men's movement? *Raleigh News and Observer,* pp. 1E, 3E.

Bailey, A. (1994). Mothering, diversity, and peace politics. *Hypatia, 9,* 188–198.

Bailey, C. (1997). Making waves and drawing lines: The politics of defining the vicissitudes of feminism. *Hypatia, 12,* 17–29.

Bailey, S., & Campbell, P. (1999). *The gender wars in education.* Groton, MA: Campbell-Kibler Associates.

Balswick, J. O. (1988). *The inexpressive male.* Lexington, MA: Lexington Books.

Balswick, J. O., & Peek, C. W. (1976). The inexpressive male: A tragedy of American society. In D. Brannon & R. Brannon (Eds.), *The forty-nine percent majority:*

The male sex-role (pp. 55–57). Reading, MA: Addison-Wesley.

Balzer, J. A., & Simonis, D. A. (1991). Are high school chemistry books gender free? *Journal of Research in Science Teaching, 28,* 353–362.

Bandura, A. (2002). Social cognitive theory of mass communication. In J. Bryant & D. Zillmann (Eds.), *Media effects: Advances in theory and research* (2nd ed., pp. 121–153). Mahwah, NJ: Erlbaum.

Bandura, A., & Walters, R. H. (1963). *Social learning and personality development.* New York: Holt, Rinehart & Winston.

Banerji, A. (1998, July 10). Telling the stories of everyday youths. *Chronicle of Higher Education,* p. A7.

Barash, D. (2002, May 24). Evolution, males, and violence. *Chronicle of Higher Education,* pp. B7–B9.

Barash, D., & Lipton, J. (2002). *Gender gap: The biology of male-female differences.* New Brunswick, NJ: Transaction Publishers.

Bardewell, J. R., Cochran, S. W., & Walker, S. (1986). Relationship of parental education, race, and gender to sex role stereotyping in 5-year-old kindergartners. *Sex Roles, 15,* 275–281.

Barnett, R., & Rivers, C. (1996). *She works, he works: How two-income families are happier, healthier, and better off.* San Francisco: HarperCollins.

Baron, L., & Straus, M. A. (1989). *Four theories of rape in American society.* New Haven, CT: Yale University Press.

Barry, K. (1998a). Radical feminism. In W. Mankiller, G. Mink, M. Navarro, B. Smith, & G. Steinem (Eds.), *The reader's companion to U.S. women's history* (pp. 217–218). New York: Houghton Mifflin.

Barry, K. (1998b). Sexual slavery. In W. Mankiller, G. Mink, M. Navarro, B. Smith, & G. Steinem (Eds.), *The reader's companion to U.S. women's history* (pp. 539–540). New York: Houghton Mifflin.

Basinger, J. (2001, April 27). Struggling for a balanced life as a president. *Chronicle of Higher Education,* pp. A37–A39.

Basow, S. A. (1990). Effects of teacher expressiveness: Mediated by sex-typing? *Journal of Educational Psychology, 82,* 599–602.

Basow, S. A. (1992). *Gender: Stereotypes and roles* (3rd ed.). Pacific Grove, CA: Brooks/Cole.

Bass, A. (1995). Do slasher films breed real-life violence? In G. Dines & J. Humez (Eds.), *Gender, race and class in media* (pp. 185–189). Thousand Oaks, CA: Sage.

Baumgardner, J., & Richards, A. (2000). *ManifestA: Young women, feminism, and the future.* New York: Farrar, Straus & Giroux.

Baxter, L. A. (1990). Dialectical contradictions in relational development. *Journal of Social and Personal Relationships, 7,* 143–158.

Beal, C. (1994). *Boys and girls: The development of gender roles.* New York: McGraw-Hill.

Beck, A. T. (1988). *Love is never enough.* New York: Harper & Row.

Beck, M., & Biddle, N. (1995, December 11). Separate, not equal. *Newsweek,* pp. 86–87.

Becker, A., & Burwell, R. (1999, May 19). *Acculturation and disordered eating in Fiji.* Paper presented at the American Psychiatric Association Conference, Washington, DC.

Becker, A., Burwell, R., Gilman, S., Herzog, D., & Hamburg, P. (2002). Eating behaviours and attitudes following prolonged exposure to television among ethnic Fijian adolescent girls. *British Journal of Psychiatry, 180,* 509–514.

Becker, C. S. (1987). Friendship between women: A phenomenological study of best friends. *Journal of Phenomenological Psychology, 18,* 59–72.

Begley, S. (1995, March 27). Gray matters. *Newsweek,* pp. 48–54.

Begley, S. (2000, March 27). The nature of nurturing. *Newsweek,* pp. 64–66.

Belenky, M. F., Clinchy, B. M., Goldberger, N. R., & Tarule, J. M. (1986). *Women's ways of knowing: The development of self, voice, and mind.* New York: Basic Books.

Bell, E. L. J., & Komo, S. (2001). *Our separate ways: Black and White women and the struggle for professional identity.* Cambridge, MA: Harvard Business School Press.

Bellas, M. (2001). The gendered nature of emotional labor in the workplace. In

D. Vannoy (Ed.), *Gender mosaics* (pp. 269–278). Los Angeles: Roxbury.

Bellinger, D. C., & Gleason, J. B. (1982). Sex differences in parental directives to young children. *Sex Roles, 8,* 1123–1139.

Bem, S. (1993). *The lenses of gender: Transforming the debate on sexual inequality.* New Haven, CT: Yale University Press.

Benenson, J., Del Bianco, R., Philippoussis, M., & Apostoleris, N. (1997). Girls' expression of their own perspectives in the presence of varying numbers of boys. *International Journal of Behavioral Development, 21,* 389–405.

Beren, S., Grilo, C., Hayden, H., & Wilfley, D. (1996). The influence of sexual orientation on body dissatisfaction in adult men and women. *International Journal of Eating Disorders, 20,* 135–141.

Bergner, R. M., & Bergner, L. L. (1990). Sexual misunderstanding: A descriptive and pragmatic formulation. *Psychotherapy, 27,* 464–467.

Berlant, L., & Warner, M. (1998). Sex in public. *Critical Inquiry, 24,* 547–566.

Berndt, C. (1997). *The story of Pak Kumjoo.* Unpublished honors thesis, University of North Carolina, Chapel Hill.

Bernstein, A. (1999, February 1). Why the law should adopt more family leave. *Business Week,* p. 48.

Berscheid, E., Snyder, M., & Omoto, A. M. (1989). Issues in studying close relationships. In C. Hendrick (Ed.), *Close relationships* (pp. 63–91). Newbury Park, CA: Sage.

Bettelheim, B. (1943). Individual and mass behavior in extreme situations. *Journal of Abnormal and Social Psychology, 38,* 417–452.

Beyer, S. (2001, November 25). The women of Islam. *Time. Com.* Retrieved April 5, 2002, from http://www.time.com/

Bierhoff, H. (1996). Heterosexual partnerships: Initiation, maintenance and disengagement. In A. E. Auhagen & M. von Salisch (Eds.), *The diversity of human relationships* (pp. 173–196). New York: Cambridge University Press.

Bingham, S. (Ed.). (1994). *Conceptualizing sexual harassment as discursive practice.* Westport, CT: Praeger.

Bingham, S. (1996). Sexual harassment on the job, on the campus. In J. T. Wood (Ed.), *Gendered relationships: A reader* (pp. 233–252). Mountain View, CA: Mayfield.

Birdwhistell, R. (1970). *Kinesics and context.* Philadelphia: University of Pennsylvania Press.

Blackless, M., Charuvastra, A., Derryek, A., Fausto-Sterling, A., Lauzanne, K., & Lee, E. (2000). How sexually dimorphic are we? Review and synthesis. *American Journal of Human Biology, 12,* 151–166.

Blankenship, J., & Robson, D. (1995). A "feminine style" in women's political discourse: An exploratory study. *Communication Quarterly, 43,* 353–366.

Blanton, D., & Cook, L. (2002). *They fought like demons: Women soldiers in the American Civil War.* Baton Rouge: Louisiana State University Press.

Blee, K. (1998). Antifeminism. In W. Mankiller, G. Mink, M. Navarro, B. Smith, & G. Steinem (Eds.), *The reader's companion to U.S. women's history* (pp. 31–33). Boston: Houghton Mifflin.

Bleier, R. (1986). Sex differences research: Science or belief? In R. Bleier (Ed.), *Feminist approaches to science* (pp. 147–164). New York: Pergamon.

Blum, D. (1997). *Sex on the brain: The biological differences between women and men.* New York: Penguin.

Blum, D. (1998, September/October). The gender blur: Where does biology end and society take over? *Utne Reader,* pp. 45–48.

Bly, R. (1990). *Iron John: A book about men.* Reading, MA: Addison-Wesley.

Bocella, K. (2001, January 31). Eating disorders spread among minority girls, women. *Raleigh News and Observer,* p. 5E.

Boling, P. (1991). The democratic potential of mothering. *Political Theory, 19,* 606–625.

Bonnett, A. (1996). The new primitives: Identity, landscape and cultural appropriation in the mythopoetic men's movement. *Antipode, 28,* 273–291.

Bordo, S. (1997). *Twilight zones: The hidden life of cultural images from Plato to O.J.* Berkeley: University of California Press.

Bordo, S. (1998, May 1). Sexual harassment is about bullying, not sex. *Chronicle of Higher Education,* p. B6.

Bordo, S. (1999). *The male body: A new look at men in public and in private.* New York: Farrar, Straus & Giroux.

Bornstein, K. (1994). *Gender outlaw: On men, women and the rest of us.* New York: Vintage.

Boston Women's Health Club Book Collective. (1976). *Our bodies/ourselves* (2nd ed.). New York: Simon & Schuster.

Bourg, C., & Segal, M. (2001). Gender, sexuality, and the military. In D. Vannoy (Ed.), *Gender mosaics* (pp. 332–342). Los Angeles: Roxbury.

Bowen, W., & Bok, D. (1998). *The shape of the river.* Princeton, NJ: Princeton University Press.

Bowleg, L. (1995). Better in the Bahamas? Not if you're a feminist. In B. Findlen (Ed.), *Listen up: Voices from the next feminist generation* (pp. 45–53). Seattle: Seal Press.

Bowman, K. K. (1994, January 10). Making the transition to "power feminism." *Wall Street Journal,* p. A10.

Bradley, P. H. (1981). The folk-linguistics of women's speech: An empirical examination. *Communication Monographs, 48,* 73–90.

Brandt, M. (1994, April 25). Far beyond white gloves and teas. *Newsweek,* pp. 57–59.

Brehm, S. S. (1992). *Intimate relationships* (2nd ed.). New York: McGraw-Hill.

Bretl, D., & Cantor, J. (1988). The portrayal of men and women in U.S. commercials: A recent content analysis and trend over 15 years. *Sex Roles, 18,* 595–609.

Brod, H. (1987). Introduction: Themes and theses of men's studies. In H. Brod (Ed.), *The making of masculinities: The new men's studies* (pp. 1–17). Boston: Allen & Unwin.

Brosnan, M., & Lee, W. (1998). A cross-cultural comparison of gender differences in computer attitudes and anxieties: The United Kingdom and Hong Kong. *Computers in Human Behavior, 14,* 559–577.

Brouwer, D. (1998). The precarious visibility politics of self-stigmatization: The case of HIV/AIDS tattoos. *Text and Performance Quarterly, 12,* 114–136.

Broverman, I., Broverman, D. M., Clarkson, F. E., Rosenkrantz, P. S., & Vogel, S. R. (1970). Sex-role stereotypes and clinical judgments of mental health. *Journal of Consulting and Clinical Psychology, 34,* 1–7.

Brown, C., & Shapiro, L. (1998, June 8). Woman warrior. *Newsweek,* pp. 64–65.

Brown, J. D., Childers, K. W., Bauman, K. E., & Koch, G. G. (1990). The influence of new media and family structure on young adolescents' television and radio use. *Communication Research, 17,* 65–82.

Brown, L. (1997). *Two-spirit people.* Binghamton, NY: Haworth Press.

Brown, T., Graves, T., & Williams, S. (1997). Dual-earner families: The impact of gender and culture on this normative family structure and implications for therapy. *Family Therapy, 24,* 177–189.

Brownmiller, S. (1993, January 4). Making female bodies the battlefield. *Newsweek,* p. 37.

Brownmiller, S. (1995). *Against our will: Men, women and rape.* New York: Simon & Schuster.

Brownmiller, S. (2000). *In our time: Memoir of a revolution.* New York: Dial Press.

Brownstein, A. (2000, December 8). In the campus shadows, women are stalkers as well as the stalked. *Chronicle of Higher Education,* pp. A40–A42.

Bruess, C., & Pearson, J. (1996). Gendered patterns in family communication. In J. T. Wood (Ed.), *Gendered relationships: A reader* (pp. 59–78). Mountain View, CA: Mayfield.

Brumberg, J. (1997). *The body project: An intimate history of American girls.* New York: Random House.

Brumberg, J. J. (1988). *Fasting girls: The emergence of anorexia nervosa as a modern disease.* Cambridge, MA: Harvard University Press.

Bruner, L. (1996). Producing identities: Gender problematization and feminist argumentation. *Argumentation and Advocacy, 32,* 185–198.

Brush, L. (1999). Gender, work, and who cares? In M. Feree, J. Lorber, & B. Hess (Eds.), *Revisioning gender* (pp. 161–189). Thousand Oaks, CA: Sage.

Bryant, A., & Check, E. (2000, Fall/Winter). How parents raise boys and girls. *Newsweek,* pp. 64–65.

Buhrke, R. A., & Fuqua, D. R. (1987). Sex differences in same- and cross-sex supportive relationships. *Sex Roles, 17,* 339–352.

Burgoon, J. K., Buller, D. B., Hale, J. L., & deTurck, M. A. (1988). Relational messages associated with nonverbal behaviors. *Human Communication Research, 10,* 351–378.

Burgoon, J. K., Buller, D. B., & Woodall, G. W. (1996). *Nonverbal communication: The unspoken dialogue* (2nd ed). New York: Harper & Row.

Burgoon, J. K., & Hale, J. L. (1988). Nonverbal expectancy violations: Model elaborations and application to immediacy behaviors. *Communication Monographs, 55,* 58–79.

Burgoon, J. K., & Le Poire, B. (1999). Nonverbal cues and interpersonal judgments: Participant and observer perceptions of intimacy, dominance, and composure. *Communication Monographs, 66,* 105–124.

Burgos-Ocasio, H. (2000). Hispanic women. In M. Julia (Ed.), *Constructing gender* (pp. 109–137). Belmont, CA: Wadsworth.

Burleson, B. (1997, November). *Sex-related differences in communicative behavior: A matter of social skills, not gender cultures.* Paper presented at the National Communication Convention, Chicago.

Burn, J. (1996). *The social psychology of gender.* New York: McGraw-Hill.

Burns, A., & Homel, R. (1989). Gender division of tasks by parents and their children. *Psychology of Women Quarterly, 13,* 113–125.

Buss, D. (1994). *The evolution of desire: Strategies of human mating.* New York: Basic Books.

Buss, D. (1995). Evolutionary psychology: A new paradigm for psychological science. *Psychological Inquiry, 6,* 1–30.

Buss, D. (1996). The evolutionary psychology of human social strategies. In E. Higgins & A. Druglanski (Eds.), *Social psychology: Handbook of basic principles* (pp. 3–38). New York: Guilford.

Buss, D. (1999). *Evolutionary psychology: The new science of the mind.* Boston: Allyn & Bacon.

Buss, D., & Kenrick, D. (1998). Evolutionary social psychology. In D. Gilbert, S. Fiske, & G. Lindzey (Eds.), *The handbook of social psychology: Vol. 2* (4th ed., pp. 982–1026). Boston: McGraw-Hill.

Butaine, R., & Costenbader, V. (1997). Self-reported differences in the experience and expression of anger between girls and boys. *Sex Roles, 36,* 625–637.

Butler, D., & Geis, F. L. (1990). Nonverbal affect responses to male and female leaders: Implications for leadership. *Journal of Personality and Social Psychology, 58,* 48–59.

Butler, J. (1990). Performative acts and gender constitution: An essay in phenomenology and feminist theory. In S. Case (Ed.), *Performing feminisms: Feminist critical theory and theater* (pp. 270–282). Baltimore: Johns Hopkins University Press.

Cahill, D., & Sias, P. (1997). The perceived social costs and importance of seeking emotional support in the workplace: Gender differences and similarities. *Communication Research Reports, 14,* 231–240.

Caldera, Y. M., Huston, A. C., & O'Brien, M. (1989). Social interactions and play patterns of parents and toddlers with feminine, masculine, and neutral toys. *Child Development, 60,* 70–76.

Caldwell, M., & Peplau, L. (1982). Sex differences in same-sex friendship. *Sex Roles, 8,* 721–732.

Calhoun, C. (1995). *Critical social theory.* Oxford, England: Basil Blackwell.

Calvert, S. (1999). *Children's journeys through the information age.* New York: McGraw-Hill.

Campbell, A. (1993). *Men, women, and aggression.* New York: Basic Books.

Campbell, K. K. (1973). The rhetoric of women's liberation: An oxymoron. *Quarterly Journal of Speech, 59,* 74–86.

Campbell, K. K. (1989a). *Man cannot speak for her: I. A critical study of early feminist rhetoric.* New York: Praeger.

Campbell, K. K. (1989b). *Man cannot speak for her: II. Key texts of the early feminists.* New York: Greenwood.

Campbell, K. K. (1991). Hearing women's voices. *Communication Education, 40,* 33–48.

Campbell, K. K. (Ed.). (1993). *Women public speakers in the United States: A bio-critical sourcebook.* Westport, CT: Greenwood.

Campbell, K., & Jerry, E. (1988). Woman and speaker: A conflict in roles. In

S. Brehm (Ed.), *Seeing female: Social roles and personal lives*. New York: Greenwood.

Campo-Flores, A., & Rosenberg, Y. (2000, June 26). A return to wilding. *Newsweek*, p. 28.

Cancian, F. (1987). *Love in America*. Cambridge, MA: Cambridge University Press.

Cancian, F. (1989). Love and the rise of capitalism. In B. Risman & P. Schwartz (Eds.), *Gender in intimate relationships* (pp. 12–25). Belmont, CA: Wadsworth.

Cancian, F., & Oliker, S. (2000). *Caring and gender*. Thousand Oaks, CA: Sage.

Cann, A., & Siegfried, W. D. (1990). Gender stereotypes and dimensions of effective leader behavior. *Sex Roles, 23*, 413–419.

Cantú, L. (2004). *De ambiente:* Queer tourism and the shifting boundaries of Mexican male sexualities. In J. Spade & C. Valentine (Eds.), *The gender kaleidoscope* (pp. 521–531). Belmont, CA: Wadsworth.

Capaldi, D., Shortt, J., & Crosby, L. (2003). Physical and psychological aggression in at-risk young couples: Stability and change in young adulthood. *Merrill-Palmer Quarterly, 49*, 1–27.

Caplan, P., & Caplan, J. (1997). Do sex-related cognitive differences exist, and why do people seek them out? In P. Caplan, M. Crawford, J. Hyde, & J. Caplan (Eds.), *Gender differences in human cognition* (pp. 52–77). New York: Oxford University Press.

Carter, C. (1998). Branston, G., & Allan, S. (Eds.). *News, gender and power*. New York: Routledge.

Carty, L. (1992). Black women in academia: A statement from the periphery. In H. Bannerji, L. Carty, K. Dehli, S. Heald, & K. McKenna (Eds.), *Unsettling relations* (pp. 13–44). Boston: South End.

Cassell, J., & Jenkins, H. (1998). *From Barbie to Mortal Kombat: Gender and computer games*. Cambridge, MA: MIT Press.

Cassirer, E. (1978). *An essay on man*. New Haven, CT: Yale University Press.

Catsambis, S. (1999). The path to math: Gender and social ethnic differences in mathematics participation from middle school to high school. In L. Peplau, S. DeBro, R. Veniegas, & P. Taylor (Eds.), *Gender, culture and ethnicity* (pp. 102–119). Mountain View, CA: Mayfield.

Cegela, D., & Sillars, A. (1989). Further examination of nonverbal manifestations of interaction involvement. *Communication Reports, 2*, 39–47.

Chaiken, S., & Pliner, P. (1987). Women, but not men, are what they eat: The effect of meal size and gender on perceived femininity and masculinity. *Personality and Social Psychology Bulletin, 13*, 166–176.

Chambers, V. (1998, January 19). Family rappers. *Newsweek*, pp. 66–67.

Chapman, M., & Hendler, G. (Eds.). (1999). *Sentimental men: Masculinity and the politics of affect in American culture*. Berkeley: University of California Press.

Chase, S. (Ed.). (1991). *Defending the earth: A dialogue between Murray Bookchin and Dave Foreman*. Boston: South End.

Chatham-Carpenter, A., & DeFrancisco, V. (1998). Women construct self-esteem in their own terms: A feminist qualitative study. *Feminism & Psychology, 8*, 467–489.

Cheney, G., Christensen, L., Zorn, T., & Ganesh, S. (2004). *Organizational communication in an age of globalization*. Prospect Heights, IL: Waveland.

Chernik, A. F. (1995). The body politic. In B. Findlen (Ed.), *Listen up: Voices from the next generation of feminists* (pp. 75–84). Seattle: Seal Press.

Chesler, E. (1992). *Woman of valor: Margaret Sanger and the birth control movement in America*. New York: Simon & Schuster.

Chesler, P. (2001). *Woman's inhumanity to woman*. New York: Thunder's Mouth Press/Nation Books.

Chethik, N. (2001). *FatherLoss: How sons of all ages come to terms with the deaths of their dads*. New York: Hyperion.

Child care. (1992, August 10). *Fortune*, pp. 50–54.

Chodorow, N. J. (1978). *The reproduction of mothering: Psychoanalysis and the sociology of gender*. Berkeley: University of California Press.

Chodorow, N. J. (1989). *Feminism and psychoanalytic theory*. New Haven, CT: Yale University Press.

Chodorow, N. J. (1999). *The power of feelings: Personal meaning in psychoanalysis, gender, & culture*. New Haven, CT: Yale University Press.

Christensen, A., & Heavey, C. (1990). Gender and social structure in the demand/withdraw pattern in marital conflict. *Journal of Personality and Social Psychology, 59,* 73–81.

Christopher, F., & McQuaid, S. (1998). *Dating relationships and men's sexual aggression.* Sarasota Springs, NY: International Society for the Study of Personal Relationships.

Clair, R. (1994). Hegemony and harassment: A discursive practice. In S. Bingham (Ed.), *Conceptualizing sexual harassment as discursive practice* (pp. 59–70). Westport, CT: Praeger.

Clark, R. A. (1998). A comparison of topics and objectives in a cross section of young men's and women's everyday conversations. In D. J. Canary & K. Dindia (Eds.), *Sex differences and similarities in communication: Critical essays and empirical investigations of sex and gender in interaction* (pp. 303–319). Mahwah, NJ: Erlbaum.

Clatterbaugh, K. (1997). *Contemporary perspectives on masculinity.* Boulder, CO: Westview Press.

Clemetson, L., & Samuels, A. (2000, December 18). We have the power. *Newsweek,* pp. 54–60.

Cleveland, J., Stockdale, M., Murphy, K. (2000). *Women and men in organizations.* Mahwah, NJ: Erlbaum.

Clinton, K. (2001, May). Unplugged: Surrendered wives. *The Nation,* p. 17.

Cloud, J. (2000, June 26). The bad Sunday in the park. *Time,* pp. 32–33.

Clover, C. (1995). Her body, himself: Gender in the slasher film. In G. Dines & J. Humez (Eds.), *Gender, race, and class in media: A text reader* (pp. 169–184). Thousand Oaks, CA: Sage.

Clutter, S. (1990, May 3). Gender may affect response and outrage to sex abuse. *Morning Call,* p. D14.

Coates, J. (1986). *Women, men, and language: Studies in language and linguistics.* London: Longman.

Coates, J. (Ed.). (1997). *Language and gender: A reader.* London: Basil Blackwell.

Coates, J., & Cameron, D. (1989). *Women in their speech communities: New perspectives on language and sex.* London: Longman.

Cochran, S. D., & Peplau, L. A. (1985). Value orientations in heterosexual relationships. *Psychology of Women Quarterly, 9,* 477–488.

Cohen, L. (1997, Fall). Hunters and gatherers in the classroom. *Independent School,* pp. 28–36.

Collins, P. H. (1986). Learning from the outsider within. *Social Problems, 33,* 514–532.

Collins, P. H. (1987). The meaning of motherhood in black culture. *Sage: A Scholarly Journal on Black Women, 4,* 3–10.

Collins, P. H. (1990). *Black feminist thought: Knowledge, consciousness, and the politics of empowerment.* Boston: Unwin Hyman.

Collins, P. H. (1996). What's in a name? Womanism, black feminism, and beyond. *Black Scholar, 26,* 9–17.

Collins, P. H. (1998). *Fighting words: Black women and the search for justice.* Minneapolis: University of Minnesota Press.

Coltrane, S. (1996). *Family man: Fatherhood, housework, and gender equity.* New York: Oxford University Press.

Coltrane, S. (1998). *Gender and families.* Newbury Park, CA: Pine Forge Press.

Coltrane, S., & Adams, M. (2001). Men, women and housework. In D. Vannoy (Ed.), *Gender mosaics* (pp. 145–154). Los Angeles: Roxbury.

Condry, S. M., Condry, J. C., & Pogatshnik, L. W. (1983). Sex differences: A study of the ear of the beholder. *Sex Roles, 9,* 697–704.

Conway, M., & Vartanian, L. (2000). A status account of gender stereotypes: Beyond commonality and agency. *Sex Roles, 43,* 181–199.

Cooper, L. (1998, Winter). Images of women in popular song lyrics. *Popular Music and Society,* pp. 28–41.

Cordes, H. (1994, September/October). There's no such thing as a mothering instinct. *Utne Reader,* pp. 15–16.

Cose, E. (1997, October 13). . . . Promises. *Newsweek,* pp. 30–31.

Cose, E. (2003, March 3). The Black gender gap. *Newsweek,* pp. 46–51.

Costin, F., & Schwartz, N. (1987). Beliefs about rape and women's social roles: A four-nation study. *Journal of Interpersonal Violence, 2,* 46–56.

Cowan, G., Lee, C., Levy, D., & Snyder, D. (1988). Dominance and inequality in X-rated videocassettes. *Psychology of Women Quarterly, 12,* 299–311.

Cowan, G., & O'Brien, M. (1990). Gender and survival vs. death in slasher films: A content analysis. *Sex Roles, 23,* 187–196.

Cowell, S. (1992, September/October). Work and family: The missing movement. *Democratic Left,* pp. 14–15.

Cowley, G. (2003, June 16). Why we strive for status. *Newsweek,* pp. 66–70.

Craft, C. (1988). *Too old, too ugly, and not deferential to men: An anchorwoman's courageous battle against sex discrimination.* Rockland, CA: Prima.

Crane, D. (1999). Gender and hegemony in fashion magazines. *Sociological Quarterly, 40,* 541–563.

Crawford, M., & MacLeod, M. (1990). Gender in the college classroom: An assessment of the "chilly climate" for women. *Sex Roles, 23,* 101–122.

Crittenden, A. (2001). *The price of motherhood: Why the most important job in the world is still the least valued.* New York: Metropolitan.

Crittenden, D. (1999). *What our mothers didn't tell us: Why happiness eludes the modern woman.* New York: Simon & Schuster.

Cronk, L. (1993). Parental favoritism toward daughters. *American Scientist, 81,* 272–279.

Croteau, D., & Hoynes, W. (1999). *Media/ Society* (2nd ed.). Thousand Oaks, CA: Sage.

Crouch, R. (1998). Betwixt and between: The past and the future of intersexuality. *Journal of Clinical Ethics, 9,* 372–384.

Crowston, K., & Kammeres, E. (1998). Communicative style and gender differences in computer-mediated communications. In B. Ebo (Ed.), *Cyberghetto or cybertopia* (pp. 185–202). Westport, CT: Praeger.

Cuklanz, L. (1996). *Rape on trial: How the media construct legal reforms and social change.* Philadelphia: University of Pennsylvania Press.

Currie, D. (1998). Violent men or violent women? Whose definition counts? In R. K. Bergen (Ed.), *Issues in intimate violence* (pp. 97–111). Thousand Oaks, CA: Sage.

Danner, L., & Walsh, S. (1999). "Radical" feminists and "bickering" women: U.S. media coverage of the United Nations Fourth World Conference on Women.

Critical Studies in Mass Communication, 16, 63–84.

Davies-Popelka, W. (2000). Mirror, mirror on the wall: Weight, identity, and self-talk in women. In D. O. Braithwaite & J. T. Wood (Eds.), *Case studies in interpersonal communication* (pp. 52–60). Belmont, CA: Wadsworth.

Davis, F. (1991). *Moving the mountain: The women's movement in America since 1960.* New York: Simon & Schuster.

Davis, S. (1990). Men as success objects and women as sex objects: A study of personal advertisements. *Sex Roles, 23,* 43–50.

Davis, S., & Gergen, M. (1997). Toward a new psychology of gender: Opening conversations. In M. Gergen & S. Davis (Eds.), *Toward a new psychology of gender* (pp. 1–27). New York: Routledge.

Davis, T. (1995). Gender differences in masking emotions: Ability or motivation? *Developmental Psychology, 31,* 660–667.

Davison, K., & Birch, L. (2001). Weight, status, parent reaction, and self-concept in five-year-old girls. *Pediatrics, 107,* 42–53.

Deal, J., & Stevenson, M. (1998). Perceptions of female and male managers in the 1990s: *Plus ça change. . . . Sex Roles, 38,* 287–300.

Deaux, K., & LaFrance, M. (1998). Gender. In D. Gilbert, S. T. Fiske, & G. Lindzey (Eds.), *Handbook of social psychology* (pp. 788–827). New York: McGraw-Hill.

Deed, M. (1998). Abuse. In W. Mankiller, G. Mink, M. Navarro, B. Smith, & G. Steinem (Eds.), *The reader's companion to U.S. women's history* (pp. 606–607). New York: Houghton Mifflin.

Deffenbacher, J., & Swaim, R. (1999). Anger expression in Mexican-American and white non-Hispanic adolescents. *Journal of Counseling Psychology, 46,* 61–69.

Deford, F. (2000, June 5). Anna Kournikova. *Sports Illustrated,* pp. 95–110.

DeFrancisco, V., & Chatham-Carpenter, A. (2000). Self in community: African American women's views of self-esteem. *Howard Journal of Communication, 11,* 73–92.

Degler, C. N. (1980). *At odds: Women and the family in America from the Revolution to the present.* New York: Oxford University Press.

Delamont, S. (2001). *Changing women, unchanged men?* Buckingham, UK: Open University Press.

Delk, J. L., Madden, R. B., Livingston, M., & Ryan, T. T. (1986). Adult perceptions of the infant as a function of gender labeling and observer gender. *Sex Roles, 15,* 527–534.

DeLucia, J. L. (1987). Gender role identity and dating behavior: What is the relationship? *Sex Roles, 17,* 153–161.

Demare, D., Briere, J., & Lips, H. M. (1988). Violent pornography and self-reported likelihood of sexual aggression. *Journal of Research in Personality, 22,* 140–153.

Deutsch, F. (2001). Equally shared parenting. *Current Directions in Psychological Science, 10,* 25–28.

Deutsch, F., & Saxon, S. (1998). Traditional ideologies, nontraditional lives. *Sex Roles, 38,* 331–361.

Devor, H. (1997). *FTM: Female-to-male transsexuals in society.* Bloomington: Indiana University Press.

The Diagram Group. (1977). *Woman's body: An owner's manual.* New York: Bantam.

Diamond, I., & Orenstein, G. F. (Eds.). (1990). *Reweaving the world: The emergence of ecofeminism.* San Francisco: Sierra Club.

Diamond, M. (1997). Sexual identity and sexual orientation in children with traumatized or ambiguous genitalia. *Journal of Sex Research, 34,* 199–211.

Dicker, R., & Piepmeier, A. (2003). *Catching a wave: Reclaiming feminism for the 21st century.* Boston: Northeastern University Press.

Dienhart, A. (1998). *Reshaping fatherhood: The social construction of shared parenting.* Thousand Oaks, CA: Sage.

Dietz, T. (1998). An examination of violence and gender role portrayals in video games: Implications for gender socialization and aggressive behavior. *Sex Roles, 38,* 187–201.

Dirie, W. (1998). *Desert flower.* New York: Morrow.

Doctor: Girl not ready for breast implants. (2001, January 6). *Raleigh News & Observer,* p. 18A.

Donnerstein, E., Linz, D., & Penrod, S. (1987). *The question of pornography: Research findings and policy implications.* New York: Free Press.

Douglas, A. (1977). *The feminization of American culture.* New York: Knopf.

Dow, B. (1996). *Prime-time feminism.* Philadelphia: University of Pennsylvania Press.

Dow, B. J. (1992). Femininity and feminism in "Murphy Brown." *Southern Journal of Communication, 57,* 143–155.

Dow, B. J. (2000). Feminism, Miss America, and media mythology. *Rhetoric & Public Affairs, 6,* 127–149.

Dow, B. J. (2003). Feminism, Miss America, and media mythology. *Rhetoric and Public Affairs, 6,* 127–160.

Dow, B., & Tonn, M. B. (1993). Feminine style and political judgment in the rhetoric of Ann Richards. *Quarterly Journal of Speech, 79,* 286–302.

Downey, D., Ainsworth-Darnell, J., & Dufur, M. (1998). Sex of parent and children's well-being in single-parent households. *Journal of Marriage and the Family, 60,* 878–893.

Doyle, J. (1989). *The male experience* (2nd ed.). Dubuque, IA: William C. Brown.

Doyle, J. A. (1997). *The male experience* (3rd ed.). Dubuque, IA: Brown & Benchmark.

Doyle, L. (2001). *Surrendered wife: A practical guide for finding intimacy, passion and peace with your man.* New York: Fireside.

Dreger, A. (1998). "Ambiguous sex"—or ambivalent medicine? Ethical issues in the treatment of intersexuality. *Hastings Center Report, 28,* 24–35.

Dreger, A. (2000). *Hermaphrodites and the medical invention of sex.* Cambridge, MA: Harvard University Press.

Dreier, P., & Freer, R. (1997, October 24). Saints, sinners, and affirmative action. *Chronicle of Higher Education,* pp. B6, B7.

Dreifus, C. (2000, July 11). A conversation with Nawal Nour. *New York Times,* p. D7.

Dresser, N. (1996). *Multicultural manners.* New York: Wiley.

Drummond, K., & Hopper, R. (1993). Acknowledgment tokens in series. *Communication Reports, 6,* 47–53.

Dubois, D., Serbin, L., & Derbyshire, A. (1998). Toddlers' intermodal and verbal knowledge about gender. *Merrill-Palmer Quarterly, 44,* 338–351.

Duck, S. W. (1988). *Relating to others.* Chicago: Dorsey.

Duck, S. W., & Wright, P. (1993). Re-examining gender differences in same-gender friendships: A close look at two kinds of data. *Sex Roles, 28,* 709–727.

DuPlessis, R., & Snitow, A. (Eds.). (1999). *The feminist memoir project: Voices from women's liberation.* Three Rivers, MI: Three Rivers.

Dyson, M. E. (1995). *Between God and gangsta rap.* New York: Oxford University Press.

Dyson, M. E. (1996). *Race rules: Navigating the color line.* New York: Addison-Wesley.

Dyson, M. E. (2003). *Why I love Black women.* New York: Basic Books.

Eagly, A. H. (1996). Differences between women and men. *American Psychologist, 51,* 158–159.

Eagly, A. H., & Johnson, B. T. (1990). Gender and leadership style: A meta-analysis. *Psychological Bulletin, 108,* 233–256.

Eagly, A. H., & Karau, S. J. (1991). Gender and the emergence of leaders: A meta-analysis. *Journal of Personality and Social Psychology, 60,* 687–710.

Edrut, O. (Ed.). (2000). *Body outlaws.* Seattle, WA: Seal Press.

Ehrenreich, B. (1990, Fall). Sorry, sisters, this is not the revolution (Special issue). *Time,* p. 15.

Ehrenreich, B. (1999, November 28). Doing it for ourselves: Can feminism survive class polarization? *In These Times,* p. 10.

Ehrenreich, B. & Hochschild, A. (Eds.). (2002). *Global women: Nannies, maids and sex workers in the new economy.* New York: Metropolitan.

Eichenbaum, L., & Orbach, S. (1983). *Understanding women: A feminist psychoanalytic approach.* New York: Basic Books.

Eichenbaum, L., & Orbach, S. (1987). *Between women: Love, envy, and competition in women's friendships.* New York: Viking.

Eldridge, N. S., & Gilbert, L. A. (1990). Correlates of relationship satisfaction in lesbian couples. *Psychology of Women Quarterly, 14,* 43–62.

Elias, M. (1992, August 3). Difference seen in brains of gay men. *USA Today,* p. 8-D.

Entman, R. M. (1994). Representation and reality in the portrayals of blacks on network television news. *Journalism Quarterly, 71,* 509–520.

Erkut, S. (2001, Spring/Summer). Learning from leaders. *Wellesley Center for Women Research Report,* pp. 7–10.

Espiritu, Y. L. (1997). *Asian American women and men.* Thousand Oaks, CA: Sage.

Estioko-Griffin, A., & Griffin, P. (1997). Woman the hunter: The Agta. In C. Brettell & C. Sargent (Eds.), *Gender in cross-cultural perspectives* (pp. 123–149). Englewood Cliffs, NJ: Prentice Hall.

Evans, D. (1993, March 1). The wrong examples. *Newsweek,* p. 10.

Evelyn, J. (2001, June 1). Changing times. *Chronicle of Higher Education,* p. A6.

Eyer, D. E. (1992). *Mother-infant bonding: A scientific fiction.* New Haven, CT: Yale University Press.

Fabes, R. (1994). Physiological, emotional, and behavioral correlates of sex segregation. In C. Leaper (Ed.), *Childhood sex segregation: Causes and consequences.* San Francisco: Jossey-Bass.

Fagot, B. I. (1985). A cautionary note: Parents' socialization of boys and girls. *Sex Roles, 12,* 471–476.

Fagot, B. I., Hagan, R., Leinbach, M. D., & Kronsberg, S. (1985). Differential reactions to assertive and communicative acts of toddler boys and girls. *Child Development, 56,* 1499–1505.

Fagot, B. I., & Leinbach, M. D. (1987). Socialization of sex roles within the family. In B. Carter (Ed.), *Current conceptions of sex roles and sex typing: Theory and research* (pp. 89–100). New York: Praeger.

Fagot, B. I., & Leinbach, M. D. (1989). The young child's gender schema: Environmental input, internal organization. *Child Development, 60,* 663–672.

Fagot, B., Leinbach, M. D., & Hagan, R. (1986). Gender labeling and the development of sex-typed behaviors. *Developmental Psychology, 4,* 440–443.

Faludi, S. (1991). *Backlash: The undeclared war against American women.* New York: Crown.

Faludi, S. (1999). *Stiffed: The betrayal of the American man.* New York: Morrow.

Farrell, C., & Matthews, D. (2000). *The reasonable woman as a standard for men.* New York: New York University Press.

Farrell, C., & Matthews, D. (2000). *A law of her own.* New York: New York University Press.

Farrell, W. (1991, May/June). Men as success objects. *Utne Reader,* pp. 81–84.

Fausto-Sterling, A. (2000). *Sexing the body: Gender politics and the construction of sexuality.* New York: Basic Books.

Feinberg, L. (1996). *Transgender warriors: Making history from Joan of Arc to RuPaul.* Boston, MA: Beacon.

Feingold, A. (1990). Gender differences in effects of physical attractiveness on romantic attraction: A comparison across five research paradigms. *Journal of Personality and Social Psychology, 59,* 981–993.

Ferguson, A. A. (2004). Bad boys: Public schools in the making of Black masculinity. In J. Spade & C. Valentine (Eds.), *The kaleidoscope of gender: Prisms, patterns, and possibilities* (pp. 193–204). Belmont, CA: Wadsworth.

Ferguson, S. (2000). Challenging traditional marriage: New married Chinese-American and Japanese-American women. *Gender and Society, 14,* 136–159.

Ferraro, S. (2001, February 15). Gender affects the course of disease, researchers say. *Raleigh News and Observer,* p. 2E.

Fiebert, M. (1987). Some perspectives on the men's movement. *Men's Studies Review, 4,* 8–10.

Fields, A. (2003). *Katharine Dexter McCormick: Pioneer for women's rights.* Westport, CT: Praeger.

Findlen, B. (Ed.). (1995). *Listen up! Voices from the next feminist generation.* Seattle: Seal Press.

Finnerty, A. (1999, May 9). The body politic. *New York Times Magazine,* p. 22.

Finstein, K. (1993, Fall). Media-made beauty. *Carolina Alumni Review,* pp. 74–83.

Fisher, H. (2000). *The first sex.* New York: Bantam.

Fishman, P. M. (1978). Interaction: The work women do. *Social Problems, 25,* 397–406.

Fivush, R., Brotman, M., Buckner, J., & Goodman, S. (2000). Gender differences in parent-child emotion narratives. *Sex Roles, 42,* 223–253.

Fixmer, N. (2003). "Revisioning the political: Feminism, difference, and solidarity in a new generation." Unpublished master's thesis, University of North Carolina at Chapel Hill.

Fixmer, N., & Wood, J. T. (in press). The political is personal: Difference, solidarity, and embodied politics in a new generation of feminists.

Flanagon, D., Baker-Ward, L., & Graham, L. (1995). Talk about preschool: Patterns of topic discussion and elaboration related to gender and ethnicity. *Sex Roles, 32,* 1–15.

Flanders, L. (1990, November/December). Military women and the media. *New Directions for Women,* pp. 1, 9.

Fletcher, J. (1999). *Disappearing acts: Gender, power and relational practice at work.* Cambridge, MA: MIT Press.

Fletcher, J., Jordan, J., & Miller, J. (2000). Women and the workplace: Applications of a psychodynamic theory. *American Journal of Psychoanalysis, 60,* 243–261.

Floyd, K. (1995). Gender and closeness among friends and siblings. *Journal of Psychology, 129,* 193–202.

Floyd, K. (1996a). Brotherly love I: The experience of closeness in the fraternal dyad. *Personal Relationships, 3,* 369–385.

Floyd, K. (1996b). Communicating closeness among siblings: An application of the gendered closeness perspective. *Communication Research Reports, 13,* 27–34.

Floyd, K. (1997a). Brotherly love II: A developmental perspective on liking, love, and closeness in the fraternal dyad. *Journal of Family Psychology, 11,* 196–209.

Floyd, K. (1997b). Communicating affection in dyadic relationships: An assessment of behavior and expectancies. *Communication Quarterly, 45,* 68–80.

Folb, E. (1985). Who's got room at the top? Issues of dominance and nondominance in intracultural communication. In L. A. Samovar & R. E. Porter (Eds.), *Intercultural communication: A reader* (4th ed., pp. 119–127). Belmont, CA: Wadsworth.

Forell, C. (1993, March). Sexual and racial harassment: Whose perspective should control? *Trial,* pp. 70–76.

Foss, K., Edson, B., & Linde, J. (2000). What's in a name? Negotiating decisions about marital names. In D. O. Braithwaite & J. T. Wood (Eds.), *Case studies in interpersonal communication* (pp. 18–25). Belmont, CA: Wadsworth.

Fowler, R., & Fuehrer, A. (1997). Women's marital names: An interpretive study of name retainers' concepts of marriage. *Feminism & Psychology, 7,* 315–320.

Fox-Genovese, E. (1991). *Feminism without illusions: A critique of individualism.* Chapel Hill: University of North Carolina Press.

Fox-Genovese, E. (1996). *Feminism is not the story of my life.* New York: Nan A. Talese/Doubleday.

Franek, M. (1994, March 30). Code of honor. *Independent Weekly,* p. 8.

Franklin, D. (2001). *What's love got to do with it? Understanding and healing the rift between Black men and women.* New York: Simon & Schuster.

Franzoi, S. L. (1991, August). *Gender role orientation and female body perception.* Paper presented at the meeting of the American Psychological Association, San Francisco.

Franzoi, S. L., & Koehler, V. (1998). Age and gender differences in body attitudes: A comparison of young and elderly adults. *International Journal of Aging and Human Development, 47,* 1–10.

Freiberg, P. (1991, May). Separate classes for black males? *APA Monitor,* p. 33.

Frieze, I., & Davis, K. (2000). Introduction to stalking and obsessive behavior in everyday life. *Violence and Victims, 15,* 3–5.

French, M. (1992). *The war against women.* New York: Summit.

Freud, S. F. (1957). *The ego and the id* (J. Riviere, Trans.). London: Hogarth.

Friedan, B. (1963). *The feminine mystique.* New York: Dell.

Friedan, B. (1981). *The second stage.* New York: Summit.

Fritz, J. (1997). Men's and women's organizational peer relationships: A comparison. *Journal of Business Communication, 34,* 27–46.

Fuentes, A. (1998, January 14). Rape statistics too good to be true. *Raleigh News and Observer,* p. 13A.

Futuyama, D., & Risch, S. (1984). Sexual orientation, sociobiology, and evolution. *Journal of Homosexuality, 9,* 157–168.

Gaard, G., & Murphy, P. (Eds.). (1999). *Ecofeminist literary criticism.* Urbana: University of Illinois Press.

Gabriel, S. L., & Smithson, I. (Eds.). (1990). *Gender in the classroom: Power and pedagogy.* Urbana: University of Illinois Press.

Gaines, S. O., Jr. (1995). Relationships between members of cultural minorities. In J. T. Wood & S. Duck (Eds.), *Understanding relationship processes, 6: Understudied relationships: Off the beaten track* (pp. 51–88). Thousand Oaks, CA: Sage.

Garlick, B., Dixon, S., & Allen, P. (Eds.). (1992). *Stereotypes of women in power: Historical perspectives and revisionist views.* Westport, CT: Greenwood Press.

Garrett, W. (2001). Personal communication.

Garrison, J. (2001, April 28). Researchers scramble over day-care study. *Raleigh News and Observer,* p. 6A.

Garrod, A., Ward, J., Robinson, T., & Kilkenny, R. (Eds.). (1999). *Souls looking back: Life stories of growing up Black.* New York: Routledge.

Gary, L. E. (1987). Predicting interpersonal conflict between men and women: The case of black men. In M. S. Kimmel (Ed.), *Changing men: New directions in research on men and masculinity* (pp. 232–243). Newbury Park, CA: Sage.

Gastil, J. (1990). Generic pronouns and sexist language: The oxymoronic character of masculine generics. *Sex Roles, 23,* 629–643.

Gates, A. (2000, April 9). Men on TV: Dumb as posts and proud of it. *New York Times,* p. 2-1.

Gaylin, W. (1992). *The male ego.* New York: Viking/Penguin Press.

Gelernter, D. (1996, February). Why mothers should stay home. *Commentary,* pp. 25–28.

Gelles, R., & Straus, M. (1988). *Intimate violence.* New York: Simon & Schuster.

Gender difference in how brain "reads." (1995, February 16). *San Francisco Chronicle,* p. A4.

Gerber, R. (2003, April 23). Finally equalize sexes in combat. *USA Today,* p. 11A.

Gerhart, A. (1999, August 5). Young women increasingly choose plastic surgery. *Raleigh News and Observer,* p. 4E.

Gerson, K. (1986). *Hard choices. How women decide about work, career, and motherhood.* Berkeley: University of California Press.

Gerson, K. (1994). *No man's land: Men's changing connections to family and work.* New York: Basic Books.

Gerson, K. (1998). Gender and the future of the family: Implications for the post-industrial workplace. In D. Vannoy & P. Dubeck (Eds.), *Challenges for work and family in the twenty-first century* (pp. 11–21). New York: Aldine de Gruyter.

Gerson, K. (2004). Moral dilemmas, moral strategies, and the transformation of gender: Lessons from two generations of work and family change. In J. Spade & C. Valentine (Eds.), *The kaleidoscope of gender: Prisms, patterns, and possibilities.* (pp. 413–424). Belmont, CA: Wadsworth.

Gilligan, C. (1982). *In a different voice: Psychological theory and women's development.* Cambridge, MA: Harvard University Press.

Gilligan, C., & Pollack, S. (1988). The vulnerable and invulnerable physician. In C. Gilligan, J. V. Ward, & J. M. Taylor, with B. Bardige (Eds.), *Mapping the moral domain* (pp. 245–262). Cambridge, MA: Harvard University Press.

Gilligan, C., Ward, J. V., and Taylor, J. M., with Bardige, B. (Eds.). (1988). *Mapping the moral domain.* Cambridge, MA: Harvard University Press.

Gilman, S. (1999). *Making the body beautiful: A cultural history of aesthetic surgery.* Princeton, NJ: Princeton University Press.

Glenn, D. (2002, November 22). Practices, identities, and desires. *Chronicle of Higher Education,* pp. A20–A21.

Goldner, V., Penn, P., Sheinberg, M., & Walker, G. (1990). Love and violence: Gender paradoxes in volatile attachments. *Family Process, 19,* 343–364.

Goldsmith, D., & Dun, S. (1997). Sex differences and similarities in the communication of social support. *Journal of Social and Personal Relationships, 14,* 317–337.

Goldsmith, D., & Fulfs, P. (1999). "You just don't have the evidence": An analysis of claims and evidence in Deborah Tannen's *You Just Don't Understand.* In M. Roloff (Ed.), *Communication Yearbook, 22,* pp. 1–49.

Goldstein, A. (2000, February 27). Breadwinning wives alter marital equation. *Washington Post,* p. A1.

Goldstein, J. (1998). Immortal combat: War toys and violent video games. In J. Goldstein (Ed.), *Why we watch* (pp. 53–68). New York: Oxford University Press.

Gonzales, A., & Kertész, J. (2001). Engendering power in Native North America. In D. Vannoy (Ed.), *Gender mosaics* (pp. 43–52). Los Angeles: Roxbury.

Good, S. (2000, February 28). As it turns out, you haven't come a long way, baby. *Insight on the News, 16,* 4.

Goode, E. (2001, August 1). 20% of girls report abuse by a date. *Raleigh News and Observer,* p. 10A.

Goodman, E. (1996, April 9). Freedom from mutilation. *Raleigh News and Observer,* p. 9A.

Goodman, E. (1999, May 29). Western culture pounds away at paradise. *Raleigh News and Observer,* p. 24-A.

Goodman, E. (2001, April 28). Playing with the numbers in child care. *Raleigh News and Observer,* p. 18A.

Goodnow, J. J. (1988). Children's household work: Its nature and functions. *Psychological Bulletin, 103,* 5–26.

Goodwin, M. H. (1990). *He said, she said: Talk as social organization among Black children.* Bloomington: Indiana University Press.

Gordon, L. (1976). *Woman's body, woman's right: A social history of birth control in America.* New York: Grossman.

Gordon, L. (1988). *Heroes of their own lives.* New York: Viking.

Gordon, L. (1998). Women's colleges. In W. Mankiller, G. Mink, M. Navarro, B. Smith, & G. Steinem (Eds.), *The reader's companion to U.S. women's history* (pp. 642–644). New York: Houghton Mifflin.

Gose, B. (2001, June 8). Supreme Court rejects appeal of a decision that cited "Bakke" to defend affirmative action. *Chronicle of Higher Education,* p. A24.

Gray, J. (1992). *Men are from Mars, women are from Venus: A practical guide for improving communication and getting what you want in your relationships.* New York: HarperCollins.

Gray, J. (1995). *Mars and Venus in the bedroom: A guide to lasting romance and passion.* New York: HarperCollins.

Gray, J. (1996a). *Mars and Venus in love.* New York: HarperCollins.

Gray, J. (1996b). *Mars and Venus together forever.* New York: HarperCollins.

Gray, J. (1998). *Mars and Venus on a date: A guide for navigating the five stages of dat-*

ing to create a loving and lasting relationship. New York: HarperCollins.

Gray, P., & Feldman, J. (1997). Patterns of age mixing and gender mixing among children and adolescents at an ungraded democratic school. *Merill-Palmer Quarterly, 43,* 67–86.

Greenberg, S. (2001, January 8). Time to plan your life. *Newsweek,* pp. 54–55.

Greene, R., & Dalton, K. (1953). The premenstrual syndrome. *British Medical Journal, 1,* 1007–1014.

Greenfield, L. (1997). *Fast forward: Growing up in the shadow of Hollywood.* New York: Knopf.

Greenfield, L. (2002). *Girl culture.* San Francisco: Chronicle Books.

Greenhouse, S. (2003, July 13). Going for the look, but risking discrimination. *The New York Times International,* p. 10YT.

Greenstein, T. (1996). Husbands' participation in domestic labor: The interactive effects of wives' and husbands' gender ideologies. *Journal of Marriage and the Family, 58,* 585–595.

Greer, G. (1992). *The change: Women, aging, and menopause.* New York: Knopf.

Greif, G. (1990). *The daddy track and the single father.* Lexington, MA: Lexington Books.

Griffin, C. (1996). Review of *Listen up! Voices from the next feminist generation. Journal of Applied Communication Research, 24,* 116–119.

Griffin, S. (1981). *Pornography and silence: Culture's revenge against nature.* New York: Harper & Row.

Griffith, R. (1997, October 17). The affinities between feminists and evangelical women. *Chronicle of Higher Education,* pp. B6, B7.

Griggs, C. (1998). *S/he: Changing sex and changing clothes.* New York: Berg/NYU Press.

Grinalds, J. (2000, February 15). New look, proven values at The Citadel. *Raleigh News and Observer,* p. 9A.

Gross, D. (1990, April 16). The gender rap. *New Republic,* pp. 11–14.

Gross, M. (2000, June). The lethal politics of beauty. *George,* pp. 53–59, 99–100.

Grover, M. B. (1999, September 6). Daddy stress. *Forbes,* pp. 202–208.

Gruenbaum, E. (2001). *The female circumcision controversy: An anthropological*

perspective. Philadelphia: University of Pennsylvania Press.

Guerrero, L. (1997). Nonverbal involvement across interactions with same-sex friends, opposite-sex friends, and romantic partners: Consistency or change? *Journal of Social and Personal Relationships, 14,* 31–58.

Guerrero, L., DeVito, J., & Hecht, M. (Eds.). (1999). *The nonverbal communication reader: Classic and contemporary readings* (2nd ed.). Prospect Heights, IL: Waveland Press.

Guerrilla Girls. (1995). *Confessions of the Guerrilla Girls.* New York: Harper-Perennial.

Gunter, N. C., & Gunter, B. G. (1990). Domestic division of labor among working couples: Does androgyny make a difference? *Sex Roles, 14,* 355–370.

Gutzman, K. (2003, June 10). Hillary's soft sell. *Raleigh News & Observer,* pp. 1E, 3E.

Guy-Sheftall, B. (2003). African American women: The legacy of Black feminism. In R. Morgan (Ed.), *Sisterhood is forever* (pp. 176–187). New York: Washington Square Press.

Haag, P. (2000). *Voices of a generation: Teenage girls report about their lives today.* New York: Marlowe.

Hacker, A. (2003a, June 20). How the B. A. gap widens the chasm between men and women. *Chronicle of Higher Education,* pp. B10–B11.

Hacker, A. (2003b). *Mismatch: The growing gulf between women and men.* New York: Scribner.

Hagan, K. (1998). Men's movement. In W. Mankiller, G. Mink, M. Navarro, B. Smith, & G. Steinem (Eds.), *The reader's companion to U.S. women's history* (p. 366). Boston: Houghton Mifflin.

Halberstadt, A. G., & Saitta, M. B. (1987). Gender, nonverbal behavior, and perceived dominance: A test of the theory. *Journal of Personality and Social Psychology, 53,* 257–272.

Hale, J., Tighe, R., & Mongeau, P. (1997). Effects of event type and sex on comforting messages. *Communication Research Reports, 14,* 214–220.

Hale-Benson, J. E. (1986). *Black children: Their roots, culture, and learning styles* (Rev. ed.). Provo, UT: Brigham Young University Press.

Hales, D. (1999). *Just like a woman.* New York: Bantam.

Hall, D., & Langellier, K. (1988). Storytelling strategies in mother–daughter communication. In B. Bate & A. Taylor (Eds.), *Women communicating: Studies of women's talk* (pp. 107–126). Norwood, NJ: Ablex.

Hall, E. T. (1959). *The silent language.* Greenwich, CT: Fawcett.

Hall, E. T. (1966). *The hidden dimension.* New York: Anchor/Doubleday.

Hall, J. A. (1998). How big are nonverbal sex differences? The case of similarity and sensitivity to nonverbal cues. In D. Canary & K. Dindia (Eds.), *Sex differences and similarities in communication: Critical essays and empirical investigations of sex and gender in interaction* (pp. 155–178). Mahwah, NJ: Erlbaum.

Hall, J. A., Halberstadt, A. G., & O'Brien, C. E. (1997). "Subordination" and nonverbal sensitivity: A study and synthesis of findings based on trait measures. *Sex Roles, 37,* 295–317.

Hall, J. A., & Taylor, M. C. (1985). Psychological androgyny and the masculinity–femininity interaction. *Journal of Personality and Social Psychology, 49,* 429–435.

Hall, R. M., with Sandler, B. R. (1982). *The classroom climate: A chilly one for women?* Washington, DC: Association of American Colleges, Project on the Status and Education of Women.

Hall, R. M., & Sandler, B. R. (1984). *Out of the classroom: A chilly campus climate for women.* Washington, DC: Association of American Colleges, Project on the Status and Education of Women.

Halper, D. (2001). *Invisible stars: A social history of women in American broadcasting.* Armonk, New York: M. E. Sharpe.

Halpern, D. (1996). Public policy implications of sex differences in cognitive abilities. *Psychology, Public Policy, and Law, 2,* 561–574.

Hamilton, M. C. (1991). Masculine bias in the attribution of personhood: People–male, male–people. *Psychology of Women Quarterly, 15,* 393–402.

Hammer, J. (2001). *What it means to be a daddy: Fatherhood for Black men living away from their children.* New York: Columbia University Press.

Hammer, R. (2002). *Antifeminism and family terrorism: A critical feminist perspective.* New York: Rowman & Littlefield.

Hammonds, E. (1998). Science and gender. In W. Mankiller, G. Mink, M. Navarro, B. Smith, & G. Steinem (Eds.), *The reader's companion to U.S. women's history* (pp. 521–522). New York: Houghton Mifflin.

Hanisch, C. (1970). What can be learned? A critique of the Miss America protest. In L. Tanner (Ed.), *Voices from women's liberation* (pp. 132–136). New York: Signet Classics.

Hanson, S. (1988). Divorced fathers with custody. In P. Bronstein & C. P. Cowan (Eds.), *Fatherhood today: Men's changing role in the family* (pp. 166–194). New York: Wiley.

Harding, S. (1991). *Whose science? Whose knowledge? Thinking from women's lives.* Ithaca, NY: Cornell University Press.

Harding, S. (1998). *Can feminism be multicultural?* Ithaca, NY: Cornell University Press.

Harris, J. (1998). *The nurture assumption.* New York: Simon & Schuster/Free Press.

Harrison, C. E. (1988). *On account of sex: The politics of women's issues, 1945–1968.* Berkeley: University of California Press.

Hartlage, L. C. (1980, March). *Identifying and programming for differences.* Paper presented at the Parent and Professional Conference on Young Children with Special Needs, Cleveland.

Hartman, S. (1998). *The other feminists: Activists in the liberal establishment.* New Haven, CT: Yale University Press.

Hartmann, E. (1991). *Boundaries in the mind: A new psychology of personality.* New York: Basic Books.

Hasenauer, H. (1997). Taking on domestic violence. *Soldiers, 52,* 34–36.

Hattery, A. (2000). *Women, work and family: Balancing and weaving.* Thousand Oaks, CA: Sage.

Haugaard, J. (2000). The challenge of defining child sexual abuse. *American Psychologist, 55,* 1036–1039.

Hawkes, B., & Spade, J. (1998, July). Women and men engineering students: Anticipations of family and work roles. *Journal of Engineering Education,* 1–8.

Hearn, J. (1987). *The gender of oppression: Men, masculinity and the critique of Marxism.* New York: St. Martin's Press.

Heath, D. (1991). *Fulfilling lives: Paths to maturity and success.* San Francisco: Jossey-Bass.

Hegde, R. (1999a). Sons and m(others): Framing the maternal body and the politics of reproduction in a south Indian context. *Women's Studies in Communication, 22,* 1–20.

Hegde, R. (1999b). Marking bodies, reproducing violence: A feminist reading of female infanticide in south India. *Violence Against Women, 5,* 507–524.

Hegel, G. W. F. (1807). *Phenomenology of mind.* (J. B. Baillie, Trans.). Germany: Wurzburg & Bamburg.

Heilbrun, A. B. (1986). Androgyny as type and androgyny as behavior: Implications for gender schema in males and females. *Sex Roles, 14,* 123–139.

Heilbrun, A. B., & Han, Y. (1984). Cost-effectiveness of college achievement by androgynous men and women. *Psychological Reports, 55,* 977–978.

Helgesen, S. (1990). *The female advantage: Women's ways of leadership.* New York: Doubleday Currency.

Heller, S. (1993, February 3). Scholars debate the Marlboro Man: Examining stereotypes of masculinity. *Chronicle of Higher Education,* pp. A6–A8, A15.

Hemmer, J. D., & Kleiber, D. A. (1981). Tomboys and sissies: Androgynous children? *Sex Roles, 7,* 1205–1211.

Hendrick, C., & Hendrick, S. (1986). A theory and method of love. *Journal of Personality and Social Psychology, 50,* 392–402.

Hendrick, C., & Hendrick, S. (1996). Gender and the experience of heterosexual love. In J. T. Wood (Ed.), *Gendered relationships: A reader.* Mountain View, CA: Mayfield.

Henley, N. (1989). Molehill or mountain? What we know and don't know about sex bias in language. In M. Crawford & M. Gentry (Eds.), *Gender and thought: Psychological perspectives* (pp. 59–78). New York: Springer-Verlag.

Henley, N. M. (1977). *Body politics: Power, sex and nonverbal communication.* Englewood Cliffs, NJ: Prentice-Hall.

Henley, N. M., & Freeman, J. (1995). The sexual politics of interpersonal behavior. In J. Freeman (Ed.), *Women: A feminist perspective* (5th ed.), (pp. 79–91). Mountain View, CA: Mayfield.

Henley, N. M., & LaFrance, M. (1996). On oppressing hypotenses: Or differences in nonverbal sensitivity revisited. In L. Radtke & H. Stam (Eds.), *Power/gender: Social relations in theory and practice. Inquiries in social construction* (pp. 287–311). Thousand Oaks, CA: Sage.

Hennesee, J. (1999). *Betty Friedan: A biography.* New York: Random House.

Henriques, G., Calhoun, L., & Cann, A. (1996). Ethnic differences in women's body satisfaction: An experimental investigation. *Journal of Social Psychology, 136,* 689–697.

Henry, S. (2002, January 24). Gender salary gap widening, study says. *Raleigh News and Observer.* P. 4A.

Herdt, G. (Ed.). (1996). *Third sex, third gender.* Chicago: New Zone Books.

Herdt, G. (1997). *Same sex, different cultures.* Boulder, CO: Westview.

Herlinger, C. (2001, December 7). Afghan women seek new role. *Raleigh News and Observer,* p. 4E.

Hernández, D., & Rehman, B. (Eds.). (2002). *Colonize this! Young women of color on today's feminism.* Seattle: Seal Press.

Herrup, M. J. (1995). Virtual identity. In R. Walker (Ed.), *To be real: Telling the truth and changing the face of feminism* (pp. 239–252). New York: Anchor.

Hewlett, S. (1986). *A lesser life: The myth of female liberation in America.* New York: Morrow.

Hewlett, S. (1991). *When the bough breaks: The cost of neglecting our children.* New York: Basic Books.

Hewlett, S. (2002). *Creating a life: Professional women and the quest for children.* New York: Hyperion.

Heywood, L. (1998, September 4). Hitting a cultural nerve: Another season of "Ally McBeal." *Chronicle of Higher Education,* p. B9.

Heywood, L., & Drake, J. (Eds.). (1997). *Third wave agenda: Being feminist, doing feminism.* Minneapolis: University of Minnesota Press.

Hicks, J. (1998a, February 12). Eating disorders screening offered. *Raleigh News and Observer*, p. 2E.

Hicks, J. (1998b, November 5). A thin line. *Raleigh News and Observer*, pp. 1E, 3E.

Hine, D., & Thompson, K. (1998). *A shining thread of hope: The history of Black women in America.* New York: Broadway.

Hines, M. (1992, April 19). [Untitled report]. *Health Information Communication Network, 5,* 2.

Hirdman, Y. (1998). State policy and gender contracts: The Swedish experience. In E. Drew, R. Emerek, & E. Mahon (Eds.), *Women, work, and the family in Europe* (pp. 36–46). London: Routledge.

Hochschild, A. (1975). The sociology of feeling and emotion: Selected possibilities. In M. Millman & R. M. Kanter (Eds.), *Another voice* (pp. 180–207). New York: Doubleday/Anchor.

Hochschild, A. (1979). Emotion work, feeling rules, and social structure. *American Journal of Sociology, 85,* 551–595.

Hochschild, A. (1983). *The managed heart: Commercialization of human feeling.* Berkeley: University of California Press.

Hochschild, A. (1989). The economy of gratitude. In D. Franks & E. D. McCarthy (Eds.), *The sociology of emotions: Original essays and research papers* (pp. 95–113). Greenwich, CT: JAI Press.

Hochschild, A., with Machung, A. (2003). The second shift: *Working parents and the revolution at home* (Rev. ed.). New York: Viking/Penguin Press.

Hoffman, B. (1998). Pink collar ghetto. In W. Mankiller, G. Mink, M. Navarro, B. Smith, & G. Steinem (Eds.), *The reader's companion to U.S. women's history* (pp. 450–451). New York: Houghton Mifflin.

Holland, D., & Eisenhart, M. (1992). *Educated in romance: Women, achievement, and college culture.* Chicago: University of Chicago Press.

Hollands, J. (2001). *Same game, different rules: How to get ahead without being a bully broad, ice queen or other Ms. Understood.* New York: McGraw-Hill.

Holt, P. (1998, June 29). Unraveling the secret life of a man who was a woman. *San Francisco Chronicle*, pp. D1, D5.

Holtzman, L. (2000). *Media messages: What film, television, and popular music teach us about race, class, gender, and sexual orientation.* New York: M. E. Sharpe.

Honolagneu-Sotelo, P. (2001). *Domestica: Immigrant workers cleaning and caring in the shadows of affluence.* Berkeley: University of California Press.

hooks, b. (1981). *Ain't I a woman? Black women and feminism.* Boston: South End Press.

hooks, b. (1990). Definitions of difference. In D. L. Rhode (Ed.), *Theoretical perspectives on sexual difference* (pp. 185–193). New York: Yale University Press.

hooks, b. (1994). *Outlaw culture.* New York: Routledge.

hooks, b. (1995, August). Appearance obsession: Is the price too high? *Essence, 26,* 69–71.

hooks, b. (2000b). *Feminist theory: From margin to center* (2nd ed.). Boston: South End Press.

hooks, b. (2002a). *Feminism is for everybody.* Boston: South End Press.

Hoover, E. (2001, June 8). New scrutiny for powerful Greek systems. *Chronicle of Higher Education*, pp. A35–A37.

Hooyman, N. (1999). Research on older women: Where is feminism? *Gerontologist, 39,* 115–116.

Hopkins, A. (2001). Personal communication.

Hopkins, A., & Walsh, M. (1996). *So ordered: Making partner the hard way.* Amherst: University of Massachusetts Press.

Horn, D. (1997). Comfort women. *Endeavors* (pp. 8–9). Chapel Hill, NC: Office of Graduate Studies and Research, University of North Carolina.

Horowitz, D. (1998). *Betty Friedan and the making of the feminine mystique: The American left, the cold war, and modern feminism.* Amherst: University of Massachusetts Press.

Hosken, F. (1992). *The Hosken report: Genital and sexual mutilation of females.* Lexington, KY: WIN News.

House, A., Dallinger, J., & Kilgallen, D. (1998). Androgyny and rhetorical sensitivity: The connection of gender and communicator style. *Communication Reports, 11,* 11–20.

How boys and girls teach each other. (1992, October). *Working Mother*, p. 116.

Howard, J. A., Blumstein, P., & Schwartz, P. (1986). Sex, power, and influence factors in intimate relationships. *Journal of Personality and Social Psychology, 51,* 102–109.

Howard, J. A., & Hollander, J. (1996). *Gendered situation: Gendered selves.* Thousand Oaks, CA: Sage.

Howey, N. (2002). *Dress codes: Of three girlhoods: My mother's, my father's and mine.* New York: Picador USA.

Howry, A. (1999). *The next feminist generation: Negotiating contradiction and ambiguity.* Unpublished master's thesis, University of North Carolina, Chapel Hill, North Carolina.

Howry, A., & Wood, J. T. Something old, something new, something borrowed: Themes in the voices of a new generation of feminists. *Southern Journal of Communication, 66,* 323–336.

Hudson, L., & Jacot, B. (1992). *The way men think.* New Haven, CT: Yale University Press.

Hughes, J. O., & Sandler, B. R. (1986). *In case of sexual harassment: A guide for women students.* Washington, DC: Association of American Colleges, Project on the Status and Education of Women.

Hunt, A. (1994, June 23). O.J. and the brutal truth about marital violence. *Wall Street Journal,* p. A15.

Hunter, J., & Mallon, G. P. (2000). Lesbian, gay and bisexual adolescent development: Dancing with your feet tied together. In B. Greene & G. Croom (Eds.), *Education, research, and practice in lesbian, gay, bisexual, and transgendered psychology* (pp. 226–243). Thousand Oaks, CA: Sage.

Huppert, J., Yaacoby, J., & Lazarowitz, R. (1998). Learning microbiology with computer simulations: Students' academic achievement by method and gender. *Research in Science and Technological Education, 16,* 231–245.

Hurtado, A. (2001). *Voicing Chicana feminisms: Young women speak out on sexuality and identity.* New York: New York University Press.

Husbands are battered as often as wives. (1994, June 23). *USA Today,* p. D8.

Huston, M., & Schwartz, P. (1996). Gendered dynamics in gay and lesbian relationships. In J. T. Wood (Ed.), *Gendered relationships: A reader* (pp. 89–121). Mountain View, CA: Mayfield.

Hyde, B., & Texidor, M. (1994). Childbearing and parental roles: A description of the fathering experience among Black fathers. In R. Staples (Ed.), *The Black family: Essays and studies* (pp. 157–164). Belmont, CA: Wadsworth.

Hyde, J. S. (1984). Children's understanding of sexist language. *Developmental Psychology, 20,* 697–706.

Ickes, W. (1993). Traditional gender roles: Do they make and then break our relationships? *Journal of Social Work, 49,* 71–85.

In their words. (2003, June 24). *Raleigh News and Observer,* p. 5A.

Ingraham, L. (1997, July 15). Feminists welcome the Promise Keepers. *Raleigh News and Observer,* p. 11A.

Ingrassia, M. (1993, August 30). Endangered family. *Newsweek,* pp. 17–29.

Ingrassia, M. (1995, April 24). The body of the beholder. *Newsweek,* pp. 66–67.

Ingrassia, M., & Beck, M. (1994, July 4). Patterns of abuse. *Newsweek,* pp. 26–33.

Inman, C. (1996). Friendships between men: Closeness in the doing. In J. T. Wood (Ed.), *Gendered relationships: A reader* (pp. 95–110). Mountain View, CA: Mayfield.

Jacklin, C. N. (1989). Female and male: Issues of gender. *American Psychologist, 44,* 127–133.

Jackman, M. R. (2003). Violence in social life. *Annual Review of Sociology, 28,* 387–415.

Jackson, L. A. (1983). The perception of androgyny and physical attractiveness: Two is better than one. *Personality and Social Psychology Bulletin, 9,* 405–430.

Jackson, M. (1999, February 14). For dads, "leave" has meant "stay." *Raleigh News and Observer,* p. 6E.

Jacobson, J. (2001, March 9). Why do so many female athletes enter ACL hell? *Chronicle of Higher Education,* p. A45.

Jacobson, N., & Gottman, J. (1998). *When men batter women: New insights into ending abusive relationships.* New York: Simon & Schuster.

James, K. (1989). When twos are really threes: The triangular dance in couple conflict. *Australian and New Zealand Journal of Family Therapy, 10,* 179–186.

Jamieson, K. H. (1995). *Beyond the double bind: Women and leadership.* New York: Oxford University Press.

Jamila, S. (2002). Can I get a witness? Testimony from a hip-hop feminist. In D. Hernández & D. Rehman (Eds.), *Colonize this! Young women of color on today's feminism* (pp. 382–394). New York: Seal Press.

Janeway, E. (1971). *Man's world, woman's place: A study in social mythology.* New York: Dell.

Jegalian, K., & Lahn, B. (2001). Why the Y is so weird. *Scientific American, 284,* 56.

Jena, S. (1999). Job, life satisfaction and occupational stress of women. *Social Science International, 15,* 75–80.

Jenkins, C. (2003). Standing by: Women in broadcast media. In R. Morgan (Ed.), *Sisterhood is forever* (pp. 418–429). New York: Washington Square Press.

Jhally, S., & Katz, J. (2001, Winter). Big trouble, little pond: Reflections on the meaning of the campus pond rapes. *UMass,* pp. 26–31.

Johnson, C. B., Stockdale, M. S., & Saal, F. E. (1991). Persistence of men's misperceptions of friendly cues across a variety of interpersonal encounters. *Psychology of Women Quarterly, 15,* 463–465.

Johnson, D. (2002, March 25). Until dust do us part. *Newsweek,* p. 41.

Johnson, F. (1996). Friendships among women: Closeness in dialogue. In J. T. Wood (Ed.), *Gendered relationships: A reader* (pp. 79–94). Mountain View, CA: Mayfield.

Johnson, F. (2000). *Speaking culturally: Language diversity in the United States.* Thousand Oaks, CA: Sage.

Johnson, F. L. (1989). Women's culture and communication: An analytical perspective. In C. M. Lont & S. A. Friedley (Eds.), *Beyond boundaries: Sex and gender diversity in communication* (pp. 301–316). Fairfax, VA: George Mason University Press.

Johnson, F. L., & Young, K. (2002). Gendered voices in children's television advertising. *Critical Studies in Media Communication, 19,* 461–480.

Johnson, J. W. (1912/1989). *Autobiography of an ex-coloured man.* New York: Vintage-Random.

Jones, A. (1994). *Next time she'll be dead: Battering and how to stop it.* Boston: Beacon.

Jones, A. (1998a). Battered women. In W. Mankiller, G. Mink, M. Navarro, B. Smith, & G. Steinem (Eds.), *The reader's companion to U.S. women's history* (pp. 607–609). New York: Houghton Mifflin.

Jones, A. (1998b). Domestic violence. In W. Mankiller, G. Mink, M. Navarro, B. Smith, & G. Steinem (Eds.), *The reader's companion to U.S. women's history* (p. 609). New York: Houghton Mifflin.

Jones, D. C. (1991). Friendship satisfaction and gender: An examination of sex differences in contributors to friendship satisfaction. *Journal of Social and Personal Relationships, 8,* 167–185.

Jones, J. (2000). Concern mounts over female genital mutilation. *British Medical Journal, 321,* 262.

Jones, K., Evans, C., Byrd, R., & Campbell, K. (2000). Gender equity training and teacher behavior. *Journal of Instructional Psychology,* 173–178.

Jorgenson, J. (2000). Interpreting the intersection of work and family: Frame conflicts in women's work. *The Electronic Journal of Communication, 10.* Retrieved from http://www.cios.org/www/ejrec2.htm

Joseph, R. (2000). The evolution of sex differences in language, sexuality and visual-spatial skills. *Archives of Sexual Behavior, 29,* 55–66.

Kafai, Y. (1999). Video game designs by girls and boys: Variability and consistency of gender differences. In M. Kinder (Ed.), *Kids' media culture* (pp. 293–314). Durham, NC: Duke University Press.

Kahn, A., & Mathie, V. (1994). Rape scripts and rape acknowledgment. *Psychology of Women Quarterly, 18,* 53–66.

Kahn, J. (1997, April 11). Therapist says male depression widespread and widely denied. *Raleigh News and Observer,* p. 5D.

Kang, M. (1997). The portrayal of women's images in magazine advertisements: Goffman's gender analysis revisited. *Sex Roles, 37,* 979–997.

Kanter, R. M. (1977). *Men and women of the corporation.* New York: Basic Books.

Kantrowitz, B., & Kalb, C. (1998, May 11). How to build a better boy. *Newsweek,* pp. 55–60.

Kaplan, E. A. (1992). *Motherhood and representation.* New York: Routledge.

Karp, M., & Stoller, D. (1999). *The BUST guide to the new girl order.* New York: Penguin Press.

Kaschak, E. (1992). *Engendered lives.* New York: Basic Books.

Kassindja, F. (1998). *Do they hear you when you cry?* New York: Delacorte.

Kato, D. (1993, March 9). Read 'em and weep, women. *Raleigh News and Observer,* pp. E1, E3.

Katz, J. (1995). Advertising and the construction of violent White masculinity. In G. Dines & J. Humez (Eds.), *Gender, race and class in media* (pp. 133–141). Thousand Oaks, CA: Sage.

Katz, J. (2000). MVP trainer's guide for working with male high school students. (Available from MVP Strategies: Gender Violence Prevention Education and Training, mvpstrat@aol.com).

Katz, J., Earp, J., & Jhally, S. (1999). *Tough guise: Violence, media & the crisis in masculinity* (video). Northhampton, MA: Media Education Foundation.

Katz, J., & Jhally, S. (1999, May 2). The national conversation in the wake of Littleton is missing the mark. *The Boston Globe,* p. E1.

Katz, J., & Jhally, S. (2000, June 25). Put the blame where it belongs: On men. *The Los Angeles Times,* p. M5.

Kaufman, M. (1995). The construction of masculinity and the triad of men's violence. In M. Kimmell & M. Mesner (Eds.), *Men's lives* (3rd ed., pp. 13–25).

Kaye, L. W., & Applegate, J. S. (1990). Men as elder caregivers: A response to changing families. *American Journal of Orthopsychiatry, 60,* 86–95.

Keen, S. (1991). *Fire in the belly: On being a man.* New York: Bantam.

Keller, E. F. (1983). *A feeling for the organism: The life and work of Barbara McClintock.* New York: Freeman.

Keller, E. F. (1985). *Reflections on gender and science.* New Haven, CT: Yale University Press.

Kellner, D. (1995). *Media culture: Cultural studies, identity, and politics between the modern and the postmodern.* New York: Routledge.

Kelly, L., & Radford, J. (1998). Sexual violence against women and girls. In R. Dobash & R. Dobash (Eds.), *Rethinking violence against women* (pp. 53–76). Thousand Oaks, CA: Sage.

Kelly-Gadol, J. (1977). Did women have a renaissance? In R. Bridenthal & C. Koonz (Eds.), *Becoming visible: Women in European history* (pp. 136–164). Boston: Houghton Mifflin.

Kemper, S. (1984). When to speak like a lady. *Sex Roles, 10,* 435–443.

Kern-Foxworth, M. (1994). *Aunt Jemima, Uncle Ben, and Rastus: Blacks in advertising, yesterday, today, and tomorrow.* Westport, CT: Greenwood Press.

Kerr, B. (1997). *Smart girls: A new psychology of girls, women, and giftedness.* Scottsdale, AZ: Gifted Psychology Press.

Kerr, B. (1999, March 5). When dreams differ: Male-female relations on campuses. *Chronicle of Higher Education,* pp. B7–B8.

Kessler, S. (1998). *Lessons from the intersexed.* New Brunswick, NJ: Rutgers University Press.

Kessler, S., & McKenna, W. (1978). *Gender: An ethnomethodological approach.* New York: Wiley.

Kilbourne, J. (1999). *Deadly persuasion: Why women and girls must fight the addictive power of advertising.* New York: Free Press.

Kilbourne, J. (2004). The more you subtract, the more you add: Cutting girls down to size. In J. Spade & C. Valentine (Eds.), *The kaleidoscope of gender: Prisms, patterns, and possibilities* (pp. 234–244). Belmont, CA: Wadsworth.

Kim, G., & Roloff, M. (1999). Attributing sexual consent. *Journal of Applied Communication Research, 27,* 1–23.

Kimball, M. M. (1986). Television and sex-role attitudes. In T. M. Williams (Ed.), *The impact of television: A natural experiment in three communities* (pp. 265–301). Orlando: Academic Press.

Kimbrell, A. (1991, May/June). A time for men to pull together. *Utne Reader,* pp. 66–71.

Kimmel, M. (1995). (Ed.). *The politics of manhood: Profeminist men respond to the mythopoetic men's movement (and the mythopoetic leaders answer).* Philadelphia: Temple University Press.

Kimmel, M. (1996). *Manhood.* New York: Free Press.

Kimmel, M. (2000a). *The gendered society.* Cambridge, MA: Oxford University Press.

Kimmel, M. (2000b, January 12). What about the boys? Keynote speech at the Center for Research on Women's 6th Annual Gender Equity Conference, Boston, MA.

Kimmel, M. (2002, February 8). Gender, class and terrorism. *Chronicle of Higher Education,* pp. B11–B12.

Kimmel, M., & Mosmiller, T. (Eds.). (1992). *Against the tide.* Collingdale, PA: Diane Publishing Company.

Kimura, D. (1999). *Sex and cognition.* Cambridge, MA: MIT Press.

Kindlon, D., & Thompson, M. (1999). *Raising Cain: Protecting the emotional life of boys.* New York: Ballantine.

Kinney, T. A., Smith, B. A., & Donzella, B. (2001). The influence of sex, gender, self-discrepancies, and self-awareness on anger and verbal aggressiveness among U.S. college students. *Journal of Social Psychology, 141,* 245–276.

Kirby, E., & Krone, K. (2002). "The policy exists but you can't really use it": Communication and the structuration of work-family policies. *Journal of Applied Communication Research, 30,* 50–77.

Kirkpatrick, M. (1989). Middle age and the lesbian experience. *Women's Studies Quarterly, 17,* 87–96.

Kishkovsky, S. (2003, September 17). Bolshoi decides it's over before "fat lady dances." *New York Times,* pp. A1, A6.

Kivel, P. (1999). *Boys will be men: Raising our sons for courage, caring, and community.* Gabriola Island, B.C.: New Society Press.

Klatch, R. (1998). Conservativism and the right wing. In W. Mankiller, G. Mink, M. Navarro, B. Smith, & G. Steinem (Eds.), *The reader's companion to U.S. women's history* (pp. 125–128). Boston: Houghton Mifflin.

Klein, E. (1984). *Gender politics: From consciousness to mass politics.* Cambridge: Harvard University Press.

Klein, S., Stafford, L., & Miklosovic, J. (1996). Women's surnames: Decisions, interpretations, and associations with relational qualities. *Journal of Social and Personal Relationships, 13,* 593–617.

Klerman, J. A., & Liebowitz, A. (1999). Job continuity among new mothers. *Demography, 36,* 145–155.

Kluwer, E., Heesink, J., & Vliert, E. (1996). The marital dynamics of conflict over the division of labor. *Journal of Marriage and the Family, 59,* 635–653.

Kneidinger, L. M., Maple, T. L., & Tross, S. A. (2001). Touching behavior in sport: Functional components, analysis of sex differences, and ethological considerations. *Journal of Nonverbal Behavior, 25,* 43–62.

Knudson-Martin, C., & Mahoney, A. (1996). Gender dilemmas and myths in the construction of marital bargains: Issues for marital therapy. *Family Process, 35,* 137–153.

Kohlberg, L. (1958). *The development of modes of thinking and moral choice in the years 10 to 16.* Unpublished doctoral dissertation, University of Chicago.

Kohlberg, L. (1966). A cognitive-developmental analysis of children's sex-role concepts and attitudes. In E. M. Maccoby (Ed.), *The development of sex differences* (pp. 82–173). Stanford, CA: Stanford University Press.

Kolbe, R., & Albanese, P. (1997). The functional integration of sole-male images into magazine advertisements. *Sex Roles, 36,* 813–835.

Kollwitz, K., & Kahlo, F. (2003). Women and the art world: Diary of the feminist masked avengers. In R. Morgan (Ed.), *Sisterhood is forever* (pp. 437–444). New York: Washington Square Press.

Konner, M. (2003, June 16). Bridging our differences. *Newsweek,* pp. 74, 77.

Koss, M. P., Gidycz, C. J., & Wisniewski, N. (1987). The scope of rape: Incidence and prevalence of sexual aggression and victimization in a national sample of higher education students. *Journal of Consulting and Clinical Psychology, 55,* 162–170.

Kovacs, P., Parker, J., & Hoffman, L. (1996). Behavioral, affective and social correlates of involvement in cross-sex friendships in elementary school. *Child Development, 67,* 2269–2286.

Kramarae, C. (1981). *Women and men speaking: Frameworks for analysis.* Rowley, MA: Newbury House.

Kramarae, C. (1992). Harassment and everyday life. In L. F. Rakow (Ed.), *Women making meaning: New feminist directions in communication* (pp. 100–120). New York: Routledge.

Kreps, G. L. (Ed.). (1992). *Communication and sexual harassment in the workplace.* Cresskill, NJ: Hampton.

Krupnick, C. G. (1985, May). Women and men in the classroom: Inequality and its remedies. *On Teaching and Learning: The Journal of the Harvard-Danforth Center for Teaching and Learning,* 18–25.

Kuczynski, A. (2001, April 9). Magazines try to help teens. *Raleigh News and Observer,* p. 3E.

Kulwicki, A. D. (2000). Arab women. In M. Julia (Ed.), *Constructing gender* (pp. 89–108). Belmont, CA: Wadsworth.

Kurdek, L. A., & Schmitt, J. P. (1986a). Early development of relationship quality in heterosexual married, heterosexual cohabiting, gay, and lesbian couples. *Developmental Psychology, 22,* 305–309.

Kurdek, L. A., & Schmitt, J. P. (1986b). Interaction of sex-role self-concept with relationship quality and relationship belief in married, heterosexual cohabiting, gay, and lesbian couples. *Journal of Personality and Social Psychology, 51,* 365–370.

Kurdek, L. A., & Schmitt, J. P. (1986c). Relationship quality of partners in heterosexual married, heterosexual cohabiting, and gay and lesbian relationships. *Journal of Personality and Social Psychology, 51,* 711–720.

Kurdek, L. A., & Schmitt, J. P. (1987). Partner homogamy in married, heterosexual cohabiting, gay, and lesbian couples. *Journal of Sex Research, 23,* 212–232.

Kurth, S., Spiller, B., & Travis, C. B. (2000). Consent, power and sexual scripts: Deconstructing sexual harassment. In C. B. Travis & J. W. White (Eds.), *Sexuality, society, and feminism* (pp. 323–354). Washington, DC: American Psychological Association.

Labov, W. (1972). *Sociolinguistic patterns.* Philadelphia: University of Pennsylvania Press.

Lakoff, R. (1975). *Language and woman's place.* New York: Harper & Row.

Lakoff, R. (1998). Language and power. In W. Mankiller, G. Mink, M. Navarro, B. Smith, & G. Steinem (Eds.), *The reader's companion to U.S. women's history* (pp. 314–316). New York: Houghton Mifflin.

Lally, K. (1996, January 7). For girls now, adolescence a perilous rite. *Richmond Times Dispatch,* pp. G1, G2.

Lamb, M. E. (1986). The changing roles of fathers. In M. E. Lamb (Ed.), *The father's role: Applied perspectives* (pp. 3–27). New York: Wiley.

Lamb, S. (1991). Acts without agents: An analysis of linguistic avoidance in journal articles on men who batter women. *American Journal of Orthopsychiatry, 61,* 87–102.

Lamb, S. (1999). (Ed.). *New versions of victims.* New York: New York University Press.

Lamb, S. (2002). *The secret lives of girls: Sex, play, aggression, and their guilt.* New York: Free Press.

Lamke, L. K. (1982). The impact of sexual orientation on self-esteem in early adolescence. *Child Development, 53,* 1530–1535.

Lamke, L., Sollie, D., Durbin, R., & Fitzpatrick, J. (1994). Masculinity, femininity, and relationship satisfaction: The mediating role of interpersonal competence. *Journal of Social and Personal Relationships, 11,* 535–554.

Lang, S. S. (1991, January 20). When women drink. *Parade,* pp. 18–20.

Langer, S. K. (1953). *Feeling and form: A theory of art.* New York: Scribner's.

Langer, S. K. (1979). *Philosophy in a new key: A study in the symbolism of reason, rite and art* (3rd ed.). Cambridge, MA: Harvard University Press.

Langreth, R. (1997, June 12). Hey guys, for the next party, try borrowing women's genes. *Wall Street Journal,* p. B1.

Lansberg, M. (2000). White Ribbon Campaign: Canadian feminists' uneasy alliance with men challenging violence. *Voice Male,* p. 15.

Lawson, C. (1993, February 16). Genderbenders. *Raleigh News and Observer,* p. E1.

Leaper, C. (1991). Influence and involvement in children's discourse: Age, gender, and partner effects. *Child Development, 62,* 797–811.

Leaper, C. (Ed.). (1994). *Childhood gender segregation: Causes and consequences.* San Francisco: Jossey-Bass.

Leaper, C. (1996). The relationship of play activity and gender to parent and child sex-typed communication. *International Journal of Behavioral Development, 19,* 689–703.

Leaper, C. (2000). The social construction and socialization of gender. In P. Miller & E. Scholnick (Eds.), *Towards a feminist developmental psychology* (pp. 127–152). New York: Routledge.

Leaper, C., Anderson, K., & Sanders, P. (1998). Moderators of gender effects on parents' talk to their children: A meta-analysis. *Developmental Psychology, 34,* 3–27.

Leaper, C., Leve, L., Strasser, T., & Schwartz, R. (1995). Mother–child communication sequences: Play activity, child gender, and marital status effects. *Merrill-Palmer Quarterly, 41,* 307–327.

Lee, P. C., & Gropper, N. B. (1974). Sex-role culture and educational practice. *Harvard Educational Review, 44,* 369–407.

Lee, S. (Director). (1997). *Get on the Bus.* (motion picture). United States: Columbia/Tristar.

Lee, V. E., & Marks, H. M. (1990). Sustained effects of the single-sex secondary school experience on attitudes, behaviors, and values in college. *Journal of Educational Psychology, 82,* 578–592.

Legato, M. (1998, May 15). Research on the biology of women will improve health care for men, too. *Chronicle of Higher Education,* pp. B4–B5.

Leland, J., & Chambers, V. (1999, July 12). Generation N. *Newsweek,* pp. 52–58.

Leo, J. (1997, March 31). Boy, girl, boy again. *Newsweek,* p. 17.

LePoire, B. A., Burgoon, J. K., & Parrott, R. (1992). Status and privacy restoring communication in the workplace. *Journal of Applied Communication Research, 4,* 419–436.

Lepowksy, M. (1998). The influence of culture on behavior and the case of aggression: Women, men, and aggression in an egalitarian society. In D. Anselmi & A. Law (Eds.), *Questions of gender: Perspectives and paradoxes* (pp. 159–172). New York: McGraw-Hill.

Leslie, C. (1998, March 23). Separate and unequal? *Newsweek,* p. 55.

Levesque, J. (2001, May 1). News flash: Pretty faces sell. *Raleigh News and Observer,* p. 5E.

Levinson, D. (1989). *Family violence in cross-cultural perspective.* Newbury Park, CA: Sage.

Levinson, R., Powell, B., & Steelman, L. C. (1986). Social location, significant others, and body image among adolescents. *Social Psychology Quarterly, 49,* 330–337.

Levy, A., & Paludi, M. (1997). *Workplace sexual harassment.* Englewood Cliffs, NJ: Prentice Hall.

Levy, G. D. (1998). Effects of gender constancy and figure's height and sex on young children's gender-type attributions. *Journal of General Psychology, 125,* 65–89.

Levy, G. D. (1999). Gender-typed and non-gender-typed category awareness in toddlers. *Sex Roles, 39,* 851–861.

Lewis, E. T., & McCarthy, P. R. (1988). Perceptions of self-disclosure as a function of gender-linked variables. *Sex Roles, 19,* 47–56.

Lightfoot-Klein, H. (1989). *Prisoners of ritual: An odyssey into female genital circumcision in Africa.* New York: Harrington Park.

Liner, E. (2001, May 24). Women's TV enters a new golden age. *Raleigh News and Observer,* p. 9E.

Lingard, B., & Douglas, P. (1999). *Men engaging feminism: Profeminism, backlashes, and schooling.* Philadelphia: Open University Press.

Lippa, R. (2001). *Gender, nature, and nurture.* Mahwah, NJ: Erlbaum.

Lister, L. (1997, Fall). Among school girls. *Independent School,* pp. 42–45.

Lively, K. (2000, June 16). Women in charge. *Chronicle of Higher Education,* pp. A33–A35.

Livingston, J., & Testa, M. (2000). Qualitative analysis of women's perceived vulnerability to sexual aggression in a hypothetical dating context. *Journal of Social and Personal Relationships, 17,* 729–741.

Lobel, T., & Bar, E. (1997). Perceptions of masculinity and femininity of kibbutz and urban adolescents. *Sex Roles, 37,* 283–289.

Logwood, D. (1997, Summer). Ghetto feminism. *Hues,* pp. 36–37.

Logwood, D. (1998, Winter). One million strong. *Hues,* pp. 15–19.

Lont, C. (Ed.). (1995). *Women and media: Content, careers, criticism.* Belmont, CA: Wadsworth.

Lont, C. (2001). The influence of media on gender images. In D. Vannoy (Ed.), *Gender mosaics* (pp. 114–122). Los Angeles: Roxbury.

Lont, C. M. (1990). The roles assigned to females and males in non-music radio programming. *Sex Roles, 22,* 661–668.

Lorber, J. (1997). A woman's rights/cultural conflict. *Democratic Left, 2,* 3–5.

Lorber, J. (2001). *Gender inequality: Feminist theories and politics* (2nd ed.). Los Angeles: Roxbury.

Loscocco, K. (1997). Work-family linkages among self-employed women and men. *Journal of Vocational Behavior, 50,* 204–226.

Lott, B. (1989). Sexist discrimination as distancing behavior: II. Prime-time television. *Psychology of Women Quarterly, 13,* 341–355.

Loury, G. (1996, January/February). Joy and doubt on the mall. *Utne Reader,* pp. 70–71.

Lucal, B. (1995). The problem with "battered husbands." *Deviant Behavior: An Interdisciplinary Journal, 16,* 95–112.

Luebke, B. F. (1989). Out of focus: Images of women and men in newspaper photographs. *Sex Roles, 20,* 121–133.

Lugones, M., & Spelman, E. (1983). Have we got a theory for you! Feminist theory, cultural imperialism, and the demand for "the woman's voice." *Women's Studies International Forum, 6,* 573–581.

Lunneborg, P. W. (1990). *Women changing work.* Westport, CT: Greenwood Press.

Lydersen, K. (2003, June 9). The disappeared. *In These Times,* p. 5.

Lyman, P. (1987). The fraternal bond as a joking relationship: A case of the role of sexist jokes in male group bonding. In M. S. Kimmel (Ed.), *Changing men: New directions in research on men and masculinity* (pp. 148–163). Newbury Park, CA: Sage.

Lynch, J., & Kilmartin, C. (1999). *The pain behind the mask: Overcoming masculine depression.* Binghamton, New York: Haworth Press.

Lytton, H., & Romney, D. M. (1991). Parents' differential socialization of boys and girls: A meta-analysis. *Psychological Bulletin, 109,* 267–296.

Maccoby, E. E. (1990). Gender and relationships: A developmental account. *American Psychologist, 45,* 513–520.

Maccoby, E. E. (1998). *The two sexes: Growing up apart, coming together.* Cambridge, MA: Harvard University Press, Belknap.

Maccoby, E. E., & Jacklin, C. N. (1974). *The psychology of sex differences.* Stanford, CA: Stanford University Press.

Maccoby, E. E., & Jacklin, C. N. (1987). Gender segregation in childhood. *Advances in Child Development and Behavior, 20,* 239–287.

MacKinnon, C. A. (1987). *Feminism unmodified: Discourses on life and law.* Cambridge, MA: Harvard University Press.

Mahlstedt, D. (1992). *Female survivors of dating violence and their social networks.* Unpublished manuscript.

Major, B., Schmidlin, A. M., & Williams, L. (1990). Gender patterns in social touch: The impact of setting and age. *Journal of Personality and Social Psychology, 58,* 634–643.

Malandro, L. A., & Barker, L. L. (1983). *Nonverbal communication.* Reading, MA: Addison-Wesley.

Maltz, D. N., & Borker, R. (1982). A cultural approach to male–female miscommunication. In J. J. Gumpertz (Ed.), *Language and social identity* (pp. 196–216). Cambridge, England: Cambridge University Press.

The Man Poll. (2003, June 16). *Newsweek,* n.p.

Mansbridge, J. (1986). *Why we lost the ERA.* Chicago: University of Chicago Press.

Mapstone, E. (1998). *War of words: Women and men argue.* London: Random House.

Marble, M. (1994). Reconciling race and reality. *Media Studies Journal, 8,* 11–18.

Marcus, I. (1998). Violence against women. In W. Mankiller, G. Mink, M. Navarro, B. Smith, & G. Steinem (Eds.), *The reader's companion to U.S. women's history* (pp. 602–606). New York: Houghton Mifflin.

Marleau, J., Saucier, J. Borgeat, F., Bernazzani, O., & David, H. (1997). Mental representations concerning the sex of the fetus in pregnant nulliparous women who wished for a boy or a girl. *Psychological Reports, 80,* 273–274.

Marshall, C. (Ed.). (1996). *Feminist critical policy analysis: A perspective from primary and secondary schooling.* Washington, DC: Falmer.

Marshall, C. S., & Reihart, J. (1997). Gender issues in the classroom. *Clearinghouse, 70,* 333–338.

Martin, C. (1991). The role of cognition in understanding gender effects. In H. Reese (Ed.), *Advances in child development and behavior, 23* (pp. 110–142). San Diego: Academic Press.

Martin, C. (1994). Cognitive influences on the development and maintenance of gender segregation. In C. Leaper (Ed.), *New directions for child development* (pp. 87–116). San Francisco: Jossey-Bass.

Martin, C. (1997). *Gender cognitions and social relationships.* Paper presented at the meeting of the American Psychological Association, Chicago.

Martin, P. Y., & Hummer, R. A. (1989). Fraternities and rape on campus. *Gender and Society, 3,* 457–473.

Martin, T., & Doka, K. (2000). *Men don't cry . . . women do: Transcending gender stereotypes of grief.* Philadelphia: University of Pennsylvania Press.

Maslin, J. (1990, June 17). Bimbos embody retro rage. *New York Times,* pp. H13, H14.

Matthaei, J. (1998). Double day. In W. Mankiller, G. Mink, M. Navarro, B. Smith, & G. Steinem (Eds.), *The reader's companion to U.S. women's history* (p. 156). New York: Houghton Mifflin.

Maume, D. (1999). Glass ceilings and glass escalators. *Work & Occupations, 26,* 483–509.

Maume, D. (2001). Work-family conflict: Effects for job segregation and career perceptions. In D. Vannoy (Ed.), *Gender mosaics* (pp. 240–248). Los Angeles: Roxbury.

Maushart, S. (2001). *Wifework: What marriage really means for women.* New York: Bloomsbury.

May, L. (1998a). Many men still find strength in violence. *Chronicle of Higher Education,* p. B7.

May, L. (1998b). *Masculinity and morality.* Ithaca, NY: Cornell University Press.

Mayberry, K. (Ed.), (1996). *Teaching what you're not: Identity politics in higher education.* New York: New York University Press.

Mazur, E. (1989). Predicting gender differences in same-sex friendships from affiliation motive and value. *Psychology of Women Quarterly, 13,* 277–291.

Mazur, E., & Olver, R. (1987). Intimacy and structure: Sex differences in imagery of same-sex relationships. *Sex Roles, 16,* 533–558.

Mazzarella, S., & Pecora, N. (Eds.). (1999). *Growing up girls: Popular culture and the construction of identity.* New York: Peter Lang.

McAdoo, J. (Ed.). (1997). *Black families.* Thousand Oaks, CA: Sage.

McClish, G., & Bacon, J. (2002). "Telling the story her own way": The role of feminist standpoint theory in rhetorical studies. *Rhetoric Society Quarterly, 32,* 27–55.

McCloskey, D. (1999). *Crossing: A memoir.* Chicago: University of Chicago Press.

McCreary, D., Newcomb, M., & Sadava, S. (1998). Dimensions of the male gender role: A confirmatory analysis in men and women. *Sex Roles, 39,* 81–95.

McDowell, A. (1998, Winter). Making it big. *Hues,* p. 8.

McFarlane, J., & Wilson, P. (2000). Intimate partner violence: A gender comparison. *Journal of Interpersonal Violence, 15,* 158–169.

McGowen, K. R., & Hart, L. E. (1990). Still different after all these years: Gender differences in professional identity formation. *Professional Psychology: Research and Practice, 21,* 118–223.

McGuffey, S., & Rich, L. (2004). Playing in the gender transgression zone: Race, class, and hegemonic masculinity in middle childhood. In J. Spade & C. Valentine (Eds.), *The kaleidoscope of gender: Prisms, patterns and possibilities.* (pp. 172–183). Belmont, CA: Wadsworth.

McHale, S. M., Bartko, W. T., Crouter, A. C., & Perry-Jenkins, M. (1990). Children's housework and psychosocial functioning: The mediating effects of parents' sex-role behaviors and attitudes. *Child Development, 61*, 1413–1426.

Mead, G. H. (1934). *Mind, self, and society.* Chicago: University of Chicago Press.

Mead, M. (1935/1968). *Sex and temperament in three primitive societies.* New York: Dell.

Mealy, L. (2000). *Sex differences: Development and evolutionary strategies.* San Diego: Academic Press.

Mechling, E., & Mechling, J. (1994). The Jung and the restless: The mythopoetic men's movement. *Southern Communication Journal, 59*, 97–111.

Meckler, L. (1996, May 2). Report supports Family Leave Act. *Raleigh News and Observer,* p. 5A.

Medved, M. (2000, May 15). Macho military makes comeback. *USA Today,* p. 23A.

Mehrabian, A. (1981). *Silent messages: Implicit communication of emotion and attitudes* (2nd ed.). Belmont, CA: Wadsworth.

Mellor, M. (1998). *Feminism and ecology.* New York: New York University Press.

Meloy, R. (1998). *The psychology of stalking: Clinical and forensic perspectives.* New York: Academic Press.

Men use half a brain to listen, study finds. (2000, November 29). *Raleigh News and Observer,* p. 8A.

Menopause. (1992, May 25). *Newsweek,* pp. 71–80.

Mernissi, F. (2004). Size 6: The Western woman's harem. In J. Spade & C. Valentine (Eds.), *The kaleidoscope of gender: Prisms, patterns and possibilities.* (pp. 297–301). Belmont, CA: Wadsworth.

Merritt, B. (2000). Illusive reflections: African American women on primetime television. In A. González, M. Houston, & V. Chen (Eds.), *Our voices* (pp. 47–53). Los Angeles: Roxbury.

Messner, M. (1997a). Boyhood, organized sports, and the construction of masculinities. In E. Disch (Ed.), *Reconstructing gender* (pp. 57–73). Mountain View, CA: Mayfield.

Messner, M. (1997b). *Politics of masculinities: Men in movements.* Thousand Oaks, CA: Sage.

Messner, M. (1998). Masculinities and athletic careers. In M. Anderson & P. Collins (Eds.), *Race, class and gender* (3rd ed.) (pp. 195–208). Belmont, CA: Wadsworth.

Messner, M. (2000). Barbie girls versus sea monsters: Children constructing gender. *Gender and Society, 7*, 121–137.

Messner, M. (2001). When bodies are weapons: Masculinity and violence in sports. In D. Vannoy (Ed.), *Gender mosaics* (pp. 94–105). Los Angeles: Roxbury.

Messner, M. (2002, December 6). Needed: A fair assessment by a "budgetary umpire." *Chronicle of Higher Education,* pp. B8–B9.

Meyers, M. (1994). News of battering. *Journal of Communication, 44*, 47–62.

Meyers, M. (1997). *News coverage of violence against women: Engendering blame.* Thousand Oaks, CA: Sage.

Mickelson, A., & Smith, S. (1992). Education and the struggle against race, class, and gender inequality. In M. Andersen & P. H. Collins (Eds.), *Race, class, and gender: An anthology* (pp. 359–376). Belmont, CA: Wadsworth.

Mickelson, A., & Smith, S. (1998). Can education eliminate race, class, and gender equality? In M. Anderson & P. Collins (Eds.), *Race, class, and gender* (3rd ed.) (pp. 328–340). Belmont, CA: Wadsworth.

Middlebrook, D. (1998). *Suits me: The double life of Billy Tipton.* New York: Houghton Mifflin.

Mignon, S. (1998). Husband battering: A review of the debate over a controversial social phenomenon. In N. Jackson & G. Oates (Eds.), *Violence in intimate relationships* (pp. 137–154). Boston: Butterworth-Heinmann.

Mihalic, S., & Elliot, D. (1997). A social learning theory model of marital violence. *Journal of Family Violence, 12*, 21–47.

Milbank, D. (1997, October 3). More dads raise families without mom. *Wall Street Journal,* pp. B1, B2.

Miller, C. L. (1987). Qualitative differences among gender-stereotyped toys: Implications for cognitive and social development. *Sex Roles, 16*, 473–487.

Miller, J. B. (1986). *Toward a new psychology of women* (2nd ed.). Boston: Beacon.

Miller, M. (2003, June 16). Stop pretending nothing's wrong. *Newsweek,* pp. 71–72.

Million, J. (2003). *Woman's voice, woman's place: Lucy Stone and the birth of the women's rights movement.* Westport, CT: Praeger.

Million Family March picks up where men's march ended 5 years before. (2000, October 14). *Raleigh News and Observer,* p. 6B.

Mills, C. J., & Bohannon, W. E. (1983). Personality, sex-role orientation, and psychological health in stereotypically masculine groups of males. *Sex Roles, 9,* 1161–1169.

Mills, J. (1985, February). Body language speaks louder than words. *Horizon,* pp. 8–12.

Mills, R., Nazar, J., & Farrell, H. (2002). Child and parent perceptions of hurtful messages. *Journal of Social and Personal Relationships, 19,* 731–754.

Mills, S. (1999). Discourse competence: Or how to theorize strong women. In C. Hendricks & K. Oliver (Eds.), *Language and liberation* (pp. 81–97). Albany, NY: State University of New York Press.

Mink, G. (1998). Title IX. In W. Mankiller, G. Mink, M. Navarro, B. Smith, & G. Steinem (Eds.), *The reader's companion to U.S. women's history* (pp. 593–594). New York: Houghton Mifflin.

Minnich, E. (1998). Education. In W. Mankiller, G. Mink, M. Navarro, B. Smith, & G. Steinem (Eds.), *The reader's companion to U.S. women's history* (pp. 163–167). New York: Houghton Mifflin.

Mintz, L., & Betz, N. (1986). Sex differences in the nature, realism, and correlates of body image. *Sex Roles, 15,* 185–195.

Mischel, W. (1966). A social learning view of sex differences in behavior. In E. E. Maccoby (Ed.), *The development of sex differences* (pp. 93–106). Stanford, CA: Stanford University Press.

Moller, L., & Serbin, L. (1996). Antecedents of toddler gender segregation: Cognitive consonance, gender-typed toy preferences and behavioral compatibility. *Sex Roles, 35,* 445–460.

Molloy, B., & Herzberger, S. (1998). Body image and self-esteem: A comparison of African-American and Caucasian women. *Sex Roles, 38,* 631–643.

Monaghan, P. (1998, March 6). Beyond the Hollywood myths: Researchers examine stalkers and their victims. *Chronicle of Higher Education,* pp. A17, A20.

Money, J. (1986). *Venuses penuses: Sexology, sexosophy, and exigency theory.* Buffalo, NY: Prometheus.

Money, J. (1988). *Gay, straight, and in-between: The sexology of erotic orientation.* New York: Oxford University Press.

Money, J., & Ehrhardt, A. (1972). *Man and woman: Boy and girl.* Baltimore: Johns Hopkins University Press.

Moniz, D., & Pardue, D. (1996, June 23). Uncounted casualties. *Raleigh News and Observer,* pp. 21A, 22A.

Monsour, M. (1992). Meanings of intimacy in cross- and same-sex friendships. *Journal of Social and Personal Relationships, 9,* 277–295.

Monsour, M. (2002). *Women and men as friends: Relationships across the life span in the 21st century.* Mahwah, NJ: Erlbaum.

Morgan, M. (1973). *The total woman.* New York: Pocket.

Morgan, M. (1987). Television, sex-role attitudes, and sex-role behavior. *Journal of Early Adolescence, 7,* 269–282.

Morgan, R. (2002, September 27). The men in the mirror. *Chronicle of Higher Education,* pp. A53–A54.

Morgan, R. (Ed.). (2003). *Sisterhood is forever: The women's anthology for a new millennium.* New York: Washington Square Press.

Morgana, C., & Anzaldúa, G. (Eds.). (1983). *This bridge called my back: Writings by radical women of color.* New York: Kitchen Table: Women of Color Press.

Morin, R., & Rosenfeld, M. (1998, April 19). Men and women: What still divides us? *Raleigh News and Observer,* pp. 23A, 24A.

Morrison, A. M., & Von Glinow, M. A. (1990). Women and minorities in management. *American Psychologist, 45,* 200–208.

Mulac, A. (1998). The gender-linked language effect: Do language differences really make a difference? In D. J. Canary & K. Dindia (Eds.), *Sex differences and similarities in communication: Critical essays and empirical investigations of sex and gender in interaction* (pp. 127–153). Mahwah, NJ: Erlbaum.

Mulac, A., Jansma, L., & Linz, D. (2003). Men's behavior toward women after viewing sexually explicit films: Degradation makes a difference. *Communication Monographs, 69*, 311–328.

Mulac, A., Wiemann, J. M., Widenmann, S. J., & Gibson, T. W. (1988). Male/female language differences and effects in same-sex and mixed-sex dyads: The gender-linked language effect. *Communication Monographs, 55*, 315–335.

Mullen, P., & Pathé, M. (2000). *Stalkers and victims.* Cambridge, MA: Cambridge University Press.

Murnen, S., & Smolak, L. (1997). Femininity, masculinity and disordered eating: A meta analytic review. *International Journal of Eating Disorders, 22*, 231–242.

Murphy, B., & Zorn, T. (1996). Gendered interaction in professional relationships. In J. T. Wood (Ed.), *Gendered relationships: A reader* (pp. 213–232). Mountain View, CA: Mayfield.

Murphy, B. C. (1997). Difference and diversity: Gay and lesbian couples. In M. Duberman (Ed.), *A queer world* (pp. 345–357). New York: New York University Press.

Murphy-Milano, S. (1996). *Defending our lives.* New York: Anchor/Doubleday.

Murray, C. B. (1996). Estimating achievement performance: A confirmation bias. *Journal of Black Psychology, 22*, 67–85.

Murrell, A. J., Frieze, I. H., & Frost, J. L. (1991). Aspiring to careers in male- and female-dominated professions. A study of Black and White college women. *Psychology of Women Quarterly, 15*, 103–126.

Myers, P. N., & Biocca, F. A. (1992). The elastic body image: The effect of television advertising on body image distortion in young women. *Journal of Communication, 3*, 108–133.

Nadesan, M., & Trethewey, A. (2000). Performing the enterprising subject: Gendered strategies of success. *Text and Performance Quarterly, 20*, 223–250.

Namaste, V. (2000). *Invisible lives: The erasure of transsexual and transgendered people.* Chicago: University of Chicago Press.

Nanda, S. (2004). Multiple genders among North American Indians. In J. Spade & C. Valentine (Eds.), *The kaleidoscope of gender* (pp. 64–70). Belmont, CA: Wadsworth.

Natalle, E. (1996). Gendered issues in the workplace. In J. T. Wood (Ed.), *Gendered relationships: A reader* (pp. 253–274). Mountain View, CA: Mayfield.

National Coalition Against Domestic Violence. (1999, July 10). Retrieved from http:www.ncadv.org

Navarro, M. (1998, Winter). Fashion a la mode. *Hues,* p. 9.

Neinas, C. M. (2002, December 6). Can we avoid unintended consequences for men? *Chronicle of Higher Education,* p. B8.

Nelson, E. (1996, March 18). Why Johnny can't empathize: No girls in his class? *Wall Street Journal,* pp. B1, B6.

Nelson, M. B. (1994b). *The stronger women get, the more men love football: Sexism and the American culture of sports.* New York: Harcourt Brace.

Nesbitt, P., Baust, J., & Bailey, E. (2001). Women's status in the Christian church. In D. Vannoy (Ed.), *Gender mosaics* (pp. 386–396). Los Angeles: Roxbury.

Neuborne, E. (1995). Imagine my surprise. In B. Findlen (Ed.), *Listen up: Voices from the next feminist generation* (pp. 29–35). Seattle: Seal Press.

A new court decision. (1992, September). *The Newsletter,* p. 5.

Newburger, E. (1999). *The men they will become: The nature and nurture of male character.* Cambridge, MA: Perseus Books.

Newcombe, N. (2002, December 14). Is sociobiology ready for prime time? *Chronicle of Higher Education,* pp. B10–B11.

Nichter, M. (2000). *Fat talk: What girls and their parents say about dieting.* Cambridge, MA: Harvard University Press.

Nigro, G. N., Hill, D. E., Gelbein, M. E., & Clark, C. L. (1988). Changes in the facial prominence of women and men over the last decade. *Psychology of Women Quarterly, 12*, 225–235.

Nikken, P., & Peeters, A. L. (1988). Children's perceptions of television reality. *Journal of Broadcasting and Electronic Media, 32*, 441–452.

Noble, B. P. (1993, January 2). Bias up against pregnant workers. *Raleigh News and Observer,* pp. A1, A8.

Noddings, N. (2002). *Starting at home: Caring and social policy.* Berkeley: University of California Press.

Nolen-Hoeksema, S. (2003). *Women who think too much.* New York: Henry Holt.

Noller, P. (1986). Sex differences in nonverbal communication: Advantage lost or supremacy regained? *Australian Journal of Psychology, 38,* 23–32.

Northrup, C. (1995). *Women's bodies, women's wisdom.* New York: Bantam.

Nussbaum, J. F. (1992). Effective teacher behaviors. *Communication Education, 41,* 167–180.

Nussbaum, M. (1992, October 18). Justice for women! *New York Review of Books,* pp. 43–48.

Oakley, A. (2002). *Gender on planet earth.* New York: The New Press.

O'Connell, L. (1995, April 21). Internal, external: Women and men handle stress differently. *Raleigh News and Observer,* p. D5.

O'Kelly, C. G., & Carney, L. S. (1986). *Women and men in society* (2nd ed.). Belmont, CA: Wadsworth.

Okin, S. M. (1989). *Gender, justice and the family.* New York: Basic Books.

O'Leary, V. E., & Ickovics, J. R. (1991). Cracking the glass ceiling. Overcoming isolation and alienation. In U. Sekeran & F. Long (Eds.), *Pathways to excellence: New patterns for human utilization.* Beverly Hills: Sage.

Olien, M. (1978). *The human myth.* New York: Harper & Row.

Oliker, S. (1989). *Best friends and marriage: Exchange among women.* Berkeley: University of California Press.

Oliker, S. (2001). Gender and friendship. In D. Vannoy (Ed.), *Gender mosaics* (pp. 195–204). Los Angeles: Roxbury.

O'Meara, J. D. (1989). Cross-sex friendship: Four basic challenges of an ignored relationship. *Sex Roles, 21,* 525–543.

Orenstein, P. (2000). *Flux: Women on sex, work, love, kids and life in a half-changed world.* New York: Doubleday.

Orion, D. (1997). *I know you really love me: A psychiatrist's journal of erotomania, stalking, and obsessive love.* New York: Macmillan.

Orr, C. (1997). Charting the currents of the third wave. *Hypatia, 12,* 29–46.

Ossana, S., Helms, J., & Leonard, M. (1992). Do "womanist" identity attitudes influence college women's self-esteem and perceptions of environmental bias? *Journal of Counseling and Development, 70,* 179–185.

Otten, A. L. (1995, January 27). Women and men still see things differently. *Wall Street Journal,* p. B1.

Oyler, C., Jennings, G., & Lozada, P. (2001). Silenced gender: The construction of a male primary educator. *Teaching and Teacher Education, 17,* 367–379.

Paetzold, R., & O'Leary-Kelly, A. (1993). The legal context of sexual harassment. In G. L. Kreps (Ed.), *Sexual harassment: Communication implications* (pp. 63–77). Cresskill, NJ: Hampton.

Painter, N. (1996). *Sojourner Truth: A life, a symbol.* New York: Norton.

Palm, G. (1993). Involved fatherhood: A second chance. *Journal of Men's Studies, 2,* 139–155.

Palmer, H. T., & Lee, J. A. (1990). Female workers' acceptance in traditionally male-dominated blue-collar jobs. *Sex Roles, 22,* 607–625.

Panee, B. (1994). Defending the "date-rape crisis": A critical discussion of Katie Roiphe's *The morning after: Sex, fear, and feminism on campus.* Paper submitted in Communication Studies 111, Chapel Hill, University of North Carolina.

Paradise, L. V., & Wall, S. M. (1986). Children's perceptions of male and female principals and teachers. *Sex Roles, 14,* 1–7.

Parlee, M. B. (1973). The premenstrual syndrome. *Psychological Bulletin, 80,* 454–465.

Parlee, M. B. (1979, May). Conversational politics. *Psychology Today,* pp. 48–56.

Parlee, M. B. (1987). Media treatment of premenstrual syndrome. In B. E. Ginsburg & B. F. Carter (Eds.), *Premenstrual syndrome.* New York: Plenum Press.

Pastore, A. L., & Maguire, K. (Eds.). (2001). *Sourcebook on criminal justice statistics.* Retrieved April 2, 2003, from http://www.albany.edu/sourcebook

Patterson, C. J. (2000). Family relationships of lesbians and gay men. *Journal of Marriage and the Family, 62,* 1052–1069.

Paul, E., & White, K. (1990). The development of intimate relationships in late adolescence. *Adolescence, 25,* 375–400.

Pearson, J. C. (1985). *Gender and communication.* Dubuque, IA: William C. Brown.

Pearson, J., West, R., & Turner, Ly. (1995). *Gender and communication* (3rd ed). Dubuque, IA: Brown and Benchmark.

Peirce, K. (1990). A feminist theoretical perspective on the socialization of teenage girls through *Seventeen* magazine. *Sex Roles, 23,* 491–500.

Pendergast, T. (2000). *Creating the modern man: American magazines and consumer culture, 1900–1950.* Columbia: University of Missouri Press.

Pereira, J. (1994, September 23). Oh, boy! In toyland, you get more if you're male. *Wall Street Journal,* pp. B1, B3.

Peterson, C. D., Baucom, D. H., Elliott, M. J., & Farr, P. A. (1989). The relationship between sex role identity and marital adjustment. *Sex Roles, 21,* 775–787.

Peterson, S. B., & Kroner, T. (1992). Gender biases in textbooks for introductory psychology and human development. *Psychology of Women Quarterly, 16,* 17–36.

Phillips, G. M., Gouran, D. S., Kuehn, S. A., & Wood, J. T. (1993). *Professionalism: A survival guide for beginning academics.* Cresskill, NJ: Hampton.

Piaget, J. (1932/1965). *The moral judgment of the child.* New York: Free Press.

Pike, K., & Striegel-Moore, R. (1997). Disordered eating and eating disorders. In S. Gallant, G. Keita, & R. Royak-Schaler (Eds.), *Healthcare for women* (pp. 97–114). Washington, DC: American Psychological Association.

Pinsky, L., Erickson, R., & Schimke, R. (Eds.). (1999). *Genetic disorders of human sexual development.* New York: Oxford University Press.

Pitts, L., Jr. (1993, June 30). Music's new wave of sexism is especially discordant. *Miami Herald,* pp. 1E, 7E.

Pleck, E. (1987). *Domestic tyranny: The making of American social policy against family violence from colonial times to the present.* New York: Oxford University Press.

Pleck, J. H. (1981). *The myth of masculinity.* Cambridge, MA: MIT Press.

Pollack, W. (1990). Sexual harassment: Women's experience vs. legal definitions. *Harvard Women's Law Review, 13,* 35–85.

Pollack, W. (2000). *Real boys: Rescuing ourselves from the myths of boyhood.* New York: Owl Books.

Pollitt, K. (1994). *Reasonable creatures: Essays on women and feminism.* New York: Knopf.

Pollitt, K. (1996, May 13). Women's rights, human rights. *Progressive,* p. 9.

Pollitt, K. (1999, March 29). Women's rights: As the world turns. *The Nation,* p. 9.

Pollitt, K. (2000, May 1). Abortion history 101. *The Nation,* p. 8.

Pomerleau, A., Bolduc, D., Malcuit, G., & Cossette, L. (1990). Pink or blue: Environmental stereotypes in the first two years of life. *Sex Roles, 22,* 359–367.

Ponton, L. (1997). *The romance of risk: Why teenagers do the things they do.* New York: Basic Books.

Pope, H., Phillips, K., & Olivardia, R. (2002). *The Adonis complex: The secret crisis of male body obsession.* New York: Simon & Schuster.

Popenoe, D. (1996). *Life without father.* New York: Free Press.

Posavac, H., Posavac, S., & Posavac, E. (1998). Exposure to media images of female attractiveness and concern with body weight among young people. *Sex Roles, 38,* 187–201.

Powell, A., & Kahn, A. (1995). Racial differences in women's desire to be thin. *Journal of Eating Disorders, 17,* 191–195.

Powlishta, K. (2000). The effect of target age on the activation of gender stereotypes. *Sex Roles, 42,* 271–282.

Powlishta, K., Serbin, L., & Moller, L. (1993). The stability of individual differences in gender typing: Implications for understanding gender segregation. *Sex Roles, 29,* 723–788.

Preves, S. (1998). For the sake of the children: De-stigmatizing intersexuality. *Journal of Clinical Ethics, 9,* 411–420.

Preves, S. (2004). Sexing the intersexed: An analysis of sociocultural responses to intersexuality. In J. Spade & C. Valentine (Eds.), *The kaleidoscope of gender: Prisms, patterns, and possibilities* (pp. 31–45). Belmont, CA: Wadsworth.

Promise Keepers: "Men have dropped the ball." (1997, October 1). *USA Today,* p. 14A.

Public Agenda Foundation. (1990). *Remedies for racial inequality: Why progress has stalled, what should be done.* Dubuque, IA: Kendall/Hunt.

Puka, B. (1990). The liberation of caring: A different voice for Gilligan's different voice. *Hypatia, 5,* 59–82.

Purcell, P., & Stewart, L. (1990). Dick and Jane in 1989. *Sex Roles, 22,* 177–185.

Quindlen, A. (1994, March 20). The unending nightmare of violence against women. *Raleigh News and Observer,* p. A23.

Quindlen, A. (2003, April 7). Not so safe back home. *Newsweek,* p. 72.

Quinn, J. (2000, July 17). Revisiting the mommy track. *Newsweek,* p. 44.

Rabidue v. Osceola Refining Company. 805F 2nd 611, 626 Cir (6th Cir 1986).

Radford-Hill, S. (2000). *Further to fly: Black women and the politics of empowerment.* Minneapolis, MN: University of Minnesota Press.

Ragsdale, D. (1996). Gender, satisfaction level, and the use of relational maintenance strategies in marriage. *Communication Monographs, 63,* 354–369.

Rakow, L. F. (1992). "Don't hate me because I'm beautiful": Feminist resistance in advertising's irresistible meanings. *Southern Communication Journal, 57,* 132–141.

Ransom, F. (1993, December 23). Black women man the ramparts for war on "gangsta rap" sexism. *Raleigh News and Observer,* p. A6.

Ranson, G. (2001). Men at work: Change or no change in the era of the "new father?" *Men and Masculinities, 4,* 3–26.

Rapoport, R., Bailyn, L., Kolb, D., & Fletcher, J. (1998). Relinking life and work: Toward a better future. *Innovations in Management Series.* Waltham, MA: Pegasus.

Rapping, E. (1994, May). Women are from Venus, men are from Mars. *Progressive,* pp. 40–42.

Rasmussen, J. L., & Moley, B. E. (1986). Impression formation as a function of the sex role appropriateness of linguistic behavior. *Sex Roles, 14,* 149–161.

Real, T. (1997). *I don't want to talk about it: Overcoming the secret legacy of male depression.* New York: Scribner's.

Reay, D. (2001). "Spice girls," "nice girls," "girlie girls," and "tomboys": Gender discourses: Girls' culture and femininities in the primary classroom. *Gender & Education, 13,* 153–167.

Reeder, H. (1996). A critical look at gender differences in communication research. *Communication Studies, 47,* 318–330.

Reich, M. (1991). *Toxic politics: Responding to chemical disasters.* Ithaca: Cornell University Press.

Reich, N. (2003). "Identity matters: Articulations of women's identities in relation to gendered violence: Efficacious rhetorical strategies for women and organizations within the ongoing social movement to end gendered violence." Unpublished doctoral dissertation, The University of North Carolina at Chapel Hill.

Reis, H. T. (1998). Gender differences in intimacy and related behaviors: Context and process. In D. Canary & K. Dindia (Eds.), *Sex differences and similarities in communication* (pp. 203–232). Mahwah, NJ: Erlbaum.

Reisberg, L. (1999, November 5). Violence-studies program takes aim at social evils and student attitudes. *Chronicle of Higher Education,* A60–A61.

Reisman, J. M. (1990). Intimacy in same-sex friendships. *Sex Roles, 23,* 65–82.

Reiss, D. (2000). *The relational code: Genetic and social influences on social development.* Cambridge, MA: Harvard University Press.

Reuther, R. R. (Ed.). (1974). *Religion and sexism: Images of woman in the Jewish and Christian traditions.* New York: Simon & Schuster.

Reuther, R. R. (1975). *New woman/new earth: Sexist ideologies and human liberation.* New York: Seabury.

Reuther, R. R. (1983). *Sexism and God-talk: Toward a feminist theology.* Boston: Beacon.

Reuther, R. R. (2001). Ecofeminism and healing ourselves, healing the earth. In D. Vannoy (Ed.), *Gender mosaics* (pp. 406–414). Los Angeles: Roxbury.

Rhodes, J. (1995). Television's realist portrayal of African-American women and the case of *L. A. Law.* In G. Dines & J. Humez (Eds.), *Gender, race, and class in media: A text reader* (pp. 424–429). Thousand Oaks, CA: Sage.

Rice, J. K., & Hemmings, A. (1988). Women's colleges and women achievers: An update. Signs: *Journal of Women in Culture and Society, 13,* 546–559.

Rich, A. (1979). *On lies, secrets and silences: Selected prose, 1966–1978.* New York: Norton.

Richmond, V., & McCroskey, J. (2000). *Nonverbal behavior in interpersonal relations* (4th ed). Boston: Allyn & Bacon.

Riechmann, D. (1996, February 22). Single-sex classes get a star for achievement. *Raleigh News and Observer,* p. 8A.

Riessman, C. K. (1990). *Divorce talk: Women and men make sense of personal relationships.* New Brunswick, NJ: Rutgers University Press.

Risman, B., & Godwin, S. (2001). Twentieth-century changes in economic work and family. In D. Vannoy (Ed.), *Gender mosaics* (pp. 134–144). Los Angeles: Roxbury.

Risman, B. J. (1989). Can men mother? Life as a single father. In B. J. Risman & P. Schwartz (Eds.), *Gender in intimate relationships* (pp. 155–164). Belmont, CA: Wadsworth.

Rives, K. (2003, April 13). What are the stakes? *Raleigh News & Observer,* pp. 27A–28A.

Rodin, J., Silberstein, L., & Striegel-Moore, R. H. (1985). Women and weight: A normative discontent. In T. B. Sonderegger (Ed.), *Nebraska symposium on motivation 1984: Psychology and gender* (Vol. 32, pp. 267–307). Lincoln: University of Nebraska Press.

Roe v. Wade at twenty-five (1998, February). *The Progressive,* pp. 8–9.

Rogers, M. (1999). *Barbie culture.* Thousand Oaks, CA: Sage.

Rohlfing, M. (1995). "Doesn't anybody stay in one place anymore?" An exploration of the understudied phenomenon of long-distance relationships. In J. T. Wood & S. W. Duck (Eds.), *Understanding personal relationships, 6: Understudied relationships: Off the beaten track* (pp. 173–196). Thousand Oaks, CA: Sage.

Roiphe, K. (1993). *The morning after: Sex, fear, and feminism on campus.* Boston: Little, Brown.

Romaine, S. (1999). *Communicating gender.* Mahwah, NJ: Erlbaum.

Root, M. P. P. (1990). Disordered eating in women of color. *Sex Roles, 22,* 525–536.

Rose, S., & Frieze, I. H. (1989). Young singles' scripts for a first date. *Gender and Society, 3,* 258–268.

Rosen, R. (2001). *The world split open: How the modern women's movement changed America.* New York: Viking.

Rosener, J. (1990, November/December). Ways women lead. *Harvard Business Review,* pp. 119–125.

Rosenfeld, M. (2001, January 9). Sugar and spice and POW! *Raleigh News and Observer,* pp. 1E, 3E.

Rosenthal, R., & DePaulo, B. M. (1979). Sex differences in eavesdropping on nonverbal cues. *Journal of Personality and Social Psychology, 37,* 273–285.

Rosenwasser, S. M., Lingenfelter, M., & Harrington, A. F. (1989). Nontraditional gender role portrayals on television and children's gender role perceptions. *Journal of Applied Developmental Psychology, 10,* 97–105.

Ross, S. I., & Jackson, J. M. (1991). Teachers' expectations for Black males' and Black females' academic achievement. *Personality and Social Psychology Bulletin, 17,* 78–82.

Roth, M. (1994). *Mother journey.* New York: Spinster's Ink.

Rothenberg, P., Schafhausen, N., & Schneider, C. (Eds.). (2000). *Race, class and gender in the United States: An integrated study.* New York: Worth.

Rowe, M. (1990). Barriers to equality: The power of subtle discrimination to maintain unequal opportunity. *Employee Responsibilities and Rights Journal, 3,* 153–163.

Rowling, M. (2002, July 22). Europe crawls ahead. *In These Times,* pp. 15–17.

Rubin, B. M. (1994, April 17). The daddy track. *Raleigh News and Observer,* p. A17.

Rubin, J. Z., Provenzano, F. J., & Luria, Z. (1974). The eye of the beholder: Parents' views on sex of newborns. *American Journal of Orthopsychiatry, 44,* 512–519.

Rubin, L. (1985). *Just friends: The role of friendship in our lives.* New York: Harper & Row.

Ruble, D., & Martin, C. (1998). Gender development. In W. Damon (Ed.), *The handbook of child psychology* (pp. 933–1017). New York: Wiley.

Ruddick, S. (1989). *Maternal thinking: Toward a politics of peace.* Boston: Beacon.

Rudman, L. A. (1998). Self-promotion as a risk factor for women: The costs and benefits of counter stereotypical impression management. *Journal of Personality and Social Psychology ,74,* 629–645.

Rugg, M. (1995). LA difference vive. *Nature, 373,* 561–562.

Rundblad, G. (2001). Gender, power, and sexual harassment. In D. Vannoy (Ed.), *Gender mosaics* (pp. 352–362). Los Angeles: Roxbury.

Rusbult, C. (1987). Responses to dissatisfaction in close relationships: The exit-voice-loyalty-neglect model. In

D. Perlman & S. W. Duck (Eds.), *Intimate relationships: Development, dynamics, and deterioration* (pp. 209–238). London: Sage.

Russell, D. E. H. (Ed.). (1993). *Feminist views on pornography.* Cholchester, VT: Teachers College Press.

Rutter, V., & Schwartz, P. (1996). Same-sex couples: Courtship, commitment, and context. In A. Auhagen & M. von Salisch (Eds.), *The diversity of human relationships* (pp. 197–226). New York: Cambridge University Press.

Ryan, B. (2004). Identity politics in the women's movement. In J. Spade & C. Valentine (Eds.), *The kaleidoscope of gender: Prisms, patterns and possibilities.* (pp. 104–113). Belmont, CA: Wadsworth.

Ryan, K., & Kanjorski, J. (1998). The enjoyment of sexist humor, rape attitudes, and relationship aggression in college students. *Sex Roles, 38,* 743–755.

Ryan, M. (1979). *Womanhood in America: From colonial times to the present* (2nd ed.). New York: New Viewpoints.

Sadker, M., & Sadker, D. (1984). *The report card on sex bias.* Washington, DC: Mid-Atlantic Center for Sex Equity.

Sadker, M., & Sadker, D. (1986, March). Sexism in the classroom: From grade school to graduate school. *Phi Delta Kappan,* pp. 512–515.

Sadker, M., & Sadker, D. (1994). *Failing at fairness: How America's schools cheat girls.* New York: Simon & Schuster.

Sagrestano, L., Heavey, C., & Christensen, A. (1998). Theoretical approaches to understanding sex differences and similarities in conflict behavior. In D. J. Canary & K. Dindia (Eds.), *Sex differences and similarities in communication: Critical essays and empirical investigations of sex and gender in interaction* (pp. 287–302). Mahwah, NJ: Erlbaum.

Sales, K. (1987, September 26). Ecofeminism—a new perspective. *The Nation,* pp. 302–305.

Sallinen-Kuparinen, A. (1992). Teacher communicator style. *Communication Education, 41,* 153–166.

Samovar, L., Porter, R., & Stefani, L. (1998). *Communication between cultures* (2nd ed). Belmont, CA: Wadsworth.

Samuels, A. (1997, November 24). Black beauty's new face. *Newsweek,* p. 68.

Samuels, A. (2003, March 3). Time to tell it like it is. *Newsweek,* pp. 52–55.

Sanday, P. R. (1986). Rape and the silencing of the feminine. In S. Tomaselli & R. Porter (Eds.), *Rape* (pp. 84–101). Oxford, England: Basil Blackwell.

Sanders, M., & Rock, M. (1988). *Waiting for prime time: The women of television news.* Urbana: University of Illinois Press.

Sandler, B. (1996, June 27). Letter to the editor. *Wall Street Journal,* p. A19.

Sandler, B. (2004). The chilly climate: Subtle ways in which women are often treated differently at work and in classrooms. In J. Spade & C. Valentine (Eds.), *The kaleidoscope of gender: Prisms, patterns, and possibilities* (pp. 187–190). Belmont, CA: Wadsworth.

Sandler, B. R., & Hall, R. M. (1986). *The campus climate revisited: Chilly for women faculty, administrators, and graduate students.* Washington, DC: Association of American Colleges, Project on the Status and Education of Women.

Sandler, B. R., Silverberg, L. A., & Hall, R. M. (1996). *The chilly classroom climate: A guide to improve the education of women.* Washington, DC: National Association for Women in Education.

Sanger, M. (1914, June). Suppression. *The woman rebel,* p. 1.

Sarkela, S. J., Ross, S. R., & Lowe, M. A. (2003). *From megaphones to microphones: Speeches of American women, 1920–1960.* Westport, CT: Praeger.

Sartre, J. P. (1966). *Being and nothingness: An essay in phenomenological ontology.* New York: Citadel.

Saucier, D., & Kimura, D. (1998). Intrapersonal motor, but not extra-personal targeting skill is enhanced during the midluteal phase of the menstrual cycle. *Developmental Neuropsychology, 14,* 385–398.

Saurer, M. K., & Eisler, R. M. (1990). The role of masculine gender roles' stress in expressivity and social support network factors. *Sex Roles, 23,* 261–271.

Scarf, M. (1987). *Intimate partners.* New York: Random House.

Scelfo, J. (2002, December 9). Kneed to know. *Newsweek,* pp. 88, 90

Schaef, A. W. (1981). *Women's reality.* St. Paul, MN: Winston.

Schein, V. E. (2001). A global look at psychological barriers to women's progress in management. *Journal of Social Issues, 57,* 675–688.

Schellhardt, T. (1997, March 31). Dropping out. *Wall Street Journal,* p. 12.

Scheper-Hughes, N. (1994). *Death without weeping.* Berkeley: University of California Press.

Scheuble, L., & Johnson, D. R. (1993). Marital name change: Plans and attitudes of college students. *Journal of Marriage and the Family, 55,* 747–754.

Schiebinger, L. (1999). *Has feminism changed science?* Cambridge, MA: Harvard University Press.

Schmetzer, U. (1997, August 13). From abused wife to India's avenging angel. *Raleigh News and Observer,* p. 13A.

Schmidt, P. (1998, October 30). U. of Michigan prepares to defend admissions policy in court. *Chronicle of Higher Education,* pp. A32–A34.

Schmidt, P. (2001, May 18). Debating the benefits of affirmative action. *Chronicle of Higher Education,* pp. A25–A26.

Schmidt, P. (2003, April 11). Supreme Court signals caution on affirmative action. *Chronicle of Higher Education,* pp. A31–A33.

Schmitt, E. (2001, May 15). For first time, nuclear families drop below 25% of households. *New York Times,* p. A1.

Schneider, B., & Stevenson, D. (1999). *The ambitious generation.* Cambridge, MA: Yale University Press.

Schneider, B. E., & Gould, M. (1987). Female sexuality: Looking back into the future. In B. B. Hess and M. M. Ferree (Eds.), *Analyzing gender: A handbook of social science research* (pp. 120–153). Newbury Park, CA: Sage.

Schneider, J., & Hacker, S. (1973). Sex role imagery and use of the generic "man" in introductory texts: A case in the sociology of sociology. *American Sociologist, 8,* 12–18.

Schroedel, J. R. (1990). Blue-collar women: Paying the price at home and on the job. In H. Y. Grossman & N. L. Chester (Eds.), *The experience and meaning of work in women's lives* (pp. 241–260). Hillsdale, NJ: Erlbaum.

Schroeder, L. O. (1986). A rose by any other name: Post-marital right to use maiden name: 1934–1982. *Sociology and Social Research, 70,* 290–293.

Schrof, J. M. (1994, April 11). A sporting chance? *U.S. News and World Report,* pp. 51–53.

Schutzman, M. (1999). *The real thing: Performance, hysteria, and advertising.* Hanover, NH: Wesleyan University Press.

Schwalbe, M. (1996). *Unlocking the cage: The men's movement, gender, politics, and American culture.* Cambridge, MA: Oxford University Press.

Schwartz, B., & Cellini, H. (1995). Female sex offenders. In B. Schwartz & H. Cellini (Eds.), *The sex offender: Corrections, treatment, and legal practice* (Vol. 1, pp. 5-1–5-22). Kingston, NJ: Civic Research Institute.

Schwartz, F. (1989, January/February). Management women and the new facts of life. *Harvard Business Review,* pp. 65–76.

Schwartz, P. (1994). *Peer marriage: How love between equals really works.* New York: Free Press.

Schwartz, P., & Rutter, V. (1998). *The gender of sexuality.* Newbury Park, CA: Pine Forge Press.

Schwichtenberg, C. (1989). The "motherlode" of feminist research: Congruent paradigms in the analysis of beauty culture. In B. Dervin, L. Grossberg, B. J. O'Keefe, & E. Wartella (Eds.), *Rethinking communication* (Vol. 2, pp. 291–306). Beverly Hills: Sage.

Schwichtenberg, C. (1992). Madonna's postmodern feminism: Bringing the margins to center. *Southern Communication Journal, 57,* 120–131.

Scott, R., & Tetreault, L. (1987). Attitudes of rapists and other violent offenders toward women. *Journal of Social Psychology, 124,* 375–380.

Scrivner, R. (1997). Gay men and nonrelational sex. In R. Levant & G. Brooks (Eds.), *Men and sex* (pp. 229–257). New York: Wiley.

Scully, D. (1990). *Understanding sexual violence: A study of convicted rapists.* Boston: Unwin Hyman.

Secunda, V. (1992). *Women and their fathers.* New York: Delta.

Segal, A. T., with Zellner, W. (1992, June 8). Corporate women: Progress? Sure. But the playing field is still far from level. *Business Week,* pp. 74–78.

Segerstråle, U. (2000). *Defenders of the truth: The battle for science in the sociobiology debate and beyond.* UK: Oxford University Press.

Seiter, E. (1995). Different children, different dreams. In G. Dines & J. Humez (Eds.), *Gender, race and class in media* (pp. 99–108). Thousand Oaks, CA: Sage.

Seligmann, J. (1994, May 2). The pressure to lose. *Newsweek,* pp. 60–61.

Sen, A. (1999). *Development as freedom.* New York: Anchor.

Seplow, S. (1996, January 19). "Old boy" networks fall. *Raleigh News and Observer,* pp. 1D, 5D.

Sexism in the schoolhouse. (1992, February 24). *Newsweek,* p. 62.

Sexually harassed male guard awarded $3.75 million. (1999, May 30). *Raleigh News and Observer,* p. 9A.

Seymour, E. (1995). The loss of women from science, mathematics, and engineering undergraduate majors: An explanatory account. *Science Education, 74,* 437–473.

Shalit, W. (1999). *A return to modesty: Discovering the lost virtue.* New York: Free Press.

Shandler, S. (1999). *Ophelia speaks: Adolescent girls write about their search for self.* New York: HarperPerennial.

Shapiro, J., & Kroeger, L. (1991). Is life just a romantic novel? The relationship between attitudes about intimate relationships and the popular media. *American Journal of Family Therapy, 19,* 226–236.

Shapiro, L. (1990, May 28). Guns and dolls. *Newsweek,* pp. 56–65.

Sharkey, B. (1993, February). You've come a long way, Madison Avenue. *Lear's,* p. 94.

Sharpe, R. (1994, January 31). Education of girls trails that of boys in many countries. *Wall Street Journal,* p. B5.

Shea, C. (1998, January 30). Why depression strikes more women than men: "Ruminative coping" may provide answers. *Chronicle of Higher Education,* p. A14.

Sheehan, R. (1999, February 28). Mom's working doesn't harm child, study finds. *Raleigh News and Observer,* pp. 1A, 12A.

Shellenbarger, S. (1993, December 17). More dads take off to look after baby. *Wall Street Journal,* p. B1.

Shellenbarger, S. (1997, April 30). Women indicate satisfaction with role of big breadwinner. *Wall Street Journal,* B1.

Sheridan, V. (2001). *Crossing over: Liberating the transgendered Christian.* Cleveland, OH: Pilgrim.

Sherrod, D. (1989). The influence of gender on same-sex friendships. In C. Hendrick (Ed.), *Close relationships* (pp. 164–186). Newbury Park, CA: Sage.

She's a woman, offer her less. (2001, May 7). *Business Week,* p. 12.

Shields, V. R., & Heinecken, D. (2001). *Measuring up: How advertising affects self-image.* Philadelphia, PA: University of Pennsylvania Press.

Shimron, Y. (1997, January 22). Men unite to live their faith. *Raleigh News and Observer,* pp. 1A, 6A.

Shimron, Y. (2002, July 21). Promise Keepers fill the house—and heart. *Raleigh News and Observer,* pp. 1A, 17A.

Siever, M. D. (1988, August). *Sexual orientation, gender, and the perils of sexual objectification.* Paper presented at the American Psychological Association, Atlanta.

Silverstein, L., & Auerbach, C. (1999). Deconstructing the essential father. *American Psychologist, 54,* 397–407.

Silverstein, L., Auerbach, C., Grieco, L., & Dunkel, F. (1999). Do Promise Keepers dream of feminist sheep? *Sex Roles, 40,* 665–688.

Simmons, R. (2002). *Odd girl out: The hidden culture of aggression in girls.* New York: Harcourt.

Simon, R. J., & Danziger, G. (1991). *Women's movements in America: Their successes, disappointments, and aspirations.* Westport, CT: Praeger.

Simonton, A. F. (1995). Women for sale. In C. Lont (Ed.), *Women and media: Content, careers, criticism* (pp. 143–177). Belmont, CA: Wadsworth.

Slack, A. (1988). Female circumcision: A critical appraisal. *Human Rights Quarterly, 10,* 432–446.

Smith, B. (1998). Black feminism. In W. Mankiller, G. Mink, M. Navarro, B. Smith, & G. Steinem (Eds.), *The reader's* companion to U.S. women's history (pp. 202–204). New York: Houghton Mifflin.

Smith, D. (2004). Schooling for inequality. In J. Spade & C. Valentine (Eds.), *The kaleidoscope of gender: Prisms, patterns, and possibilities* (pp. 183–186). Belmont, CA: Wadsworth.

Smith, J. E., Waldorf, V. A., & Trembath, D. L. (1990). "Single White male looking for thin, very attractive . . ." *Sex Roles, 23,* 675–685.

Smith, L. (1995, March 21). How do fathers nurture? *Raleigh News and Observer,* p. E1.

Smith, N. (1998). Guerrilla girls. In W. Mankiller, G. Mink, M. Navarro, B. Smith, & G. Steinem (Eds.), *The reader's companion to U.S. women's history* (p. 250). New York: Houghton Mifflin.

Smith, V. (1998). *Not just race, not just gender: Black feminist readings.* New York: Routledge.

Snarey, J. (1994). *How fathers care for the next generation.* Cambridge, MA: Harvard University Press.

Sommers, C. (2000). *The war against boys: How misguided feminism is harming our young men.* New York: Simon & Schuster.

South, S. J., & Felson, R. B. (1990). The racial patterning of rape. *Social Forces, 69,* 71–93.

Spade, J. (2001). Gender and education in the United States. In D. Vannoy (Ed.), *Gender mosaics* (pp. 85–93). Los Angeles: Roxbury.

Spain, D. (1992). *Gendered spaces.* Chapel Hill: University of North Carolina Press.

Spayde, J. (1998, September/October). Indefinable heroes. *Utne Reader,* pp. 52–55.

Spelman, E. V. (1988). *Inessential woman: Problems of exclusion in feminist thought.* Boston: Beacon.

Spence, J., & Buckner, C. (2000). Instrumental and expressive traits, trait stereotypes and sexist attitudes: What do they signify? *Psychology of Women Quarterly, 24,* 44–62.

Spender, D. (1984a). *Man made language.* London: Routledge and Kegan Paul.

Spender, D. (1984b). Defining reality: A powerful tool. In C. Kramarae, M. Schultz, & W. O'Barr (Eds.), *Lan-*

guage and power (pp. 195–205). Beverly Hills: Sage.

Spitz, R. (1952). Authority and masturbation. *Psychoanalytic Quarterly, 21,* 38–52.

Spitzack, C. (1990). *Confessing excess.* Albany: State University of New York Press.

Spitzack, C. (1993). The spectacle of anorexia nervosa. *Text and Performance Quarterly, 13,* 1–21.

Spitzack, C., & Carter, K. (1987). Women in communication studies: A typology for revision. *Quarterly Journal of Speech, 73,* 401–423.

Spitzberg, B. (1998). Sexual coercion in courtship relations. In B. Spitzberg & W. Cupach (Eds.), *The dark side of close relationships* (pp. 179–232). Mahwah, NJ: Erlbaum.

Spitzberg, B., Nicastro, A., & Cousins, A. (1998). Exploring the interactional phenomenon of stalking and obsessive relational intrusion. *Communication Reports, 11,* 33–47.

Stacey, J. (1990). *Brave new families: Stories of domestic upheaval in late twentieth-century America.* New York: Basic Books.

Stacey, J. (1996). *In the name of the father: Rethinking family values in a postmodern age.* Boston: Beacon.

Stafford, D. (2003, March 2). New parents failing to take more leave. *Raleigh News & Observer,* p. 4E.

Stafford, L., Dutton, M., & Haas, S. (2000). Measuring routine maintenance: Scale revision, sex versus gender roles, and the prediction of relational characteristics. *Communication Monographs, 67,* 306–323.

Stafford, L., & Kline, S. (1996). Women's surnames and titles: Men's and women's views. *Communication Research Reports, 13,* 214–224.

Stamp, G., & Sabourin, T. (1995). Accounting for violence: An analysis of males' spousal abuse narratives. *Journal of Applied Communication Research, 23,* 284–307.

Stancill, J. (1999, April 17). In triangle, women rise to the top of higher-learning realm. *Raleigh News and Observer,* pp. 1A, 15A.

Stanley, J. P. (1977). Paradigmatic woman: The prostitute. In D. L. Shores & C. P.

Hines (Eds.), *Papers in language variation* (pp. 303–321). Tuscaloosa: University of Alabama Press.

Statham, A., Richardson, L., & Cook, J. A. (1991). *Gender and university teaching: A negotiated difference.* Albany: State University of New York Press.

Status Report. (2000, June). *Smart Money,* p. 82.

Steele, S. (1990). *The content of our character.* New York: St. Martin's Press.

Steil, J. M. (2000). Contemporary marriage: Still an unequal partnership. In C. Hendrick & C. Hendrick (Eds.), *Close relationships: A sourcebook* (pp. 125–136). Thousand Oaks, CA: Sage.

Steil, J. M., & Weltman, K. (1991). Marital inequality: The importance of resources, personal attributes, and social norms on career valuing and the allocation of domestic responsibilities. *Sex Roles, 24,* 161–179.

Stein, R. (1995, August 15). Is affirmative action necessary? *Investor's Business Daily,* p. B1.

Steinberg, C. (1999, May 9). Not doing what the Romans do. *New York Times,* p. 8.

Steinberg, R. (2001). How sex gets into your paycheck and how to get it out: The gender gap in pay and comparable worth. In D. Vannoy (Ed.), *Gender mosaics* (pp. 258–268). Los Angeles: Roxbury.

Stern, M., & Karraker, K. H. (1989). Sex stereotyping of infants: A review of gender labeling studies. *Sex Roles, 20,* 501–522.

Stewart, L. P., Stewart, A. D., Friedley, S. A., & Cooper, P. J. (1996). *Communication between the sexes: Sex differences, and sex role stereo-types* (3rd ed.). Scottsdale, AZ: Gorsuch Scarisbrick.

Stewart, M. (1998). Gender issues in physics education. *Educational Research, 40,* 283–293.

Stewart, S., Stinnett, H., & Rosenfeld, L. (2000). Sex differences in desired characteristics of short-term and long-term relationship partners. *Journal of Social and Personal Relationships, 17,* 843–853.

Stockdale, M., Visio, M., & Batra, L. (1999). The sexual harassment of men: Evidence for a broader theory of sexual harassment and sex discrimination. *Psychology, Public Policy and Law, 5,* 630–664.

Stoller, D., & Karp, M. (Eds.). (1999). *The Bust guide to the new girl order.* New York: Penguin Press.

Stoltenberg, J. (1995). Male virgins, blood covenants, and family values. *On the Issues, 4,* n.p.

Straus, R., & Goldberg, W. (1999). Self and possible selves during the transition to fatherhood. *Journal of Family Psychology, 13,* 244–259.

Straus, S. (2004). Escape from animal house. In J. Spade & Catherine Valentine (Eds.), *The kaleidoscope of gender* (pp. 462–465). Belmont, CA: Wadsworth.

Strine, M. S. (1992). Understanding how things work: Sexual harassment and academic culture. *Journal of Applied Communication Research, 4,* 391–400.

Stroup, K. (2001, May 7). Newsmakers. *Newsweek,* p. 75.

Stryker, S. (1997). Over and out in academe: Transgender studies come of age. In G. Israel & D. Tarver II (Eds.), *Transgender care: Recommended guidelines, practical information, and personal accounts* (pp. 241–244). Philadelphia, PA Temple University Press.

Stryker, S. (1998). The transgender issue: An introduction. *GLQ: A Journal of Lesbian and Gay Studies, 4,* 145–158.

Study links high testosterone to male urge for upper hand. (1991, July 17). *Raleigh News and Observer,* pp. A1, A8.

Study links men's cognitive abilities to seasonal cycles. (1991, November 11). *Raleigh News and Observer,* p. A3.

Study says women face glass walls as well as ceilings. (1992, March 3). *Wall Street Journal,* pp. B1, B2.

Stumpf, H., & Stanley, J. (1998). Stability and change in gender-related differences on the college board advanced placement and achievement tests. *Current directions in Psychological Science, 7,* 192–196.

Suggs, W. (1999, May 21). More women participate in collegiate sports. *Chronicle of Higher Education,* pp. A44–A49.

Suggs, W. (2000, July 7). Poll finds strong public backing for gender equity in college athletics. *Chronicle of Higher Education,* p. A40.

Suggs, W. (2001, May 4). Woman who wanted to play football at Duke wins another round in court. *Chronicle of Higher Education,* p. A51.

Suggs, W. (2003a, July 25). Colleges make slight progress toward gender equity in sports. *Chronicle of Higher Education*, pp. A30–A32.

Suggs, W. (2003b, July 25). Education Department stands pat on Title IX. *Chronicle of Higher Education*, p. A33.

Sullivan, P. J., & Short, S. E. (2001). *Furthering the construct of effective communication: A second version of the Scale for Effective Communication in Team Sports.* Paper presented at the North American Society for the Psychology of Sport and Physical Activity (NASPSPA), St Louis, MO.

Surrey, J. L. (1983). The relational self in women: Clinical implications. In J. V. Jordan, J. L. Surrey, & A. G. Kaplan (Speakers), *Women and empathy: Implications for psychological development and psychotherapy* (pp. 6–11). Wellesley, MA: Stone Center for Developmental Services and Studies.

Swain, S. (1989). Covert intimacy: Closeness in men's friendships. In B. J. Risman & P. Schwartz (Eds.), *Gender and intimate relationships* (pp. 71–86). Belmont, CA: Wadsworth.

Switzer, J. Y. (1990). The impact of generic word choices: An empirical investigation of age- and sex-related differences. *Sex Roles, 22,* 69–82.

Talbot, M. (2002, October 13). Men behaving badly. *New York Times Magazine.* pp. 52–57, 82, 84, 95.

Tannen, D. (1986). *That's not what I meant! How conversational style makes or breaks relationships.* New York: Ballantine.

Tannen, D. (1990a). Gender differences in conversational coherence: Physical alignment and topical cohesion. In B. Dorval (Ed.), *Conversational organization and its development.* (Vol. XXXVIII, pp. 167–206). Norwood, NJ: Ablex.

Tannen, D. (1990b). *You just don't understand: Women and men in conversation.* New York: Morrow.

Tannen, D. (1991, June 19). Teachers' classroom strategies should recognize that men and women use language differently. *Chronicle of Higher Education*, pp. B1, B3.

Tannen, D. (1995). *Talking 9 to 5: Women and men in the workplace.* New York: Avon.

Tanouye, E. (1996, June 28). Heredity theory says intelligence in males is "like mother, like son." *Wall Street Journal*, p. B1.

Tavris, C. (1992). *The mismeasure of woman.* New York: Simon & Schuster.

Tavris, C. (2002, July 5). Are girls really as mean as books say they are? *Chronicle of Higher Education*, pp. B7–B9.

Tavris, C., & Baumgartner, A. (1983, February). How would your life be different? *Redbook*, pp. 92–95.

Tavris, C., Meginnis, K., & Bardari, K. (2000). Beauty, sexuality and identity: The social control of women. In C. Tavris & J. White (Eds.), *Sexuality, society, and feminism* (pp. 237–272). Washington, DC: American Psychological Association.

Taylor, B., & Conrad, C. R. (1992). Narratives of sexual harassment: Organizational dimensions. *Journal of Applied Communication Research, 4,* 401–418.

Taylor, V., & Rupp, L. (1998). Lesbian organizations. In W. Mankiller, G. Mink, M. Navarro, B. Smith, & G. Steinem (Eds.), *The reader's companion to U.S. women's history* (pp. 330–332). New York: Houghton Mifflin.

Tetenbaum, T. J., & Pearson, J. (1989). The voices in children's literature: The impact of gender on the moral decisions of storybook characters. *Sex Roles, 20,* 381–395.

3rd Wave. (1999, May 24). Web site. Retrieved May 24, 1999, from http://www.io.com/~wwwave/

Thomas, V. G. (1989). Body-image satisfaction among Black women. *Journal of Social Psychology, 129,* 107–112.

Thomas, V. G., & James, M. D. (1988). Body image, dieting tendencies, and sex-role traits in urban Black women. *Sex Roles, 18,* 523–529.

Thompson, E. H., Jr. (1991). The maleness of violence in dating relationships: An appraisal of stereotypes. *Sex Roles, 24,* 261–278.

Thompson, E. H., Jr., & Pleck, J. H. (1987). The structure of male role norms. In M. S. Kimmel (Ed.), *Changing men: New directions in research on men and masculinity* (pp. 25–36). Newbury Park, CA: Sage.

Thompson, L., & Walker, A. J. (1989). Gender in families: Women and men in marriage, work, and parenthood. *Journal of Marriage and the Family, 51,* 845–871.

Thompson, T., & Zerbinos, E. (1995). Television cartoons: Do children notice it's a boy's world? *Sex Roles, 37,* 415–432.

Thompson, T., & Zerbinos, E. (1997). Gender roles in animated cartoons: Has the picture changed in 20 years? *Sex Roles, 32,* 651–673.

Thurer, S. L. (1994). *The myths of motherhood.* New York: Houghton Mifflin.

Tidball, M. E. (1989). Women's colleges: Exceptional conditions, not exceptional talent, produce high achievers. In C. S. Pearson, D. L. Shavlik, & J. G. Touchton (Eds.), *Educating the majority: Women challenge tradition in higher education* (pp. 157–172). New York: American Council on Education/Macmillan.

Tiffs, S., & VanOsdol, P. (1991, February 4). A setback for pinups at work. *Time,* p. 61.

Timmers, M., Fischer, A. H., & Manstead, A. S. (1998). Gender differences in motives for regulating emotions. *Personality and Social Psychology Bulletin, 24,* 974–985.

Tjaden, P., & Thoennes, N. (1998). *Prevalence, incidence, and consequences of violence against women: Findings from the National Violence Against Women Survey.* Atlanta, GA: Centers for Disease Control and Prevention, Center for Injury Prevention and Control.

Tjaden, P., & Thoennes, N. (2000). Prevalence and consequences of male to female and female to male intimate partner violence as measured by the National Violence Against Women Survey. *Violence Against Women, 6,* 142–161.

Tobias, S. (1997). *The faces of feminism.* Boulder, CO: Westview.

Toubia, N. (1993). *Female genital mutilation: A call for global action.* New York: Women, Ink.

Toubia, N. (1994). Female circumcision as a public health issue. *New England Journal of Medicine, 331,* 712–716.

Transgrud, K. (1994). Female genital mutilation: Recommendations for education and policy. *Carolina Papers in International Health and Development, 1,* n.p.

Treichler, P. A., & Kramarae, C. (1983). Women's talk in the ivory tower. *Communication Quarterly, 31,* 118–132.

Tretheway, A. (2000). Revisioning control: A feminist critique of disciplined bodies. In P. M. Buzzanell (Ed.), *Rethinking organizational and managerial communication from feminist perspectives* (pp. 107–127). Thousand Oaks, CA: Sage.

Trexler, R. (1997). *Sex and conquest.* Ithaca, NY: Cornell University Press.

Trinh, M. (1989). *Woman, native, other: Writing postcoloniality and feminism.* Bloomington: Indiana University Press.

Trouble at the top. (1991, June 17). *U.S. News and World Report,* pp. 40–48.

Trudeau, M. (1996, June 4). Morning news. Public Broadcasting System.

Truman, D., Ttokar, D., & Fischer, A. (1996). Dimensions of masculinity: Relations to date rape, supportive attitudes, and sexual aggression in dating situations. *Journal of Counseling and Development, 74,* 555–562.

Turner, R. (1998, December 14). Back in the Ms. biz. *Newsweek,* p. 67.

Tyre, P. & McGinn, D. (2003, May 12). She works, he doesn't. *Newsweek,* 44–54.

Ueland, B. (1992, November/December). Tell me more: On the fine art of listening. *Utne Reader,* pp. 104–109.

Ugwu-Oju, D. (2000, December 4). My turn: Should my tribal past shape Delia's future? *Newsweek,* p. 14.

Ullman, S., Karabatsos, G., & Koss, M. (1999). Alcohol and sexual assault in a national sample of college women. *Journal of Interpersonal Violence, 14,* 603–625.

Umberson, D., Chen, M., House, K., Hopkins, & Slaten, E. (1996). The effect of social relationships on psychological well-being: Are men and women really so different? *American Sociological Review, 61,* 837–857.

Unger, R. (1998). *Resisting gender: Twenty-five years of feminist psychology.* Thousand Oaks, CA: Sage.

United States Bureau of the Census. (1998). *Statistical abstract of the United States, 1999.* Washington, DC: U.S. Bureau of the Census.

United States Bureau of the Census. (2000). *Statistical abstract of the United States* (118th ed.). Washington, DC: U.S. Government Printing Office.

United States Bureau of Labor Statistics (2000). Median weekly earnings of full-time and salary workers by detailed occupation and sex. *Employment and Earnings, 47,* 213–218.

Valian, V. (1998). *Why so slow? The advancement of women.* Boston: MIT Press.

Van der Kwaak, A. (1992). Female circumcision and gender identity: A questionable alliance? *Social Science Medicine, 35,* 777–787.

Vavrus, M. D. (2002). Domesticating patriarchy: Hegemonic masculinity and television's Mr. Mom. *Critical Studies in Media Communication, 19,* 352–375.

Veniegas, R., & Peplau, L. (1997). Power and the quality of same-sex friendships. *Psychology of Women Quarterly, 21,* 279–297.

Vigorito, A., & Curry, T. (1998). Marketing masculinity: Gender identity and popular magazines. *Sex Roles, 38,* 135–152.

Villarosa, L. (1994, January). Dangerous eating. *Essence,* pp. 19–21, 87.

Violent crime's era of decline is over, report says. (2001, May 31). *Raleigh News and Observer,* p. 7A.

Vobejda, B., & Perlstein, L. (1998, June 7). Girls catching up with boys in ways good and bad, study finds. *Raleigh News and Observer,* pp. 1A, 14A.

Wadsworth, B. (1996). *Piaget's theory of cognitive and affective development.* New York: Addison-Wesley.

Wagenheim, J. (1990, September/October). The secret life of men. *New Age Journal,* pp. 40–45, 106–118.

Wagenheim, J. (1996, January–February). Among the Promise Keepers. *Utne Reader,* pp. 74–77.

Waggoner, C., & O'Brien Hallstein, L. (2001). Feminist ideologies meet fashionable bodies: Managing the agency/constraint conundrum. *Text and Performance Quarterly, 21,* 26–46.

Wajcman, J. (1998). *Managing like a man: Women and men in corporate management.* University Park, PA: Pennsylvania State University Press.

Walker, A. (1983). *In search of our mothers' gardens.* New York: Harcourt Brace Jovanovich.

Walker, K. (2004). Men, women, and friendship: What they say, what they do. In J. Spade & C. Valentine (Eds.), *The kaleidoscope of gender: Prisms, patterns, and possibilities* (pp. 403–413). Belmont, CA: Wadsworth.

Walker, R. (Ed.). (1995). *To be real: Telling the truth and changing the face of feminism.* New York: Anchor.

Walt, V. (1997, March 31). The cutting edge. *Wall Street Journal,* p. 14.

Wamboldt, F. S., & Reiss, D. (1989). Defining a family heritage and a new relationship identity: Two central tasks in the making of a marriage. *Family Process, 28,* 317–335.

Warm, J. (2000). The attainment of self-consistency through gender in young children. *Sex Roles, 40,* 209–231.

Warren, K. (2000). *Ecofeminist philosophy: A Western perspective on what it is and why it matters.* Rowman & Littlefield.

Wartik, N. (2002, June 23). Hurting more, helped less? *New York Times,* pp. 15-1, 15-6,7.

Waterman, A. S., & Whitbourne, S. K. (1982). Androgyny and psychological development among college students and adults. *Journal of Personality, 50,* 121–133.

Watzlawick, P., Beavin, J., & Jackson, D. D. (1967). *Pragmatics of human communication.* New York: Norton.

Way, N. (1998). *Everyday courage.* New York: New York University Press.

Weedon, C. (1987). *Feminist practice and poststructuralist theory.* New York: Basil Blackwell.

Weiler, K. (1988). *Women teaching for change: Gender, class and power.* New Haven, CT: Yale University Press.

Weiner, J. (1999, November 18). Youths' media time is mostly TV. *Raleigh News and Observer,* p. 7A.

Weisman, L. K. (1992). *Discrimination by design: A feminist critique of the man-made environment.* Chicago: University of Chicago Press.

Weiss, D. M., & Sachs, J. (1991). Persuasive strategies used by preschool children. *Sociology, 97,* 114–142.

Welch, L. B. (Ed.). (1992). *Perspectives on minority women in higher education.* Westport, CT: Praeger.

Wellington, E. (1999, May 12). The single dad. *Raleigh News and Observer,* pp. 1E, 3E.

Welter, B. (1966). The cult of true womanhood: 1820–1960. *American Quarterly, 18,* 151–174.

Werking, K. (1997). *We're just good friends: Women and men in nonromantic relationships.* New York: Guilford.

West, C., & Zimmerman, D. H. (1983). Small insults: A study of interruptions in cross-sex conversations between unacquainted persons. In B. Thorne, C. Kramarae, & N. Henley (Eds.), *Language, gender and society* (pp. 102–117). Rowley, MA: Newbury House.

West, C., & Zimmerman, D. H. (1987). "Doing gender." *Gender and Society, 1,* 125–151.

West, J. T. (1995). Understanding how the dynamics of ideology influence violence between intimates. In S. Duck & J. T. Wood (Eds.), *Understanding relationship processes, 5: Confronting relationship challenges* (pp. 129–149). Thousand Oaks, CA: Sage.

West, L., Anderson, J., & Duck, S. (1996). Crossing the barriers to friendship between women and men. In J. T. Wood (Ed.), *Gendered relationships: A reader* (pp. 111–127). Mountain View, CA: Mayfield.

West, R. (1913, November 13). Untitled. *The Clarion,* n.p.

Wetherell, M. (1997). Linguistic repertoires and literary criticism. New directions for a social psychology of gender. In M. Gergen & S. Davis (Eds.), *Toward a new psychology of gender* (pp. 149–165). New York: Routledge.

Wharton, A. S. (2004). Feminism at work. In J. Spade & C. Valentine (Eds.), *The kaleidoscope of gender: Prisms, patterns and possibilities* (pp. 347–356). Belmont, CA: Wadsworth.

What about this backlash? (1994, March 16). *Independent Weekly,* pp. 14–15.

Wheeler, D. (1998, April 24). Researchers explore gender-related differences in response to pain. *Chronicle of Higher Education,* p. A18.

Wheeless, V. E. (1984). A test of the theory of speech accommodation using language and gender orientation. *Women's Studies in Communication, 7,* 13–22.

Whitaker, S. (2001). Gender politics in men's movements. In D. Vannoy (Ed.), *Gender mosaics* (pp. 343–351). Los Angeles: Roxbury.

White, B. (1989). Gender differences in marital communication patterns. *Family Process, 28,* 89–106.

White, J., & Bondurant, B. (1996). Gendered violence between intimates. In J. T. Wood (Ed.), *Gendered relationships: A reader* (pp. 197–210). Mountain View, CA: Mayfield.

White Ribbon Campaign. (n.d.). Retrieved May 20, 2003 from www.whiteribbon .com

Whitehead, B. (1997, October 3). Soccer dads march on Washington. *Wall Street Journal,* p. A10.

Whiteley, S. (2000). *Women and popular music: Sexuality, identity, and subjectivity.* New York: Routledge.

Whiting, B., & Edwards, C. (1973). A cross-cultural analysis of sex differences in the behavior of children aged three through eleven. *Journal of Social Psychology, 91,* 171–188.

Whitley, B. E. (1997). Gender differences in computer-related attitudes and behavior: A meta-analysis. *Computers in Human Behavior, 13,* 1–22.

Will, G. (2003, May 26). High noon for "diversity." *Newsweek,* p. 76.

Williams, D. (1985). Gender, masculinity, femininity, and emotional intimacy in same-sex friendship. *Sex Roles, 12,* 587–600.

Williams, J. (2000, December 15). What stymies women's academic careers? It's personal. *Chronicle of Higher Education,* p. B10.

Williams, J. E., & Best, D. L. (1990). *Measuring sex stereotypes: A multi-nation study* (Rev. ed.). Newbury Park, CA: Sage.

Williams, J. H. (1973). Sexual role identification and personality functioning in girls: A theory revisited. *Journal of Personality, 41,* 1–8.

Willis, E. (1992). *No more nice girls: Countercultural essays.* Hanover, NH: Wesleyan University Press.

Wills, T. A., Weiss, R. L., & Patterson, G. R. (1974). A behavioral analysis of the determinants of marital satisfaction. *Journal of Consulting and Clinical Psychology, 42,* 802–811.

Wilson, E. (1975). *Sociobiology: The new synthesis.* Cambridge, MA: Harvard University Press, Belknap.

Wilson, R. (2001, May 4). Proportion of part-time faculty members leveled off from 1992 to 1998, data show. *Chronicle of Higher Education,* p. A14.

Wilson, T. (2000, October 24). Census: Mothers return to work. *Raleigh News and Observer*, pp. 1A, 9A.

Winbush, G. (2000). African American women. In M. Julia (Ed.), *Constructing gender: Multicultural perspectives in working with women* (pp. 11–34). Belmont, CA: Wadsworth.

Winkler, K. (1997, November 7). Girls at risk: A passionate historian surveys culture and physiology. *Chronicle of Higher Education*, pp. A15, A16.

Winstead, B. A. (1986). Sex differences in same-sex friendships. In V. J. Derlega & B. A. Winstead (Eds.), *Friendship and social interaction* (pp. 81–99). New York: Springer-Verlag.

Wise, S., & Stanley, L. (1987). *Georgie Porgie: Sexual harassment in everyday life*. New York: Pandora.

Witt, S. D. (1996). Traditional or androgynous: An analysis to determine gender role orientation of basal readers. *Child Study Journal, 26*, 303–318.

Wolf, N. (1991). *The beauty myth*. New York: Morrow.

Wolf, N. (1993). *Fire with fire: The new female power and how it will change the 21st century*. New York: Random House.

Wolfe, D., & Feiring, C. (2000). Dating violence through the lens of adolescent romantic relationships. *Child Maltreatment, 5*, 360–363.

Women on Words and Images. (1972). *Dick and Jane as victims*. Princeton, NJ: Author.

Women usually attacked by people they know. (1996, December 19). *Raleigh News and Observer*, p. 9A.

Woo, D. (2001). The gap between striving and achieving: The case of Asian American women. In M. Anderson & P. H. Collins (Eds.), *Race, class, and gender: An anthology* (4th ed., pp. 243–251). Belmont, CA: Wadsworth.

Wood, J. T. (1992a). *Spinning the symbolic web: Human communication and symbolic interaction*. Norwood, NJ: Ablex.

Wood, J. T. (1992b). Telling our stories: Narratives as a basis for theorizing sexual harassment. *Journal of Applied Communication Research, 4*, 349–363.

Wood, J. T. (1993a). Engendered relationships: Interaction, caring, power, and responsibility in close relationships. In S. Duck (Ed.), *Processes in close relationships: Contexts of close relationships* (Vol. 3, pp. 26–54). Beverly Hills: Sage.

Wood, J. T. (1993b). Engendered identities: Shaping voice and mind through gender. In D. Vocate (Ed.), *Intrapersonal communication: Different voices, different minds* (pp. 145–167). Hillsdale, NJ: Erlbaum.

Wood, J. T. (1993c). From "woman's nature" to standpoint epistemology: Gilligan and the debate over essentializing in feminist scholarship. *Women's Studies in Communication, 15*, 1–24.

Wood, J. T. (1993d). Issues facing nontraditional members of academe. In G. M. Phillips, D. S. Gouran, S. A. Kuehn, & J. T. Wood, *Professionalism: A survival guide for beginning academics* (pp. 55–72). Cresskill, NJ: Hampton.

Wood, J. T. (1993e). Gender and relationship crises: Contrasting reasons, responses, and relational orientations. In J. Ringer (Ed.), *Queer words, queer images: The (re)construction of homosexuality* (pp. 238–264). New York City: New York University Press.

Wood, J. T. (1993f). Defining and studying sexual harassment as situated experience. In G. L. Kreps (Ed.), *Communication and sexual harassment in the workplace* (pp. 6–23). Cresskill, NJ: Hampton.

Wood, J. T. (1994a). Saying it makes it so: The discursive construction of sexual harassment. In S. Bingham (Ed.), *Discursive conceptualizations of sexual harassment* (pp. 17–30). Greenwood, NJ: Praeger.

Wood, J. T. (1994b). *Who cares: Women, care, and culture*. Carbondale: Southern Illinois University Press.

Wood, J. T. (1995). *Relational communication: Continuity and change in personal relationships*. Belmont, CA: Wadsworth.

Wood, J. T. (1996a). Dominant and muted discourses in popular representations of feminism. *Quarterly Journal of Speech, 82*, 171–185.

Wood, J. T. (Ed.). (1996b). *Gendered relationships: A reader*. Mountain View, CA: Mayfield.

Wood, J. T. (1998). *But I thought you meant . . . Misunderstandings in human communication*. Mountain View, CA: Mayfield.

Wood, J. T. (2000). He says/she says: Misunderstandings in communication between women and men. In D. O. Braithwaite &

J. T. Wood (Eds.), *Case studies in interpersonal communication* (pp. 93–100). Belmont, CA: Wadsworth.

Wood, J. T. (2001a). A critical response to John Gray's Mars and Venus portrayals of men and women. *Southern Communication Journal, 67,* 201–210.

Wood, J. T. (2001b). The normalization of violence in heterosexual romantic relationships: Women's narratives of love and violence. *Journal of Social and Personal Relationships, 18,* 239–262.

Wood, J. T. (in press). Monsters and victims: Male felons' accounts of intimate partner violence. *Journal of Social and Personal Relationships.*

Wood, J. T., & Conrad, C. R. (1983). Paradox in the experience of professional women. *Western Journal of Speech Communication, 47,* 305–322.

Wood, J. T., & Inman, C. (1993). In a different mode: Recognizing male modes of closeness. *Journal of Applied Communication Research, 21,* 279–295.

Wood, J. T., & Lenze, L. F. (1991a). Strategies to enhance gender sensitivity in communication education. *Communication Education, 40,* 16–21.

Wood, J. T., & Lenze, L. F. (1991b). Gender and the development of self: Inclusive pedagogy in interpersonal communication. *Women's Studies in Communication, 14,* 1–23.

Wood, W., Christensen, P., Hebl, M., & Rothgerber, H. (1997). Conformity to sex-typed norms, affect, and the self-concept. *Journal of Personality and Social Psychology, 73,* 523–535.

Worley, J., & Vannoy, D. (2001). The challenge of integrating work and family life. In D. Vannoy (Ed.), *Gender mosaics* (pp. 165–173). Los Angeles: Roxbury.

Wriggins, J. (1998). Rape. In W. Mankiller, G. Mink, M. Navarro, B. Smith, & G. Steinem (Eds.), *The reader's companion to U.S. women's history* (pp. 612–614). New York: Houghton Mifflin.

Wright, P. H. (1982). Men's friendships, women's friendships, and the alleged inferiority of the latter. *Sex Roles, 8,* 1–20.

Wright, P. H. (1988). Interpreting research on gender differences in friendship: A case for moderation and a plea for caution. *Journal of Social and Personal Relationships, 5,* 367–373.

Wright, P. H., & Scanlon, M. B. (1991). Gender role orientations and friendship: Some attenuation but gender differences still abound. *Sex Roles, 24,* 551–566.

The wrong weight. (1997, November). *Carolina Woman,* p. 7.

Wyn, J., & White, R. (1997). *Rethinking youth.* Thousand Oaks, CA: Sage.

Yellin, J. F. (1990). *Women and sisters: Antislavery feminists in American culture.* New Haven, CT: Yale University Press.

Yildirim, A. (1997). Gender role influences on Turkish adolescents' self-identity. *Adolescence, 32,* 216–231.

Yogman, M., Cooley, J., & Kindlon, D. (1988). Fathers, infants, and toddlers: A developing relationship. In P. Bronstein & C. Cowan (Eds.), *Fatherhood today: Men's changing role in the family* (pp. 53–78). New York: Wiley.

Young, C. (1992, October 4). Female trouble. *Washington Post,* pp. C1, C4.

Zaharlick, A. (2000). Southeast Asian-American Women. In M. Julia (Ed.), *Constructing gender* (pp. 177–204). Belmont, CA: Wadsworth.

Zimbalist, A. (2000, March 3). Backlash against Title IX: An end run around female athletes. *Chronicle of Higher Education,* p. B9.

Zimmerman, D. H., & West, C. (1975). Sex roles, interruptions and silences in conversation. In B. Thorne & N. Henley (Eds.), *Language and sex: Difference and dominance* (pp. 105–129). Rowley, MA: Newbury House.

Zinn, H. (1995). *A people's history.* New York: HarperCollins.

Zinn, M., & Dill, B. (1996). Theorizing difference from multiracial feminism. *Feminist Studies, 22,* 321–331.

Ziv, L. (1997, May). The horror of female genital mutilation. *Cosmopolitan,* pp. 242–245.

Zoch, L., & Turk, J. (1998). Women making news: Gender as a variable in source selection and use. *Journalism and Mass Communication Quarterly, 75,* 762–775.

Zuckerman, M. B. (1993, August 2). The victims of TV violence. *U.S. News and World Report,* p. 64.

Baumgardner, Jennifer, 4
beauty, norms of, 25, 164, 292. *See also*
    physical appearance
Belenky, Mary, 70
bias
    diversity training and, 229
    in education, 29, 195–98, 199–202
    in judicial system, 29
    in language, 105–6
    in media, 107–8, 246–49
    in workplace, 220
biological theory, 38–44, 299
biology, 19–22
birth control. *See* reproductive rights
Blacks. *See* African Americans
Black Women Organized for Action, 73
Blum, Deborah, 47
Bly, Robert, 92–94
body, pathologizing of, 251–54
bodybuilding, 252
body hair, 252–53
body image, 140–44, 250. *See also* physical
    appearance
Bowleg, Lisa, 80
boy code, 162
bra burning, not, 64, 246
brain structure, 40–42, 132
breadwinner
    burden of role, 91–92
    family leave and, 217
    as gender role, 52, 160, 161, 294
    media portrayals of, 242–43
    power dynamics and, 183–84
    stereotype of, 213
breast size, 253
Breedlove, Mark, 46
bride burning, 275
Brown v. Board of Education, 223
Bully Broads, 212
Bush, Laura, 292, 293

Campbell, Karlyn Khors, 70
Cancian, Françoise, 172
care, expressing, 164, 179–81
career aspirations, 192, 214
caregiving
    in dual-worker families, 184–85
    gender stereotypes, 52, 164, 182, 242–43
    in media, 235
    by men, 54–55, 185
    parental modeling, 157–58
Carmichael, Stokely, 63
Cassirer, Ernst, 105
Caucasians. *See* European Americans
censorship, 255

change, 285–93
    agent of, 8–9, 282
    in attitudes, 16–17
    communication and, 11–12, 23–24, 215,
        287–88
    in education, 289–90
    in gender themes, 166
    history of, 11
    influence, forms of, 296–97
    in media, 291–92
    need for, 9, 10–11, 274
    in relationships, 288–89
Charlie's Angels, 237–38
Chavis, Benjamin, Jr., 98
Chethik, Neil, 94
Chicanas, 75, 155
children
    advertising and, 240
    aggression in, 248
    custody of, 29
    play of, 117–19, 133–34, 155–56
    sex changes in, 42
    sexual assault of, 262
    stereotypes and, 250
    television and, 242, 250, 251
children, care of
    aggression and day care, 248
    media portrayals of, 235
    by men, 54–55, 185
    parental modeling, 157
    women, stereotypical role of, 52, 164, 182,
        184–85, 242–43
children's books, sexism in, 68
Chodorow, Nancy J., 44
choice, 12, 166, 167, 293–97
chores, household, 152, 156
chromosomes, 19–20, 38–39, 41
circumcision, 271, 302. *See also* genital
    surgery
The Citadel (military school), 17
civil rights, 223–24
Civil Rights Act of 1964, 223
class, 1, 157
classism, 197
classroom climate, 199–205
classroom communication, 199–205
Clinton, Bill, 287–88
Clinton, Hillary Rodham, 108, 292, 293
clitoridectomy, 272, 274, 299
closeness
    in dialogue, 173–74, 179–80
    in doing, 175–76, 180
clothing, 134, 155
CNN, 237
coalition-building, 78

cognitive development theory, 47–48, 132, 151, 196, 299
colleges. *See* education
combat, women in, 16–17
comfort women (Japan), 264
commercials. *See* advertising
commitment, 179–87
communality, 144–45
communication, 30–33, 104–47, 299
  as changeable, 215
  change and, 11–12, 23–24, 287–88
  defining, 30, 299
  as dynamic process, 30, 115–16
  electronic, 292
  feminine style of, 119–21
  future of, 288
  gender identity and, 116
  gender socialization and, 117–19
  levels of meaning, 31–32
  by men, 287–88
  nature of, 105
  nonverbal (*See* nonverbal communication)
  organizational, 208–29
  from parents, 154–56
  in schools, 189–206
  society structured through, 28
  static views of, 215
  symbolic interaction, 32–33
  as system, 30–31
  value of studying, 12, 14–16
  verbal, 104–27
  by women, 119–21, 287
communication climate, 204, 219–20
companions, 175, 177
competition, 117–18, 119, 161, 174, 204
complementary copy, 243, 300
computers, 202
confidantes, 173
conflict, 186
connection, 181
consciousness-raising groups, 64–65, 87, 282
consent, informed, 261–62, 301
content level of meaning, 31, 126, 300
control, 132–33
conversational command, 122
conversational maintenance work, 120
cosmetics, 134
cosmetic surgery, 140, 253
counseling, 279
covert intimacy, 175–76
cross-dressing, 27
Crouching Tiger, Hidden Dragon, 239
cult of domesticity, 60–63

cultural practices and beliefs
  body image, 144, 250
  dowry deaths, 259, 275, 282–83
  educational bias, 200
  and gender, 24–25, 27, 28–30
  genital surgery, 259, 271–74
  maternity leave, 218
  menopause, 252
  nonverbal communication and, 136, 144–45
  partner abuse, comparison of, 187
  personal space, 135
  prostitution, forced, 264
  on sex and sexual orientation, 6
  value of female vs. male children, 154, 274–75
  violence and, 261, 274–75, 277, 280, 282–83
cultural (structural or difference) feminism, 59, 300
cultural structures, 23, 28–30, 282–83
cultural theories of gender, 48–55
culture of romance, 201, 300
culture(s), 28–30, 300
  definition of, 28, 300
  gender variation across, 24–25, 27, 49–51
  gender variation within, 18–19, 25
  matriarchal, 109
  patriarchal, 29, 68, 135, 136
  redefining, 295–96
  value of studying, 12, 14–16
cumulative impact, 205
curriculum
  content of, 195–98, 289
  hidden, 189, 205, 289–90, 301
cycles
  hormonal, 40
  of intimate partner violence, 265–66

daddy track, 217
date rape, 110, 261, 263, 288
Davis, Flora, 296
d'Eaubonne, Françoise, 70–71
Declaration of Sentiments, 60
decoding skill, 132
demand-withdraw pattern, 181
denial, 4
dependence and independence, 240–42
depression, 162
determination vs. influence, 43, 154
devaluing of women. *See also* violence
  in educational settings, 198–99
  gender intimidation, 260–61
  gender socialization and, 165
  parental communication and, 154

devaluing of women *(continued)*
  as sex objects, 209, 237, 243–46
  through language, 105
  violence in media, effect of, 255
Devi, Phoolan, 283
dialogue
  closeness in, 173–74, 179–80
  internal, 149
dieting, 141–43, 163, 250, 252, 253
difference(s). *See also* sex differences
  metaphors for, 295–96
  respecting, in nonverbal communication, 145–46
  responding to, 295–96
  third-wave feminism and, 78
difference (structural or cultural) feminism, 59, 300
direct power, 296
disclaimers, 122–23
discrimination
  in education, 223–24, 289–90
  against homosexuals, 209
  microinequities, 222
  reverse, 227–28
  in workplace, 209, 210, 211–12, 220, 222–24, 290
diversity training, 229
divorce laws, 288
dolls, 134, 155, 163
domesticity, cult of, 60–63
domestic violence. *See* abuse between intimates; violence
Dominican Republic, 50
double standard
  for appearance, 163
  for sexual activity, 113
Douglass, Frederick, 60, 82
dowry deaths, 259, 275, 282–83
dual-worker families, 165–66, 183–85, 213, 288–89. *See also* working women

eating disorders, 141, 143, 144, 163, 250
ecofeminism, 70–72, 300
education, 189–206
  affirmative action in, 225–27
  attention to students in, 199–205
  bias in, 29, 198–99
  career aspirations and, 192
  communication in, 189–206
  curricular content of, 195–98
  in future, 289–90
  inequities in, 190–92, 193
  instructional style in, 203–5
  organization of schools, 190–95
  processes of, 198–205

sex discrimination in, 223–24, 289–90
  sexism in, 196–98
  sex-segregated, 194–95
  technology, 202
  of women, 189, 190
  worldwide, 201
EEOC (Equal Employment Opportunity Commission), 223–24
ego boundaries, 152–54, 173–74, 300
emotions
  expression of, 170–73
  focus on, 182
  interpretation of, 131, 132
  repression of, 161, 171
entertainment. *See* media
environmental factors vs. biology, 43
envy, 174
equality (liberal or middle-class) feminism, 59, 66–67, 72, 83, 286–87, 301–2
equal opportunity laws, 223–24, 300
Equal Pay Act (1963), 211
Equal Rights Amendment (ERA), 84, 100–101
erotica and pornography, 245, 276–77, 300
essentialist views, 18
essentializing, 18, 300
estrogen, 39
ethnocentricity, 274
European Americans
  affirmative action and, 226
  body image, 141
  child care, 157
  gender constructions among, 25
  informal networks, 221
  nonverbal communication, 131
  parental expectations, 155
  standpoints, and gender identity, 54
evolutionary theory, 39
excision (clitoridectomy), 272, 274, 299
exclusionary language, 105–6
eye contact, 130, 131, 132, 138–39

fainting spells, 27–28
Faludi, Susan, 91, 101
families, 148–68. *See also* fathers; mothers; parental influence
  dual-worker, 165–66, 183–85, 213, 288–89
  gender identity and, 149–50
  role modeling in, 151–52, 156–58
  violence in, 266, 277
Family and Medical Leave Act, 216–17, 219, 291
family leave, 216–17, 218, 219, 290–91
Farrakhan, Louis, 98
Farrell, Warren, 91

Fascinating Womanhood Movement, 100
fashion, 245–46
father hunger, 94, 300
fathers
   caregiving by, 54–55, 185
   daddy track for, 217
   gender socialization and, 133, 152, 155
   identification with, 151, 152
   increasing commitment of, 86, 158, 185
   influence of, 158–59
   loss of, 94
   media portrayals of, 235
   paternity leave for, 217
   relationship with child, 157–58, 159
   rights of, 91
   single, 158
feelings. *See* emotions
femicide, 275, 300
feminine, growing up, 45–46, 162–66
feminine gender identity, 150–54
Feminine Mystique (Friedan), 66, 67
feminine ruler, 172
feminine speech community, 116–27
feminine style of communication, 119–21
femininity. *See also* women
   changing views of, 16–17, 22, 24–25,
      27–28, 294
   defining, 166, 294
   language and, 112
   learning competence in, 46–47, 47–48
   physical standards of, 141–44
   social expectations of, 134
   themes of, 162–66
feminism, 3–5, 58, 59–80
   backlash against, 99–102, 241, 246–47,
      286, 299
   cultural (structural or difference), 59, 300
   defining, 3–4
   ecofeminism, 70–72, 300
   first wave of, 59–63
   in future, 286–87
   lesbian, 69, 301
   liberal (equality or middle-class), 59,
      66–67, 72, 83, 286–87, 301–2
   male, 83–90, 302
   misunderstandings of, 3, 246
   multiracial, 74–76, 302
   power, 76–77, 303
   as process, 4–5
   radical, 63–65, 303–4
   revalorist, 69–70, 304
   second wave of, 63–80, 241, 246, 286–87
   separatist, 68–69, 304
   socialist, 304
   third wave of, 77–80, 305

   victim, 77
   womanism, 72–74, 305
   women's rights and, 59–63
fetus, development of, 20
fighter, stereotype of, 213
foot binding, 274
Ford, Maggie, 194
formal practices, in organizations, 216–18
freedom of speech, 255
Free Men, 90–92, 300–301
Freud, Sigmund, 44, 150
Friedan, Betty, 66, 67, 68
friendships, 173–77
   long-distance, 175
   between men, 172, 174–76
   sex differences in, 171
   between women, 172, 173–74
   between women and men, 176–77
future, 285–97
   communication in, 287–88
   education in, 289–90
   feminism in, 286–87
   media in, 292–93
   relationships in, 288–89
   sexual harassment in, 293
   violence in, 293
   women's and men's movements in,
      286–87

G. I. Joe doll, 134
"gals," 113
games, 117–19, 155–56
gangsta rap, 241, 246, 276
gate keeping, 296–97
gay bashing, 260
gays
   affection, expression of, 108
   brain development in, 41–42
   commitment and, 179
   conflict in relationships, 186
   eating disorders and, 144
   intimacy and, 178
   masculine identity and, 160
   power dynamics, 183
   rights of, 90
   sex-object stereotype, 209
Gelernter, David, 99
gender, 19, 22–28, 301
   cultural practices and, 28–30
   defined by language, 105–10
   language, cultural views in, 105–16
   parental attitudes about, 154–56
   parental communication about, 154–56
   as personal quality, 22–23, 294
   as relational concept, 27–28

as unearned, 1–2
  between women and men, 190–92,
    217–23, 288–89
  in workplace, 217–23
infanticide, female, 274–75
infibulation, 272–73, 301
influence, 296–97
informal network, 220–21
informal practices, in organizations, 218–23
information, 1, 7, 12
informed consent, 261–62, 301
institutions
  future of gender in, 290–93
  masculine norms for, 213–16
  normalization of violence and, 277–80
  sexual harassment and, 279
  sustaining of gender roles and, 29, 190,
    217–23
instructional style, 203–5
instrumentality, 121–22, 175, 180, 182
intercultural beliefs. *See* cultural practices
  and beliefs
internal dialogues, 149
internalization, 52–53, 150–52
Internet, 292
interpersonal theories, 44–48
interruptions, 32, 122
Intersex Society of North America (ISNA),
  20
intersexuals and intersexuality, 21, 301
  freedom of choice, 67
  and gender construction, 25, 27
  genetics and biology of, 20–21
  polarized language and, 112
  social views of, 20
  testes, undescended, 50
intimacy. *See also* friendships;
  relationships
  covert, 175–76
  gays and lesbians and, 178
  in men, compared to women, 171–72
  romantic, 177–78
intimate partner violence. *See* abuse
  between intimates
intimidation, gender, 260–61, 301
Iron John (Bly), 93, 94
iron maiden, stereotype of, 211–12, 215

Jackson, Jesse, 76, 296
Japan, 131, 264
job segregation, 210, 222–23
Johnson, Lyndon, 224
Jones, Irma, 74
journals, 15, 82–83
judicial system, 29

Katz, Jackson, 89
Keller, Evelyn Fox, 70
Kiatbusaba, Parinyua, 27
kinesics, 138–39, 301
King, Martin Luther, Jr., 76

labor, division of, 184
Labov, William, 116
La Feminisme ou la Mort (d'Eaubonne),
  70–71
Lakoff, Robin, 120
Langer, Suzanne, 116
language
  devaluing of women in, 105
  exclusionary, 105–6
  gender-defining, 105–10
  gender evaluated by, 112–14
  hypothetical thought and, 114
  inclusive, 5
  normalization of violence and, 279–80
  perception organized through, 110–12
  as process, 115–16
  self-reflection and, 114–15
  of victims, 111
  voice, power of, 297
law enforcement, 278–79
leave policies, 216–17, 218, 219, 290–91
lesbian feminists, 69, 301
lesbians
  affection, expression of, 108
  commitment and, 179, 181–82
  conflict in relationships, 186
  intimacy and, 178
  sex-object stereotype, 209
levels of meaning, 31–32
  content, 31, 126, 300
  relationship, 32, 119–20, 123–24, 129,
    130–33, 304
liberal (equality or middle-class) feminism,
  59, 66–67, 72, 83, 286–87, 301–2
liking, 132
listening noises, 124
locker rooms, 43
love, feminization of, 172

Madonna, 245, 292
male bashing, 8, 9, 88
male circumcision, 271, 302
male deficit model, 170–71, 302
male feminists, 83–90, 302
male generic language, 105–6, 302
male mode of feeling, 94
male standard bias. *See* bias
managerial style, 214–15
manliness. *See* masculinity

stereotype of, 209–10
  working outside the home, 187
Mott, Lucretia Coffin, 59–60
movies. *See* media
MR, Inc., 90
MTV, 237, 241, 244–45, 251
Mulan, 291–92
multicultural perspective. *See* cultural prac-
    tices and beliefs; culture(s)
multiracial feminism, 74–76, 302
murder. *See also* violence
  gender-based, 154, 274–75
  by intimates, 265, 268, 275
Murray, Pauli, 68
music, 236, 245, 250–51, 276, 291
mythopoetic movement, 92–95, 303

name, and marriage, 29, 108–9
name, birth, 109
naming, 108–10
National Association Opposed to Women's
    Suffrage, 100
National Black Feminist Organization, 73
National Coalition of Free Men, 90
National Organization for Men Against
    Sexism (NOMAS), 86–87
National Organization for Women (NOW),
    66, 68, 73, 286
National Organization of Men (NOM), 90
National Political Congress of Black
    Women, 246
Native Americans, 50
New Left movement, 63
nonverbal communication, 129–47, 303
  cultural context of, 144–46
  forms of, 133–44
  functions of, 129–33
  gender socialization and, 131–32, 133,
    136, 137, 139–40
  misinterpretation of, 145
  respecting differences in, 145–46
  significance of, 129
normal, social construction of
  awareness of, 29–30
  body, pathologizing of, 251–54
  heterosexuality, 2
  nonverbal communication and, 145
  violence and, 254–55, 275–80
nurturing ability, 54–55. *See also* caregiving

older people, 234
oppression, 4, 71, 76
organization, 110–12
organizational climate, 219–20
organizational communication, 208–29

organization of experience and perception,
    110–12
outsider within, 54

paralanguage, 139–40, 303
parallel language, 107
parental influence. *See also* families; fathers;
    mothers
  communication about gender and,
    154–56
  modeling, 151–52
  mothers and fathers, comparison of,
    158–59
parental leave, 216–17, 219, 290–91
pathologizing the human body, 251–54
patriarchal culture, 29, 68, 135, 136, 303
pay, 210–11, 290
peers, communication among, 202–3
peer shaming, 162, 165, 202–3
personal as political, 65, 79–80
personal relationships, 170–73, 303. *See also*
    relationships
personal space, 135–37
physical appearance, 140–44, 303
  anthropological research on, 250
  beauty, norms of, 25, 164, 292
  clothing, 134, 155
  as feminine theme, 163–64
  media and, 237
  parental modeling, 157
  pathologizing of the body, 251–54
  race and, 143–44
  workplace and, 209
Plant, Judith, 71
plastic surgery, 140, 253
play, 117–19, 133–34, 155–56, 157–58, 159
PMS, 251
polarized thinking, 111–12, 303
political as personal, 79–80
politics, 121, 287–88
Pollitt, Katha, 4
pornography, 245, 276–77, 303
post-transitional females to males (FTM),
    26
post-transitional males to females (MTF),
    26
power, 132–33
  abuse and, 186–87, 265–66, 268
  dynamics in relationships, 183–87
  influence, forms of, 296–97
  rape and, 263–64
  standpoint and, 53
power dynamics, 183–87
power feminism, 76–77, 303
Powerpuff Girls, 239

preferential treatment, 224

Pregnancy Discrimination Act (1978), 290

privilege, 1–2

problem that has no name, 66

profeminist men's movements, 83–90

professionalism, masculine definition of, 213–16

Progressive Education Movement, 190

promasculinist men's movements. *See* masculinist men's movements

Promise Keepers, 95–98, 303

prostitution, forced, 264

provider role. *See* breadwinner

proxemics, 135–37, 303

psychodynamic (psychoanalytic) theory, 44–46, 150–52, 303

psychological responsibility, 184–85, 303

psychological theories, 44, 46–48

public speaking, 126

qualifiers, 120

quid pro quo sexual harassment, 269, 303

quotas, 227–29, 303

Rabidue v. Osceola Refining Company, 270–71

race. *See also* African Americans

  affirmative action, 224–27

  goals and quotas, 227–29

  inequities based on, 1

  multiracial feminism, 74–76

  physical ideals and, 143–44, 164

  responsiveness and, 131

  standpoints and, 54, 55

  womanism and, 72

racism, 197

radical feminism, 63–65, 303–4

radio, 250

rape, 261–64

  African American men, fear of, 160

  cultural ideologies and, 280

  date or acquaintance, 110, 261, 263, 288

  definitions of, 261, 293

  marital, 29, 262, 288

  masculinity and, 161

  myths and facts about, 263

  pornography and, 276–77

  power and, 77, 263–64

  prevalence of, 258, 259, 261, 262

rape script, 262

rap groups, 64

rap music, 236, 241, 246, 276

real men, 90–91, 162

reasonable man standard, 270–71

reasonable woman standard, 271

re-covering, 70

reform. *See* change

regulation of interaction, 130

relationship experts, women as, 170–71

relationship level of meaning, 32, 304

  in feminine speech, 119–20

  in masculine speech, 123–24

  nonverbal communication and, 129, 130–33

relationships, 169–88. *See also* abuse between intimates

  changes in, 288–89

  commitment in, 179–87

  cultural association of women with, 108

  divisiveness in, 289

  family (*See* families)

  friendships, 173–77

  in future, 289

  gendered patterns in, 170–73

  heterosexual, 1, 177–87

  meaning of, 170–73

  mentor, 221–22

  personal, 170–73, 303

  psychodynamic theory and, 44

  responsibility for health of, 181–82

  romantic, 177–87

  stereotypical images of, 240–46

  workplace, 216, 219–22

relationship talk, 126, 174

reproductive rights, 62, 247

responsibility

  psychological, 184–85, 303

  for relationships, 181–82

  for violence, 281–82

responsiveness, 120, 123–24, 130–32, 174

Reuther, Rosemary Radford, 71

revalorists, 69–70, 304

reverse discrimination, 227–28

rhetoric, 58

rhetorical movements, 58–80

Richards, Amy, 4

rights

  civil, 223–24

  equal, 84, 100–101

  of fathers, 91

  of gays, 90

  reproductive, 62, 247

  voting, 60, 61–62

  of women, 59–63

Roiphe, Katie, 76

role, 52–53, 304

role models

  for adolescents, 48

  of alternatives to traditional views, 23–24

  in families, 156–58, 159

feminine, 47–48, 152
masculine, 47–48, 151, 152
in media, 48, 250–51
in schools, 192–95
romance, culture of, 201, 300
Ruddick, Sara, 54, 70

Saheli, 282–83
salaries, 210–11, 290
Sanger, Margaret, 62
Saudi Arabia, 136
Schlafly, Phyllis, 101
schools. *See* education
Schwalbe, Michael, 95
scripts
  gender, 53
  rape, 262
  for romance, 177–78
second shift, 184–85, 304. *See also* working
  women
second-wave feminism, 63–80, 241, 246,
  286–87
segregation. *See* sex segregation
self, 51–53, 148–49, 152–53
self-as-object, 149, 304
self-defense, 267, 268
self-disclosure, 124, 171
self-esteem
  androgyny and, 115
  violence and, 268
self-reflection, 114–15
self-reliance, 161
self-talk, 149
Seneca Falls Convention, 60, 99
separate but equal doctrine, 194, 223
separatism, 68–69
separatists, 304
sex, 19–22, 304
sex differences, 18–22, 39–42
  in brain structure, 40–42
  in chromosomal structure, 38–39
  in friendships, 170–73
  in hormones, 20–21, 39–40
sex discrimination. *See* discrimination
sexism
  awareness of, 66–67
  in children's books, 68
  in education, 196–98
sex object, 209, 237, 243–46
sex segregation, 117, 176–77
  in education, 194–95
  in workplace, 210, 222–23
sexual, directive for men to be, 161, 252
sexual abuse, 260–61
sexual assault, 261–64, 304. *See also* rape

sexual harassment, 268–71, 304
  cross-cultural, 136
  in education, 198–99
  in future, 293
  in hostile environment, 219, 269–70
  informal networks and, 221
  institutions and, 279
  naming of, 109–10
  prevalence of, 259
  quid pro quo sexual harassment, 269, 303
  same-sex, 269, 270
  standards for assessing, 270–71
  stereotyping and, 209
  touch as, 137
sexual orientation. *See also* gays; lesbians
  biology and, 41–42
  inequities based on, 1
  intimacy and, 178, 179
  masculinity and, 160
  multicultural perspectives on, 6
  and normal, construction of, 2
shaming from peers, 162, 165, 202–3
Shrek, 292
signals, 132
Simpson, O. J., 278–79, 280
single-sex schools, 194–95
smiling, 131, 138
social construction
  of gender, 22–28, 52–53, 159–67, 285–86,
    295
  of heterosexuality as normal, 2
  of inequality, 2–3, 9
  of normal, 2, 29–30, 50, 145, 251–55,
    275–80
socialization. *See* gender socialization
social learning theory, 46–47, 132, 304
social movements
  men's, 82–102, 287
  women's, 58, 59–80, 246–49, 286–87
sociobiology, 39
Sojourner of God's Truth, 61
The Sopranos (TV), 232, 239
space, personal, 135–37
speech
  freedom of, 255
  of men, 121–24
  of women, 119–21
speech communities. *See* gendered speech
  communities
splenium, 41
sports
  aggression and, 160–61
  discrimination in, 43
  gender constructions and, 23
  in schools, 43, 191–92, 194